SOCIAL WORK, SOCIAL JUSTICE, & HUMAN RIGHTS

SOCIAL WORK

SOCIAL JUSTICE & HUMAN RIGHTS

A STRUCTURAL APPROACH TO PRACTICE

SECOND EDITION

COLLEEN LUNDY

 UNIVERSITY OF TORONTO PRESS

Library and Archives Canada Cataloguing in Publication

Lundy, Colleen, 1946–
     Social work, social justice, & human rights : a structural approach to practice / Colleen
Lundy. — 2nd ed.

Previous title: Social work and social justice.
Includes bibliographical references and index.
ISBN 978-1-4426-0039-3

     1. Social service—Textbooks. I. Lundy, Colleen, 1946–   . Social work and social justice.
II. Title. III. Title: Social work, social justice and human rights.

HV41.L85 2011   361.3'2   C2011-906365-4

We welcome comments and suggestions regarding any aspect of our publications—please
feel free to contact us at news@utphighereducation.com or visit our Internet site at
www.utppublishing.com.

North America
5201 Dufferin Street
North York, Ontario, Canada,
M3H 5T8

2250 Military Road
Tonawanda, New York, USA, 14150

ORDERS PHONE: 1-800-565-9523
ORDERS FAX: 1-800-221-9985
ORDERS E-MAIL: utpbooks@utpress.utoronto.ca

UK, Ireland, and continental Europe
NBN International
Estover Road, Plymouth, PL6 7PY, UK
ORDERS PHONE: 44 (0) 1752 202301
ORDERS FAX: 44 (0) 1752 202333
ORDERS E-MAIL: enquiries@nbninternational.com

This book is printed on paper containing 100% post-consumer fibre.

The University of Toronto Press acknowledges the financial support for its publishing activities
of the Government of Canada through the Canada Book Fund.

Printed in Canada.

This book is dedicated to the memory of my mother Hymmi Mikkola Lundy (1912–2008) who worked hard so that I could have the educational opportunities she was denied.

CONTENTS

FIGURES AND TABLES

FIGURES

TABLES

ABBREVIATIONS

9/11	11 September 2001 terrorist attacks in New York City and Washington, DC
ACSW	Alberta College of Social Workers
ADD	Attention Deficit Disorder
ADHD	Attention Deficit Hyperactivity Disorder
AIT	Agreement on Internal Trade (Canada)
ASWB	Association of Social Work Boards (US)
CAP	Canada Assistance Plan
CAS	Children's Aid Society
CASW	Canadian Association of Social Workers
CCF	Cooperative Commonwealth Foundation (Canada)
CCPR	Covenant on Civil and Political Rights (UN)
CEDAW	Convention on the Elimination of All Forms of Discrimination against Women (UN)
CEO	chief executive officer
CETA	Comprehensive Economic and Trade Agreement
CHST	Canada Health and Social Transfer
COS	Charity Organization Societies (Canada and the US)
COSW	community-oriented social work
CSWE	Council on Social Work Education (US)
CTO	Community Treatment Order (Canada)
CUPE	Canadian Union of Public Employees
DSM	*Diagnostic and Statistical Manual of Mental Disorders*
DSM-III	*Diagnostic and Statistical Manual of Mental Disorders*, 3rd edition

DSM-IV-TR	*Diagnostic and Statistical Manual of Mental Disorders, Text Revisions, 4th edition*
ECOSOC	Economic and Social Council (UN)
EFT	emotionally focused therapy
EI	Employment Insurance (Canada)
EPS	extrapyramidal symptoms
FAFIA	Canadian Feminist Alliance for International Action
FAST	Free and Secure Trade program
FTAA	Free Trade Agreement of the Americas
G6/G8/G20	Group of (6, 8, 20) the most powerful capitalist countries
GABA	gamma-aminobutyric acid
GAF	global assessment of functioning
GARS	government-assisted refugees (Canada)
GATS	General Agreement on Trade in Services
GATT	General Agreement on Tariffs and Trade
HRC	Human Rights Council (UN)
IASSW	International Association of Schools of Social Work
ICESCR	International Covenant on Economic, Social, and Cultural Rights (UN)
ICSW	International Council on Social Welfare
IFH	Interim Federal Health Program (Canada)
IFSW	International Federation of Social Workers
IMF	International Monetary Fund
INCO	International Nickel Company
LGBT	lesbian, gay, bisexual, and transgendered persons
LICO	Low-Income Cut-Off (Statistics Canada)
LINC	Language Instruction for Newcomers to Canada
MAO	monoamine oxidase
MBM	market-basket measure (Statistics Canada)
NAACP	National Association for the Advancement of Colored People
NAFTA	North American Free Trade Agreement
NASW	National Association of Social Workers (US)
NATO	North Atlantic Treaty Organization
NGOS	non-governmental organizations
NUPGE	National Union of Public and Government Employees (Canada)
NWT	Northwest Territories (Canada)
OASW	Ontario Association of Social Workers
OCAP	Ontario Coalition Against Poverty
OCCSW	Ontario College of Certified Social Workers

OCF	Ontario Common Front
OPTSQ	Ordre professionnel des travailleurs sociaux du Québec
PRWORA	Personal Responsibility and Work Opportunity Reconciliation Act (US)
PSAC	Public Sector Alliance of Canada
PSRS	privately sponsored refugees (Canada)
PTSD	post-traumatic stress disorder
RAP	Resettlement Assistance Program (Canada)
SIF	supervised injection facilities
SPP	Security and Prosperity Partnership of North America
SQ	Sûreté du Québec
SSRIS	selective serotonin reuptake inhibitors
TA	transactional analysis
TILMA	Trade, Investment and Labour Mobility Agreement (Canada)
UDHR	Universal Declaration of Human Rights (UN)
UN	United Nations
UNHCR	UN High Commissioner for Refugees
UNCHR	UN High Commissioner for Human Rights
UNICEF	Children's Fund (UN)
US	United States
WHO	World Health Organization (UN)
WPP/WILPF	Women's Peace Party, which re-formed as the Women's International League for Peace and Freedom
WTO	World Trade Organization

FOREWORD

OCIAL WORK HISTORY IS CHARACTERIZED by a constant preoccupation with the dual focus on individual and social change. The difficulty that has persisted since the inception of social work as a profession is that of relating these two levels of concern. Each generation identifies the dual focus on its own terms. Mary Richmond's "wholesale" and "retail" methods, Porter Lee's "cause" and "function," and Clarke Chambers' "prophets" and "priests" identify the struggle involved in relating the "private" and the "public," the "individual" and the "social," the "personal" and the "political." Many other writers, too, have emphasized the tension of the dual focus in social work. Some propose choosing one over the other; others encourage maintenance and extension of the duality, placing different social work practitioners in each sphere; still others place social workers outside the duality, arguing that they provide a mediating force between the social and the individual. Finally, some contributors to the debate seek to integrate the two perspectives into a single, more effective practice by suggesting that the "personal is political" and that individual services and social action are parts of the same act. The challenge has been the development of theoretical frameworks and practice approaches that reflect such an orientation.

Professor Colleen Lundy has the merit of providing a coherent theoretical framework and an original practice model that move from a dualistic view of the "personal" and the "social" to a dialectical one. Her historical analysis of the evolution to a "structural" perspective is very instructive and also quite relevant for any educator or practitioner interested in bridging the gap between "micro" and "macro" interventions. She clarifies the many ambiguities that are often present in the use of the concept "structural" and offers a clearer definition of its theoretical foundations. She also demonstrates that a progressive perspective such as the structural approach is more than a theoretical, ideological, or analytical exercise.

The originality of her contribution is the conceptualization of the direct practice component of this perspective in a manner that is amenable to practitioners working with individuals, families, small groups, and communities. She articulates the helping process within a structural perspective through a creative use of practice situations where the helping relationship is clearly defined in dialogical terms. Assessment tools such as genograms, ecological and social network maps, and a life line are identified along with assessment formats, all within a human needs and human rights perspective. The characteristics of ethical and accountable practice are particularly well defined. The author provides an interesting and convincing argument for the use of a structural approach in her description of the nature of the change process that occurs at the direct practice level, i.e., connecting the structural and the personal, through empathy, critical consciousness, and empowerment.

The section on professional associations and union membership is particularly illuminating. Social workers experience a tension between practicing in an ethical and competent manner and implementing policies and program regulations in the context of program cutbacks and mean-spirited governments. There may be a crisis in the social services, but the author correctly suggests that it is not a crisis stemming from social work incompetence as some regulatory bodies tend to advocate. Rather, it is a crisis of underfunding and of structures that perpetuate inequalities and oppression.

The structural approach was developed in the 1970s within a socio-economic and political climate that lent itself to change. We were witnessing the rise of the civil rights and anti-poverty movements, the women's movement, and student militancy. This was followed by a period of severe cutbacks in social welfare institutions and heavy criticism of the function and effectiveness of social work practice. The structural approach argued for a critical/generalist perspective in connecting the "personal" and the "social" that moved away from the "blaming the victim" perspectives to ones that sought to alleviate and transform the conditions in which oppressed clients found themselves. But what about its relevance today, in a context of globalization and neoliberalism?

In the global market the decline of social reform is increasingly leaving social needs unanswered. More than ever social workers must understand the nature of the inequalities and oppression that stem from globalization and neoliberal policies. Within this context the structural approach's focus on establishing the link between "public issues" and "personal troubles" while maintaining its commitment to social change and social justice is particularly relevant.

Professor Lundy provides a much needed and helpful analysis of the nature of oppression, its causes and sources, its production and reproduction, its dynamics, its effects on the oppressed—including its internalization—and the social functions it carries out in the interest of the dominant groups in society. I believe that her contribution goes a long way in preparing social workers to confront the challenge of globalization and neoliberalism and their impact on clients and social work practice.

Roland Lecomte
Professor, School of Social Work
University of Ottawa

PREFACE

Above all. Always be capable of feeling deeply any injustice committed against anyone, anywhere in the world. This is the most beautiful quality of a revolutionary.　　　　—Che Guevara[1]

I think social work has to find its soul and its conscience again. There needs to be a revolution in the profession.

　　　　　　　　　　　　　　　　—Dr. David Woodsworth[2]

THE CHALLENGE FOR SOCIAL WORK

PEOPLE WORKING IN THE FIELD OF SOCIAL WORK often face a dilemma in providing "help" to clients. On the one hand, much of the "help" that we are trained to provide targets personal and interpersonal change. At the same time, many of the issues and problems facing the people with whom we work are rooted in broad social, political, and economic conditions, and only a change in those conditions will "solve" them. This dilemma has sparked a series of debates within the profession about where social workers should place their efforts. Does building a profession or working for social change deserve most of our attention? Should we concentrate on individual casework or do community organization and social policy changes make more sense?

Of course, for most social workers this is very much an individual professional and career choice based on their own interests and goals. One of the main purposes of this book is to stimulate social work students and practitioners to consciously examine the relationship between the two approaches and the choices they make as professionals. While social workers are not limited to an either/or choice on this issue, this book argues that it is in their interests and those of their clients that they at least understand the relationship between individual problems and social conditions. Furthermore, a central theme is that individual recovery or change is often related to, if not determined by, change in social structures. Although an individual may approach a social worker with a seemingly individual concern such as alcohol overuse, the use of alcohol may be a way to survive an unbearable reality. For example, a fox caught in a leg-hold trap may begin to gnaw off its foot rather than die of star-vation or the cold.[3] A distant observer may not see the trap beneath the snow and conclude that the fox is self-destructive and acting abnormally. Similarly social workers need to look for the traps in the lives of people. Finally, this book advocates for an understanding of social conditions, social problems, and social change as a means of strengthening our social work practice.

Despite decades of debate within the profession, we still tend to divorce the critical analysis required for understanding broader social conditions (social welfare) from the personal and interpersonal theories and skills needed for working directly with individuals and families. Seldom are human needs viewed as human rights. For example, there may be an attempt to understand the ideas, behaviour, and feelings of individuals in the context of the socialization of their families, but there is little attempt to extend this analysis to a broader social context. Themes related to social analysis, oppression, power, and diversity are noticeably absent from these discussions. Often disparate theories and per-spectives are in direct conflict with one another. The result is a tendency in direct intervention practice to individualize and pathologize problems that are often symptomatic of broader social, political, and economic conditions. How-ever, integrating a critical analysis of broader social conditions into our day-to-day work with individuals and families does not mean that *all* of the problems individuals face are necessarily rooted in the larger social and political structure. Nor does it imply that individual problems can automatically be solved with changes at the societal level or that individuals do not have responsibility for their actions. Certainly it does not also mean that social work should ignore an individual's pain and suffering if it is rooted in larger social structures.

A central thesis of this book is to situate and understand the socio-economic or structural context of individual problems and how these power arrangements and societal forces create social conditions that generate stress, deprivation, and other forms of individual problems. Such an analysis can only strengthen our individual, family, and community practice. Structural analysis involves developing an awareness of the ways in which individuals and families learn to adapt and conform to their social conditions, as well as the ways they resist and challenge them. Central to this is an understanding of social and economic conditions as well as the role of ideology in shaping the way in which individual and social problems are perceived within society. It also involves a critical awareness of the role of the social work profession in the delivery of social services within a larger socio-economic and political context.

This book argues for a social change framework in social work practice. It builds on recent attempts to develop a critical analysis of class inequality, sexism, and racism along with other forms of oppression and their impact on social work practice; essentially, it offers a structural approach to social work practice. The second edition has expanded on these areas and has added four new chapters that include human rights and social work practice in mental health, refugee and immigrant settlement, and working with families and couples. The text is designed for social work students, social work practitioners, and others interested in developing a structural analytical perspective as well as entry level generic skills for practice in a variety of social service settings. Finally, there has been some debate in the profession regarding the term used for those who come to us for help. While some use "client" others prefer "service user" or "consumer." Throughout the book I refer to "the person" or "the family" and at times use the term "client." I do not believe that it is demeaning or that a person would be offended by it. After all, it is the nature of the helping relationship and the equalizing of the power differential that is most important.

ORGANIZATION OF THE CHAPTERS

This second edition of *Social Work, Social Justice, and Human Rights* divides the discussion into two parts. Part 1 outlines the structural and theoretical framework that underpins and guides social work practice. This section begins by situating the social welfare state and the delivery of social services within a broader context of the enlarging global capitalist economy. Chapter 1 explores the impact of the economic recession, globalization, and increased international trade liberalization on the social welfare of the population. Chapter 2 turns to social work's role in pursuing social justice, human rights, and peace. In Chapter 3 an historical account of social work developments in theory and practice is summarized to provide an understanding of the roots of common practice perspectives as well as the ongoing tension between individual helping and advocacy for social change.

Chapter 4 distinguishes theory from models and approaches while discussing the ideology guiding them and suggests an organizing framework in which to understand the ideological and philosophical differences. The chapter also outlines the development and foundations of the structural approach to social work. Included here is a discussion of social structures and human rights and social justice, as well as principles for practice.

In Chapter 5 attention is placed on structural injustice and inequality in society while examining the multiple social factors that influence the lives of individuals on a day-to-day basis. An awareness of the role of social relationships based on social class, race and ethnicity, sexual orientation, disability, and gender is viewed as central in responding to client problems and difficulties. Chapter 6 outlines the ethics of social work practice in addition to offering some direction in responding to ethical dilemmas and difficult situations. The role and importance of recording in social work is also discussed.

Part II focuses on social work practice. Chapter 7 presents assessment, analysis, and practice skills in working with individuals and their families. The anticipated outcome of social work practice, whether with individuals, families, or communities, is positive change, yet little is known regarding the nature of change and how it comes about. Chapter 8 continues with a process for achieving change and considers the influence of objective conditions on one's subjective reality while assessing the importance of critical consciousness and empowerment in the process. Chapter 9 focuses on sensitive and effective social work responses with refugees and immigrants; it outlines the immigration and refugee process and summarizes concerns of newcomers. In Chapter 10 the focus is on mental health concerns and includes attention to diagnostic categories, psychopharmacology, and social work responses. Chapter 11 offers an overview of the impact of personal, social, and economic conditions on couples and families and discusses approaches to support them when they face difficult situations. Chapter 12 highlights theory and practice in group work. Chapter 13 moves the discussion into social work practice with communities and suggests strategies for joining with participants to organize for change.

Increasingly, social workers encounter stress from the nature of the social and individual problems they face in practice, funding cuts to their agencies, and expanding case-loads. The final chapter, Chapter 14, is devoted to the working conditions of social workers and the role of professional associations and unions in advancing social work practice and social justice.

Like David Woodsworth, I too believe that in many ways social work has drifted from its past social justice/human rights orientation. While this orientation has not always been prevalent or dominant within the profession, it is only through reasserting the strengths and benefits of such an approach that it will be kept as a visible option for social workers. This is especially true in a time, as we now face, where social programs are being eroded and dismantled, where individuals with problems are left more and more to their own devices and support of friends and family, and ideologies that apologize for this state of affairs are becoming more and more fashionable. It is my hope that this text will engender "fire in the hearts" of social workers and offer some guidance in the task before us of responding to individual trauma and problems while supporting positive structural change and working toward a more just society.

NOTES

1 Che Guevara, *To His Children: Che's Letter of Farewell*, trans. Carmen Gonzalez; ed. José Marti (Havana: Artex, 1995) 11.

2 David Woodsworth, "An Interview with Dr. David Woodsworth, Emeritus Professor of Social Work, McGill University," *Canadian Social Work* 2.2 (Fall 2000): 149.

3 The metaphor is credited to Bruce K. Alexander, "The Empirical and Theoretical Bases for an Adaptive Model of Addiction," *The Journal of Drug Issues* 20.1 (1990): 37–65.

ACKNOWLEDGEMENTS

THIS BOOK DRAWS ON THE IDEAS of many scholars and practitioners, and I am indebted to their contributions. In particular, I wish to acknowledge the passion and vision for social justice that Maurice Moreau instilled in students and colleagues and infused in his development of a structural approach to social work. He left behind a legacy of social justice advocacy.

I also wish to recognize the students, faculty, and other staff colleagues at Carleton University. It is a privilege to teach in a department where critical discussion, debate, and camaraderie fill the classrooms and offices.

Anne Brackenbury of the University of Toronto Press was unfaltering in her support and encouragement. Her professional excellence and responsiveness have made the publishing process a pleasant one. Betsy Struthers provided exceptional copy-editing. Her close attention to detail and suggestions are greatly appreciated. My thanks are due to all those who offered invaluable feedback on the first edition, to the anonymous reviewers who took the time to offer suggestions and encouragement, and to Roland Lecomte who graciously agreed to write the foreword for the first edition.

I am indebted to Yohannes Drar and Adnan Türegün who readily engaged in discussions on mental health concerns and refugee and immigrant settlement, shared their expertise, and directed me to relevant sources. My nephew Allan Dubé assisted with the production of several graphics.

On a more personal note, I am particularly grateful to friends, especially my "forever young friends," family, and companion animals who provided much welcomed diversion during the writing process.

PART ONE

STRUCTURAL & THEORETICAL FRAMEWORK

CHAPTER 1

SOCIAL WORK, SOCIAL WELFARE, AND THE GLOBAL ECONOMY

OCIAL WORK AS A PROFESSION HAS HISTORICALLY HELD a central role in the development and delivery of social welfare. The need for an organized group of socially committed professionals to respond to the social and economic needs of people emerged out of the industrialization and urbanization of the late nineteenth century and the social problems they wrought. Initially the practice of social work developed within charity organizations and gradually expanded as the responsibility for social welfare shifted more and more to the state. Social work has increasingly taken on legitimacy as a profession. Social workers are front-line witnesses to the often harmful impact of economic and political policies on the lives of ordinary people. The response by the profession over the years has been to both advocate for immediate services and resources for those in need as well as to promote social change strategies aimed at eliminating and transforming structural inequalities. Political and economic changes, both in the national and international spheres, continue to have an impact on how social workers do their jobs and, in particular, on the role of social work in social welfare delivery.

THE GLOBAL CAPITALIST ECONOMY

These are particularly challenging times both for those who are responsible for the front-line delivery of social welfare services and for those who access those services. People are feeling the effects of more than three decades of downsizing and cuts to social programs with the consequent erosion of social benefits. This situation is now compounded by the economic recession that began in 2008 in the United States (US) and quickly spread to Europe; this is now noted as the worst economic downturn since 1929 and the Great Depression. Global capitalism is in crisis, and the most vulnerable are incurring the greatest suffering.

Within the context of increased mobility of capital, power has shifted even further from nation-states to transnational corporations, a shift that is being solidified through international trade agreements.[1] The process that Karl Marx and Friedrich Engels identified in 1848 as the move to "universal interdependence of nations" continues today:

> All old-established national industries have been destroyed or are daily being destroyed. They are dislodged by new industries, whose introduction becomes a life and death question for all civilised nations, by industries that no longer work up indigenous raw material, but raw material drawn from the remotest zones; industries whose products are consumed, not only at home, but in every quarter of the globe.[2]

What is different, some argue, is the accelerated speed of trade liberalization and accumulation of capital on a global scale with its attendant erosion of sovereignty and democracy within nation-states. The conversion of public services into commodities to be bought and sold on the private market is now a reality in our municipalities and provinces. Transnational organizations now determine the social, economic, and political policies of countries. The result is a profound increase in the polarization of wealth and disparity within and among countries as growing numbers of people within the global village lack the basic needs for survival, while a small number of others accumulate the riches of the world.[3]

This capitalist globalization process, under the banner of the World Trade Organization (WTO) and recent trade agreements such as the North American Free Trade Agreement (NAFTA) and the proposed Free Trade Agreement of the Americas (FTAA), ensures rights for transnational corporations while eroding the power of nation-states, and their citizens, to determine their own destiny. Ironically, "democracy" is being upheld as the necessary criterion in order to gain membership and participation in these agreements.

While there has been an expanding world market throughout the history of the capitalist mode of production, the period after World War II marked a qualitative shift to a global economy and commodity production with the removal of trade barriers. During this time global trade and investment grew dramatically, and the world domination of the US was established through new economic structures.[4] Gary Teeple notes that the origins of these new global institutions date back to 1944 when, under American auspices, the future members of the United Nations (UN) held a conference at Bretton Woods and developed institutions to regulate and liberalize world trade. An exchange rate mechanism set the parities of national currencies against the US dollar, and two institutions, the International Monetary Fund (IMF) and the World Bank (WB) were created. The General Agreement on Tariffs and Trade (GATT) followed in 1947 and further freed commerce by providing the institutional means for the removal of all national barriers to world trade.[5] Since the creation of the GATT there have been nine rounds of multilateral trade negotiations. In 1995 at the Uruguay Round (1986–94) the WTO was established to administer and regulate international trade among the 141 members.

The WTO is a powerful institution based in Geneva and managed by a 500-person secretariat, which administers legal agreements such as the GATT, the General Agreement on Trade in Services (GATS), and the agreement on Trade-Related Intellectual Property Rights. The WTO joins the IMF and WB as the administrative core that manages economic interests and the global financial system.[6] The functions of the WTO include "facilitating the implementation and operation of the Multilateral Trade Agreements, providing a forum for negotiations, administering the dispute settlement mechanism, providing multilateral surveillance of trade policies, and cooperating with the WB and the IMF to achieve greater coherence in global economic policy-making."[7]

Climate change and environmental destruction have resulted in a global water crisis and the devastation of tropical forests and oceans. This grave situation requires an international response; however, the primacy of trade and the accumulation of capital are preventing needed urgent changes. The most current round of WTO negotiations—the Doha Round (2001)—produced the Doha Declaration upholding WTO members' conviction that the aims of "an open trading system, protecting the environment, and promoting sustainable development *must be* mutually supportive."[8] Each country enters trade negotiations with the intent of expanding foreign markets for its own exports. Governments can launch trade challenges using WTO agreements against countries that may attempt to impose environmental regulations and policies to stop climate change.

In 2008 unleashed and unregulated "free market" capitalism, often referred to as neoliberalism or the Washington consensus (deregulation, privatization, spending cuts, wage controls, and the elimination of trade barriers), resulted in a global recession creating hardship for many. While there is a history of financial volatility under neoliberal capitalism, in this case the cause was deregulation of the US banking system and the introduction of "sub-prime" mortgages with low interest rates to applicants who were not required to demonstrate financial stability to assume home ownership. When interest rates increased, the only choice for thousands of homeowners was to walk away from their home and equity.[9] In communities such as Fort Myers, Florida, considered the foreclosure capital, there are streets of abandoned homes. Although the impact of the recession has been less severe in Canada, mainly due to a regulated banking system and surplus that the current government inherited, Canadians still find themselves more vulnerable than in the 1929 depression mainly because personal debt is at a record high.

The leaders of the most powerful capitalist countries meet on a regular basis to oversee the stabilization of global capitalism and the neoliberal economic and social policies. The Group of Six (G6) was formed in 1975; later Canada joined to form the G7 and Russia to form the G8. The G20 was created in response to the Asian crisis and the importance of adding emerging powers such as South Africa, Brazil, and India.[10] Although there are 192 countries in the world (often referred to as the G192), the G20 represents 75 per cent of the world's GDP. The G8 meets annually, the G20 semi-annually. In June 2010 the G8 and G20 meetings were in Ontario, in Huntsville and Toronto respectively, and the focus was on the impact of the international financial crisis and the coordination of an economic recovery. The summit in Toronto came with a price tag of over $1.24 billion, the most expensive meeting to date, and resulted in the arrests of over 1,000 protesters, one of the largest mass arrests in Canadian history. It was later revealed that Ontario had invoked a so-called secret law that was likely "illegal and unconstitutional" and resulted in a massive sweep of arrests.[11] The G20 agreed to implement austerity measures, which include cuts to public spending, thereby strengthening the neoliberal agenda.[12]

While world leaders were meeting, activists from around the world gathered in Toronto's Massey Hall to expose the summit's agenda. Maude Barlow, head of the Council of Canadians, was a key speaker. Barlow presented the facts: "The richest 2% own more than half the household wealth in the world. The richest 10% hold 85% of total global assets and the bottom half of humanity owns less than 1% of the wealth of the world. The three richest men in the world have more money than the poorest 48 countries."[13]

Despite the recession, chief executive officers (CEOs) of major corporations continue to pocket large salaries, many topped up by bonuses. In 2008 the average pay of the 50 highest paid CEOs was 243 times the pay of an average worker, a dramatic increase since 1995 when it was 85 times the average pay. By the time many Canadians returned from lunch on their first working day in January 2010, each CEO had already earned the annual income of most of them.[14]

NEOLIBERALISM

Capitalism has developed over the years and its latest phase is referred to as global neoliberal capitalism, representing the most advanced stage of capitalist imperialism.[15] Neoliberalism is the transformation of social structures, institutional arrangements, and economic policies and practices along market lines. To facilitate the movement of capital, goods, and services the removal of trade barriers and deregulation are required. This includes reduced wages, non-unionized workers, and the elimination of price controls, privatization, and minimizing regulation by the state—in other words, the privileging of free enterprise.

Increasingly public services are transferred to private companies. Most institutions in Canada—universities, hospitals, prisons, and schools—have out-sourced their essential services such as cleaning, maintenance, food production, laundry, and parking. The companies providing these services are often international corporations and have little commitment or investment in the overall quality of service. The diminished role of the state has resulted in the restructuring of welfare with the movement away from active welfare to the implementation of short-term life skills employment and training programs. Welfare recipients must demonstrate their readiness to work, no matter how short term or low paying the job is. More and more the responsibility of poverty is placed on the individual and not on changing social structures.[16]

The policies of deregulation and market liberalization, imposed by financial institutions such as the IMF and the WB, produced the 2007 US crisis that quickly became global. Joseph Stiglitz points out how "The crisis exposed deep flaws in notions of market fundamentalism, the theory that unfettered markets would lead to efficient and stable outcomes."[17] Financial crises are a feature of capitalism, and although this is not the first, it is the worst since the Great Depression.

THE ROLE OF THE MILITARY

Globalization "can neither survive nor function without the military powers as its backbone" since at times force is required to suppress resistance to WB/IMF policies and to ensure the expansion of imperialism.[18] As far as global military institutions, there are three: the armed forces of the US, the North Atlantic Treaty Organization (NATO), and the UN. The UN has the second largest deployed force after the US; in 2006 there were 100,000 soldiers, police, and civilians under its control.[19] As new markets are developed to distribute raw materials and access cheap labour, political and military policies protect these interests.[20]

Sharma and Kumar document how imperialist powers have militarily intervened in countries and discuss four categories that render countries vulnerable:

1) countries unable to repay debt or interest on it; 2) countries in which the people and the government resist the imposition of WB/IMF conditions;

3) countries with socialist, semi-socialist, nationalist or left populist economies; and 4) countries that resist MNCs [multinational corporations], try to develop regional alliances and struggle to present a model of development other than that of neo-liberalism.[21]

The authors also point out how imperialist countries reward countries that "voluntarily" submit to their political, economic, and military requirements and withdraw support from those who resist. For example, during the bombing of Afghanistan in 2001 after 9/11, agreement by Pakistan to accommodate the US airforce was rewarded by a lifting of trade sanctions by the US and Japan, the provision of $500 million in US aid, and an IMF loan of $1.3 billion.

Steven Staples, in a recent review of Canada's military spending, documents how "globalization, the arms industry, and military allies such as the US and NATO push for Canada to spend more on defence—much more than is required for our basic needs."[22] Canada is already one of the top military spenders in the world, ranking thirteenth, the sixth highest among the 28 members of NATO, and will spend an estimated $23 billion on its military forces in the 2010–11 fiscal year.[23] The military spending is now higher than it has been in the last 60 years and is 20 times the size of the federal budget for the environment department.[24] In July 2010 the Conservative Harper government announced the plan to purchase 65 F-35 stealth fighter aircraft from the US firm Lockheed Martin without a competition. The estimated total cost will reach approximately $16 billion, not including the actual cost of operation and the fact that the aircraft are not needed for current domestic and expeditionary military roles.[25]

However, it is the US that is the top nation in military spending. With the permanent War on Terror, US military spending reached $1 trillion in 2007.[26] The US accounts for 43 per cent of the 2009 worldwide military spending of $1.52 trillion (US dollars).[27]

Although Canada promotes its image as a peacekeeping nation, in reality the government heavily subsidizes the Canadian arms industry. Between 2003 and 2006 these industries profited from close to $7.5 billion in exports to 85 foreign governments, the majority to the US. These exports supported armed conflict in most of the countries receiving them.[28]

Social workers have voiced their opposition to militarization and war. The US National Association of Social Workers (NASW) recognizes the US dominance in the global economy and over the pillars of capitalism, the WB, the IMF, and the WTO. The association was firmly opposed to a unilateral, pre-emptive military attack by the US against Iraq. In a policy statement the association recognizes that "Beyond the destruction and trauma of war is the continual drain on human and material resources—the diversion of energies and goods and services to meet military needs—while the social welfare of millions of people in the United States and abroad goes unmet."[29] In 2003 and the aftermath of the bombardment of Iraq the International Federation of Social Workers (IFSW) released a statement entitled "Go on using your voice for peace" and shared profound sadness over what lay ahead for the people of Iraq.[30] The IFSW also called for an immediate implementation of the ceasefire called for by the UN Security Council against the 2008 Israeli air strikes against Hamas facilities in Gaza, which resulted in the deaths of hundreds of Palestinian civilians.[31] The next chapter on human rights continues the discussion of militarism, war, and the role of social work.

IMPOSED STRUCTURAL ADJUSTMENT PROGRAMS

Many developing countries, including those in Latin America and the former Soviet Union, must adhere to imposed Structural Adjustment Programs in order to receive IMF/WB loans to advance their economies. The imposed structural adjustment measures, a component to neoliberalism, require countries to embrace international investment and to put out the "welcome mat" of low wages, compliant unions, environmental deregulation, privatization of public services, and diminished role of the state in social protection and social programs. Under Structural Adjustment Programs countries are required

- to abandon domestic industry in favour of transnational corporate interests;
- turn their best agricultural lands over to export crops to pay off their national debt;
- curtail spending on social programs and abandon universal health care, education, and social security programs;
- deregulate their electricity, transportation, energy, and national resources sectors;
- remove regulatory impediments to foreign investment.[32]

According to Tony Clarke, the Structural Adjustment Programs, applied to both developed and developing countries and promoted by business, include "the deregulation of foreign investment and national economies; the privatization of crown corporations and public utilities and services; the negotiation and implementation of free trade regimes; the reduction of public deficits through massive social spending cuts; the erosion of national controls over monetary policy; and the reduction of public revenues through lower corporate taxes and higher interest rates."[33] Countries must agree to allow foreign investors to purchase businesses and land. Lower corporate taxes and diminished controls over corporations are accompanied by lower wages, less social spending, and lower environmental standards.

The far reach of the IMF at every level is demonstrated in a recent case in Jamaica. According to reports, the IMF demanded the closure of Air Jamaica due to its level of debt, while supporting a new airline, Caribbean Airlines, to take its place.[34]

WHAT DO INTERNATIONAL TRADE AGREEMENTS HAVE TO DO WITH SOCIAL WORK?

This book is not about international trade agreements. However, in order to effectively respond to social concerns we need to understand the financial underpinnings of our world. The international trade agreements noted above influence the delivery of services that are essential to the social welfare of Canadians, because trade agreements are no longer just about trade in goods such as automobiles, steel, or lumber, they are increasingly about trade in services. This is made clear by the GATS, which is currently being renegotiated to liberalize trade in services including health care, dental care, child and elder care, museums, libraries, social services, education, utilities, water, publishing, tourism, and postal services, thus paving the way for corporate privatization of these services with no restrictions. The idea is to create a level playing field for competition among private industries, whereby governments play little or no part in supporting their workers or families. In her assessment of the GATS, Maude Barlow notes that "not only is the ability to deliver these services in the public sector threatened, but as well governments' authority to regulate any service— public or private—is under attack."[35] Foreign corporations established in Canada will not be obligated to hire Canadian workers or adhere to environmental, health, or social security standards. The social and health services under attack by these policies employ the majority of social workers.

There is growing criticism of NAFTA, which was launched in 1994 by Canada, the US, and Mexico. In 2009 a coalition of noted Canadian organizations called for a renegotiation of the trilateral agreement. The gap between the rich and poor has continued to increase in all three countries; overall, working people have been adversely affected. In Mexico over 1 million farmers have been displaced and 15 million people have been driven into poverty.[36] In order to facilitate the movement of goods, the NAFTA Superhighway, including railways and pipelines, is being constructed from Mexico to the western Canadian border. Initiatives such as the Free and Secure Trade (FAST) program ensure border mobility for preferred citizens who represent capital.[37]

The coalition also calls for the end to the secret Security and Prosperity Partnership of North America (SPP), which is reportable only to business. Decisions made by the SPP include the reduction of Canada's higher pesticide standards to match those in the US.[38] Also Canada has linked its immigration policy to the SPP in order to increase the number of migrant workers.

Summing up the influence of these agreements and pro-globalization structures, Clarence Bolt emphasizes that the "control of Canada's destiny will not be in the hands of Canadian legislatures, but in the hands of organizations like NAFTA, the WTO, the IMF and the WB, that are beyond the reach of our governments—organizations that have no loyalty or accountability to Canada or its people."[39] In response, non-governmental organizations (NGOs), social coalitions, and labour unions have effectively informed citizens about the impact of the trade agreements and have mobilized them to act. Opposition to neoliberal globalization structures has taken to the streets in massive demonstrations, such as the "Battle of Seattle" in 1999 where the presence of 50,000 protesters closed down the WTO meeting. Seattle was a pivotal point in the challenge to neoliberalism and demonstrated the potential of coalition forces. In response to such demonstrations, state repression became increasingly violent. Two years later, demonstrators opposing the Summit of the Americas in Quebec City and the proposed FTAA met with one of the biggest security operations in Canadian peacetime history.

An important point to stress is that the effects of global capitalism are not felt just in the developing world. Corporate influences outside of Canada have had a profound impact on internal decision-making. Chossudovsky points out that it was the credit rating of Canada's public debt by Moody's (a financial market) that was a factor in the 1995–96 national restructuring that resulted in massive cuts to social programs and reduction of the government workforce.[40] Also, the role of the IMF in the cuts to social welfare in Canada is now evident. As a member country, Canada's economic performance is regularly evaluated by the IMF, which then makes "suggestions" for structural readjustment. Copies of these IMF memos to former Finance Minister Paul Martin, obtained by *The CCPA Monitor*, reveal that he *voluntarily* followed IMF suggestions in budget decisions to implement $29 billion in spending cuts over three years, including "$7.4 billion slashed from health care, education and social assistance transfers to the provinces; the elimination of 45,000 public sector jobs; large reductions in UI benefits and eligibility; the privatization of the Canadian National Railway, all airports, and the air traffic control system; the end of federal funding for social housing; the cancellation of the Liberals' oft-promised national child-care program."[41]

The trade treaties signed by Canada also apply to the northern territories

(Yukon, Northwest Territories (NWT), and Nunavut). While the Yukon and the NWT were able to participate in the negotiations of the NAFTA, Nunavut came into existence several years later in 1999 and was not able to introduce exceptions to protect its interests. There are four key issues facing the North: the economy, the environment, governance, and social services. Since treaties represent global corporate interests over local priorities, the North is in a vulnerable position with its sparse population, large geographic area, and unique concerns.[42]

Canada is currently negotiating a trade agreement with the European Union, the Comprehensive Economic and Trade Agreement (CETA). The document is alarming in that it takes aim at the use of progressive government purchasing policies and will impact essentially on every facet of life and services in Canada. This will include "all entities operating in the so-called M.A.S.H. sector (municipalities, municipal organizations, school boards and publicly funded academic, health and social service entities) as well as any corporation or entity owned or controlled by one or more of the preceding."[43] CETA's reach will also include airports, transport, ports, and municipal transit authorities such as VIA rail; the distribution of electricity; and all central government entities such as the Canadian Space Agency, Bank of Canada, House of Commons, Senate of Commons, Revenue Canada Taxation, National Film Board, and Transport Canada. Sinclair warns that "If CETA proceeds as planned, Canada would be on the verge of ceding democratic control over most provincial, territorial and municipal procurement, effectively abolishing the use of purchasing to lever economic, environmental and social benefits."[44] The agreement threatens to privatize and deregulate the public services on which Canadians rely: health care, social programs, water treatment, mail delivery, and so on. Needless to say, powerful European corporations are poised to take advantage of this giveaway and assume these services.

Since the economy is fundamental in shaping lives, permitting the market to be an arbiter of social priorities has a destabilizing influence on Canadian society, to say the least. More and more people are trying to piece together a living by combining a number of part-time jobs. Full-time unionized jobs have been replaced with temporary contract work, and Canadians are working more and earning less under harsher conditions.

Not surprisingly, this austere economic climate, compounded by an uncharitable political sentiment, is bound to have a profound impact on the psychological, social, and physical health of Canadians and on their opportunities for education and employment. Governments, both federal and provincial, have abdicated their responsibility for social welfare provision by reducing funding to health care, education, the environment, and social programs. There is a disturbing trend toward privatization as governments hand over public utilities and social and health services to the lowest bidder, thereby encouraging substandard services that are more costly to those who depend on them. These trends can only increase under trade regimes that look for profits for transnational corporations.

Globalization and trade agreements are also shaping social work as a profession. Guy Standing clearly outlines how neoliberalism impacts on the profession and its autonomy. "Commodification occurs as a craft or profession loses control of its ability to reproduce itself (setting standards of practice, levels of acceptable qualification, training methods and so on), or loses the capacity to operate its own association (the way it runs itself), or loses control of its work, the ability to determine what quality is acceptable, the ability to control the timing and extent of work to be performed, what goes on in the workplace, the market for its services and its relation to the state."[45]

Capital needs global labour mobility, and for professions that means removing restrictions on entry. On 18 July 1994 the federal, provincial, and territorial governments of Canada signed the Agreement on Internal Trade (AIT) to remove trade barriers and increase the mobility of goods, services, and workers throughout Canada. In March 2007 nine social work regulatory bodies signed the Mutual Recognition on Labour Mobility for Social Workers in Canada in order to comply with obligations under the AIT. Newfoundland and Labrador did not sign.[46] Similarly, there is pressure for countries to harmonize around the structure of regulation. The impact of trade agreements and the changing scope of social work practice is more fully addressed in the final chapter.

UNEMPLOYMENT, POVERTY, AND SOCIAL PROTECTION

Unemployment, part-time jobs, limited contracts, and casual jobs are features of global capitalism. The current recession has resulted in closed businesses, job losses, the foreclosure of homes, and devastating stress in the lives of individuals and their families. In Canada within one year 486,000 full-time jobs were wiped out; 80 per cent of the unemployed were in Ontario, British Columbia, and Alberta. Men and young workers are highly represented in the statistics.[47] There are also indicators that more and more people are experiencing economic hardship if not abject poverty. In 2010 the unemployment rate in Canada for women was 7.2 per cent, while for men it was 8.7 per cent.[48] That same year the US unemployment rate reached double digits; approximately 10 per cent of Americans were unemployed, the highest rate since 1983. All major race and ethnicity groups in the US were affected; 15.8 per cent of African Americans were out of work. Hidden are the large numbers of discouraged workers, those who have given up on searching for jobs.[49] In Canada temporary and part-time work now accounts for 40 per cent of the workforce.[50] This situation is compounded by the fact that Employment Insurance (EI) has been severely undermined and is highly inadequate: approximately six out of ten unemployed are not eligible for EI benefits.[51] Others who do qualify exhaust their claims before finding a new job. Workers who started collecting in late 2008 were running out of benefits by the fall of 2009. Currently claimants are eligible for between 19 and 50 weeks of benefits depending on how many hours they worked during the 52-week qualifying period plus the regional unemployment rate.[52]

Unemployed and underemployed people have a greater reliance on social programs. However, even with all possible income security assistance, people remain trapped in poverty. Particularly disadvantaged in terms of inadequate income and housing are persons with disabilities, Aboriginal peoples, recent immigrants and refugee claimants, and single parents. Whether on reserves or in cities, Aboriginal people are poorer and live in inadequate housing as compared to their non-Aboriginal counterparts.[53] Based on data from Canada's last three censuses—1996, 2001, and 2006—Aboriginal people (First Nations, Inuit, and Métis) experience greater income inequality, higher rates of unemployment, and lower levels of education compared to the rest of Canada. It is no surprise that accompanying this poverty are higher rates of suicide, substance abuse, and imprisonment.[54]

While people find themselves without resources to sustain dignity and health, services offered by hospitals and social agencies have been cut or closed, and social assistance has been reduced to provide less to fewer people. Insurance for the unemployed, social assistance, and other welfare benefits fail to provide for even the most basic needs of housing, food, and clothing, let alone essential toiletries, school supplies, bus fares, and non-prescription drugs.

The only alternative for many people is to rely on charity. Food banks, non-existent in 1980, now provide food for many people, including families, on a regular basis. Line-ups at soup kitchens and the increasing numbers of street people and homeless have become part of the social landscape. Between March 2008 and March 2009 there was a 17.6 per cent increase in the use of food banks. Children represented the largest single group at 37.2 per cent while 13.6 per cent were unemployed.[55] The ever-increasing number of hungry and homeless men, women, and children is a gauge of the depth of the social crisis and the inadequacy of the "safety net" in meeting their basic needs.[56]

The lack of subsidized housing combined with increasing rents has resulted in family homelessness. Family shelters are full of destitute families who now represent the largest single group seeking shelter accommodation.[57] Homelessness is a visible sign of the failure of the social welfare state and the income security system. It costs $48,000 a year for each homeless person, yet only $28,000 to provide housing for them.[58] In December 2010 in Ottawa shelter beds were full, forcing 114 families to be placed in motel rooms without cooking facilities.[59]

Poverty is not only an economic concern but a violation of human rights. There is a direct connection between living in poverty and ill health. Dennis Raphael concludes that the "high levels of poverty in Canada pose the greatest threat to the health and quality of life of Canadians." He points out that the incidences of death from heart disease, diabetes, arthritis, HIV/AIDS, and mental illness are strongly related to a life in poverty.[60] Among First Nations and Inuit people mortality rates were almost 1.5 times higher than the national rate and infant mortality rates were close to 3.5 times the national rate.[61]

There is solid evidence that unemployment and financial stress take a devastating toll on mental health, resulting in depression and suicides. The Canadian Institute for Health found that people in more disadvantaged urban areas face higher rates of hospitalization. Not surprisingly, experts in Canada's Mental Health Commission concluded that the toll of unemployment or the threat of job loss will increase levels of depression, anxiety, and suicide.[62] In Windsor, Ontario where there were lay-offs in the auto industry due to the recession, the demand for mental-health services increased 50 per cent in 2009. This reality is also reflected in a survey of family physicians in Canada; 88 per cent reported seeing patients undergoing stress due to the uncertain economy. A tragic example of the hopelessness that can accompany the uncertainty and stress of unemployment occurred on 1 January 2009 in Chicoutimi, Quebec. Recently unemployed and bankrupt, parents of three children carried out a murder-suicide pact to end their financial problems. The desperate act resulted in three children and their father dead and the mother seriously injured.[63]

Michael Kirby, Chair of the Mental Health Commission of Canada, states that "instead of cutting social-service budgets in times of crisis, we should nurture a culture of community support for the unemployed."[64] However, government and public discussions more and more are based on the ideology of blaming the victims for their poverty and misfortune.[65] Addressing societal inequalities and social structures that contribute to such conditions are no longer part of the political agenda, if they ever were.

Measuring Poverty

The 2009 Report Card on Child Poverty Campaign 2000 reports that 637,000 children—that is, one in ten—and their families were living in poverty in 2007. Among First Nations families, one in four children lives in poverty.[66] While it is the reality for many, the debate over how best to define and measure poverty continues. In the US the Census Bureau sets an income threshold that reflects a family's needs according to the number of its members. These thresholds do not vary geographically but are updated yearly for inflation using the Consumer Price Index.

Currently one in seven (14.3 per cent) people in the US are living in poverty, the highest number since 1959 when tracking poverty started.[67] Although the Canadian government has no mandated definition of poverty, the concept of relative poverty, by which a person's situation is considered relative to others in the same region of the country, is used to measure poverty. Statistics Canada's Low-Income Cut-Off (LICO), an unofficial measure of poverty, defines people as poor if they spend more than 55 per cent of their income on food, shelter, and clothing. Social policy analysts with the Fraser Institute, a conservative think tank, disagree with the LICO, claiming that it inflates the number of poor and arguing that poverty ought to be defined in terms of basic necessities of food, shelter, and clothing. Statistics Canada introduced the market-basket measure (MBM) that determines a poverty level according to a shopping basket of basic life essentials such as food, clothes, rent, and transportation.[68] As a result, Ernie Lightman points out, the child poverty rate in Canada of around 18 per cent when measured by LICO dropped to 12 per cent when the MBM was used.[69] The limitations of these poverty measures are evident. Poverty ought to describe people's incomes and standard of living in relation to the average income earners in the society in which they live; otherwise, the poor face social exclusion and are denied opportunities to actively participate in their communities.

Poverty statistics indicate that more and more Canadians and Americans have slipped below government poverty lines. The process of globalization and the withdrawal of state support for social security have created conditions in which the fundamental human rights of citizens are being violated. Federal governments in both Canada and the US have downloaded responsibility for social welfare on the provinces and states resulting in a lowering of benefits, tightening of eligibility criteria, and the elimination of much-needed social programs. It is quite striking how the developments in both countries have taken a similar path. In Canada in 1996 the Canada Health and Social Transfer (CHST) replaced the Canada Assistance Plan (CAP) and introduced a single block funding that includes health, post-secondary education, and social welfare funding. With an elimination of federal standards, provinces were free to reduce social welfare benefits and impose workfare or training for work conditions for eligibility. In the US the 1997 Personal Responsibility and Work Opportunity Reconciliation Act (PRWORA) converted welfare from a federal entitlement into a block grant administered by the states. The block funding is contingent on conditions such as a mandatory work requirement for welfare recipients and a five-year lifetime limit on benefits from federal funds.[70] While the majority of states have imposed the ban, others have not.

While all families are affected by economic restructuring and an erosion of social welfare programs, sole support women and their children are among the most vulnerable. Concerned with the economic impact on women of the significant cuts to social assistance and funding to women's shelters by the Ontario government in 1996, the Ontario Association of Transition Houses submitted a report to the UN Rapporteur on Violence against Women. The report documented the conditions endured by women fleeing abuse and called the government's actions a human rights violation. In the US so-called welfare reform has "pushed thousands of women off the rolls into low-paid jobs, but also into dangerous welfare hotels, drug-plagued streets, and unsafe relationships."[71] The impact of joblessness, low wage employment, cuts to social welfare, and poverty is hard felt by many individuals and families. Sometimes the effects can be deadly, as demonstrated in the case of Kimberly Rogers.[72]

A survey of social workers in Eastern Ontario provides a glimpse into the despair and desperation they encounter in their clients. They reported that, along with relying on food banks in their struggle to survive, clients are moving to less expensive housing (or in with other family members), not filling much-needed medical prescriptions, cancelling phone service, and selling possessions. Parents forgo food for themselves in order to feed their children, have no money for celebrating birthdays and holidays, and often report feeling depressed and suicidal.[73] As a last resort, some families are requesting that the Children's Aid Society provide care for their children, while other clients report turning to prostitution as a source of income or a place to stay.

Disadvantaged youth are adversely impacted by the erosion of social welfare programs and the uncertainty of the changing labour market. Jobs lost through corporate restructuring have resulted in some older workers taking jobs normally done by young workers. Older workers now manage newspaper routes, check out and bag groceries, and work in the fast food industry.

Stiglitz argues that "social protection is not only an instrument of social justice but also a tool of economic stabilization. Well-designed social protection systems make the economy more resilient to shocks by increasing the automatic stabilizers."[74] Among these stabilizers are insurance against risks and progressive redistribution of wealth. Inequalities are lessened as resources are present.

UNDERSTANDING INDIVIDUAL AND SOCIAL PROBLEMS
IN A STRUCTURAL CONTEXT

The previous section outlined a series of important economic and social problems that face all of us living in Canada. How our society is organized and how it distributes material and social resources determine the general health of a population. Inequality impacts on the health and well-being of the most vulnerable. Bruce Alexander in his latest book, *The Globalization of Addiction*, highlights the devastating impact of capitalism on people: "A society structured by free-market economics generates enormous material wealth and technical innovation and, at the same time, breaks down every traditional form of social cohesion and belief, creating a kind of dislocation or poverty of the spirit that draws people into addiction and other psychological problems."[75]

A structural approach to social work practice starts with an understanding of these developments. An awareness of these problems can help guide the practice of social workers and inform understanding of social relations, as well as personal troubles and the various resistance and coping strategies of those affected. Such an analysis can help social workers illuminate the obstacles to, as well as the strategies for, achieving advocacy, providing education, and promoting social change. Too often the social, political, and economic underpinnings of people's problems are not considered. Such a lack of understanding is more likely to lead to social workers focusing on individual deficiency and promoting only social control measures such as medical treatment, monitoring, and incarceration, rather than progressive social change and social justice.

Even if the first priority of social workers is not to challenge social inequality and advocate on behalf of women, racial/ethnic minorities, or an exploited class of people, an understanding of the principal divisions within society can only assist them in their many areas of practice. For example, understanding the influence of large multinational corporations and their emphasis on the production of goods and services that can be sold in the marketplace for a profit, their ruthless competition with other corporations, and the need to maximize profits in the long run explains their efforts to keep workers' wages and benefits as low as possible in order to intimidate workers and increase their productivity while laying off others. It helps explain the closure of Cape Breton coal mines in Nova Scotia. Men who had spent almost 30 years underground lost their jobs and do not qualify for a pension; the result is social strife and the intensification of various social problems for them, their families, and everyone who relies on the mining industry.[76]

Coal miners also experience the long-term impact of the chronic injustice that accompanies cyclical unemployment, underemployment, and poverty, as well as racial exploitation. David Cattell-Gordon, a native of West Virginia, observed symptoms of depression, futility, anger, numbing of the spirit, and fatalism among miners and their families and identified this as part of a traumatic stress syndrome that may affect several generations.[77] As Father Bob Neville of New Waterford, Cape Breton explains, coal mining has left many men old before their time: "After twenty years in the pit, a man's body, if uninjured in an accident, is full of aches and pains and his lungs have silicosis. For many, the stress caused by the constant darkness and danger leads to life styles which are destructive to themselves and to their families."[78]

It is also important to note that not all social conflict is unhealthy. Much of it is a "natural" response to unfair policies or social inequalities. For example, when 1,600 Cape Breton miners decided to launch a wildcat strike to fight the closure of the mine, it was reported that the confidence, the self-assurance, and the laughter were back, despite the fact that 200 RCMP were sent to the Prince Mine to contain their resistance. As one miner's wife said of her husband: "I don't care if he's right or wrong or wins or loses. Right now he feels like a man. And that's all that's important to me."[79] Fighting back, and even winning, does not address all of the social problems faced by Cape Breton coal-mining families, but it is an illustration of how resistance and social cohesion can play a positive role and make a difference.

Workers now face particular challenges when their workplace is sold to an international transnational corporation. In 2006 a Brazilian multinational, Vale SA, purchased the International Nickel Company (INCO) based in Sudbury, Ontario for $20 billion. When the United Steelworkers contract was up for renewal, Vale made demands for concessions, most notably to the pension plan, and the 3,000 union members refused to lose gains already fought for and went on strike in mid-July 2009. In early August the strike was joined by workers at Vale Inco refinery in Port Colbourne on Lake Erie and at the mine at Voisey's Bay in Labrador. On 8 July 2010 an agreement was reached for a five-year collective agreement, ending the longest strike in INCO history. Wayne Fraser of the United Steelworkers commented, "If this had been the old INCO, I think that we would have settled in a couple of months. The old INCO cared about its community and cared about its employees."[80] In 2008 Vale SA reaped US $13.2 billion in profits.

Although profits rather than the needs of people and their community determine the nature and extent of production within capitalism, this situation is intensified with foreign ownership of companies in Canada. The federal government needs to place some conditions on foreign ownership so that workers are not exploited and left to battle multinationals on their own.

A comprehensive data analysis of an international comparison of countries demonstrates that the quality of our social relations is closely connected to material conditions. The authors conclude that raising material standards improves the quality of life. There is evidence that unequal societies result in unhealthy societies with problems that include mental illness, drug and alcohol addiction, obesity, low educational performance, homicides, and high imprisonment rates.[81] Russia is a prime example; the collapse of the former Soviet Union and the sudden move to a market economy in the early 1990s was accompanied by a rapid rise in income inequality that resulted in a dramatic decline in life expectancy. This is in stark contrast to Cuba, a socially responsive state, which rivals industrial countries in population health.[82]

THE ROLE OF THE STATE

There is a need to understand the role of the state within Canadian society. Whether the state at any level is perceived as a problem creator or problem solver essentially depends on who is asked and what their experience has been. The state in Canada can be viewed as including institutions such as schools and child protection and family agencies, as well as such bureaucratic structures as the Departments of Finance and National Defence. For the most part, Canadians tend to believe that the state's role is to mediate between different groups of people for the benefit of the larger society, but many argue that the state usually functions in the interests of the rich and powerful.[83]

Our conception and understanding of the state can affect how we as social workers function within it. It can also affect our support for others who do challenge state policies and actions. For example, what do we think is the role of the state when it comes to Aboriginal peoples in Canada? How do we view the events of the summer of 1990 at the Mohawk barricades at Oka when Canadian Armed Forces were called in to assist the Sûreté du Québec (SQ) to put a stop to the uprising against expansion of a golf course into an area unsettled by land claims?[84] How do social workers view the role of the state when police are used to repress peaceful demonstrations during the G20 meetings in Toronto in 2010?

While not all of us will become involved in social protests or even openly sympathize with them, an understanding of the problems that lay behind and are the core of such struggles can enhance our practice as social workers. In *The Fiscal Crisis of the State*, James O'Connor argues that, while the state maintains the conditions in which profitable capital accumulation is possible, "the state must also create the conditions for social harmony."[85] In *Regulating the Poor*, Richard Cloward and Frances Piven provide an historical examination of social welfare practices and conclude that social welfare exists primarily to control the poor.[86] A final example of studies that can inform our practice is Gary Teeple's work in which he argues that the welfare state can be seen as "a capitalist *society* in which the state has intervened in the form of social policies, programs, standards, and regulation in order to mitigate class conflict *and* to provide for, answer, or accommodate certain social needs for which the capitalist mode of production in itself has no solution or makes no provision"(italics in original).[87] As contradictory and inadequate as these programs are, they do redistribute income, provide social security, and represent the gains made by workers and their unions, as well as other social movements. It is for these reasons that they must be defended.[88]

Sam Gindin points out how an increase in equality and security for workers and a strengthening of social programs can actually threaten capitalism. It is for this reason that he believes that the push for neoliberalism and the rapid globalization of the economy is intentional in order to preserve capitalism.[89]

This book focuses on the practice of social workers. Ann Withorn poignantly sums it up when she states that social workers "face the human result of all the contradictions and inefficiencies of a capitalist, racist, sexist society as well as the sheer pain and suffering that is part of life."[90] In regards to offering direct help, social workers often find themselves with two contradictory functions—the care versus control dilemma. Sue Wise views our role as carrying out the "policing of minimum standards of care for, and the protection of the rights of, the most vulnerable members of our society."[91] When we work in child protection, apprehending abused and neglected children and monitoring the progress of someone who is court-mandated to our service, we are carrying out the function of social control. At the same time we engage in the care function by offering individual and family counselling and advocating for much-needed social programs. If social work plays a contradictory role, it is because the society we live in is conflicted and uncommitted to the social well-being of its people.

In conclusion, for social workers to be consistent with their values and ethics, they must understand the inequalities in society and develop a practice approach that responds to the structural needs of individuals and families.

NOTES

1 Doug Henwood, author of *Wall Street: How It Works and For Whom* (New York: Verso, 1999), points out that organizations such as the WB hold the view that globalization as we know it is inevitable and unstoppable and notes that, even on the left, many speak of globalization instead of capitalism or imperialism to describe the process of corporate accumulation and power on an international scale. Henwood comments that "Once you understand capitalism, you see that it's always been an international and internationalizing system. Maybe we can say that the pace of that has picked up, but I don't think there is anything particularly newly international about the political economy today." In "The 'New Economy' and the Speculative Bubble: An Interview with Doug Henwood," *Monthly Review* 52.11 (April 2000): 72.

2 Karl Marx and Friedrich Engels, "*The Communist Manifesto* (1848)," in *The Communist Manifesto Now: Socialist Register*, ed. Leo Panitch and Colin Leys (Halifax: Fernwood, 1998) 243.

3 Those, such as Fidel Castro, who oppose the new globalization acknowledge its reach. "Globalization is an objective reality underlining the fact that we are all passengers on the same vessel—this planet where we all live. But passengers on this vessel are traveling in very different conditions. A trifling minority is traveling in luxurious cabins furnished with the internet, cell phones, and access to global communication networks … 85 per cent of the passengers on this ship are crowded together in its dirty hold, suffering hunger, disease, and helplessness." Fidel Castro, "Third World Must Unite or Die: Opening of the

South Summit, Havana," in *Capitalism in Crisis: Globalization and World Politics Today*, ed. David Deutschman (New York: Ocean Press, 2000) 279.

4 Gary Teeple, *Globalization and the Decline of Social Reform: Into the Twenty-First Century* (Toronto: Garamond, 2000). Teeple reminds us that the US was the only victor in World War II in terms of capital since other industrial powers were "economically exhausted and/or indebted to the United States" (57).

5 Teeple, *Globalization* 54.

6 The fourth ministerial meeting of the WTO took place in Dohar, Qatar, on 9–13 November 2001. At the same time there were anti-WTO meetings held around the world. In Havana, the Cuban government hosted the "Enuentro Hemisferico de Lucha Contra ACLA" [Hemispheric Meeting for the Struggle Against the FTAA] (13–16 November 2001). Over 800 delegates from 34 countries met to discuss the FTAA and their resistance to it.

7 Bernard M. Hoekman and Michel M. Kostecki, *The Political Economy of the World Trading System* (New York: Oxford University Press, 2001) 51. The authors are summarizing Article III of the Agreement Establishing the World Trade Organization.

8 Ellen Gould, *First, Do No Harm: The Doha Round and Climate Change* (Ottawa: *Canadian Centre for Policy Alternatives*, March 2010) 2; emphasis added.

9 John Bellamy Foster and Fred Magdoff, *The Great Financial Crisis: Causes and Consequences* (New York: Monthly Review Press, 2009).

10 Paul Martin, the Canadian Finance Minister, had a central role in expanding the G8 to G20 and was the inaugural chair. The G20 includes only 19 countries with the European Union taking the twentieth seat as a symbolic presence. John Ibbitson and Tara Perkins, "Secret Origins and the New Order," *Globe and Mail*, 19 June 2010: F1 and F6–7.

11 *Ottawa Citizen*, "G20 Abuses 'Will Live in Infamy,' Watchdog Says in Scathing Report," 8 December 2010: A3.

12 Justin Podur, "The G20 Debacle," *The Bullet*, E-Bulletin No. 380, 2 July 2010: 1–6, http://www.socialistproject.ca/bullet/380.php; Brent Patterson, "Challenging the Monstrosity of the G8 and G20 and Winning over Public Opinion along the Way," *Canadian Perspectives* (Autumn 2010): 21–22. Shamefully Canada's development contribution for maternal health was only $1.1 billion.

13 Maude Barlow, "The World Has Divided into Rich and Poor as at No Time in History," *Democracy Now!* 2 July 2010: 1, http://www.commondreams.org.

14 Hugh MacKenzie, *A Soft Landing: Recession and Canada's 100 Highest Paid CEOs* (Ottawa: Canadian Centre for Policy Alternatives, January 2010) 1–17.

15 Berch Berberoglu, ed., *Globalization in the 21st Century: Labor, Capital, and the State on a World Scale* (New York: Palgrave MacMillan, 2010).

16 Dean Herd, Ernie Lightman, and Andrew Mitchell, "Searching for Solutions: Making Welfare Policy on the Ground in Ontario," *Journal of Progressive Human Services* 20, no. 2 (2009): 129–51.

17 Joseph E. Stiglitz, *The Stiglitz Report: Reforming the International Monetary and Financial Systems in the Wake of the Global Crisis* (New York: New Press, 2010) ix. The President of the UN General Assembly approached Stiglitz to chair a Commission of Experts to write an independent report on the crisis and offer directions forward. The book is the result and reflects contributions from the 18 commission members.

18 Sohan Sharma and Surinder Kumar, "The Military Backbone of Globalisation," *Race and Class* 44.3 (January–March 2003): 23.

19 Jerry Harris, "US Imperialism after Iraq," *Race and Class* 50.1 (2008): 37–58.

20 Alan J. Spector, "Neoliberal Globalalization and Capitalist Crises in the Age of Imperialism," in *Globalization in the 21st Century: Labor, Capital, and the State on a World Scale*, ed. Berch Berberoglu (New York: Palgrave MacMillan, 2010): 33–56.

21 Sharma and Kumar, "The Military Backbone" 27.

22 Steven Staples, *Breaking Rank: A Citizen's Review of Canada's Military Spending* (Ottawa: The Polaris Institute, 2002) 29.

23 Bill Robinson, *Canadian Military Spending 2010–11* (Ottawa: Canadian Centre for Policy Alternatives, March 2011).

24 Bill Robinson, *Canadian Military Spending 2009* (Ottawa: Canadian Centre for Policy Alternatives, December 2009) 1.

25 Steven Staples, *Pilot Error: Why the F-35 Stealth Fighter is Wrong for Canada*, Foreign Policy Series (Ottawa: Canadian Centre for Policy Alternatives, October 2010) 1–8.

26 John Bellamy Foster, Hannah Holleman, and Robert McChesney, "The us Imperial Triangle and Military Spending," *Monthly Review* 60.5 (October 2008): 1–19.

27 Robinson, *Canadian Military Spending 2010–11*.

28 Richard Sanders, "Fuelling Wars, Supplying the Warmongers: Canadian Government Heavily Subsidizing Our Military Companies," *The CCPA* Monitor (March 2010): 12–15.

29 National Association of Social Workers, "Peace and Social Justice," *Social Work Speaks: National Association of Social Workers Policy Statements 2000–2003* (Washington, DC: NASW Press, 2000) 238; Also can be found at http://www.naswdc.org. The NASW opposes unilateral, pre-emptive military action by the us against Iraq. See, e.g., the 7 October 2002 letter to President George W. Bush from Terry Mizrahi, President of NASW, found at the same web site.

30 Imelda Dodds and Tom Johannesen, "Go On Using Your Voice for Peace" (Sydney/Bern: IFSW 18 March 2003).

31 David N. Jones and Tom Johannesen, "Statement on the Gaza Conflict" (London: IFSW 13 January 2009).

32 Maude Barlow, *The Free Trade Areas of the Americas and the Threat to Social Programs, Environmental Sustainability, and Social Justice in Canada and the Americas* (Ottawa: Council of Canadians, 18 January 2001) 4.

33 Tony Clarke, "Transitional Corporation Agenda Behind the Harris Regime," in *Mike Harris's Ontario: Open for Business: Closed to People*, ed. Diana Ralph, Andre Regimbald, and Nérée St-Amand (Halifax: Fernwood, 1990) 29. Clarke also draws our attention to how the NAFTA and the GATT are bills of rights for transnational corporations and how these rights supersede those for citizens of countries.

34 Ewart Walters, "Caribbean Airline Takes Over, Air Jamaica: The Love Bird Flies No More," *Spectrum* 27.5 (2010): 1.

35 Maude Barlow, "The Fourth Ministerial Meeting of the World Trade Organization—An Analysis," 16 October 2001, http://canadians.org/trade/documents/maude-wto.pdf.

36 Harsha Walia, "Transient Servitude: Migrant Labour in Canada and the Apartheid of Citizenship," *Race and Class* 52.1 (2010): 71–84.

37 The FAST card program began after 9/11 as a strategy to secure the us borders without jeopardizing the flow of trade. A FAST membership card can be used as proof of identity and citizenship for approved participants to expedite border clearance.

38 Linda Diebel, "It's Time to Renegotiate NAFTA, Critics Tell Harper," *The Star*, 14 February 2009, http://www.thestar.com/News/Canada/article/587628.

39 Clarence Bolt, "Our Destiny to be Decided More by TNCs Than by MPs," *The CCPA Monitor*

6.6 (1999): 18. It is for these reasons that some 40,000 protesters, representing 800 grass-roots organizations from over 75 countries, gathered at the meeting of the WTO in Seattle in November 1999, voicing their opposition to growing corporate control of nation-states and the imposed economic restructuring. Similarly, in April 2001 in Quebec City, 60,000 people gathered to highlight the harmful impact the FTAA will have in terms of human rights and on social, economic, and environmental conditions.

40 Michel Chossudovsky, *The Globalization of Poverty: Impacts of IMF and the World Bank Reforms* (London: Zed Books, 1997). This text offers a comprehensive analysis of globalization and the impact on both developed and developing countries. The author is scathing in his critique of this new international order: "The new international financial order feeds on human poverty and the destruction of the natural environment. It generates social apartheid, encourages racism and ethnic strife, undermines the rights of women, and often precipitates countries into destructive confrontations between nationalities" (34).

41 Canadian Centre for Policy Alternatives, Editorial, "Structurally Maladjusted," *The CCPA Monitor* 9.2 (June 2002): 2.

42 Noel Schacter, Jim Beebe, and Luigi Zanasi, *Globalization and the North* (Ottawa: Canadian Centre for Policy Alternatives, 2004).

43 Scott Sinclair, *Negotiating from Weakness: Canada-EU Trade Treaty Threatens Canadian Purchasing Policies and Public Services* (Ottawa: Canadian Centre for Policy Alternatives, April 2010): 13. A copy of CETA is provided in the report's appendix. See also, Jim Stanford, *Out of Equilibrium: The Impact of the EU-Canada Free Trade on the Real Economy* (Ottawa: Centre for Policy Alternatives, October 2010) 1–42.

44 Scott, *Negotiating from Weakness* 19.

45 Guy Standing, *Work after Globalization: Building Occupational Citizenship* (Cheltenham, UK: Edward Elgar, 2009) 147.

46 Newfoundland and Labrador Association of Social Workers (NLASW) did not sign the agreement because they wanted to maintain the Bachelor of Social Work degree as entry to practice and did not want to accept individuals registered as social workers in the provinces of Alberta and Saskatchewan on the basis of college diploma and certificates. NLASW has since obtained an exception and signed on.

47 Canadian Centre for Policy Alternatives, *Getting Canada Working Again: A Six Point Jobs Plan*, Alternative Federal Budget (Ottawa: Canadian Centre for Policy Alternatives, March 2010) 1–5.

48 Human Resources and Skills Development Canada, 27 May 2011, http://www4.hrsdc.gc.ca/.3ndic.1t.4r@-eng.jsp?iid=16.

49 Steven F. Hipple, "The Labor Market in 2009: Recession Drags On," *Monthly Labour Review* (March 2010): 1–20, http://www.bls.gov/opub/mlr/2010/03/art1full.pdf.

50 Senate Standing Committee on Social Affairs, Science, and Technology, "In From the Margins: A Call to Action on Poverty, Housing, and Homelessness" (December 2009): 42. http://www.parl.gc.ca/Content/SEN/Committee/402/citi/rep/rep02dec09-e.pdf.

51 Armine Yalnizyan, *Exposed: Revealing Truths about Canada's Recession* (Ottawa: Canadian Centre for Policy Alternatives, April 2009) 3–43.

52 Canadian Centre for Policy Alternatives, *Getting the Job Done Right*, Alternative Federal Budget (Ottawa: Canadian Centre for Policy Alternatives, 2010).

53 Senate Standing Committee, "In From the Margins."

54 Daniel Wilson and David Macdonald, *The Income Gap between Aboriginal Peoples and the Rest of Canada* (Ottawa: Canadian Centre for Policy Alternatives, April 2010) 1–34.

55 Canadian Centre for Policy Alternatives, *Getting the Job Done Right*.

56 Statistics compiled by the City of Ottawa in 2001 suggest that between 40 and 50 homeless people have died in shelters and on the streets in each of the previous three years. See *Ottawa Citizen*, "Mission to Add Hospice for Homeless," 15 March 2001: F6.

57 *Ottawa Citizen*, "Families Stuck in Costly 'Last Resort' Motels," 22 October 2001.

58 Senate Standing Committee, "In From the Margins" 107.

59 Jessica Sims, "Increased Demand for Shelter Beds Points to 'Community Situation,'" *Ottawa Citizen*, 22 December 2010: C1 and C5.

60 Dennis Raphael, *Poverty and Policy in Canada: Implications for Health and Quality of Life* (Toronto: Canadian Scholars Press, 2007) 203.

61 Raphael, *Poverty and Policy in Canada* 215.

62 Canadian Centre for Policy Alternatives, *Getting the Job Done Right* 65.

63 *Globe and Mail*, "Tragedy in Chicoutimi: Kids Killed in Parents' Suicide Pact: Police," 5 January 2009: A1 and A4.

64 Michael Kirby, "Everybody Hurts in a Social Recession," *Globe and Mail*, 26 August 2009: A13.

65 An excellent analysis of this practice can be found in William Ryan, *Blaming the Victim* (New York: Pantheon Books, 1971).

66 Campaign 2000, "Annual Report Card on Child and Family Poverty," 24 November 2009. http://www.campaign2000.ca/reportCards.

67 Paul Koring, "Almost 44 Million Americans Living Below the Poverty Line," *Globe and Mail*, 17 September 2010: A14.

68 *Globe and Mail*, "New Poverty Gauge Based on Survival," 9 January 2003: A3.

69 Ernie Lightman, *Social Policy in Canada* (Don Mills, ON: Oxford University Press, 2003).

70 Under the PRWORA, Temporary Assistance for Needy Families (TANF) replaced Aid to Families with Dependent Children. See Dorothy C. Miller, "What is Needed for True Equality: An Overview of Policy Issues for Women," *Building on Women's Strengths: A Social Work Agenda for the Twenty-First Century*, ed. K. Jean Peterson and Alice A. Lieberman (New York: The Haworth Social Work Practice Press, 2001) 45–65.

71 Mimi Abramovitz, *Under Attack, Fighting Back: Women and Welfare in the United States* (New York: Monthly Review Press, 2000) 25.

72 On 9 August 2001, Kimberly Rogers—40 years old, eight months pregnant, and battling depression—died. Ms. Rogers had made the mistake of enrolling in a social service worker program and receiving student loans while remaining on social assistance (a practice that was once allowed). She was charged with welfare fraud, convicted, banned from social assistance for life, and placed under house arrest except for three hours on Wednesday mornings. A legal challenge was successful in getting temporary reinstatement of welfare benefits of $520 a month. Of her monthly income, 10 per cent was automatically withdrawn for loan restitution, and $450 went for rent, leaving her with $18 a month for food and other essentials. See, e.g., Laura Etherden, "Criminalization of the Poor: Government Complicity in the Death of Kim Rogers," *NAPO News* 81 (December 2001): 9; *Globe and Mail*, "Bleak House," 18 August 2001. One year later, after an inquiry, the coroner's jury decided that Ms. Rogers had taken an overdose of antidepressants and ruled that the ban was a contributing factor in her death. However, the Ontario government

refused to lift the life-time ban; see, *Globe and Mail*, "Ontario to Maintain Lifetime Welfare Ban," 20 December 2002: A11.

73 OASW, Eastern Branch Survey, "Observations of Social Workers in Eastern Ontario on Effects on Clients/Families of Recent Funding and Policy Changes and Strategies Clients/Families are Using to Cope" (January–February 1996).

74 Stiglitz, *The Stiglitz Report*, 30.

75 Bruce Alexander, *Globalization of Addiction: A Study of Poverty of the Spirit* (Oxford: Oxford University Press, 2008) 12.

76 For a year prior to the shutdown and strike, the miners and their families lived in an atmosphere of uncertainty, abandonment, and powerlessness. The effect has been devastating, leading to heart attacks, family problems, and a questioning of their own worth. See, e.g., Reverend Robert Neville, "Commentary," *CBC Morning* (January 2000, reproduced with permission). Reverend Neville kindly sent me a copy of the commentary.

77 David Cattell-Gordon, "The Appalachian Inheritance: A Culturally Transmitted Traumatic Stress Syndrome?," *Journal of Progressive Human Services* 1, vol. 1 (1990): 41–57.

78 Neville, "Commentary." On 16 May 2001, the Prince mine workers and their families found out about the closure of the mine by hearing the news on the radio. The federal minister was not courteous enough to inform them directly.

79 Neville, "Commentary."

80 Peter Koven, "Despite Deal, Vale Tensions Remain," *Ottawa Citizen*, 6 July 2010: C7.

81 Richard Wilson and Kate Pickett, *The Spirit Level: Why Equality is Better for Everyone* (New York: Bloomsbury Press, 2009).

82 Colleen Lundy and Therese Jennissen, "Social Development and Human Rights during Economic Transition: Women in Russia and Cuba," in *International Social Work: Canadian Perspectives*, ed. Gayle Gilchrist James, Richard Ramsey, and Glenn Drover (Toronto: Thompson Educational, 2009) 127–49.

83 For example, Joanne Naiman outlines how the state serves the interests of the capitalist class, composed primarily of Anglo-Saxon, wealthy, white, heterosexual, and able-bodied men and women, by the three functions of accumulation, legitimation, and coercion. Accumulation is when the state tries to create or maintain the conditions for growth of profits and capital accumulation. Legitimation is when the state tries to maintain social harmony, in large measure by legitimating the current class structure and the right of the ruling class to rule. Coercion involves the state using force to suppress the subordinate classes on behalf of the dominant class. Joanne Naiman, *How Societies Work: Class, Power, and Change in a Canadian Society* (Concord, ON: Irwin, 1997) 161.

84 For an understanding of the uprising, see Kahn-Tineta Horn, "Interview: Oka and Mohawk Sovereignty," *Studies in Political Economy* 35 (Summer 1991): 29–41; Harry Swain, *Oka: A Political Crisis and its Legacy* (Vancouver: Douglas and McIntyre, 2010).

85 James O'Connor, *The Fiscal Crisis of the State* (New York: St. Martin's Press, 1973) 6.

86 Frances Fox Piven and Richard A. Cloward, *Regulating the Poor: The Functions of Public Welfare*, rev. ed. (New York: Vintage Books, 1993).

87 Teeple, *Globalization* 15.

88 The fact is that the taxes paid by the working class in Canada pay for all social welfare expenditures plus military and other budgets as well. See, e.g., Ardeshir Sepehri and Robert Chernomas, "Who Paid for the Canadian Welfare State between 1955–1988?," *Review of Radical Political Economics* 24.1 (Spring 1992): 71–88.

89 Sam Gindin, "Social Justice and Globalization: Are They Compatible?," *Monthly Review* 54.2 (June 2002): 1–11.

90 Ann Withorn, *Serving the People: Social Service and Social Change* (New York: Columbia University Press, 1984) 89.

91 Sue Wise. "Becoming a Feminist Social Worker," in *Feminist Praxis*, ed. Liz Stanley (London: Routledge, 1990) 236.

CHAPTER 2

PURSUING SOCIAL JUSTICE, HUMAN RIGHTS, AND PEACE

I want a world that is human-centred and genuinely democratic—a world that builds and protects peace, equality, justice, and development. I want a world where human security, as envisioned in the principles of the UN Charter, replaces armaments, violent conflicts, and wars. I want a world where everyone lives in a clean environment with a fair distribution of the earth's resources and where human rights are protected by a body of international law.

—Doug Roche[1]

SOCIAL WORK IS THE ONLY HELPING PROFESSION that has a rich history of social justice as its fundamental value and concern. The long commitment to social and economic justice, human rights, and peace permeates the mandates and codes of ethics of current provincial, national, and international social work organizations.[2]

However, social work has not fully incorporated the elements of human rights within its theory, policies, and practices. Today the urgency of this task is even greater as the impact of neoliberalism and economic globalization increasingly undermines human rights and the possibilities for social justice. There is a need not only for more robust human rights and greater social justice but also for clarity in how social workers might engage them in their social work practice. A number of recent contributions from social work scholars have contributed to this task.[3]

Social justice and equality need to be seen as integrally linked to the need for economic security and access to better social services and programs. Social workers have also turned their attention to the impact of militarism and the environmental crisis on well-being. The inclusion of a human rights framework strengthens social work's social change response.

This chapter outlines the role of the United Nations and the involvement of social work. It includes the development of human rights, both at the international and national level, and addresses some of the dilemmas and challenges facing social workers as they attempt to advocate for them and question exploitative structures that are creating hardship for so many.

THE UNITED NATIONS AND THE EMERGENCE OF HUMAN RIGHTS

The United Nations was formed in 1945 at the end of World War II, with an initial membership of 51 nation-states, to serve as a structure to oversee international law and to protect future generations from the atrocities of war. One of its first tasks was to develop international human rights. The UN's Universal Declaration of Human Rights (UDHR) was adopted by the UN General Assembly on December 10, 1948 as a common standard for economic, civil, cultural, and social rights (see Appendix A). It was the first international human rights instrument and was drafted by John Humphrey, a Canadian professor. In summary, all people have:

> the right to a standard of living that is adequate for the health and well-being of all people and their families, without exception, and the essential resources to meet such a standard; the right to adequate food and nourishment; the right to adequate clothing; the right to adequate housing; the right to basic health care; the right to an education; the right to security in the event of unemployment, sickness, disability, widowhood, old age, or other lack of livelihood beyond one's control; the right to necessary social services; and the right not to be subjected to dehumanizing punishment.[4]

These rights are considered essential for equality and a life of dignity. The declaration is not a binding instrument but rather a formal enunciation of general principles and obligations with the expectation that countries would abide by it. It was intended to represent the minimum standards necessary to ensure human dignity and to which all states should adhere. The UN is responsible for monitoring the UDHR as well as other human rights laws through a main body, the Office of the High Commissioner for Human Rights, which includes the Human Rights Council (HRC). However, there is no mechanism in place that holds noncompliant states accountable.

The General Assembly, made up of all member nation-states, is the main decision-making body. Member states make decisions at the UN on resolutions, declarations, conventions, and protocols, and each has one vote. The Security Council that oversees the maintenance of international peace and security is the only body that has binding resolutions.

Social Work and the United Nations

The International Federation of Social Workers (IFSW), established in 1928, is the global social work association. IFSW represents social work associations in 90 countries with a total membership of more than 745,000 social workers. The IFSW, the International Association of Schools of Social Work (IASSW), and the International Council on Social Welfare have taken a leadership role in advancing a human rights and social justice perspective and have been granted consultative status as NGOs. They offer advice but are not part of the decision-making.[5] Both the Canadian Association of Social Workers (CASW) and the National Association of Social Workers (NASW) uphold the standards set in the UDHR in their codes of ethics and place an emphasis on the social worker's ethical responsibility for social change and the promotion of social justice.[6]

IFSW has consultative status with the UN's Economic and Social Council (ECOSOC) and its Children's Fund (UNICEF). The association also has a close working relationship with the World Health Organization (WHO), the Office of the UN High Commissioner for Refugees (UNHCR), and the office of the UN High Commissioner for Human Rights (OHCHR). In 1988 the IFSW established a Human Rights Commission to support and advocate on behalf of social workers who are at risk and persecuted as they practice their profession. IFSW's mandate has consistently included human rights, and it has participated in the yearly meeting of the Commission on Human Rights, which was replaced in 2006 by the HRC.[7]

THE DEVELOPMENT OF HUMAN RIGHTS

Human rights are an evolving concept that has advanced over three generations. The first generation of human rights, often referred to as negative rights, gives primacy to civil and political rights (the rights to vote, freedom of speech, free assembly, and citizenship). The second generation includes economic, social, and cultural rights such as health, housing, social security, and education to ensure a life of dignity. These are generally referred to as positive rights since more involvement of the state is required for their realization. The third generation is not based on a UN covenant but refers to collective rights, those shared by a community or a population, and include peace, a healthy environment, and the right to self-determination. These collective rights are central to community development. Ife examines the impact of globalization and capitalist market forces and advocates for some collective universal rights over economic development and the protection of the environment.[8]

It is ironic that both the UDHR and the major pillars of the economic structure of the global economic system were established at the same time.[9] The parallel development of a move toward greater human rights and global capitalism has not been without its tensions. This was noted by Sergio Vieira de Mello, a former UN High Commissioner for Human Rights (1997–2002), when he described international financial institutions such as the WTO, IMF, and the WB as posing fundamental obstacles to the realization of human rights.[10]

Because the UDHR is an international agreement and not a legal instrument, the initial intention was to establish a treaty that would contain a mechanism to monitor and enforce components of the declaration. However, the US was opposed to including health care and social and economic rights in a binding treaty and insisted that the UDHR be divided into two treaties, one that addressed social, economic, and cultural rights and the other political and civil rights. The International Covenant on Economic, Social, and Cultural Rights (ICESCR) and the Covenant on Civil and Political Rights (CCPR) were adopted by the UN General Assembly in December 1966. However, they did not come into force for another decade until the required 35 states ratified both instruments. By 2009, 60 of the 195 UN member states had ratified the ICESCR, and 164 states had ratified the CCPR. The US only ratified the latter.[11] Since Canada is a signatory of both, social workers can use the UDHR as an example when holding the federal and provincial/territorial governments accountable for eliminating social inequities. The human rights provisions of the UN Charter, the UDHR, and the two International Covenants on Human Rights are referred to as the International Bill of Rights.[12]

The ICESCR expands on the UDHR and outlines the following rights:

> The right to work; the right to the enjoyment of just and favorable conditions of work; the right to form and join a trade union; the right to social security, including social insurance; the right to the protection of family; the right to an adequate standard of living; the right to the enjoyment of the highest attainable standard of physical and mental health; the right of everyone to education; the right to take part in cultural life.[13]

In the US and Canada, as in most capitalist economies, the CCPR tends to take precedence over the ICESCR since the protection of civil and political rights requires few economic resources while social and economic rights require the redistribution of basic goods and services to each person. Civil and political rights are free; economic, social, and cultural rights require a safety net.

All the provinces in Canada as well as the federal government have human rights legislation that is administered by a Human Rights Commission. Also, the Canadian Charter of Rights and Freedoms, introduced in 1982, addresses civil and political rights. The Charter outlines four fundamental freedoms: freedom of religion; freedom of thought, belief, opinion, and expression, including freedom of the press and other media; freedom of peaceful assembly; and freedom of association. The Charter also upholds democratic rights, legal rights, and the two official languages in Canada. Neither the Bill of Rights of the US Constitution or the Canadian Charter of Rights and Freedoms contain all of the rights in the UDHR; most notably missing are socio-economic rights.

The advance of social and economic rights and social justice has been uneven at best, and a substantial number of people are still unaware of these rights and have never possessed them. Moreover, as Teeple notes, human rights "remain abstractions unless people have the means to realize them and live in a system in which they can be realized."[14] The full realization of civil and political rights is not possible without economic, social, and cultural rights. In regards to the latter, unless services and policies actually exist, and there is substantial redistribution of wealth, these rights cannot be met. Gwen Brodsky, lawyer and international expert on equality rights, explains how poverty is a human rights violation since it denies people their universal human rights: "In the lived experience of people who are poor, civil and political rights can be meaningless. Poor people have much less access to justice, and they are criminalized because of their poverty."[15] Social worker Hugh Shewell questions the potential of liberal democracies such as Canada, characterized by class inequality and exploitation, to advance human rights. He explains that, since democracy is inherently about human equality, "people are only free if the conditions in which they live allow for their full human development."[16]

Since 1948 various covenants, laws, and international agreements have strengthened the UDHR. Other instruments providing protection are the Convention on the Prevention and Punishment of the Crime of Genocide (1948), International Convention on the Elimination of All Forms of Racial Discrimination (1965), Convention on the Elimination of All Forms of Discrimination against Women (1979), Convention against Torture and Other Inhuman or Degrading Treatment or Punishment (1984), Convention on the Rights of the Child (1989), International Convention on the Protection of the Rights of All Migrant Workers and Members of Their Families (1990), Convention on the Rights of Persons with Disabilities (2006), and International Convention on the Protection of all Persons from Enforced Disappearance (2006). The latter has not been ratified by either Canada or the US.[17] Nor has Canada ratified the Convention on the Protection of the Rights of All Migrant Workers and Members of Their Families. A state is not legally bound to implement the treaty until it has ratified it.

In 2007, Canada was one of four nations (with Australia, New Zealand, and the US) that refused to sign the UN Declaration on the Rights of Indigenous Peoples.[18] It is notable that these four nations have substantial populations of indigenous peoples, all struggling for their rights. Although the declaration is an endorsement of the 370 million indigenous people worldwide and was more than 20 years in development followed by three years of ratification discussions, the federal government claimed that it contravenes Canadian law.[19] Following endorsements by Australia and New Zealand, and a pledge by the US to reconsider its decision, and after much contentious debate and widespread Aboriginal support for the declaration, the Conservative government reversed its decision on 12 November 2010 and announced that Canada would be a signatory after all.[20]

None of the UN human rights documents include specific mention of sexual orientation in order to ensure that gay, lesbian, bisexual, and transgendered persons have the same rights and are not discriminated against. It was not until 1996 that the Canadian Human Rights Act was amended to include sexual orientation.[21] All provinces (except Alberta) and territories have added "sexual orientation" to their human rights laws. The Northwest Territories also includes "gender identity."

The sixtieth anniversary of the UDHR came on 10 December 2007. The hopeful vision that everyone could live free of political violence and have the basic necessities of life has not yet been realized for many and appears even more tenuous and out of reach.

We are now witnessing human rights violations around the world. One obstacle to achieving greater social and economic justice is the globalization of the market economy and the attendant erosion of sovereignty and democracy within nation-states, deregulation and privatization of essential services, and an increase in disparity among members of the population. According to Craig, in order to achieve social justice, such inequities and problems must be understood as an integral feature of global capitalism.[22] However, despite the fact that the hardship many people experience is directly linked to multinational capitalism and imposed structural adjustment programs and debt, reference to capitalism is generally absent from UN reports.[23]

MILITARISM, ARMED CONFLICT, AND NON-STATE TERRORISM

Along with world financial institutions and globalization, increased military spending and armed conflicts have resulted in human rights violations and have become obstacles to social justice and equality. Human rights are intricately connected to militarization and war, growing social and economic inequality within and between countries, the erosion of social welfare, and environmental destruction. States that are dominant in military and economic terms also dominate international human rights, according to de Feyter,[24] and these rights may be limited in order to advance national and corporate interests. In her examination of voting on UN resolutions, Guest reports that those that addressed transnational exploitation, such as foreign debt and structural adjustment programs, were split between countries in the North and South.[25]

A War with No End

The events of 9/11 were followed by the "War on Terror," which resulted in a military buildup, and the "Bush doctrine" that justifies the use of pre-emptive military force when there is the possibility of capturing terrorist suspects.[26] Subsequently, the US invaded Iraq with a "shock and awe" bombardment, though those responsible for 9/11 were not from there, and accusations that Iraq was harbouring weapons of mass destruction were not confirmed. The US government, after the destruction of Iraq's infrastructure and the capture of its president, Saddam Hussein, established an occupation that was devastating to both the country and the people. Current conditions in Iraq are bleak; the 12 years of sanctions and seven years of occupation have resulted in vast unemployment, while basic services such as electricity, water, and health care are in short supply or nonexistent. In October 2001 the US and the UK entered Afghanistan to remove the al-Qaeda terrorist organization and the Taliban, the perceived perpetrators of 9/11, and NATO quickly assumed control of the war, which is now referred to as the longest war. In both Iraq and Afghanistan normal life has been seriously disrupted, and civilian casualties continue to mount. We are now "at war" with an entity that we cannot recognize nor confine—a war with no end.

It was not long after the invasion of Iraq that human rights violations were documented. Scott Harding sees it as an example of "human-created disasters," which he defines as "conditions that result from a range of policies and deliberate state actions" and includes "war, actions of repressive regimes, failure to halt the spread of preventable disease and epidemics, economic sanctions, and neoliberal economic strategies."[27] Three authors, one a social worker, effectively demonstrate how the aim of the US invasion was to destroy the Iraqi state in order to remake it as a puppet regime under its control. In their well-documented book, they summarize the totality of this vast destruction:

The consequences in human and cultural terms of the destruction of the Iraqi state have been enormous: notably, the deaths of over 1 million civilians; the degradation in social infrastructure, including electricity, potable water, and sewage systems; the targeted assassination of over 400 academics and professionals and the displacement of 4 million refugees and internally displaced people. All of these terrible losses are compounded by unprecedented levels of cultural devastation, attacks on national archives and monuments that represent the historical identity of the Iraqi people.[28]

Since the 2003 invasion of Iraq, an estimated 650,000 Iraqi civilians—men, women, and children—have been killed.[29] The cost of war on humanity is great while the military industrial complex profits. War is itself terrorism. Cluster munitions are weapons that disperse up to as many as 600 bomblets. The US peppered both Iraq and Afghanistan with cluster bombs, inflicting death and injury to civilians including children.[30] Depleted uranium shell-casings were used in Iraq; their long-term effects on both the civilian and military population are yet to be seen. However, recent research indicates that the long-term impact of US bombing is now responsible for the major increase in cancers and birth defects in Iraq. The dramatic rise of birth defects in the city of Falluja is unprecedented and presents a serious public health crisis.[31]

The War on Terror includes not only the invasion of Iraq and Afghanistan but the illegal retaining of individuals without charge, the use of torture, and the restriction on human rights through such things as wiretapping of phones without a warrant.[32] American soldiers returning home are often suffering from post-traumatic stress syndrome and are at high risk for alcohol and drug overuse. In 2009 approximately 140 returning US soldiers took their own lives.[33] Similar documentation on Canadian soldiers has not been revealed publicly.

The NASW has been particularly active in upholding human rights and speaking out when violations occur and was quick to condemn the plans for the invasion of Iraq put forward by former President George W. Bush. The NASW emphasized social work's history "of advocating the elimination of all weapons of mass destruction—chemical, biological, and nuclear, including the country's arsenal" and related concern that such actions would "result in substantial loss of liberties, the harassment of Arab and Muslim communities within and outside the US, the curtailing of individual freedoms and privacy rights, and the self-censorship of the media that would limit healthy debate."[34]

In January 2008, NASW endorsed and participated in the demonstration on the National Mall in Washington, DC, to protest the use of torture of any kind, the rendition or the sending of prisoners to countries where torture can be conducted, and the lack of due process for US detainees; it also called for the closure of the Guantanamo Bay detention facility in Cuba.[35] The CASW has not issued any statements regarding the War on Terror.

War is a crime against humanity and contributes to global insecurity. US President Barack Obama ended the combat mission in Iraq in August 2010. However, 50,000 troops remain there, apparently to train and advise Iraqi military, prompting Congressman Dennis Kucinich to point out that "You can't be in and out at the same time."[36] At one point in the campaign for the US presidency, Obama pointed out that it was not just a matter of getting out but changing the mindset that got the US into Iraq.[37] However, that mindset has not changed, and the US remains an expansionist and imperialist power whose solutions to problems are military solutions. Any honest criticism of military interventions is labeled as unpatriotic.

While Canada planned to end its combat role in Afghanistan in 2011, in November 2010 Prime Minister Harper announced that Canada will stay there in a training mission. Military presence in Afghanistan is not bringing democracy and stability to the country, nor has the condition of Afghani women improved. Colin Kenny, a former chair of the Senate Committee on Security and Defence, claims that the Afghan mission has been a failure. He points out that al-Qaeda had departed before the mission began, the Taliban is now strengthened, a corrupt government was put in place, and the drug trade is burgeoning. The cost has been immense: billions of dollars, the lives of 2,579 NATO and 157 Canadian soldiers, as well as 8,832 Afghan civilians.[38] However, amidst a financial crisis and unprecedented global inequality and the revelation of US military war crimes, President Obama has ordered that 17,000 more troops be sent to Afghanistan. The US involvement is not entirely altruistic. Afghanistan is vital to the US as a natural gas pipeline route linking the natural gas resources of Turkmenistan, Pakistan, and India. Turkmenistan has the world's fourth largest reserves of gas.[39]

On 17 August 2010 Congressman Kucinich wrote a letter to his fellow members of Congress urging them to withdraw all US troops and to end the "Longest War in US History." Although $104 billion was allocated to Afghanistan between January and August 2010, over 270 US soldiers died and civilian causalities rose by 31 per cent in the last year. Kucinich, among others, believes that there is no war to be won in Afghanistan.[40]

The austerity measures placed on social welfare spending are in stark contrast to budget support of the military. World military expenditures are well over $1 trillion or $306 billion per day, $128 million per hour, $2.1 million a minute.[41] Since 2001 the acknowledged US defence spending has increased almost 60 per cent in real dollar terms to a level in 2007 of $553 billion, representing 45 per cent of world military expenditures. The actual budget is $1 trillion.[42]

Nuclear weapons threaten global peace and security. While the 15 kiloton atomic bomb caused devastation in Hiroshima and Nagasaki, the average nuclear warhead today is 100 kilotons, while some are 250 kilotons and 5 megatons.[43] The Nuclear Non-Proliferation Treaty, signed in 1970, is an agreement by 177 non-nuclear nations not to acquire nuclear weapons and for the top five

(US, Britain, France, China, and Russia) to dismantle theirs. The US and allies are the world's biggest nuclear proliferators. Canada provides around 40 per cent of the world's uranium and exports 76 per cent to the US, mostly for weapons production. The distribution of uranium for weapons is in direct violation of the Nuclear Non-Proliferation Treaty.[44] Similarly, initiatives to ban nuclear testing (such as the Comprehensive Nuclear Test Ban Treaty) have been ignored by the US, China, India, Pakistan, Israel, and North Korea.

Opposing Militarism

Military spending is at its highest level since the end of World War II, and there appears to be no shortage of money to participate in ongoing military missions. It is estimated that the Canadian military costs for the Afghanistan mission are close to $13–$16 billion to date.[45] It is no surprise that as military budgets increase, social welfare funding does not, despite the growing number of those who are unemployed and homeless.

The reasons for opposing militarization and war were eloquently stated by President Dwight Eisenhower in 1953.

> Every gun that is made, every warship launched, every rocket fired signifies, in the final sense, a theft from those who hunger and are not fed, those who are cold and not clothed. This world in arms is not spending money alone. It is spending the sweat of its laborers, the genius of its scientists, the hopes of its children. This is not a way of life at all in any true sense. Under the cloud of threatening war, it is humanity hanging from a cross of iron.[46]

The War on Terror justifies the curbing of civil liberties and the increase in spending on defence and homeland security at the expense of better social programs and services. Yet when world leaders pledged to reduce poverty in half by 2015 at the UN Millennium Summit in 2000, they stated that they did not have the financial resources to achieve the Millennium Goals.[47] Peace is not only the absence of war but also the absence of injustice. Jane Addams in *Peace and Bread in Time of War* addressed the costs of militarism and emphasized the importance of shelter, health, education, human dignity, and freedom from suppression.[48]

SOCIAL INJUSTICE IS KILLING PEOPLE

Capitalist expansion globally intensifies social and economic inequality, and the inequalities within and between countries is astounding. One half of the world's population is living in severe poverty, while the other half reaps the riches. World poverty is responsible for one-third of all human deaths (50,000 deaths per day, 18 million a year) yet eradication would require no more than 1 per cent of the global product.[49]

The WHO recently released a report on the determinants of health and concluded that social justice is a matter of life and death and that social injustice is killing people on an alarming scale.[50] The report highlights how the conditions in which people live and die are shaped by political, social, and economic forces.

Dennis Raphael, a physician in Canada, points out that "high levels of poverty in Canada pose the greatest threat to the health and quality of life of Canadians."[51] He and a colleague, Juha Mikkonen, outline the social determinants of health in Canada (see Table 2.1) and conclude that "the primary factors that shape the health of Canadians are not the medical treatments or lifestyle choices but rather the living conditions they experience."[52] There is evidence that an increase in material conditions immensely improves the quality of human life.

Social workers increasingly see clients who lack adequate housing and a living wage to support themselves and their families. Graham Riches reminds us that in 1976 Canada ratified the ICESCR and is therefore obligated to protect "the right of everyone to an adequate standard of living ... including food, cloth-

TABLE 2.1
THE SOCIAL DETERMINANTS OF HEALTH AND MENTAL HEALTH IN CANADA

- Aboriginal status or background
- Access to health services
- Disability
- Early life
- Education
- Employment and working conditions
- Food insecurity
- Health services
- Gender
- Housing
- Income and income distribution
- Racialization or race
- Social exclusion
- Social supports
- Unemployment and job security

Source: Juha Mikkonen and Dennis Raphael, *Social Determinants of Health: The Canadian Facts*, 1–6, p. 9. Publication available at http://www.thecanadianfacts.org/.

ing and housing" (Article 11.1).[53] Food is a fundamental human right, yet more and more families are desperate and rely on food banks for their survival. Although the first food bank was established in 1981 in Edmonton, they are now an established component of the social welfare net. It is no longer a surprise to find individuals and families who are unable to meet their basic needs for food, clothing, and shelter. Overall, 2.7 million Canadians experience food insecurity, that is, an inadequate diet in terms of quality and quantity.[54] Over the past two years, there has been an unprecedented 28 per cent rise in food bank use in Canada. Of those accessing food banks, 38 per cent are children or youth under 18 years of age.[55] Food bank use in Canada has reached its highest level on record, demonstrating the urgent need for a national poverty reduction plan.

The capacity to provide sufficient food for the global population exists. However, more and more land is being devoted to supporting the demand for biofuels and is contributing to food shortages. Over 30 per cent of US farm land will go to supply ethanol (crops designated to produce the biofuel additive for gasoline).[56] This development, along with the growth and power of agribusinesses, has created an acute crisis in food supplies and prices.

Excessive weather and environmental destruction in the past year has been linked to man-made global warming. "Earthquakes, heat waves, floods, volcanoes, super typhoons, blizzards, landslides and droughts killed nearly 260,000 people in 2010—the deadliest year in more than a generation. More people were killed worldwide by natural disasters this year than have been killed in terrorism attacks in the past 40 years combined."[57] Many more are left homeless and struggle with disease and hunger. Yet the attempts at the 2010 UN meeting in Cancun to reach a global agreement among countries to reduce emissions of greenhouse gases resulted in only modest goals, likely not sufficient to avert further catastrophic change to the earth's climate.[58]

There is currently a global water crisis that has left large numbers of people without access to clean drinking water. Many areas of the world are facing a water scarcity, including the mid-western US, Florida, and Arizona. In fact, Arizona now imports all of its drinking water. Worldwide, "more children are killed by dirty water than by war, malaria, HIV/AIDS and traffic accidents combined."[59] Maude Barlow convincingly argues that without a major change in direction, two-thirds of the world population will face a scarcity of water within 15 years.

In April 2008 the *Canadian Medical Association Journal* reported that there were 1,766 boil-water advisories in areas that were not First Nations communities. However, numerous Aboriginal communities often do not have access to clean drinking water. Eight hundred of the 1,500 residents of Kashechewan, a Cree community in northern Ontario near James Bay, were evacuated from their homes in 2005 because of E.coli contamination of the water.[60] Although plagued by contaminated water over the years, the evacuation solicited national attention when members were evacuated and temporarily housed in Timmins, Sudbury, Geraldton, and Cochrane.

On 28 July 2010 the efforts of the Council of Canadians resulted in a positive outcome. The UN General Assembly overwhelmingly agreed to a resolution that declared safe and clean drinking water and sanitation as a human right. The Bolivian government introduced the resolution, and 122 countries voted in its favour, while 41 countries—including Canada—abstained.[61]

SOCIAL JUSTICE AND HUMAN RIGHTS: THE CHALLENGE TO THE PROFESSION

The social work profession promotes social change, problem solving in human relationships, and the empowerment and liberation of people to enhance well-being. Utilising theories of human behaviour and social systems, social work intervenes at the points where people interact with their environments. Principles of human rights and social justice are fundamental to social work.[62]

Social workers by their very positions and commitment are human rights workers, advocating for individual and collective rights every day. As a profession, social work has consistently linked the issues of peace and social justice.[63] In 1988 the IFSW declared that historically social work has been a human rights profession.[64] Human rights are intrinsic to social work, and, as discussed above, these rights are closely connected to economic, political, environmental, and social forces. Social and personal problems are often rights denied and the failure of governments to live up to the obligations that accompany domestic human rights legislation and international commitments made to UN declarations and conventions. Poverty is fundamentally a denial of rights.

Unfortunately, the federal human rights legislation, the Charter of Rights and Freedoms and the federal Human Rights Act do not explicitly recognize poverty or homelessness as human rights. However, Section 7 of the Charter refers to "security of the person"—and there is no security in hunger or homelessness. Hugh Shewell advances the argument that "human welfare represents a set of rights that constitute social rights and that these rights are human rights."[65]

While social work has a long history of promoting the principles of social

justice and human rights, often these principles are not demonstrated in practice approaches and social work responses.[66] What is meant by social justice,
and how do we practice within a social justice framework? As professionals,
how do we buy in without selling out? Moreover, the relationship between social
justice and social work "is decidedly uneasy, fraught with tension, contradiction,
and conflict at both the ideological, conceptual, and theoretical levels as well
as the levels of policy and practice."[67] Social workers hold a key and, at the same
time, contradictory position in society as they establish principles of social justice within a political and economic context that is based on, and supports,
exploitation and inequality.

Michael Reisch provides an account of the development of the concept of
social justice in social work and the current challenges facing social workers
practicing within a social justice framework. He points out that social justice
was initially viewed as an alternative to charity. However, the establishment
and growth of the welfare state in the 1930s, viewed by many as a means to
address the structural inequalities in society, has not been a successful means
for achieving social justice. With the ongoing privatization and erosion of social
welfare programs, and the implementation of authoritarian welfare policies by
agencies, there is the concern that instead of tackling social injustice, social
work has internalized the new right-wing doctrines.[68] Since capitalism is the
fundamental cause of much of the social and economic injustice that the poor
experience, the degree to which social justice is possible within a market economy has been questioned.[69] Moyo goes further to challenge social workers: "In
my view, the current lovefest of charity, volunteerism, and social services speaks
to the maintenance of cultures of inequalities and therefore a perpetuation of
injustices."[70]

Gary Craig, a professor of social justice, argues that in order to achieve social
justice governments must confront the inequities of capitalism. Craig views
social justice as:

> a framework of political objectives, pursued through social, economic, envi-
> ronmental, and political policies, based on an acceptance of difference and
> diversity, and informed by values concerned with:
> • achieving fairness, and equality of outcomes and treatment;
> • recognizing dignity and equal worth and encouraging the self-
>   esteem of all;
> • the meeting of basic needs;
> • maximizing the reduction of inequalities in wealth, income, and life
>   chances; and
> • the participation of all, including the most disadvantaged.[71]

It is clear that conditions of injustice and inequality violate the basic human rights of people. This results in an erosion of support for social welfare and the creation of harsh social and economic conditions for citizens, particularly the poor and working people. Women, children, the ill and disabled, unemployed and under-employed, and the elderly are among the most vulnerable and yet reliant on a well-funded system of social security. The right to the necessities of life (adequate food, water, clothing, and housing) and basic health and social services and programs must become an objective of any social justice movement. These goals present tremendous challenges for the profession of social work.

CALL TO ACTION

Social workers are recognized as key participants in the promotion and protection of human rights and have had an active role at the UN since its birth in 1945.[72] Lynne Healy, however, is more hesitant in regards to our recognition or visibility within the larger global human rights movement.[73] Whether it is locally, nationally, or internationally, social workers ought to advocate for human rights and social justice. Adopting a human rights approach can guide social workers to gain an awareness of the structural conditions facing their clients and to move from a need to rights approach in response.

In 1992, as a result of collaboration, the UN Centre for Human Rights, the IFSW, and the IASSW published *Human Rights and Social Work: A Manual for Schools of Social Work and the Social Work Profession*. The purpose of the manual, revised in 1994, reprinted in 2000, and currently under revision, is to provide social work students, professors, and practitioners with "an understanding and awareness of human rights and concerns for social justice."[74] It defines human rights and summarizes the basic instruments, the UN bodies concerned with human rights, issues for social work practice, and the dilemmas facing social workers and teaching about human rights.

As social workers, we are citizens of the world, closely interconnected to events and people in other parts of the globe whether it is in the context of armed conflicts, ecological disasters, financial crises, or international health epidemics. There is urgency to our work; addressing global poverty and environmental destruction and addressing human rights cannot wait if we are to survive as a species. Eleanor Roosevelt offered some direction in this regard:

Where, after all, do universal human rights begin? In small places, close to home—so close and so small that they cannot be seen on any map of the world. Yet they are the world of the individual person, the neighborhood he

[she] lives in; the school or college he [she] attends; the factory, farm, or office where he [she] works. Such are the places where every man, woman, and child seeks equal justice, equal opportunity, equal dignity without discrimination. Unless these rights have meaning there, they have little meaning anywhere. Without concerted citizen action to uphold them close to home, we shall look in vain for progress in the larger world.[75]

Social workers, aware of their own history of organizing and advocating for social change, human rights, and social justice, can be spurred on to also act and speak out against injustices. Social work history also reflects the contradictions of attraction to advocacy and social/political activism and the pressure of conformity to the goals of the state, with its associated emphasis on professionalism. The next chapter traces these tensions.

NOTES

1 Douglas Roche, *The Human Right to Peace* (Toronto: Novalis, 2003) 15–16. Roche was Canada's Ambassador for Disarmament at the UN.

2 Colleen Lundy and Katherine van Wormer, "Social and Economic Justice, Human Rights, and Peace: The Challenge for Social Work in Canada and the USA," *International Social Work* 50.6 (2007): 727–39.

3 It is encouraging to see special issues on social justice recently appear in two social work journals—*British Journal of Social Work* 32 (2002) and the *Journal of Contemporary Human Services* 83.4 (2002)—and the publication of texts on human rights: Elisabeth Reichert, *Social Work and Human Rights* (New York: Columbia University Press, 2003); Elisabeth Reichert, ed., *Challenges in Human Rights: A Social Work Perspective* (New York: Columbia University Press, 2007); and J. Ife, *Human Rights and Social Work: Towards a Rights-Based Practice*, rev. ed. (Cambridge: University of Cambridge Press, 2008).

4 National Association of Social Workers, "International Policy on Human Rights," *Social Work Speaks: NASW Policy Statements* (Washington, DC: NASW Press, 2002) 181.

5 Michael Cronin, Robin Sakina Mama, Charles Mbugua, and Ellen Mouravieff-Apostol, "Social Work and the United Nations," in *Social Work: Making a Difference*, ed. Nigel Hall (n.p.: IFSW and FAFO, 2006) 209–24. Also see, e.g., http://www.ifsw.org/home; http://icsw.org/index.htm; and http://www.iassw-aiets.org/.

6 In addition, the CASW also upholds the Canadian Charter of Rights and Freedoms (1982).

7 Cronin et al., "Social Work and the United Nations."

8 Anne-Marie Skegg, "Human Rights and Social Work," *International Social Work* 48, no. 5 (2005): 667–72; Ife, *Human Rights and Social Work*.

9 In 1944, under US auspices, the future members of the UN held a conference at Bretton Woods and created the IMF and the WB, which form the administrative core and which oversee the economic interests of the developed world and the global financial system. In 1948, the UN General Assembly adopted the UDHR.

10 Sergio Vieira de Mello, "Five Questions for the Human Rights Field," *SUR—International Journal of Human Rights* 1 (2004): 165–71, http://www.surjournal.org/eng/index1.php.

11 Judith R. Blau and Albert Moncado, "Constitution and Human Rights," in *Globalization*

and America, ed. Angela J. Hattery, David G. Embrick, and Earl Smith (New York: Rowman and Littlefield, 2008) 219–30; Thomas Buergenthal, Dinah Shelton, and David P. Stewart, *International Human Rights in a Nut Shell*, 4th ed. (St. Paul, MN: West Publishing, 2009).

12 Buergenthal, Shelton, and Stewart, *International Human Rights in a Nut Shell*.

13 Buergenthal, Shelton, and Stewart, *International Human Rights in a Nut Shell* 68–69.

14 Gary Teeple, *The Riddle of Human Rights* (Aurora, ON: Garamond, 2004) 22.

15 Gwen Brodsky, "Human Rights and Poverty: A Twenty-First Century Tribute to J.S. Woodsworth and Call for Human Rights," in *Human Welfare, Rights, and Social Activism: Rethinking the Legacy of J.S. Woodsworth*, ed. Jane Pulkingham (Toronto: University of Toronto Press, 2011) 139.

16 Hugh Shewell, "Social Rights are Human Rights," in *Human Welfare, Rights, and Social Activism: Rethinking the Legacy of J.S. Woodsworth*, ed. Jane Pulkingham (Toronto: University of Toronto Press, 2011) 124.

17 UN Treaty Collection, Declarations and Reservations, http://treaties.un.org/.

18 Aziz Choudry, "What's Left? Canada's 'Global Justice' Movement and Colonial Amnesia," *Race and Class* 52.1 (2010): 97–102. The vote in the 192-member assembly was 143 in favour, four against, and 11 abstentions.

19 Pricilla Settee, "The Struggle to Right Historical Wrongs: Grim Legacy of Colonialism Blights Indigenous Peoples," *The CCPA Monitor* (December 2008–January 2009): 12–14.

20 Yale D. Belanger, "The United Declaration on the Rights of Indigenous Peoples and Urban Aboriginal Self-Determination in Canada: A Preliminary Assessment," *Aboriginal Policy Studies* 1.1 (2011): 132–61.

21 Canadian Human Rights Act (revised 1996). http://www.chrc-ccdp.ca/en/timePortals/milestones/139mile.asp.

It now reads: "For all purposes of this Act, the prohibited grounds of discrimination are race, national or ethnic origin, colour, religion, age, sex, sexual orientation, marital status, family status, disability and conviction for which pardon has been granted."

22 Gary Craig, "Poverty, Social Work, and Social Justice," *British Journal of Social Work* 32 (2002): 669–82.

23 Krysti Justine Guest, "Exploitation under Erasure: Economic, Social, and Cultural Rights Engage Economic Exploitation," *Adelaide Law Review* 19 (1997): 73–93.

24 Koen de Feyter, *Human Rights: Social Justice in the Age of the Market* (Dhaka: University Press, 2005).

25 Guest, "Exploitation Under Erasure."

26 Nicole La Violette and Craig Forcese, eds., *The Human Rights of Anti-Terrorism* (Toronto: Irwin Law, 2008).

27 Scott Harding, "Man-made Disaster and Development," *International Social Work* 50.3 (2007): 296.

28 Raymond W. Baker, Shereen T. Ismael, and Traeq W. Ismael, eds., *Cultural Cleansing in Iraq* (New York: Pluto Press, 2010) 4.

29 G. Burnham, R. Lafta, S. Doocy, and L. Roberts, "Mortality After the 2003 Invasion of Iraq: A Cross-Sectional Cluster Sample Survey," *The Lancet* 368.9545 (2006): 1421–28.

30 Chris Cobb, "Victims Recount Horrors of Cluster Bombs," *Ottawa Citizen*, 4 December 2008: A9.

31 Martin Chulov, "Research Links Rise in Falluja Birth Defects and Cancers to US Assault," *Guardian*, 30 December 30, 2010. http://www.guardian.co.uk/world/2010/dec/30/faulluja-birth-defects-iraq.

32 The Uniting and Strengthening America by Proudly Appropriating Tools Required to Intercept and Obstruct Terrorism Act of 2001 (US Patriot Act), passed by Congress with little debate, expands state power and reduces civil liberties. See, e.g., Armando T. Morales, Bradford W. Sheafor, and Malcolm E. Scott, *Social Work: A Profession of Many Faces*, 12th ed. (Boston: Allyn and Bacon, 2010).

33 Amy Goodman, *Democracy Now!*, 20 February 2009.

34 Terry Mizrahi, "A Legacy of Peace: The Role of the Social Work Profession," initially posted on the NASW web site and later published in the *NASW News* (April 2003): 1–2, http://www.socialworkers.org/pressroom/events/peace/default.asp.

35 Moya Atkinson, "The National Association of Social Workers—Supporting Social Justice and Peace—Recent Actions Opposing US Torture," 28 June 2008; this is a widely circulated statement on the NASW position.

36 *Globe and Mail*, "US Sets Firm Date for Iraq Pullout," 28 February 2009: A1.

37 Kevin Zeese, "Obama: 'I want to end the mindset that got us into the war in the first place,'" Voters For Peace, http://votersforpeace.us/perspectives/zeese020508.html.

38 Colin Kenny, "Afghan Mission Numbers Don't Add Up to Success," *Ottawa Citizen*, 14 July 2011: A13.

39 John Foster, "Afghanistan Vital to US as a Natural Gas Pipeline Route," *CCPA Monitor* 15.1 (May 2008): 1.

40 Dennis Kucinich, letter to members of Congress, 17 August 2010; CommonDreams http://www.commondreams.org.

41 Neil Burton, "'War on Terror' a Convenient Excuse for the New Global Arms Race," *The CCPA Monitor* 13.6 (November 2006): 29–30.

42 Foster, Holleman, and McChesney, "The US Imperial Triangle."

43 Mel Hurtig, "Danger of a Nuclear Holocaust is Becoming Even Greater," *The CCPA Monitor* 13.4 (October 2006): 36–37.

44 Asad Ismi and Kristin Schwartz, "Canada is Violating the Nuclear Non-Proliferation Treaty," *CCPA Monitor* 15.4 (October 2008): 20–21.

45 Robinson, "Canadian Military Spending 2010–11."

46 Dwight D. Eisenhower, speech to the American Society of Newspaper Editors, 16 April 1953, http://www.quotationspage.com/quote/9556.html.

47 Roche, *The Human Right to Peace*.

48 Jane Addams, *Peace and Bread in Time of War* (New York: MacMillan, 1922).

49 Thomas Pogge, *World Poverty and Human Rights*, 2nd ed. (Cambridge: Polity Press, 2008) 222, 264.

50 WHO, Commission on Social Determinants of Health, "Final Report: Closing the Gap in a Generation: Health Equity through Action on Social Determinants of Health" (Geneva: WHO, 2008).

51 Raphael, *Poverty and Policy in Canada* 203.

52 Juha Mikkonen and Dennis Raphael, *Social Determinants of Health: The Canadian Facts* (Toronto: York University School of Health Policy and Management, 2010), http://www.thecanadianfacts.org: 7.

53 Graham Riches, "Right to Food within Canada: International Obligations, Domestic Compliance" in *International Social Work: Canadian Perspectives*, ed. Gayle Gilchrist James, Richard Ramsey, and Glenn Drover (Toronto: Thompson Educational, 2009).

54 Mikkonen and Raphael, *Social Determinants of Health* 26.

55 Food Banks Canada, *HungerCount 2010* (Toronto: Food Banks Canada, 2010), http://foodbankscanada.ca/HungerCount.htm.

56 Edward R. Boyle, *Feed People First* (Ottawa: Canadian Centre for Policy Alternatives, February 2009) 3–9.

57 *Globe and Mail*, "Mother Nature's Wrath: The Year the Earth Struck Back," 20 December, 2010: A15.

58 Shawn McCarthy, "Goals Modest for Environmental Summit," *Globe and Mail*, 30 November 2010: A9.

59 Maude Barlow, *Blue Covenant: The Global Water Crisis and the Coming Battle for the Right to Water* (Toronto: McClelland and Stewart, 2007).

60 See Kate Hopwood, "The Sad Story of Kashechewan," *Guelph Mercury News*, 28 April 2008, http://pqasb.pqarchiver.com/guelphmercury/results.html?st=basic&publications =ALL&type=current&QryTxt=the+sad+story+of+kashechewan.

61 Council of Canadians, "Win! UN General Assembly Passes Historic Human Right to Water and Sanitation Resolution," council-of-canadians@topica.email-publisher.com.

62 International Federation of Social Workers, "Definition of Social Work," adopted by the IFSW General Meeting, Montreal, July 2000, http://www.ifsw.org/p38000208.html.

63 Colleen Lundy, "The Role of Social Work in the Peace Movement," *The Social Worker/ LeTravailleur* 55.2 (1987): 61–65; Maura Sullivan, "Social Work's Legacy of Peace: Echoes from the Early 20th Century," *Social Work* 38.5 (September 1993): 513–26; Lundy and van Wormer, "Social and Economic Justice, Human Rights, and Peace."

64 International Federation of Social Workers, "Human Rights," in *International Policy Papers* (Geneva: IFSW, 1988).

65 Shewell, "Social Rights are Human Rights" 114.

66 See note 3, above.

67 Matthew Colton, "Editorial," *British Journal of Social Work* 32 (2002): 659.

68 Colton, "Editorial" 659–67.

69 Craig, "Poverty, Social Work and Social Justice" 669–82; Gindin, "Social Justice and Globalization" 1–11; Otrude Nontobeko Moyo, "A Commitment to Social Justice in a Capitalist Democracy: Are We Being Critical Citizens or Just Moving Along Clichés?," *Journal of Progressive Human Services* 21.1 (2010): 3–7.

70 Moyo, "A Commitment to Social Justice in a Capitalist Democracy" 4.

71 Craig, "Poverty, Social Work and Social Justice" 671–72.

72 Daniel Pollack, "Social Workers and the United Nations: Effective Advocacy Strategies," *International Social Work* 50, no. 1 (2007): 113–19.

73 Lynne M. Healy, "Exploring the History of Social Work as a Human Rights Profession," *International Social Work* 51.6 (2008): 735–48.

74 International Federation of Social Workers, *Human Rights and Social Work: A Manual for Schools of Social Work and the Social Work Profession* (Geneva: United Nations Centre for Human Rights, 1994, repr. 2000) 3.

75 Eleanor Roosevelt, "In Your Hands: A Guide for Community Action for the Tenth Anniversary of the Universal Declaration of Human Rights" (1958), http://www.udhr.org/history /inyour.htm; emphasis in the original.

CHAPTER 3

HISTORICAL DEVELOPMENTS IN SOCIAL WORK

> One group who have traditionally been moved to action by "pity for the poor," we call the Charitable; the other, larger or smaller in each generation, but always fired by the "hatred of injustice" we designate as the Radicals.
>
> —Jane Addams[1]

I N THE EARLY PART OF THE LAST CENTURY, rapid economic growth and industrial expansion were accompanied by a rise in immigration, deplorable working conditions for labouring people, and substandard housing. There were also few resources for those who were impoverished or who faced serious social and health problems. This situation was exacerbated by major economic depressions, which resulted in massive unemployment.[2] Social work as a profession emerged in Canada and the US as an organized response to such social and economic conditions and the resultant problems many individuals and families experienced. Five central themes emerge as we trace the developments of the profession in these two countries over the past 80 years.

First, since its inception in the 1920s, the social work profession has aspired to two goals: providing services to those in need and advocating for change to social policy and social conditions. While all social workers have embraced the first goal, the profession has often been divided over whether the second has a place within social work. Those practitioners who see social change activity as part of the purpose of social work and strive to work to change social structures as well as assisting individuals and communities are part of the more radical wing. Those who focus on individual and family change, the development of practice approaches to individual and family problems, and the enhancement and acceptance of social work as a profession argue that participation in broad social change is not the role of professional social workers. This tension between social action and individual change is evident throughout the history of social work practice. The profession consequently has been marked by periods of conservative retrenchment as well as tides of "militant professionalism" within its ranks.[3] Most would agree that radicals have been a persistent but weak force within the profession; others see the dominance of the profession by the conservative forces as complete. Indeed, Reuben Bitensky has suggested that social work's abandonment of social action and the role of the "conscience of society" for the role of "an apologist for the *status quo*" and "devoting its efforts to adjusting clients to the existing social institutions" offered the possibility of the survival of the profession and ensured a firm footing within state-sponsored social services.[4]

Secondly, in the early years of the profession, Canadian and US social work shared a common history. Social workers attended the same conferences, belonged to the same organizations, and subscribed to the same journals. But the relationship was not equal. The Council on Social Work Education (CSWE) in the US accredited Canadian schools of social work until 1970, demonstrating the degree to which social work in Canada was influenced by theoretical and practical models from our neighbour to the south. While contributions from the UK were considered, social work in Canada was most influenced by US social work developments during these early years.[5]

Thirdly, theoretical developments and empirical research in other disciplines such as sociology, political science, economics, and psychology have informed social work practice in the past and continue to do so. The radical streams within these disciplines inform the social change approach of the profession, while more conservative theories and studies inform the individual-focused approach to practice.

Fourth, the ongoing search for a unifying practice framework that would bring social workers together under common principles and a generic base has persisted throughout the years. Given the degree of differing views within the profession, it is not surprising to learn that no unifying framework has emerged.

Finally, for the most part Canadian social workers have closely modeled US developments in regard to professionalization, initially by establishing professional associations and, more recently, regulatory bodies.

THE EARLY YEARS: RESPONDING TO POVERTY AND ESTABLISHING LEGITIMACY

Early attempts at organized response to the problems of poverty focused on the provision of charity and usually were based in Christian churches. Clergy and other church leaders established charity organizations and settlement houses for the purposes of providing food, shelter, and services to the poor. Canada's social welfare pioneers—such as the journalist J.J. Kelso (1864–1935)—laid the ground work and mobilized community support for services such as Children's Aid Societies, the first of which opened in Toronto in 1891. In 1893 Kelso was instrumental in introducing provincial child welfare legislation and was appointed as Superintendent of Neglected and Dependent Children, a position he held until 1934. Along with the expansion of Children's Aid Societies throughout Ontario, he contributed to similar developments in Nova Scotia, New Brunswick, Saskatchewan, Manitoba, and British Columbia.[6]

Unlike the rest of Canada, the Maritime region (Nova Scotia, New Brunswick, and Prince Edward Island) based their social charity response on the English Poor Laws of 1763. The system was distinguished by poor houses, homes for orphans, a "paupers list," and charity distributed according to who was deemed worthy by an appointed "Overseer of the Poor." In some counties where there were no Alms Houses, poor men, women, and children were auctioned off to farmers or shop keepers as indentured labour. The last pauper's auction of this "white slave trade" took place in King's County, New Brunswick in 1898; Nova Scotia stopped auctioning the poor in 1900.[7] In the mid-1800s so-called Houses of Industry, that is, work houses, also opened up in Montreal and Toronto as a means of housing the poor. However, up until the 1950s, the poor house remained the major form of state relief in Nova Scotia and New Brunswick.[8]

Charity Organization Societies (cos), first developed in Britain in 1869 and established in the us by 1877, advanced the practice of "scientific philanthropy," almsgiving, and rehabilitation of the poor. They identified those who were "deserving" of charity and provided a registry to insure that provisions were not duplicated by participating agencies. In 1891 Mary Richmond (1861–1928), the director of the Baltimore (Maryland) Charity Organization, advocated a "retail" approach to administering to the needy; it concentrated on a case-by-case response to individual client problems. Richmond became a leader in establishing "friendly visiting" as a profession and in developing casework as its primary activity. Her first book, *Friendly Visiting Among the Poor* (1899), was a manual to guide the practice.[9] She believed that social casework, an individualistic approach, ameliorated the impact of industrialization through advancing personal change or adaptation. In her book *The Good Neighbour* (1908), Richmond advocated for a community response to human difficulty.[10] She later turned her attention to establishing social case work as the central core of social work through the publication of two books, *Social Diagnosis* (1917) and *What is Social Case Work* (1922).[11]

At the same time, those who were socially minded—"some paternalistic, some missionary, and some even Marxist"—established settlement houses in communities where there was great social need and advocated for "wholesale" social change while focusing on individual concerns.[12] Social workers such as Jane Addams, Bertha Reynolds, Sophonisba Breckinridge, and Mary van Kleck were leaders in the early human rights movement and organized a number of international human rights organizations that still exist today.[13]

Jane Addams (1860–1935), one of the first leaders of the settlement house movement, took over the directorship of Hull House in Chicago in 1892 and gained national stature as a social change advocate. Addams was a nationally recognized political and peace activist and was a founding member of the National Association for the Advancement of Colored People (NAACP). In 1915 she established the Women's Peace Party (WPP), which re-formed as the Women's International League for Peace and Freedom (WILPF) in 1919. WILPF continues to be an active international organization. Addams paid a dear price for her anti-war position; she was vilified by the press, accused of disloyalty, placed on a list of "dangerous radicals," and was under surveillance by the Department of Justice.[14] While Addams considered herself to be "middle of the road" in politics and social reform, she found herself pushed toward the left on the subject of war and published a book on the subject, *Peace and Bread in Time of War* in 1922. In 1931 she was awarded the Nobel Peace Prize for her efforts in opposing World War I and building peace.

Her opposition to the outbreak of war in 1914 and her support for those on the left, including Socialist presidential candidate Eugene Debs, was more than social workers at the time could accept. Therefore, her influence diminished.[15] In addition to her political activism and her involvement in settlement work, between 1907 and 1916 she published six books and more than 150 essays. Meanwhile, Mary Richmond, who supported the war, set out to ensure that social workers were prepared to respond to its casualties.

The two responses to poverty and social inequality and the respective approaches taken by Richmond and Addams laid the foundation on which social work as a profession would be built, and the dichotomy would endure long after they ceased to practice.[16]

Charity Organization Societies

In response to the growing numbers of poor people in North American cities that resulted from capitalist industrialization and mass immigration from Europe, organized charity was seen as "the urban community's surest safeguard against revolution." Initially, charity was distributed by volunteers who engaged in "friendly visiting" a practice that has been characterized as "an instrument of social control which assumed not only the right, but the civic duty of intervention in the lives of the poor by their economic and social betters."[17]

The charity movement social workers, guided by a desire for professional identity and recognition, turned their attention to developing individual practice skills and techniques. Their tradition had the greatest influence on educational programs and thus on the development and direction of the newly emerging profession. Stanley Wenocur and Michael Reisch provide a thorough account of how social work followed the route taken by other established professions such as medicine in developing ties to social elites who could provide support and legitimation. It also engaged in establishing "university-based education with increasingly selective entry into the field, active professional associations to promote social work standards and to gain exclusive control over the right to practice, and development of individualistic, technological, 'scientific' methodology that would be consistent with dominant social values."[18]

Settlements

In direct contrast to the COS caseworkers who provided "friendly visiting," counseling, and material resources to those less fortunate, social workers working in the settlement house movement often lived within the community and provided assistance to the immigrant and working-class population to whom they referred as "neighbours in need."[19] Social workers practicing in the settlement tradition advanced the role of social work in the area of social justice and social activism. Emphasis was placed on group work, organizing, and community development with little interest in acquiring recognition and legitimacy for their work as a profession.

The US settlement movement was the leader in the mobilization for social reform, and its representatives actively advocated for change in working conditions, health care, housing, child labour, child welfare, and civil rights for African Americans.[20] In 1902 Evangelia Settlement opened in Toronto—the first settlement house in Canada. Unlike their US and British counterparts, Canadian settlements tended to be church-affiliated, not secular. Allan Irving, Harriet Parsons, and Donald Bellamy suggest that this is partly due to the fact that industrialization and its accompanying social problems came later in Canada. The churches viewed charity as their responsibility, and, since they had an administrative structure that could readily respond to families and children in need, they helped develop the settlements.[21]

Early settlement work also was greatly influenced by the radical social gospel movement, considered by some to have socialist and feminist elements.[22] Social gospellers established missions, such as the Fred Victor Mission in Toronto, for transient and homeless men.[23] One member of the social gospellers was James Shaver Woodsworth, who later became a leader in the Social Welfare League and the Cooperative Commonwealth Foundation (CCF), the precursor to the modern New Democratic Party.[24] Another social gospeller, Nellie McClung, an advocate for women's rights, was elected to the federal Parliament in 1921 and was one of five feminists who successfully fought in 1929 to have women in Canada regarded as persons.[25]

Settlement workers looked to sociology, economics, and political economy, as well as social gospel for a conceptual and theoretical framework to inform their activities. They varied in their analysis of social problems and their approach to alleviating them. While some limited their response to concrete services and advocacy, others such as Jane Addams and J.S. Woodsworth strove for radical reform and political action. With some exceptions, settlement workers, like their counterparts in charity organizations, generally did not engage in class conflict and radical structural change.[26]

Establishing the Foundations of the Profession

By the end of the first third of the twentieth century the foundations of the social work profession were established. The profession constituted its title, defined its basic function and purpose, and founded professional associations and educational programs.[27] As early as 1898, the COS established the first training program in social work, the New York Summer School in Philanthropic Work, in New York, which increased to a full year as the New York School of Philanthropy in 1904.[28] By 1910 there were five professional training schools in the US.[29] In the same year training courses for social workers in Canada were increased to two years, and the first university program for social workers opened at the University of Toronto in 1914, followed in 1918 by a program at McGill University in Montreal. In 1919 the University of Toronto school joined 14 US schools of social work to form the Association of Training Schools for Professional Social Work (later renamed the American Association of Schools of Social Work and finally the Council on Social Work Education) and began the work of establishing educational standards and an accrediting function.[30]

In these early years the tension in social work between whether or not to concentrate on social advocacy or casework practice was present in university programs. In a history of the School of Social Work at the University of Toronto, John Graham found that while the internal divisions among faculty influenced the theoretical framework of the program, the British influence and the focus on political economy and social policy dominated.[31] E.J. Urwick, the first Director of the Department of Social Services at the University of Toronto, placed emphasis on sociology and social philosophy over psychology and, given the choice between "approaches that emphasized the individual's need to adapt to social institutions and approaches that emphasized the need for social institutions to adapt to individual's needs," leaned toward change to social institutions.[32]

The movement toward establishing social work as a profession was not with-out its setbacks. At the 1915 National Conference on Social Welfare, Abraham Flexner, a recognized expert on professional schools, addressed the member-ship. While Flexner prefaced his comments with an admission that he lacked knowledge about social work, and questioned his competence to assess whether or not social work was a profession, he nonetheless proceeded to place emphasis on the professional attribute of "intellectual activity" and, on that basis, to con-clude that social work, unlike medicine and law, was not a profession since it did not possess a distinct activity, technique, or knowledge base.[33] Social workers were viewed as mediators, not professionals with expertise.

Many social work leaders considered this appraisal to be a serious setback for the fledgling profession and turned their attention to the work of identifying and defining a theory and practice specific to social work. In 1917 Mary Rich-mond published *Social Diagnosis*, modeled after the medical profession's text-book, to guide social workers in the practice of studying, diagnosing, and treating individual problems through an interview process. Casework was identified as the technique, and social work's attention turned almost exclusively to individual counselling and away from understanding social conditions and promoting social change.

The Diagnostic and Functional Schools

The shift away from social change toward individual change or from "cause to function" was further supported by what has been coined the "psychiatric del-uge," the adoption of Freudian psychoanalytic principles as the theoretical base for social work practice.[34] Richmond's casework had found a theory base in Freudian psychology, and the adoption of its central tenets greatly influenced the direction of the fledgling profession. The importance of social conditions in understanding individual behaviour was greatly diminished as attention was placed on childhood development and unresolved experiences, feelings, and thoughts, many of which were believed to be buried in the subconscious. The role of the social worker was to free the person from these damaging past experiences through intensive therapy. For example, after World War I, return-ing soldiers, along with their families, became a new client group in need of professional social work services, and psychoanalytic social work practice expanded.

By the mid-1920s, family agencies and child guidance clinics were estab-lished, and social workers found new settings in which to practice. During this time most graduates from the two Canadian schools of social work (Univer-sity of Toronto and McGill University) were employed mainly in private family and child welfare agencies, with a few working in hospitals, settlement houses, and municipal and provincial or federal government departments. Women and men were viewed very differently by the public and the profession. The image that the public held of a social worker, according to Joy Maines, Executive Director of the Canadian Association of Social Work, "was a female dressed in mannish suits, with a straight brimmed hat, flat-heeled shoes and a very long nose for 'snooping.'" On the other hand, male social workers usually were thought to be "either reformers, retired clergymen, or wild-eyed idealists."[35]

Psychodynamic theory largely informed by Freudian theory was to dominate social work practice from the 1920s through to the 1960s. In the process it has been argued that, "the social worker departed from the stance of a doer, a provider of concrete services, to that of passive observer" and counsellor.[36] Even during the Great Depression of the 1930s, the Freudian psychological approach remained dominant.

An alternative to the diagnostic school and psychoanalytic theory was introduced by Virginia Robinson and Jessie Taft at the Pennsylvania School of Social Work in the 1930s.[37] Called functionalism, this development prompted heated debates, which continued through the 1940s and divided the social work community.

The functional school, an approach to casework based on the psychology and personality theory of Otto Rank, was considered to be a more humanistic and self-deterministic response to dealing with the problems of poverty, because it emphasized the client/worker relationship, the importance of the client's interpretation of the problem or difficulty, and the present rather than past feelings and experiences.[38] Robinson and Taft attempted to shift social work away from a dependence on psychiatry and the determinism of Freudian psychoanalytic theory.[39] They placed emphasis on the helping relationship and the participation of clients in the process. While casework and psychotherapy continued to be used, the therapeutic relationship was not shaped by the client's ego drives but by the agency's function. The purpose of a social worker's helping was influenced by the social purpose, policies, and procedures of the agency in which she was employed. For example, the purpose of family intervention by a hospital social worker would differ from that of a child protection worker. While the focus remained on individual change with little attention to the material conditions of people coming for help and a general disregard for advocacy on behalf of the client, principles of the functional approach, such as the right to self-determination and the helping relationship, can be found in social work practice approaches today.

Professional Associations

In the immediate post-World War I years, Canadian social workers were members of the American Association of Medical Social Workers (created in 1918) and the American Association of Social Workers (created in 1922); however, they saw a need for a Canadian association. Plans to establish such a Canadian association were laid during the 1924 National Conference on Social Welfare, held in Toronto. By 1926 the Canadian Association of Social Workers (CASW) was formed, and the first general meeting was held two years later.

The purpose of the CASW in its formative years was "to bring together professional social workers for such cooperative effort as may enable them more effectively to carry out their ideals of service to the community," and the membership set out "to promote professional standards, encourage proper and adequate preparation and training, cultivate an informed public opinion which will recognize the professional and technical nature of social work, issue an official organ, maintain a professional employment service, conduct research and carry on such other activities as it may deem possible."[40] The formation of the CASW was followed quickly by the establishment of three international associations that united social workers around the world. In July 1928 at the 1st International Conference on Social Work held in Paris, the International Permanent Secretariat of Social Workers (now the International Federation of Social Workers) was established, the International Council on Social Welfare (ICSW) also in 1928, and the International Association of Schools of Social Work (IASSW) in 1929. The role of these international associations in human rights and the UN is discussed in the previous chapter.

Specialization and Fragmentation

As social work began to create specializations based on fields of practice—psychiatric, medical, and school social work—there was concern that the profession was becoming fragmented. To address this problem, a gathering of representatives from national organizations was held in Milford, Pennsylvania in 1923. The objectives of the Milford Conference were to create professional unity and formulate a generic base for casework practice that was common to all, regardless of practice setting. Those attending recognized casework as the predominant, but not sole element in social work practice and stressed the existence of common principles of "generic social case work" that could unite caseworkers into a single occupational group.[41] The final report, *Social Casework: Generic and Specific*, published in 1929, concluded that, while there were various field specializations in social work, the method of generic casework unified the profession. The report also identified the fundamental social work techniques as social case work, community organization, group work, social research, and administration and recommended that all should be included in social work training programs. However, the profession did not have a theoretical base that would unite all the different areas of practice around generic case work.

RESPONSES DURING THE GREAT DEPRESSION

The 1930s, marked by massive unemployment and unprecedented poverty, produced a situation that was not responsive to the psychological intervention being used in most private agencies. The professionalization of the previous decade had resulted in a decline in social reform activities, and social workers were caught by surprise and were unprepared for this upheaval.[42] Also, in the US settlement work was being undermined by the introduction of Community Chests controlled by conservative elites who supported private charity.[43] The economic crisis, so far-reaching in its devastation, presented a challenge within the profession and fostered a resurgence of the social action tradition, which had been set aside. In the US a group of social workers organized "The Rank and File Movement." They aligned themselves with labour and the poor, advocated political action, and, unlike Jane Addams and other settlement workers, moved beyond advocating better social conditions to directly exposing and challenging the capitalist system.[44]

Bertha Reynolds, a key figure in the Rank and File movement, articulated the choices ahead for the social work profession:

> Social work today is standing at the crossroads. It may go on with its face toward the past, bolstering up the decaying profit system, having to defend what is indefensible for the sake of money which pays for its services. On the other hand it may envision a future in which professional social services as well as education, medical services and the like shall be the unquestioned right of all, conferred not as a benefit but as society's only way of maintaining itself.[45]

She and other social workers of the Rank and File did not abandon working with individuals and families but infused their work with critical social analysis and activism. Through organizing efforts they successfully initiated important reform measures in areas such as social security and child and public welfare while seeking social changes. Unlike many professionals of the time, members of the Rank and File were active in trade unions and were sensitized to, and spoke out against, racism.[46]

While there were radical movements in Canada during this time, there does not appear to have been a social work response comparable to the Rank and File. However, Canadian social workers contributed articles to *Social Work Today*, the Rank and File journal, and financially supported the movement.[47] For many members of the CASW, social action "had rather a sinister connotation in the thirties." According to Joy Maines's recollection, a committee was set up to consider:

… the relationship of the professional body to the large numbers of unqualified workers then unemployed. There was hot and heavy discussion during these years about whether or not CASW should throw its doors of membership wide open. The relationship of trade unions to professional associations was debated. Was there danger of a "rank and file" movement in Canada such as caused considerable flurry in the United States? CASW decided not to lower its standards![48]

In spite of the CASW's general lack of regard for the work of the Rank and File and its socialist orientation, articles by Bertha Reynolds appeared in Canadian social welfare journals. In 1936 in the journal of *Child and Family Welfare*, she urged social workers to join in solidarity with all workers:

The future of social casework is the future of the right of common men and women to economic justice and civil liberties, including the right to think and to participate in the making of their own life condition. If the common men and women fail to achieve those rights, no one will have them. Professional people are learning that their fate is bound up with that of all other workers. If they do not stand courageously for all human rights, they will lose their own, including the right to practice their profession as a high and honourable calling.[49]

Since the profession did not offer a radical alternative, Canadian social workers interested in working toward economic and social justice most likely joined The League for Social Reconstruction, which set out to develop a Canadian brand of socialism. The League influenced the development of social welfare policy and produced the document "Social Planning in Canada" (1935) to guide policies of the left-leaning CCF.[50] Formed in 1932, the CCF, a federation of farmer, labour, and socialist organizations, entered federal politics in the 1935 election and captured seven seats and 8.8 per cent of the vote. J.S. Woodsworth was the first party leader. The party advocated a planned economy with public ownership of natural resources, socialized health services, support for farmers, a national labour code, and disarmament and peace.[51] Harry Cassidy and Leonard Marsh, both economists and leaders in social welfare reform and social work education, were among the League's most active members.

The Great Depression years demonstrated the inadequacy of the existing social welfare system and the need for federally supported programs. In the US members of the Rank and File were instrumental in the passing of the 1935 Social Security Act, which gave the federal government responsibility for the aged, unemployed, persons with disability, and dependent children. Although the Rank and File was not a national organization, members were successful in providing an analysis of capitalism and drawing attention to the prevalence of poverty and inadequacy of social relief. They brought trade unionism into social work and influenced the American Association of Social Workers to take a more progressive stand on the economic and social conditions of people.

While limited in scope, these developments, and the larger social upheavals of the period, prompted the profession to move beyond a psychological individual approach to social work practice. It was during this time that group work, a practice method where a social worker sees individuals in a therapeutic group, entered social work as a legitimate practice function.[52] A section on group work was included in the National Conference on Social Work in Montreal in 1935, and one year later the National Association of Group Work was formed.[53]

SOCIAL WORK IN THE ERA OF RETRENCHMENT

Social work entered a period of relative retrenchment from social change during the 1940s and 1950s when the focus was on strengthening professional associations and educational programs, as well as developing the theoretical core of social work practice. The practice approaches that emerged placed emphasis on the individual at the expense of social conditions. Herbert Bisno raised concern that the emphasis on methods and techniques placed the profession in danger of pursuing "know-how" at the expense of "know-why."[54]

During World War II, economic production increased to support the war effort, and unemployment ceased to be an urgent problem. The rise of fascism presented a common enemy, and the struggle between the working class and the capitalists subsided. The conservatism of the 1940s and 1950s and the rise of McCarthyism with its anti-communist and anti-socialist rhetoric took its toll on political activism. Left-wing or radical activities in all fields were curtailed, and the Rank and File social work movement disbanded.[55] According to Gerald Rothman, the movement was destroyed by the Red Scare, and the union was expelled for so-called communist domination. Anyone associated with the union could not find an agency job, and the profession generally distanced its relationship with members of the Rank and File and failed to support them.[56] Jennissen and Lundy document the repression of Canadian social workers who were considered subversive during the Cold War and provide a detailed account of the witch hunt against Mary Jennison, initially as a social worker and later as a peace activist. Jennison was placed on the RCMP "Red List" from 1939 until her death in 1970.[57] Lewey interviewed six social workers who were on the left and were victims of RCMP surveillance.[58]

Conservatism and McCarthyism created difficulties for social workers who were perceived as radical or socialist. For instance, Charlotte Towle was commissioned by the US Federal Bureau of Public Assistance to write a book that would provide guidelines for the supervision of public assistance workers. *Common Human Needs*, published in 1945, was quickly a success, necessitating a third printing. However, over a four-year period starting in 1949, a Commission on Government, fuelled by local business interests, questioned the efficiency of social welfare delivery and alleged that the Bureau of Public Assistance, through this publication, was promoting the maintenance of people on welfare and thereby encouraging idleness. In 1951 the bureau responded by destroying the plates for the book and removing all copies from circulation. Towle's offending sentence, which appeared on page 57, was: "Social security and public assistance programs are a basic essential for attainment of the socialized state envisioned in democratic ideology, as a way of life which so far has been realized only in slight measure."[59] Towle signed the copyright over to the American Association of Social Workers, and the book was reprinted in 1952 with a slight modification to the sentence that had created so much controversy. Towle continued to teach at the University of Chicago. Suspicions of her resurfaced when she signed a petition seeking clemency for Julius and Ethel Rosenberg, who had been charged with treason and were facing execution in 1953. As a result, she was denied a passport the following year.

As the Rank and File were driven underground, functional caseworkers reemerged as the "therapy people," professional counsellors practicing psychotherapy.[60] Humanistic psychology and behavioural theories joined psychoanalytic approaches in guiding social work practice. With the suppression of the radical elements within social work, traditional social workers returned to the task of building a profession and the further development of university-based social work programs. In 1947 the first Master's in Social Work program was established at the University of Toronto, and in 1951 the university opened its doctoral program in social work.

In the early 1950s, social work education at the Master's level in both Canada and the US was redesigned away from a focus on specializations toward a generic curriculum that included social welfare policy, human growth and development, and the three recognized methods of the day—casework, group work, and community organizing.[61] This marked the shift away from specializations toward an emphasis on a common core and a generalist social work model that would unite all social workers. This shift was also reflected at the level of professional associations. In 1955 seven US social work associations merged to create one association, the National Association of Social Workers (NASW).

Authors such as Florence Hollis continued in the psycho-social tradition with an emphasis on diagnosis and Freudian psychology. The centrality of ego psychology and the dismissal of the social context is reflected in her views on assessment:

> Since the personality theory used in the psycho social approach is primarily Freudian, the personality system is conceptualized as a set of interacting forces designated as id, ego, and superego. The functioning of the many aspects of the ego, including how the individual's defences operate, is considered of primary importance in assessing the adequacy of the client's efforts to deal with his difficulty and the extent to which he is contributing to his own problems. Ego functioning must be understood even when the causes of the problem lie primarily in the situation rather than in the client's personality.[62]

A central task of social workers practicing from the diagnostic school was to assess the client's situation and/or problem and determine an intervention. Helen Harris Perlman, in *Social Casework: A Problem Solving Process*, developed an approach based on John Dewey's principles of problem-solving, which viewed the person as an active agent in the process, rather than a passive recipient of professional assessment and services. Perlman attempted to bridge the diagnostic and functional schools by promoting problem-solving as the function of social work while retaining the foundations of ego psychology. She described the problem-solving process as gathering facts (study), assessment (diagnosis), and selection of a course of action (treatment). She also recognized that the client must have the material means—money, recreational opportunities, or child care, for example—in order to resolve the problem.[63]

However, the emphasis on ego functioning and the disregard for structural causes of client difficulties was out of step with the rediscovery of poverty and the movements for equality and justice of the 1960s. In the context of this social unrest and organized resistance, the practice of psychotherapy lost credibility. Increasing numbers of social workers were returning to community-based practice, and in 1962 the Council on Social Work Education finally recognized community organizing as a legitimate specialization. The buoyant economy of the time produced a proliferation of services and agencies and an immense growth in social work.

It was during this time that social workers considered a theoretical framework for practice that viewed people in the context of their environments. Sociologist C. Wright Mills made the distinction and connection between "private troubles and public issues" in his book *Power, Politics and People*.[64] During the Great Depression, Mills noted the difference between the personal predicament of being unemployed and the public issue of structural unemployment. William

Schwartz, drawing on this connection between "private troubles and public issues," proposed that a social worker's role was "neither to 'change the people' nor to 'change the system' but to change the ways in which they deal with each other."[65] This mediating role shifted away from strictly a psychotherapy focus and again brought attention to the social context. Lawrence Shulman, building on the interactionist perspective of Schwartz, developed a holistic, empirically based theory for practice that placed emphasis on skills of helping. In the third edition of his book, Shulman added a focus on families, along with individuals and groups, and incorporated oppression theory into the framework. In 1999 he extended skills of helping to working with communities in the fourth edition of the book.[66] Now in its seventh edition, *The Skills of Helping Individuals, Families, Groups, and Communities* remains one of the most referenced books within social work, and Shulman's framework and skills for helping have been incorporated into a number of practice approaches.[67]

IN SEARCH OF A GENERALIST PRACTICE FRAMEWORK

In the last 40 years, social work in Canada has come into its own as a profession with a proliferation of university-based social work programs, social work scholarship and journals, the further development of professional associations, and legislation to regulate social work. In 1970 the Canadian Association of Schools of Social Work took over the accrediting function held by the US Council on Social Work Education, thus signalling the independent direction of Canadian social work education.

In both the US and Canada, social workers continued to be concerned about fragmentation and the absence of a theoretical approach that would unite the profession and provide relevant practice methods. Howard Goldstein commented that the theoretical core of social work had not yet been fully developed and that the profession had "a valued and effective body of services and purpose but, like a cell without a nucleus, does not contain a substantial interior."[68] As well, there was a growing recognition that psychoanalytic approaches were limited in their application to the pressing concerns facing social workers. Therefore, there was an acute interest in identifying a conceptual framework for social work that would unify social workers and link private troubles to public issues.

While some social workers turned to functional systems theory, others looked to Marxist theory based on "socialist theory and radical analysis of society, which placed social work in a political context."[69] These two ways of viewing the client within a social context influenced social work approaches in the years to follow, each offering an organizing framework to unify and develop social work practice.[70] While both connect individual experiences to a larger social system, they differ ideologically and in their analysis of individual troubles.

Functional Systems Theory

Social workers, identifying the limitations of the individual focus of the approaches to social work, saw promise in General Systems Theory to provide the long sought-for unified framework for social work practice. Models based on this functional systems theory, such as Howard Goldstein's *Social Work Practice: A Unitary Approach* (1973) and Allen Pincus and Anne Minahan's *Social Work Practice: Model and Method* (1973), challenged the psychoanalytic approach of looking to the individual for the source of the problem; instead, they connected the person and problem with the environment.[71] They viewed society as an assembly of individuals in various sized units (called subsystems), all interacting in relative harmony within the larger system. The central assumptions were that people depend on systems and that problems are the result of a breakdown between people and the systems with which they interact, whether that be family, school, workplace, church, or welfare office. The primary goal of approaches drawing on functional systems theory was to achieve equilibrium within the family system, and although the social context was considered, the need for broad social change was disregarded.

While the authors differed in their application of systems theory, they were united in their attempt to offer models that would unify the profession and integrate the methods of casework, group work, and community practice with a focus on both the individual and society. Pincus and Minahan proposed four basic systems in social work practice: the change agent system (social worker(s) and agency colleagues); the client system (the client requesting help); the target system (people who "need to be changed to accomplish the goals of the change agent"); and the action system (change agents and others involved at work on the target system). They emphasized that "change agents are working to change *people*, not vague abstractions such as the 'community,' 'the organization,' or 'the system.'"[72] Pincus and Minahan, along with other social workers who based their practice on functional systems theory, avoided the political dimension and believed that political activity was "more suited to social reform movements and political parties than to a profession."[73] While they recognized the need for social workers to be involved in social change, they offered a contradictory warning that "society will not support any activity which has an objective of bringing about fundamental changes in the very fabric of social institutions."[74]

Other variations on the functional systems theme include Carel Germain and Alex Gitterman's *The Life Model of Social Work Practice* (1980, 1996, 2008) based on ecological thinking that "focuses on the reciprocity of person-environment exchanges, in which each shapes and influences the other over time." Germain and Gitterman emphasized the social context and acknowledged that inequality and oppression is the reality for some in society: "This abuse of power creates and maintains social pollution such as poverty, institutional racism and sexism, repressive gender roles in family, work and the community life, homophobia, and physical and social barriers to community participation by those with disabilities."[75] However, they neglected to provide an analysis of the social structures that produce such inequality or to supply social work strategies for broad social change. Carol Meyer's *Clinical Social Work in an Eco-Systems Perspective* (1983) drew on systems, eco-systems, and ecology in a conceptual framework that claimed to accommodate a number of approaches (eclecticism) including the life model.[76]

While the shift from the focus on individual deficiency prevalent in the psychodynamic approaches to attention to an individual's family and community was a welcome development, other social work scholars felt there was a lack of recognition of the political and economic power that produced unequal social relations; they turned to Marxist systems theory.

Marxist Systems Theory

Critics of functional systems theory articulated an alternative role for social work and offered a framework for practice. At different times this alternative approach in social work has been referred to as Marxist, radical, critical, or structural social work, but Marxism was the theory that most informed the early developments of this framework. Unlike functional systems theorists, there was no attempt to create social work models. Instead, a framework for practice with an emphasis on the analysis of society and social problems was the goal of Marxist practitioners. While proponents of functional systems theory were located primarily in the US, the leadership for radical practice also came from Britain, Australia, and Canada.

Radical social work approaches, based on a Marxist systems theory, placed the individual problems within common experience and explored the degree to which they were socially constructed. This attention to how material conditions influence personal development and well-being moved social workers to develop practice strategies that would contribute to social justice as well as individual change. In 1975 two influential texts in radical social work were published—*Radical Social Work*, edited by British sociologists and activists Roy Bailey and Mike Brake, and *The Politics of Social Services* by American social worker Jeffry Galper.[77] Bailey and Brake clearly stated their vision for radical social work as "understanding the position of the oppressed in the context of the social and economic structures we live in. A socialist perspective is, for us, the most human approach for social workers. Our aim is not, for example, to eliminate casework, but to eliminate casework that supports ruling-class hegemony."[78] Similarly, Galper introduced his book: "The analysis is radical, in this sense, because it roots the problems of the social services in the most fundamental organizational principles of the society. The practice that is developed is radical, since it suggests that social services will not be of full service to clients and us all unless their task is seen as a struggle for the creation of a fundamentally changed society and—we believe—for a society organized on socialist principles."[79]

During the late 1970s, conservative political parties in power in North America and Britain eroded the welfare state through downsizing and cutbacks to services. Social workers writing in the radical tradition responded by producing some of the best analyses in social work literature on social welfare, the state, and social problems. "The Critical Texts in Social Work and the Welfare State," edited by Peter Leonard, made a particularly valuable contribution in this regard. Among them were *Social Work Practice under Capitalism: A Marxist Approach*, by Paul Corrigan and Peter Leonard (1978); *Class, Capital and Social Policy*, by Norman Ginsburg (1979); and Ian Gough's *The Political Economy of the Welfare State* (1979). During the same time, the London Edinburgh Weekend Return Group of social and community workers presented an excellent understanding of social welfare provision under capitalism in the book *In and Against the State* (1979).[80]

The faculty in the School of Social Work at Carleton University were the first in Canada to move toward a radical perspective as an orientation for social work education.[81] In 1972, the shift to more fully address social inequality was supported by the Carleton University Commission on the School of Social Work, which examined the curriculum and encouraged a broadened approach to practice. The Commission concluded that "in addition to the clinical ego-psychology approach, in which the client is seen as mainly having a problem requiring intervention and necessitating assistance towards adaptation, approaches to treatment should include a range of perspectives up to and including the 'Advocacy' and 'Participatory' approaches in which institutions and social processes are seen as having causal features requiring changes in which social workers must lead."[82]

Following this inquiry, under the leadership of Maurice Moreau, the School shifted from an ego-psychology model to what became called a structural approach, leaving behind the dualistic focus of individual change or social change and adopting a dialectic position of acknowledgement that both must be addressed and that change in one promotes change in the other. Carleton quickly became known as a "structural school," as a critical analysis and response was incorporated into all courses.[83] The project was also influenced by visiting scholars from the US and Britain such as Jeffry Galper, Vic George, Peter Leonard, and Mike Brake, who later joined the faculty on a full-time basis. (The structural approach is discussed in greater detail in Chapter 4.)

During these years, while the analysis of economic and political structures and policy was clearly developed, the direct practice component was less well conceptualized. Much of the early writings from a radical perspective, while articulating a clear class analysis and critique of capitalism, placed little emphasis on personal change or on the differing experiences of women, persons with a disability, immigrant and visible minority persons, or those who identify as lesbian, gay, or transgendered. Toward the mid-1980s, these limitations were addressed by social workers who thereby transformed the framework for structural social work.[84]

One of the most important contributions to understanding individual behaviour within a Marxist systems framework came from Peter Leonard in his 1984 book *Personality and Ideology*. Leonard's development of personality under the conditions of capitalism provided the missing piece in much of Marxist social work. He outlined how the limitation of mainstream psychological theories, which hold a non-materialist view of society, "prevents them from understanding its necessarily exploitative character and therefore how this exploitative structure constructs the individual's inner experience of class, gender and ethnic status."[85] It is this understanding of the dialectic between consciousness and material existence that continues to be the core of radical social work practice.

Divisions in Social Work

The differences between those social workers who drew on functional systems theory and those who drew on Marxist systems theory were highlighted as social work educators returned to the task of conceptualizing a unified model for social work that would unite professional specializations and set out to clarify social work's mission, purpose, and common base. Much of the debate centred on defining the difference between practitioners who were considered generalists and those who were called specialists. These discussions took place at two working meetings on conceptual frameworks, and the contributions, which were published in the 1977 and 1981 issues of *Social Work*, reflect the differing views of generalist practice and the purpose of social work and its ideological underpinnings.

According to Anne Minahan and Allen Pincus, a generalist is defined as a person with "a broad view who can look at an entire social situation, analyze the interactions between people in all the resource systems connected to that situation, intervene in those interactions, determine which specialists are needed from a variety of disciplines, and coordinate and mobilize the knowledge and skills of many disciplines."[86] In their view, if the social worker has been prepared at a graduate level, he or she could become more of an expert generalist than a specialist. Specialized knowledge and skills were influenced by the practice setting, not so much by university preparation.

For others the first division of social work methods was whether or not a social worker was employed in direct service activities (counselling, advocating, providing resources and information, and making referrals) or indirect service activities (policy analysis, administration, program development and evaluation, and community planning).[87] A second level of specialization would then be determined by the specific practice setting and the client population.

Ideological difference also surfaced during these discussions. Those attending the second meeting in 1979 produced a very general "Working Statement on the Purpose of Social Work" and encouraged colleagues to make comments and critique the statement.[88] John F. Longres felt that a major limitation of the statement was its lack of attention to the ideological differences among social workers. An advocate for radical social work, he referred to the political nature of social work practice and how "theoreticians and practitioners alike are attempting to integrate radicalism into everyday, face-to-face practice with individuals, families, and communities rather than allowing it to be separated off as something that exists apart from contact with clients." Longres explained that radical practice works toward "a change *of* the system, not change *in* the system" and is guided by a socialist vision.[89] An opposing view was presented by Carol Myer, who while recognizing the reality of increasing social inequality and the need for political action, held that it should not be part of the social work role and that such activities would be detrimental to the profession: "The idea in the last decade that social workers would change the social system through professional pursuit not only has been proven wrong (the system is worse) but has shaken public confidence in what social workers have been able to do." She concluded that "social workers can be more politically conscious and active, but politics ordinarily is not the domain of professional practice."[90] While there is relative consensus that social workers are generalists, there continues to be differences as to the practice framework that best serves social work and the needs of its clients.

Postmodernism

In the 1990s, some social work practitioners and academics began to consider the merits of postmodernism as a way of better informing the profession.[91] Peter Leonard, Janis Fook, and Bob Mullaly, all of whom have made significant contributions to radical social work, now incorporate postmodern theory to some degree.[92] Iain Ferguson and Michael Lavalette note that in the past two decades, Marxism has been marginalized within social work theory and practice as "postmodern and post-structuralist approaches, fiercely hostile to any attempt to make sense of the world as a totality, have often claimed the mantle of radicalism (in our view, quite unjustifiably)."[93]

Although the complexities of, and variations in, postmodern theory cannot be elaborated here, several integral tenets should be addressed. Postmodernism is a critique of the foundations of "modernity" and its focus on science, reason, and truth; it questions the relevance of universal claims and "grand theories," "grand narratives," or "totalizing theories" such as Marxism, socialism, and capitalism,[94] which are claimed to automatically overlook individual experience and other forms of oppression. Postmodernism, rooted in linguistic theory, holds that truth is a product of language or social discourse and is not objective or universal. Postmodern thinkers or "anti-truth tellers," as described by Joan Laird, hold that "knowledge does not develop from 'proven' or empirically-tested theory or hypothesis, it does not reflect any objective truth but is a product of social discourse; particular 'knowledges' are seen as social constructions, stories that have been shaped in contexts of power relationships in which they were crafted."[95]

Bob Mullaly suggests a continuum: at one end "postmodernism is a conservative, individualistic, and nihilistic doctrine, which holds that there is no potential for solidarity among oppressed persons or for social change efforts"; at the other end are those who, based on criticism of modernity, are attempting to revitalize critical social theory.[96] Similarly, Vodde and Gallant suggest that a narrative-deconstructivist practice drawing on postmodern theory provides a solution to the micro-macro split in social work and therefore unifies clinical and social action in pursuit of social justice.[97] They, too, distinguish between the purely linguistic orientation of postmodernist practice and one that focuses on language within a social justice framework, advocating for the latter, which they believe is represented in the narrative approaches that have been largely credited to Michael White and David Epston.[98]

Narrative therapy has gained in popularity in both Canada and the US, and White has been credited for bringing family therapy into the "postmodern world."[99] The goal of narrative approaches is to help people become authors of their own "stories" and to deconstruct and revise old problematic "stories."[100] The premise is that people are held back by an "old story," which may have helped them survive in the past but is no longer useful. In the postmodern deconstruction and revision, "no person, no theory, no point of view has privilege at the expense of anyone else's."[101] The process of deconstruction is to discover realities not initially evident—to question assumptions regarding beliefs, concepts, and practices.

The acceptance of all stories as equal creates difficulty when responding to situations rooted in injustice, such as the case of women who are beaten by their partners. If all "stories" are equal, are reactionary theories and views in regards to social class, gender, and race to be accepted as valid? Joan Laird, who incorporates social constructionism and narratives in her work with women raises caution in its application. She notes that since these theories and models have emerged during an era of political conservatism, "we could be lulled into thinking that everyone has equal power to shape his or her own story, forgetting that we must always be sensitive to the fact that our individual stories take shape in a powerful sociopolitical context."[102]

The use of creative questioning, externalization of the problem, and respect for local knowledges—all components of narrative therapy—have informed a number of practice approaches and have offered some creative ways of working with individuals and families. For example, Charles Waldegrave and his colleagues at the Family Centre in New Zealand have utilized postmodern concepts to complement modern approaches to practice. "Just Therapy," guided by the principles of spirituality, justice, and simplicity, recognizes the social and economic context of colonization and the injustices to the indigenous Maori, the impact of increasing poverty among low income families, gender inequality, and racism in their society.[103] Waldegrave's social justice framework for practice is grounded in the culture, conditions, and experiences of the families which come to the Centre.

While postmodernism has its proponents, it also has its social work critics. Much of the criticism is directed at the relativism and potential conservatism in its application to social work. Feminist scholars have pointed to how postmodernism ignores power and gender relations and marginalizes feminist contributions to family therapy.[104] Others hold that its tenets are extremely problematic for any emancipatory struggle. Brotman and Pollack argue that postmodernism is inherently conservative because "an undiscerning acceptance of its principles means relinquishing social work's goal of social change."[105]

Ben Carniol questions the premise that universal truths do not exist. "From my observation, based on four decades of work with diverse individuals and communities, it is self-evident that when it comes to certain values, there are indeed universal truths. For example, real democracy is better than tyranny; respect for human beings is better than killing them; protection of our environment is better than poisoning the air, water and soil; caring for others is better than indifference, prejudice and hatred or contempt."[106]

The focus on differences and the many ways of knowing and even many truths creates an immense challenge to mobilize a united opposition that can advance an alternative vision for society. Postmodernists question the use of identity categories such as "working class" or "woman" because "these representations demand the suppression of the difference and instability that is inherent to each category."[107] Kenan Malik, in "Universalism and Difference:

Race and the Postmodernists," critiques postmodernism for failing to understand "that while difference can arise from equality, equality can never arise from difference."[108] The emancipatory potential of postmodernism is questionable when it rejects theories of capitalism, as well as historical materialism, as a method for understanding class conflict, at a time of global capitalist expansion and growing inequalities throughout the world.

Atherton and Bolland point out that postmodernism has received credit where credit was not due. They challenge the claim that postmodernism has opened up the "possibility of beginning to hear other voices—those of women, gays, Blacks and other visible minorities, colonized peoples, the working class, religious groups that were forced to keep quiet so long."[109] They are correct to point out that these voices have been raised and acknowledged by feminists and other activists working toward social justice long before postmodernism. Nonetheless, postmodernists and their attention and commitment to diversity have enriched practice approaches in this regard. Similar criticism is directed at the postmodernism critique of science. John Saul explains that "we don't need the postmodernists to remind us that there are limits to the scientificity of the social science that we practice and apply."[110]

Peter Leonard, a social work scholar who has written extensively on postmodernism, concludes that postmodern theory and analysis cannot "be accepted without substantial challenge and modification."[111] However, he remains convinced of its potential contributions and believes that it must be part of the work to continue the "emancipatory project in the form of feminist, socialist, anti-racist, anti-colonial, environmentalist, and other political struggles but also emphasizes a common ground underlying this diversity."[112] Leonard argues that "on its own, postmodernism is unable to provide an intellectual or practical basis for the kind of politics necessary to a new welfare project: only as linked to feminism and Marxism does it realize a capacity to move from deconstruction to reconstruction."[113]

It remains to be seen the degree to which postmodernism can contribute to the emancipatory project and offer a solution to social work practice and social problems in our society. In my view, broad-based social change and social justice are more likely to occur through a collective struggle based on a critique and analysis of modern society. A focus on subjectivities while retreating from the broader structures will neither serve our profession nor the people whom we serve. In reference to postmodernism, William D. Gairdner, in *The Book of Absolutes*, suggests that "although the edge of novelty is gone, it survives as kind of a confused theory still relied upon to justify a pervasive relativist attitude." In stating his objections to the relativism underlying postmodernism he comments that "if all truth claims are equally valid, then the claim that relativism is false must also be true." For Gairdner, it all depends on where we place the emphasis. All trees in a forest could be seen as different or as the same. All trees have needles or leaves, a trunk, roots, and branches, and they all rely on photosynthesis for energy. Yet, there are many varieties of trees in a forest; they are not all the same.[114]

Attention to our commonalities such as social class and to the "grand narratives" such as capitalism and socialism are more important than ever. As Paulo Freire has noted, "Society is transformed when we transform it. And we transform it when the organized and mobilized political forces of the popular classes and workers throw themselves into history to change the world, and not in someone's head."[115] While the quote is somewhat dated, the sentiment and the general approach remain as relevant as ever. The next chapter examines the realm of social work practice and the principles and practices of the structural approach.

NOTES

1 Jane Addams, The President's Address, "Charity and Social Justice," *Proceedings* of the National Conference of Charities and Corrections (St. Louis, MO: The Archer Printing Co., 1910) 1.
2 An excellent history of this period is provided in Michael J. Piva, *The Condition of the Working Class in Toronto—1900–1921* (Ottawa: University of Ottawa Press, 1979).
3 David Wagner, "Radical Movements in the Social Services: A Theoretical Framework," *Social Service Review* (June 1989): 264–84.
4 Reuben Bitensky, "The Influence of Political Power in Determining the Theoretical Developments of Social Work," *Journal of Social Policy* 2, Pt. 2 (April 1973): 119, emphasis in original. See also Harry Specht and Mark E. Courtney, *Unfaithful Angels: How Social Work Has Abandoned Its Mission* (New York: The Free Press, 1994).
5 Once Canadian schools had their own accrediting body and social work scholars began publishing texts on social work practice, the US influence lessened.
6 For historical accounts of Kelso's contributions see A. Jones and L. Rutman, *In the Children's Aid: J.J. Kelso and Child Welfare in Ontario* (Toronto: University of Toronto Press, 1981; Michael Mulroney, *Formative Influences and Early Social Welfare Work of J.J. Kelso 1864–1891, an Independent Enquiry Project* (Ottawa: Carleton University, 1993).
7 Therese Jennissen and Colleen Lundy, *One Hundred Years of Social Work: A History of the Profession in English Canada, 1900–2000* (Waterloo, ON: Wilfrid Laurier University Press, 2011).
8 Alvin Finkel, *Social Policy and Practice in Canada: A History* (Waterloo, ON: Wilfrid Laurier University Press, 2006).
9 Mary Richmond, *Friendly Visiting among the Poor* (New York: Macmillan, 1899).
10 Mary Richmond, *The Good Neighbor* (Philadelphia: Russell Sage Foundation, 1908).
11 Mary Richmond, *Social Diagnosis* (Philadelphia: Russell Sage Foundation, 1917); Mary Richmond, *What is Social Casework?* (New York: Russell Sage Foundation, 1922).
12 Gerald C. Rothman, *Philanthropists, Therapists and Activists* (Cambridge, MA: Schenkman,

1985) 26. Mary Richmond coined the terms "retail" and "wholesale" to distinguish between the efforts placed on individual change and those directed at greater societal
change.

13 See e.g. Healy, "Exploring the History of Social Work as a Human Rights Profession."

14 Eleanor M. Klosterman and Dorothy C. Stratton, "Speaking Truth to Power: Jane Addams'
Value Base for Peacemaking," *Affilia: Journal of Women and Social Work* 21.2 (Summer
2006): 158–68.

15 Jane Addams and other settlement workers participated in the six-year process of appeal
and mass demonstrations in support of Nicola Sacco and Bartolomeo Vanzetti, Italian
immigrants and anarchists who were charged in 1920 with murder and executed by the
State of Massachusetts on 23 August 1927 despite evidence pointing to their innocence.
See, e.g., Patrick Selmi, "Social Work and the Campaign to Save Sacco and Vanzetti,"
Social Service Review 75.1 (March 2001): 115–34.

16 See, e.g., Donna L. Franklin, "Mary Richmond and Jane Addams: From Moral Certainty
to Rational Inquiry in Social Work Practice," *Social Service Review* (December 1986):
504–25.

17 Roy Lubove, *The Professional Altruist: The Emergence of Social Work as a Career 1880–
1930* (Cambridge, MA: Harvard University Press, 1965) 5, 14.

18 Stanley Wenocur and Michael Reisch, *From Charity to Enterprise: The Development of
American Social Work in a Market Economy* (Chicago: University of Illinois Press, 1989) 89.

19 Karen Lundblad, "Jane Addams and Social Reform: A Role Model for the 1990s," *Social
Work* 40.5 (1995): 661–69.

20 See, e.g., Rothman, *Philanthropists, Therapists and Activists* 28.

21 Allan Irving, Harriet Parsons, and Donald Bellamy, *Neighbours: Three Social Settlements
in Downtown Toronto* (Toronto: Canadian Scholars Press, 1995).

22 Gale Wills, "Values of Community Practice: Legacy of the Radical Social Gospel," *Canadian
Social Work Review* 9, no. 1 (1992): 28–40.

23 Donald Bellamy and Allan Irving, "Pioneers," in *Canadian Social Welfare*, 3rd ed., ed.
Joanne C. Turner and Francis J. Turner (Scarborough, ON: Allyn and Bacon, 1995) 89–117.
The Fred Victor Mission's doors are still open in Toronto.

24 Bellamy and Irving, "Pioneers."

25 McClung also published 16 books. Among the most widely read is *In Times Like These*,
originally published in 1915 and more recently reissued by the Social History of Canada
Series (Toronto: University of Toronto Press, 1972).

26 See e.g. Wenocur and Reisch, *From Charity to Enterprise.*

27 A thorough account of US social work history can be found in Lubove, *The Professional
Altruist.*

28 Wenocur and Reisch, *From Charity to Enterprise.*

29 Leslie Leighninger, *Creating a New Profession: The Beginnings of Social Work Education
in the United States* (Alexandria, VA: Council on Social Work Education, 2000).

30 Shankar A. Yelaga, *An Introduction to Social Work Practice in Canada* (Scarborough, ON:
Prentice-Hall, 1985) 2–23; Wenocur and Reisch, *From Charity to Enterprise* 130.

31 John Graham, "A History of the University of Toronto School of Social Work," Ph.D. dissertation, University of Toronto, 1996.

32 Finkel, *Social Policy and Practice in Canada* 87.

33 Abraham Flexner, "Is Social Work a Profession," Proceedings of the National Conference
of Charities and Corrections (Baltimore, MD: Hildmann Printing Co., 1915): 576–90.

34 Richard Cloward and Francis Fox Piven, "The Acquiescence of Social Work," in *Strategic Perspectives on Social Policy*, ed. J. Tropman, M. Duluhy, and R. Lind (New York: Pergamon Press, 1981). In 1908 Freud's works were translated into English for the first time and appeared in American journals. In the following year he was invited to deliver a series of lectures at Clark University in Worchester, Massachusetts.

35 Joy Maines, "Through the Years in CASW," NAC, FA 1713, MG 28I441: 2.

36 Howard Goldstein, *Social Work Practice: A Unitary Approach* (Columbia, SC: University of South Carolina Press, 1979) 31. See also, Specht and Courtney, *Unfaithful Angels*.

37 See, e.g., Clarke A. Chambers, "Women in the Creation of the Profession of Social Work," *Social Service Review* (March 1986): 1–33. Clarke describes Jessie Taft and Virginia Robinson as life-long companions who adopted two children into their "Boston marriage." He holds that settlement living supported such arrangements. A thorough understanding of the functional approach can be found in Virginia Robinson, *A Changing Psychology in Social Case Work* (Chapel Hill, NC: University of North Carolina Press, 1930); Jessie Taft, *Family Casework and Counseling, A Functional Approach* (Philadelphia: University of Pennsylvania Press, 1935).

38 Martha M. Dore, "Functional Theory: Its History and Influence on Contemporary Social Work Practice," *Social Service Review* 64.3 (1990): 358–74. Taft and Robinson were so committed to the ideas of Rank that they both entered into analysis with him.

39 Noel Timms, "Taking Social Work Seriously: The Contribution of the Functional School," *British Journal of Social Work* 27 (1997): 723–37.

40 A history of the CASW from 1922 to 1977 can be found in the National Archives of Canada. See, e.g., "Through the Years," FA 1713, MG 28 I441; the quote is on page 2.

41 Leslie Leighninger, "The Generalist-Specialist Debate in Social Work," *Social Service Review* (March 1980): 1–12; American Association of Social Workers, *Social Case Work, Generic and Specific: An Outline, A Report of the Milford Conference* (New York: American Association of Social Workers, 1929).

42 Jacob Fisher, *The Response of Social Work to the Depression* (Cambridge, MA: Schenkman, 1980).

43 Judith Ann Trolander, "The Response of Settlements to the Great Depression," *Social Work* (September 1973): 92–102. Community Chests developed in both Canada and the US as fund-raising organizations and were the precursor to the present United Way. See, e.g., Jennissen and Lundy, *One Hundred Years of Social Work*.

44 The Rank and File, a group of 15,000 social workers, outnumbered the American Association of Social Workers at the time. The movement existed for four years and produced the journal *Social Work Today*. See Michael Reisch and Janice Andrews, *The Road Not Taken: A History of Radical Social Work in the United States* (New York: Bruner-Routledge, 2002); also Fisher, *The Response of Social Work to the Depression*.

45 Bertha C. Reynolds, *An Uncharted Journey, Fifty Years of Growth in Social Work* (New York: The Citadel Press, 1963) 143.

46 See Fisher, *The Response of Social Work to the Depression* 131. Fisher recounts an incident at the 1935 National Conference of Social Welfare held in Montreal where three Black social workers were denied accommodation at the six hotels they approached. The conference committee, composed of Rank and File members, issued a general statement condemning racial discrimination and developed a policy to meet only in cities that insured complete access to facilities.

47 For example, in 1939, six Canadian social workers were listed as contributors: Sophie N. Boyd, Kathleen Gorrie, Margaret Gould, Mary Jennison, Dora Wilensky, and Kathleen

Would. See, e.g., Jennissen and Lundy, *One Hundred Years of Social Work*.

48 Maines, "Through the Years in CASW" 9, 10.

49 Bertha C. Reynolds, "Social Case Work: What is it? What is its Place in the World Today?," *Child and Family Welfare* 11.6 (March 1936): 12.

50 For a history of the organization, see Michiel Horn, *The League for Social Reconstruction: Intellectual Origins of the Democratic Left in Canada 1930–1942* (Toronto: University of Toronto Press, 1980). Approximately one-third of the membership came from education, social work, and the ministry. The League never exceeded 1,000 members.

51 Alan Whitehorn, *Canadian Socialism: Essays on the CCF-NDP* (Toronto: Oxford University Press, 1992).

52 A major contribution to this end was Grace Coyle's *Social Process in Organized Groups*, published in 1930 by R.R. Smith, the first comprehensive group work text. Coyle offered a theoretical framework, and group work was legitimated as a practice.

53 Wenocur and Reisch, *From Charity to Enterprise*.

54 Herbert Bisno, "How Social Will Social Work Be?," *Social Work* 1.2 (April 1956): 12–18.

55 Senator Joseph McCarthy of Wisconsin was one of the main proponents of the Red Scare. In 1938 the House of Representatives set up the Committee on Un-American Activities, which persecuted anyone with a left-of-centre political perspective; see Leslie Leighninger and Robert Knickmeyer, "The Rank and File Movement: The Relevance of Radical Social Work Traditions to Modern Social Work Practice," *Journal of Sociology and Social Welfare* 4.2 (1976): 170.

56 Rothman, *Philanthropists, Therapists and Activists* 5. The ideas of the group were submerged and not heard again until the late 1960s.

57 Jennissen and Lundy, *One Hundred Years of Social Work*.

58 Laurel Lewey, "Anti-Communism in the Cold War and Its Impact on Six Canadian Social Workers," *Canadian Social Work* 12.2 (2010): 10–24.

59 Wendy B. Posner, "Common Human Needs: A Story from the Prehistory of Government by Special Interests," *Social Service Review* (June 1995): 201. Posner's research explains how the criticism and negative press coverage of Towle's book was part of a campaign to discredit President Harry S. Truman's attempts to establish a national health care program. See Charlotte Towle, *Common Human Needs* (London: George Allen and Unwin, 1973). The book was originally published in 1945 and has been translated into more than 10 languages.

60 Rothman, *Philanthropists, Therapists and Activists*.

61 These changes were based on "The Hollis and Taylor Report": Ernest V. Hollis and Alice L. Taylor, *Social Work Education in the United States* (New York: Columbia University Press, 1951). Since Canadian social work programs continued to be accredited by the American Council on Social Work Education, the changes influenced us as well.

62 Florence Hollis, "The Psycho Social Approach to Casework," in *Theories of Social Casework*, ed. Robert W. Roberts and Robert H. Nee (Chicago: University of Chicago Press, 1970) 53. See also Florence Hollis, *Casework: A Psycho Social Therapy* (New York: Random House, 1964).

63 Helen Harris Perlman, *Social Casework: A Problem Solving Process* (Chicago: University of Chicago Press, 1957).

64 C. Wright Mills, *Power, Politics and People* (New York: Oxford University Press, 1963).

65 William Schwartz, "Private Troubles and Public Issues," *The Social Welfare Forum* (1969): 40.

66 Lawrence Shulman, *The Skills of Helping Individuals, Families, and Groups*, 3rd ed.

(Itasca, IL: F.E. Peacock, 1992); Lawrence Shulman, *The Skills of Helping Individuals, Families, Groups and Communities*, 4th ed. (Itasca, IL: F.E. Peacock, 1999).

67 Lawrence Shulman, *The Skills of Helping Individuals, Families, Groups and Communities*, 7th ed. (Belmont, CA: Wadsworth, 2011).

68 Goldstein, *Social Work Practice* 53.

69 Wagner, "Radical Movements in the Social Services" 271.

70 The journal *Social Work* produced two conceptual framework issues in 1977 and 1981.

71 Goldstein, *Social Work Practice*; Allen Pincus and Anne Minahan, *Social Work Practice: Model and Method* (Itasca, IL: F.E. Peacock, 1973).

72 Pincus and Minahan, *Social Work Practice* 63, emphasis in original.

73 Pincus and Minahan, *Social Work Practice* 27.

74 Pincus and Minahan, *Social Work Practice* 27.

75 Carel B. Germain and Alex Gitterman, *The Life Model of Social Work Practice* (New York: Columbia University Press, 1996) 7, 19.

76 Carol H. Myer, "The Search for Coherence," *Clinical Social Work in the Eco-Systems Perspective*, ed. Carol H. Myer (New York: Columbia University Press, 1983) 5–34. For a comprehensive analysis of the eco-systems perspective, see Jerome C. Wakefield's two-part series, "Does Social Work Need the Eco-Systems Perspective? Part 1: Is the Perspective Clinically Useful?" *Social Service Review* (March 1996): 1–32; and "Part 2: Does the Perspective Save Social Work from Incoherence?" *Social Service Review* (June 1996): 183–213. In the June 1996 journal see also the Debate with Authors, an exchange between Alex Gitterman and Jerome Wakefield.

77 Roy Bailey and Mike Brake, eds., *Radical Social Work* (New York: Pantheon Books, 1975); it was first published by Edward Arnold in London. Jeffry H. Galper, *The Politics of Social Services* (Englewood Cliffs, NJ: Prentice-Hall, 1975).

78 Bailey and Brake, *Radical Social Work* 9.

79 Galper, *The Politics of Social Services* x.

80 See, e.g., Paul Corrigan and Peter Leonard, *Social Work Practice under Capitalism: A Marxist Approach* (London: Macmillan, 1978); Norman Ginsburg, *Class, Capital and Social Policy* (London: Macmillan, 1979); Ian Gough, *The Political Economy of the Welfare State* (London: Macmillan, 1979); London Edinburgh Weekend Return Group, *In and Against the State* (London: Pluto Press, 1979).

81 The development of this approach is outlined in Roland Lecomte, "Connecting Private Troubles and Public Issues in Social Work Education," in *Social Work and Social Change in Canada*, ed. Brian Wharf (Toronto: McClelland and Stewart, 1990) 31–51.

82 Commission on the School of Social Work, *Report* (Ottawa: Carleton University, June 1972) 6.

83 Faculty members included Jim Albert, Peter Findlay, Roland Lecomte, Allan Moscovitch, and Helen Levine. Levine took a leadership role in ensuring that feminist theory informed the approach. See Helen Levine, "The Personal is Political: Feminism and the Helping Professions," in *Feminism in Canada*, ed. Angela Miles and Geraldine Finn (Montreal: Black Rose Books, 1982) 175–210.

84 For a woman-centred approach, see Helen Marchant and Betsy Wearing, eds., *Gender Reclaimed: Women in Social Work* (Sydney, NSW: Hale and Iremonger, 1986); Jalna Hanmer and Daphne Statham, *Women and Social Work: Towards a Woman-Centered Practice* (London: Macmillan, 1989). On anti-racism, see Lena Dominelli, *Anti-Racist Social Work* (London: Macmillan, 1988). And for social work for persons with a disability, see Michael Oliver, *Social Work with Disabled People* (London: Macmillan, 1983).

85 Peter Leonard, *Personality and Ideology: Toward a Materialist Understanding of the Individual* (London: Macmillan, 1984) 26.

86 Anne Minahan and Allan Pincus, "Conceptual Framework for Social Work Practice," *Social Work* 22.5 (1977): 352.

87 Neil Gilbert, "The Search for Professional Identity," *Social Work* 22.5 (1977): 401–06.

88 The Working Statement can be found in Anne Minahan, "Introduction to Special Issue," *Social Work* 261 (1981): 5–6.

89 John F. Longres, "Reactions to Working Statement on Purpose," *Social Work* 26.1 (1981): 85; emphasis in the original.

90 Carol H. Mayer, "Social Work Purpose: Status by Choice or Coercion?," *Social Work* 26.6 (1981): 74.

91 Joan Laird, ed., *Revisioning Social Work Education: A Social Constructionist Approach* (New York: The Haworth Press, 1993); Adrienne S. Chambon and Allan Irving, eds., *Essays on Postmodernism and Social Work* (Toronto: Canadian Scholars Press, 1994).

92 Peter Leonard, "Knowledge/Power and Postmodernism: Implications for the Practice of a Critical Social Work Education," *Canadian Social Work Review* 11.1 (Winter 1994): 11–24; Peter Leonard, "Postmodernism, Socialism, and Social Welfare," *Journal of Progressive Human Services* 6, no. 2 (1995): 3–19; Peter Leonard, "Three Discourses on Practice: A Postmodern Re-appraisal," *Journal of Sociology and Social Welfare* 23.2 (June 1996): 7–26; Peter Leonard, *Postmodern Welfare: Reconstructing an Emancipatory Project* (London: Sage, 1997); Bob Pease and Jan Fook, eds., *Transforming Social Work Practice: Postmodern Critical Perspectives* (London: Routledge, 1999); Bob Mullaly, *Challenging Oppression: A Critical Social Work Approach* (Don Mills, ON: Oxford University Press, 2002); Bob Mullaly, *The New Structural Social Work* (Don Mills, ON: Oxford University Press, 2007).

93 Iain Ferguson and Michael Lavalette, "Beyond Power Discourse: Alienation and Social Work," *British Journal of Social Work* 34 (2004): 298.

94 Modernity generally refers to the historical period of the Enlightenment (seventeenth- and eighteenth-century Europe) and corresponds to the development of capitalism in Europe. For an overview of modernity, see, e.g., Leonard, "Knowledge/Power and Postmodernism."

95 Laird, *Revisioning Social Work Education* 4.

96 Mullaly *Challenging Oppression: A Critical Social Work Approach* 18.

97 Rich Vodde and J. Paul Gallant, "Bridging the Gap between Micro and Macro Practice: Large Scale Change and a Unified Model of Narrative-Deconstructive Practice," *Journal of Social Work Education* 38.3 (2002): 439–58.

98 Michael White and David Epston, *Narrative Means to Therapeutic Ends* (New York: Norton, 1990).

99 Alan Parry and Robert E. Doan, *Story Re-visions: Narrative Therapy in a Postmodern World* (New York: The Guilford Press, 1994).

100 Although not acknowledged, the concept of deconstructing, revisioning, and restorying is similar to script analysis in transactional analysis (TA) where a script is a life plan also discovered through narratives. See, e.g., Claude Steiner, *Scripts People Live: Transactional Analysis of Life Scripts* (New York: Grove Press, 1974).

101 Perry and Doan, *Story Re-visions* 22.

102 Joan Laird, "Changing Women's Narratives: Taking Back the Discourse," in *Building on Women's Strengths: A Social Work Agenda for the Twenty-First Century*, ed. Jean K. Peterson and Alice A. Lieberman (New York: The Haworth Social Work Practice Press, 2001) 294.

103 Charles Waldegrave, "'Just Therapy,' Social Justice and Family Therapy: A Discussion of

the Work of The Family Centre, Lower Hutt, New Zealand," Special Issue, *Dulwich Centre Newsletter* 1 (1990): 1–46.

104 Rosemary Paterson and Salli Trathen, "Feminist In (ter)ventions in Family Therapy," *ANZ Journal of Family Therapy* 15.2 (1994): 91–98.

105 Shari Brotman and Shoshana Pollack, "Loss of Context: The Problem of Merging Postmodernism with Feminist Social Work," *Canadian Social Work Review* 14.1 (Winter 1997): 9.

106 Ben Carniol, "Analysis of Social Location and Change: Practice Implications," in *Social Work: A Critical Turn*, ed. Steven Hick, Jan Fook, and Richard Pozzuto (Toronto: Thompson Educational, 2005) 155.

107 Karen Healy, "Power and Activist Social Work," in *Transforming Social Work Practice: Postmodern Critical Perspectives*, ed. Bob Pease and Jan Fook (London: Routledge, 1999) 117.

108 Kenan Malik, "Universalism and Difference: Race and the Postmodernists," *Race and Class* 37.3 (1996): 4.

109 Charles R. Atherton and Kathleen A. Bollard, "Postmodernism: A Dangerous Illusion for Social Work," *International Social Work* 45.4 (2002): 430. They quote from Allan Irving, "From Image to Simulacra: The Modern/Postmodern Divide and Social Work," *Essays on Postmodernism and Social Work*, ed. A.S. Chambron and A. Irving (Toronto: Canadian Scholars Press, 1994) 28.

110 John S. Saul, "Identifying Class, Classifying Difference," in *Fighting Identities: Race, Religion, and Ethno-Nationalism*, ed. Leo Panitch and Colin Leys (London: Merlin Press, 2002) 349.

111 Leonard, "Three Discourses on Practice" 19.

112 Leonard, "Knowledge/Power and Postmodernism" 18.

113 Leonard, *Postmodern Welfare* xiv.

114 William D. Gairdner, *The Book of Absolutes: A Critique of Relativism, and a Defence of Universals* (Montreal: McGill-Queen's University Press, 2008) 31.

115 Paulo Freire, "A Critical Understanding of Social Work," *Journal of Progressive Human Services* 1.1 (1990): 9.

CHAPTER 4

STRUCTURAL SOCIAL WORK: THEORY, IDEOLOGY, AND PRACTICE PRINCIPLES

THE REVIEW OF HISTORICAL DEVELOPMENTS in social work practice approaches in the previous chapter outlines the differing theories and ideologies that have influenced the profession in the past and continue to do so today. Although theories and ideologies implicitly guide social workers in their day-to-day practice, they often are unaware of this fact. This is not a problem only for practitioners who operate outside of academia. An awareness of ideology and theory and its role in social work practice is frequently absent in social work courses and social work literature. Whether acknowledged or implicit, theories and models of practice have ideological assumptions underpinning them. This chapter discusses a number of theories that social workers draw on and the role these theories play in shaping and legitimating practice models or approaches. In particular, the principles and practices of a structural approach to social work are outlined.

THE CONTEXT OF SOCIAL WORK PRACTICE

The ongoing challenge for social workers is to be informed about the diverse and ever changing context that shapes the lives of individuals and frames social work practice. The IFSW identifies five contexts of social work practice in the publication *Human Rights and Social Work*:

- *Geographical.* All practice is located within some set of boundaries: agency, nation-state, and region.
- *Political.* Every country has a political system. This sets the context for practice, whether the system is liberal or repressive, socialist, social democratic, or capitalist.

- *Socio-economic.* An adequate livelihood, work, health and facilities, education, and, if possible, access to social security and social services are basic human aspirations. The social cohesion of any group or nation depends, to a large extent, on an equitable sharing of available resources.
- *Cultural.* The practices, beliefs, aspirations, and culture of individuals, families, groups, communities, and nations have to be respected, though without prejudice to the evolution of certain practices and beliefs [and as long as the rights of another are not violated]. Unless this is done, discriminatory acts that are destructive for society will occur.
- *Spiritual.* No society in which social work is practiced is value-free. It is central to social work/human practice that attention is paid to the spirit, the values, the philosophies, the ethics, and the hope and ideals of those with whom social workers work and, at the same time to social workers' own values.[1]

On a recent trip to Nunavut and the Northwest Territories, I was struck at the complexities facing social workers who practice in the far north. They strive to meet individual and social concerns of the residents who live in a geographical region composed largely of a number of remote fly-in communities. Access to resources and social services is limited, while social concerns and needs are immense. The impact of colonialism and institutional racism is reflected in the high rates of suicide, alcohol and other drug use, and abject poverty within Aboriginal communities. In a major study on suicide in Nunavut, Jack Hicks noted that "The Inuit transition from a low-suicide society to a high-suicide society in a very short period is almost without parallel elsewhere on the planet."[2] Inuit suicide is most prevalent among young men and women and can be attributed to intergenerational trauma. Hicks explains that the low suicide rate among Inuit elders is in part the result of their connection to their culture.

As with social work in the north, the practice of social workers in all settings is embedded in these five contexts: geographical, political, socio-economic, and an appreciation and respect for the cultural and spiritual traditions and practices of the population. I would add to this list an awareness of the historical context.

THEORY, MODELS, AND APPROACHES

Theory is a systematically organized collection of concepts and relationships that explains a phenomenon. How we understand a certain situation is partly due to the theory on which we draw. While there is a tendency to interchange the terms theory, models, and approaches, there are distinct differences among them. Duncan Foley points out that theories offer explanations of a reality and include contradictory forces that call for change in the theory itself. "A model, on the other hand, is a representation of a theory in which these contradictory elements have been suppressed, often to allow a mathematical representation of the ideas. Models are representations not of reality but of theory," according to Foley.[3] This explains how social work models may share a similar theoretical foundation but differ in how the theory is represented. For example, functional systems theory informed the development of a number of generalist practice models in social work such as *Social Work Practice: Model and Method* (Allen Pincus and Anne Minahan), *Social Work Practice: A Unitary Approach* (Howard Goldstein), and *The Life Model of Social Work Practice* (Carol Germaine and Alex Gitterman). Similarly, postmodern theory is represented in narrative, solution-focused, and brief therapy approaches.

Foley points out that those who strictly adopt a particular model of practice run the danger of not considering the limitations of the model and how it is a static and unchanging representation of a changing reality. Criticisms of a model are often received with a counter argument by the proponent. For example, in the 1970s, a number of social workers, including the author, were influenced by transactional analysis and gestalt therapy. We attended institutes and workshops, and some received certification as recognized therapists in the field. The practice was utilized in individual, family, and group work. Once invested in and committed to the model, we were reluctant to acknowledge the limitations of its prescriptive tenets and its disregard for the changing economic and material context of clients' lives. Similarly, when the Milan family therapy approach was critiqued because it demonstrated acceptance of traditional roles that advantaged men in the family, members of the Milan team discounted the concern.[4]

Much of the theory that informs, organizes, and guides the practice responses of social workers is derived from psychology, sociology, economics, political science, and social administration. Social work approaches are more expansive than many models or theories in that they draw on a number of theories that share similar theoretical and philosophical assumptions in order to understand individual and social problems. For example, the psycho-social approach spearheaded by Florence Hollis draws on psychoanalytic theory, ego psychology, and object relations, all independent but related theories.

Since theory takes into account and contains within itself the potential for change, it is never static, and it does not offer a fixed explanation for individual or social problems. As any experienced practitioner will tell you, there is a dynamic relationship between theory and practice in that, through the application of the theory, the theory itself is transformed. This process of action and reflection, where theory informs practice and practice in turn informs theory, has been acknowledged by revolutionary theorist and practitioner Mao Tsetung.[5]

Malcolm Payne speaks to this relationship when he states that "the nature of social work and its theory are defined, not by some independent process of academic development and experimental testing but by what social workers actually do."[6] Paulo Freire's concept of "praxis," a process in which one's reflection on practice or action informs the next practice, speaks to this relationship of theory to practice.[7]

It has been said that "there is nothing as practical as a good theory."[8] Theory informs social work analysis, assessment, and intervention strategies. However, as practitioners respond to the urgent and complex situations before them, they often are not conscious of the particular theories that inform their actions and the overall theoretical framework that guides their practice. Social workers often view theory as too academic or abstract. In a study of expertise in social work, the researchers concluded that "social work theorizing may be more about underlying assumptions, the use of particular concepts and developing practice wisdom in a seemingly intuitive way than about using integrated theoretical frameworks."[9] At times it may seem like we are acting spontaneously, intuitively, yet our perceptions and our actions are never completely free of theory. The task for social workers is to strive to identify, analyze, and build on the theoretical framework that guides their practice and to insure that it corresponds to the conditions under which people live and the needs they have.

Up until the 1960s, theory development in social work, as in other disciplines, had an ethnocentric bias and neglected to adequately consider differences based on gender, race and/or ethnicity, sexual orientation, and social class. This lack of awareness informed the responses of practitioners and failed certain groups of people. For example, Kohlberg's moral development theory was based on the study of young men, framed around their development and experience, and then applied to the development of both men and women. Since Kohlberg concluded that abstract ethical principles of justice were used by these young men to resolve moral dilemmas, women were found lacking when judged against this male standard. Carol Gilligan's research on young girls revealed that they struggled with moral dilemmas by focusing on relationships and the human consequences of their choices. Gilligan's discovery of these "different voices" built on, but also critiqued the work of Kohlberg.[10]

The women's movement, feminist research, and the development of women's studies programs were instrumental in transforming knowledge by introducing a gender analysis and advancing theory in the social sciences, including social work. Challenges and contributions from visible minority women have highlighted the limitations of what currently is conceptualized as feminism and further transformed feminist thought and feminist practice.[11]

In her study of the application and development of theory within social work, Donna Baines found that a number of feminist concepts were not helpful in her work with working-class women and women of colour in an inner city hospital. For example, the general understanding that women direct their anger inward and should be encouraged to express it outwardly had no relevance for the "streetsy" women with whom she had contact and who were far from passive and had no difficulty in expressing their anger.[12] While theories are helpful in guiding our practice, we must be ever mindful not to assume that all persons of a certain social category share the same experiences. Therefore, it is imperative that social workers develop cultural sensitivity and develop knowledge to respond to the differing realities of clients.

TAKING IDEOLOGY INTO ACCOUNT

When we look at the array of models, theories, and approaches within social work and related disciplines, we discover that they all have ideologies or assumptions that are either stated or implied. A major factor influencing practitioners as they adopt theories and practice models/approaches is the fit between their beliefs and values (ideology) and those inherent in a particular theoretical approach. As Mary Bricker-Jenkins argues:

> Practice is more than stringing techniques and methods around a theoretical framework; it is also the reflection and promotion of values and beliefs. In other words, every practice model has an ideological core.... In short, ideology is the glue that holds a practice system together and binds it to human conditions, institutions, and practices.[13]

Our assumptions and beliefs form the lens through which we look to understand and respond to social and individual situations. Social attitudes toward people based on their gender, race/ethnicity, class, sexual orientation, physical and mental ability, and the problems with which they are struggling are often influenced by ideology—ideology which is embedded in the policies and practices of social institutions. For example, the act of placing the full responsibility/blame on individuals for their circumstances is rooted in a particular ideology or set of ideas and beliefs.

We are usually influenced by the dominant ideology—the political, economic, and social beliefs that permeate all structures in our society—and in Canada today that is predominantly the neoliberal ideology. It holds, among other beliefs, the view that capitalism is a sound economic system and that the accumulation of wealth by corporations and rich individuals is well-earned and somehow "trickles down" to others in need. The prevailing message is that there are opportunities for all who are motivated to work; therefore, unemployment and poverty are generally viewed as the responsibility of individuals and their families. The notion of ideology holds political connotations.

One study of the ideological and socio-political assumptions within introductory social work textbooks found that "virtually all were found to contain assumptions about the political-economic structure of society, the nature of class and social class relationships, and the nature of social change."[14] The authors found that the texts fell into three equal clusters along a left-centre-right dimension. The texts from a left perspective promote the view that the livelihoods of individuals are a product or responsibility of political, economic, and social institutions and conditions that must be improved. Those on the right place responsibility on families and individuals for their life situation and place little emphasis on larger social and material conditions.[15] Those in the centre acknowledge the importance of social conditions and engage in strategies of social reform but do not advocate significant changes to social, economic, and political structures.

Along the same lines, John Coates proposed that models of social work practice can be organized into three areas—those that stress personal deficiency, ecological factors, or the larger political economy. These correspond to conservative, liberal, and socialist/feminist ideological perspectives respectively.[16] Using Coates's distinction, social work approaches that assume that the primary source of personal difficulties lies within the individual, such as the psychoanalytic or behavioural models, can be considered as a personal deficiency approach. An ecological approach includes the models based on functional systems theory in which the broader system is considered, but not in a politically critical way. The political economy approach refers to anti-capitalist, anti-racist, and feminist models based on assumptions that individual troubles are connected to structural inequalities.

ORGANIZING FRAMEWORKS

In the 1960s, John Horton proposed that theories of social problems could be separated into two groups, conflict or order, depending on whether they viewed society as being divided by conflict or functioning in a generally ordered way.[17] Conflict models offer a critique of capitalist structures and the production of inequality and exploitation. They emphasize the importance of a critical consciousness, collective action, and a radical restructuring of society, while order models argue that the system is structurally sound. An order analysis is most often expressed by those in power within capitalist societies, while a conflict analysis is advanced by social activists and political groups on the left who are often in opposition to those governing.

Building on Horton's order-conflict axis, Burrell and Morgan organized theories of social problems along two theoretical and two philosophical dimensions. In social work Whittington and Holland, and Carniol found the framework useful and modified it for organizing social work theories/approaches and ideologies[18] (see Table 4.1).

Burrell and Morgan suggest that perspectives or theories be viewed as situated along a continuum. It does not matter simply whether or not a theory falls into either a conflict or order model, they argue, but the degree to which it adheres to the assumptions of either. Similar to Horton's order-conflict binary, the theoretical dimension of the framework situates a theory along a transformation-accommodation continuum according to the degree to which it supports radical change or the regulation of society and social problems. According to Whittington and Holland, theories of radical change assume that our society has an inherent tendency to instability and change and contains inherent con-

TABLE 4.1 ORGANIZING FRAMEWORK FOR SOCIAL WORK APPROACHES

Sources: Carniol, "Clash of Ideologies in Social Work Education"; W&H: Whittington and Holland, "A Framework for Theory in Social Work."

traditions (for example, between labour and capital); that the ideas, rules, and objectives of some groups dominate others; that radical change of prevailing rules and structures is necessary; that deprivation and alienation are widespread; and that emancipation is a prime objective. On the other end of the continuum, theories of regulation assume that "we live in a predominately stable, integrated and cohesive society; that there is a consensus on rules and objectives; that behaviour should be regulated in accord with the prevailing social rules; that there exist social institutions to satisfy the needs of individuals and the social system (the family, education, welfare); and, finally that integration and reintegration into society are prime objectives."[19]

The philosophical dimension focuses on assumptions about how knowledge is developed and how individual and social change occurs. Theories are situated according to the degree of importance placed on subjective, individual consciousness on one end of the continuum and material conditions on the other. When the philosophical dimension is added, theories can be further distinguished by their attention to either the subjective/individual or the objective/structural. The two dimensions offer a more nuanced approach to situating theories. For example, although an order theory such as functional systems theory places emphasis on the social context when assessing social and personal problems, social structures themselves are not viewed as problematic. Solutions are found within individual or family functioning and accommodation to the structure such as readjustment and/or resocialization of the troubled individual. The majority of the "traditional social work" approaches coincides with this perspective, according to Whittington and Holland. Similarly, social work approaches based on theories of social order can focus on a client's subjective experiences, as is the case with an "interactionist approach," such as the client-centred approach first developed by Carl Rogers.[20]

Conflict theories can differ in the emphasis placed on either agency or structure and the possibilities of social change. Radical humanist, radical feminist, and several approaches such as narrative therapy based on postmodern theory all emphasize individual subjective experiences and fall within a conflict approach. On the other hand, radical social work, socialist feminist, and Marxist-based approaches rely primarily on an objective/structural analysis and place emphasis on social, economic, and political conflict through collective action instead of attention to individual, subjective experiences.[21]

The structural approach is advocated in this book as the most promising and fruitful way of addressing social problems. It situates seemingly individual problems within social and material conditions and alienating social structures while at the same time emphasizes the importance of human agency while offering help to individuals and their families. Clearly, it is situated within the radical change/transformation approach, bridging both dimensions of the subjective and objective.

Surprisingly, there has been little attention paid to the relationship between ideology, theory building, and social work practice. However, as has been argued, certain theories share a common ideology—a set of beliefs, assumptions, and values—that offer differing views and interpretations than other theories and approaches.

Pursuing this theme, Ben Carniol presents four distinct ideological perspectives or world views of society that inform practice responses (see Table 4.1). Theories within the "regulation" quadrants are based on the ideological perspectives of individualism—"work hard and you can achieve"—and system functionalism in which the belief that the system—the social, economic, and political structures—is sound and contributes to individual well-being. Both perspectives take a "blaming the victim" position in understanding individual and social problems since the source of the problem and the responsibility and focus for change rests with the person not with the social structures in which they live. Within the "transformatory" quadrants, Carniol situates the ideological perspectives of radical humanism—where people are viewed as inherently co-operative and posits that a raised consciousness is instrumental in having people come together to overcome structural inequalities and create social change—and radical structuralism where emphasis is placed on a structural analysis of power and inequalities.

While I consider a structural social work approach the most useful, it is important not to simply dismiss theories or approaches that may not be considered transformatory. Any concept, theory, or approach that promotes empowerment and social change is useful and can be transformed. For example, the concept of empathy as developed by Carl Rogers is useful in developing a client-centred approach and has become a central skill in all practice approaches. Empathy is the ability to understand the client's feelings and thoughts and to communicate that understanding to the client. However, because Rogers did not critique the social structures that affect people and help us understand their problems, the approach is limited. Social work theorists and practitioners such as Janis Fook and Thomas Keefe have rectified this limitation to some extent by extending the concept of empathy to include an understanding of the social context and the role it plays in consciousness-raising.[22] Consciousness-raising was also adapted by the women's movement of the 1970s as a way of teaching women to assert themselves and advocate for social change.

A structural approach to social work can be viewed as a practice that acknowledges the role of social structures in producing and maintaining inequality and personal hardship and the importance of offering concrete help to those in need or difficulty. Clearly, it draws on an array of theories and models. And yes, it is supported by and flows from a particular ideological perspective. Situated within the transformation quadrants, a structural approach, as developed here, bridges both radical structuralism and radical humanism. While not the complete answer or solution to all our practical and theoretical problems, such an approach is more relevant than ever if we are to effectively respond to the needs of individuals and their families while at the same time engage in strategies for social change.

STRUCTURAL SOCIAL WORK

As we have seen, many of the issues and problems facing people in need are rooted in broad social, political, and economic conditions. At the same time, much of the "help" that we are prepared to provide is done at an individual level and assumes that problems are personal rather than a reflection of wider social structural problems. The tension between personal troubles and public issues is reflected in the social work practice goals of personal change through therapy or counselling versus social change through advocacy and activism. It is also reflected in the conflicts in the role of casework versus community organizing and the development and implementation of social policy. There have been numerous attempts to reduce the gap between "micro" (working with individuals and families) and "macro" practice (working in communities, social advocacy, and social change) and to acknowledge the importance of both functions for social work.

A structural approach to social work attempts to bridge the duality of the personal and the social, the individual and the community, and offers social workers an understanding of diverse populations in the context of social structures and social processes that generally support and reproduce social problems. In the US in the mid-1970s Gale Goldberg and Ruth Middleman proposed a structural approach to practice in which the goal of the social worker was "to improve the quality of the relationship between people and their social environment by changing social structures that limit human functioning and exacerbate human suffering."[23] Goldberg and Middleman based their approach on two central assumptions: "Individuals' problems are not viewed as pathology, but as a manifestation of inadequate social arrangements" and "the response of the social work profession to the need for social change is the obligation of all social workers wherever they are in the bureaucracy."[24] More recently, the authors incorporated social constructionist perspectives, rooted in postmodern philosophy, and clarify that they use the term "structures" to refer to *social* structures, such as the local school, the welfare office, or the public transit system."[25]

Maurice Moreau and his colleagues at Ottawa's Carleton University in the 1970s also set out to develop a structural approach. They turned to Marxist and feminist theories to inform their understanding of social problems and social relations in society and how social workers might respond to them.[26] This emphasis on advocacy and social change was in keeping with the profession's code of ethics, but it also addressed structural problems. Moreau identified two general social work roles: 1) to explore the socio-political and economic context of individual difficulties and to help collectivize personal troubles; and 2) to enter into a helping process that facilitates critical thinking, consciousness-raising, and empowerment.[27]

Roland Lecomte recalls how the School of Social Work at Carleton University quickly became known as a "structural school" when he and others began to integrate the structural approach into all aspects of curricula.[28] Since the pioneering work of Moreau and colleagues, a structural approach to social work has been adopted by other schools in Canada and has been developed by people in the profession. Much like the radical social workers before him, Bob Mullaly, in his book *Structural Social Work: Ideology, Theory and Practice*, views structural social work as based on a socialist ideology, grounded in critical theory, and espousing a conflict view of society. For Mullaly, "The essence of socialist ideology and of radical social work perspective is that inequality (1) is a natural, inherent (i.e., structural) part of capitalism; (2) falls along lines of class, gender, race, sexual orientation, age, ability, and geographical region; (3) excludes these groups from opportunities, meaningful participation in society, and a satisfactory quality of life; and (4) is self-perpetuating."[29]

Although an understanding of the societal context is central to the approach, attention to social structures does not deny the personal element. Janis Fook, an Australian social worker, points out that "not *all* personal problems are *totally* structurally caused," but she insists that "there is *always* a structural element in any experienced problem." According to Fook, "the structural element will always interplay with personal factors such as biography, current life events, emotional and psychological characteristics, genetic inheritance, physical health, and so on to create a unique personal situation."[30]

Clearly, focusing on the social and economic context does not imply that individual change work is ignored or set aside. Nor does it suggest that individuals are not responsible for their actions. Structural social work recognizes that one's life circumstances and difficulties are connected to one's economic and social position in society and that social work intervention at both the level of the individual and social structures is needed. In essence, since powerlessness and inequality are structurally produced, they require structural solutions. However, not all social workers whose practice goals are transformatory consider what they do as structural social work. While structural social work may share similarities with strength-based, empowerment, and anti-discriminatory approaches,[31] the primary differences are the former's critical analysis of the social structures in society and attention to social justice and human rights.

THE ROLE OF SOCIAL STRUCTURES

While the nature and role of social structures is central to a structural social work approach, they tend to be viewed as static structures in the social work literature. But as Wallace Clement points out, "Social structures are products of the dynamics of power and resistance; domination and struggle are the motors of history. In other words, the structure of any social formation is the complex outcome of ongoing class and social struggles." Clement therefore defines social structures "as sets of enduring relationships among and between key institutions, including the state, capital, and labour…. The social structure is social in the sense it is the product of relations between people; it is a structure in the sense of a relatively stable ordering of these relationships into what are often known as institutions. Social structures are as intimate as the family, based on the ideology and practice of patriarchy, or as abstract as the mode of production (the way a society produces and reproduces its material conditions, in Canada's case through capitalism)."[32]

With this in mind, a social worker who utilizes a structural approach in responding to an individual's problems and needs considers not only the material and social conditions of clients but also the social relationships and institutional formations that may be contributing to the clients' problems and acting as barriers to meeting their needs.

In the case of assisting a woman who has been physically assaulted by her male partner, an understanding of her social class, race and ethnicity, age, abilities and disabilities, and regional origin, along with an understanding of how these factors and gender inequality impact on her situation, will provide a better assessment and guide the social worker's response as a professional. For example, women in partner relationships with men who are unemployed or where the family income is below $15,000 have been shown to be more likely to suffer violence from their male partners.[33] In such situations a man's patriarchal beliefs intersect with tensions and stress that exist in the lives of many couples who struggle to support a family with very little economic resources. Also, if the woman is neither employed nor economically independent, her opportunities for alternative safe and secure housing are reduced. Women who leave shelters often return to abusive partners because they cannot support themselves and their children. Aboriginal and Black women may have experienced discrimination and racism from the police and service providers, and many women have encountered the sexism that is prevalent within social structures such as the family, schools, government, criminal justice system, and church. A woman with a disability may face inaccessible shelters and increased vulnerability. As a woman, she may also have internalized stereotypes and negative messages about her own worth from her partner, other family members, and the social institutions and structures to which she is exposed or is part of. Despite this array of oppressive factors, it is important to recognize the woman's strength and how she has survived the impact of these forces. In understanding her particular situation and the social factors that either restrict or offer possibilities, we can offer her the professional support she needs.

By our actions as social workers, in conjunction with those of many other people, we maintain or change social structures within particular interactions, while we are also restrained and curtailed by them. The view that social structures and social relationships are not fixed but a result of tensions, conflict, and contradictions is part of a dialectical understanding of society.[34] For example, although the mandate of children's aid societies is the protection of children and the support of families, the inadequate state funding of the service creates a situation in which overworked social workers in such agencies are given the impossible tasks of overseeing the care of children at risk. Furthermore, state policies are partly responsible for more and more families descending into poverty conditions that place even more demand on existing state-funded programs and services. The need for decent wages and benefits as an alternative to poverty requires an appreciation of the struggle of workers for safe working conditions and a job that provides a living wage. Similarly, the welfare state and its social programs are the product of the struggle by labour unions and other social movements and community groups. Indeed, the welfare state and programs are better understood historically as a concession by the ruling class to the working class and its allies. This concession was also a victory for the working class, although a limited victory.

PRINCIPLES AND PRACTICES OF STRUCTURAL SOCIAL WORK

Structural social work is a practice framework that acknowledges the role of social structures in producing and maintaining inequality and personal hard - ship and uses this knowledge and understanding to assist clients. Within this framework social workers draw on and at times adapt theories and practice skills that have been developed over the years and have become the core of social work practice and relationship building. Because of this, the structural social work approach prepares social workers to be generalist practitioners and to work in individual, family, group, and community practice, and in social policy and administration.

One of the traditional divisions in social work has been practice versus policy, as social workers identify with either being in direct service (individual, group, family or community work, providing referrals, advocating) or indirect service (social policy analysis and development, program development, and administration). A structural approach to social work considers this division to be an artificial one. For most social workers, knowledge and expertise are not so easily polarized. While a social worker may be employed in a direct service role as a child protection worker, with specific intervention skills, she will have a conceptual understanding of children and youth in crisis as well as the policies and laws that affect her clients and limit possible interventions. Similarly, an executive director of a community health centre will draw on her policy expertise, as well as an awareness of community and direct practice concerns and strategies in response to social welfare and social justice concerns.

Whether or not there are practice skills unique to a radical structural approach or whether helping skills can be applied within such an approach has been a topic of debate. Jeffry Galper supported the latter position. "The best practice techniques from a liberal or humanitarian perspective will provide radical practice with a methodology of intervention at the level of technique," he argued, but it is "The use to which technique is put, rather than technique itself, that distinguishes radical from conventional practice."[35] Janis Fook, also reluctant to disregard traditional approaches, argued that "Radical casework both *incorporates* potentially radical elements of traditional casework and *extends* these."[36] Similarly, Maurice Moreau believed that there were no interviewing skills specific to the approach and that various helping techniques could be utilized as long as they did not depoliticize the client's problem or mystify and further alienate and oppress the person.[37]

Moreau decided to study the application of the structural approach. He surveyed front-line social workers who were graduates of the Carleton School of Social Work and who were using the structural approach in their practice. He also examined taped examples from practice sessions submitted by the social workers. Based on an analysis of both the surveys and the taped practice sessions, Moreau and his research team were able to understand what structural social workers do in practice. They found that "Workers are primarily helping people develop and elaborate a new understanding of thoughts, feelings and behaviours, engaging in various facets of contracting, validating clients, helping to operationalize, coach and support new strategies with people and gathering data on and making links to material conditions."[38] Moreau concluded that overall there were five goals that guide structural social work practice, and he identified how these goals or practices were operationalized.[39] A discussion of the five goals and their operationalization follows.

1. Defence of the Client

Social workers help defend client entitlements and rights and encourage clients to "defend themselves against an often bewildering and unfriendly system."[40] As an ally and advocate, the social worker provides information concerning rights and entitlements and agencies' resources and structure, appeals decisions, writes letters, accompanies clients to meetings, and at times subverts and challenges oppressive agency policy and procedure.[41] Social workers with full knowledge of benefits will be able to access much-needed benefits for clients. For example, it was recently reported that thousands of senior citizens in Canada who were living in poverty did not know that they were eligible for the Guaranteed Income Supplement to the Old Age Pension, a situation that social workers could help to rectify. Social workers have knowledge about the various benefits and programs for which someone may be eligible and can offer guidance in the application process and appeals process if necessary. Challenging policy often puts the social worker in direct conflict with the employer and the state. In such situations, the social worker engages in an ethical decision-making process to assess the risks facing the client and determines the best strategy to pursue.[42] Also it is important for the social worker to have the support of a union and/or the professional association.

2. Collectivization

This goal is about helping inform clients about how their difficulties are shared by others, potentially reducing isolation and alienation. This is done by normalizing the problem by connecting clients with a support network, thus reducing isolation. The social worker also recognizes and assists the client in questioning the limits of individual solutions when there is also a need for social change through collective action.[43] One social worker described how she practiced collectivization in her group for incest survivors by taking:

> … the blame off them in terms of them seeing their situation as an individual problem. I like to talk about how other people may be in the same situation as them, and it is not because of their individual failing or inadequacy that they are in that situation. In my sexual abuse survivors group, I use educational materials, that is, other women's stories of being abused and how

they got through it and the things they did for themselves to get stronger and to change and feel better about themselves. I distribute material talking about the prevalence of sexual abuse so these women do not think "it is a private shame, it just happens to us."[44]

Collectivization normalizes and demystifies the client's problem and provides and can contribute to empowerment.

3. Materialization

Materialist analysis, a fundamental tenet of structural social work practice, is an understanding of the material conditions under which people live and the ways in which these conditions impact on their perceptions of themselves and the problems they experience. An assessment of a client's situation and particular problem is then followed by acquiring as many resources as possible— both "hard" resources such as shelter, money, food, and social services and "soft" resources such as respect, caring, and social recognition.[45] Not surprisingly, a lack of money and material resources were major concerns for many of the clients of social workers in Moreau's study. One practitioner summed up the situation:

> [Y]ou know that the real issue is that this woman doesn't need to be with a counsellor. She needs money. If she had a better roof over her head, if she had more money coming in, if she had a male partner who didn't beat her up, she wouldn't be in this office because someone told her she was crazy and needed help.[46]

The same practitioner emphasized that the structural approach to helping single mothers is not simply an intellectual or mechanical exercise.

> The orientation that I bring to my work with clients is always keeping the social analysis on the back burner so that right away when someone comes in, you're able to put them in a context, for example, single mother, there's not much money, there's no supports, she is isolated and there's a good deal of stigma in terms of being a single mother. There's a lot of being treated as a second-class citizen in terms of being a woman.[47]

Another social worker describes how a materialist understanding of violence and an applied collectivist concept can be used in helping the perpetrators of violence against women:

It is very important to understand men's behaviour as more than simply a personal response or personal behaviour that is located in that individual relationship. The first thing we try and do throughout the programme is to continually make connections between the men's behaviour that they are exhibiting in a relationship and the behaviour of men in the community, in this city, in this society, which in many ways mirrors what they are doing. Part of it is making those links between what you do in the privacy of your own home and helping men see that it has a big connection with the roles of women and men in the society in which we live.[48]

4. Increasing Client Power in the Worker-Client Relationship

Reducing the power differential between client and worker is integral to the helping relationship and can be advanced, according to Moreau and Frosst, by "maintaining respect for the client's dignity and autonomy, validating strengths, articulating limits to the professional role, clear contracting, reducing distance, sharing the rationale behind interventions, encouraging self-help and the use of groups, and self-disclosure."[49] This process can also include using first names; demystifying the social work role by employing simple language and avoiding jargon and diagnostic/medical terminology; ensuring that clients see what is written and hear what is being said about them; and protecting confidentiality. The utilization of a contract that clarifies purpose, goals, and tasks puts much of this in place. One social worker described empowerment of the client as:

> ... not me solving their problems. They solve them but I am a catalyst to connect the energy so they can increase their understanding. I don't take over other people's problems. I try to empower them to own the problems and to also own the solutions.[50]

5. Enhancing the Client's Power through Personal Change

According to Moreau and Frosst, this practice aims to "maximize the client's potential to change thoughts, feelings, and behaviours that are self-destructive and/or destructive to others while acknowledging the impact of the societal context."[51] This goal is achieved by identifying and communicating strengths, assisting the client in obtaining a critical understanding of the connection of his or her personal problem within the social context, and supporting the client in personal goals. Social workers can thus enable people to gain an understanding of their situation by joining with them in exploring the range of possibilities for changing their circumstances.

IT IS IMPORTANT TO NOTE that the goals and practices discussed above are not all in play at one time or in every case. In the client sessions submitted by self-identified structural social workers, Moreau and his associates identified a total of 1,737 interventions of which 50.7 per cent reflected the goal of enhancing client power through personal change; increasing client power in the worker-client relationship accounted for 22.3 per cent of interventions; and materialization accounted for 17 per cent, defence of client 6 per cent, and collectivization 4 per cent.

A SUMMARY

While the goal of all social work is change, it is the nature and method of change that distinguishes the structural approach from others. The structural approach is based on a critical analysis of the social, economic, and political context and promotes a restructuring of the social structures that exploit and dehumanize people. Within this framework social workers draw on, and at times adapt, theories and practice skills that have been developed over the years and have become the core of social work helping and relationship building. The focus, grounded in a long tradition within social work of advocating for social justice, is on empowerment and social change. While it is within a radical tradition, it is also in keeping with the profession's code of ethics, which places emphasis on advocacy, equality, and social justice.

NOTES

1 Centre for Human Rights, *Human Rights and Social Work: A Manual for Schools of Social Work and the Social Work Profession* (New York and Geneva: International Federation of Social Workers, United Nations, 2000).

2 Jack Hicks and the Working Group for a Suicide Prevention Strategy for Nunavut, "Qau-jiausimajuni Tunngaviqarniq: Using Knowledge and Experience as a Foundation for Action: A Discussion Paper on Suicide Prevention in Nunavut" (Nunavut: Working Group for a Suicide Prevention Strategy for Nunavut, 2009) 3.

3 Duncan K. Foley, *Understanding Capital: Marx Economic Theory* (Cambridge, MA: Harvard University Press, 1986) 10.

4 In a published interview with family therapist Mara Selvini Palazzoli, one of the founders of Milan systemic family therapy, the interviewer raises criticisms of her approach, particularly in regards to ignoring the wider social context and the inequality of women. In her response she does not acknowledge the importance of women's inequality for family practice models such as her own. See *Networker*, "An Interview with Mara Selvini Palazzoli" (September–October 1987): 26–33.

5 Mao argues that there can be no knowledge apart from practice. "Knowledge begins with practice, and theoretical knowledge that is acquired through practice must then return to practice." The process is practice, knowledge, again practice, and again knowledge.

Mao Tsetung, "On Practice," *Selected Readings From the Works of Mao Tsetung* (Peking: Foreign Languages Press, 1971) 76.

6 Malcolm Payne, *Modern Social Work Theory: A Critical Introduction* (Chicago: Lyceum Books, 1991) 35.

7 Paulo Freire, *Pedagogy of the Oppressed*, 30th anniversary ed. (New York: Continuum, 2001).

8 Kurt Lewin, "Problems of Research in Social Psychology (1943–1944)," in *Field Theory in Social Psychology: Selected Theoretical Papers*, ed. D. Cartwright (Chicago: University of Chicago Press, 1976) 155–69.

9 Jan Fook, Martin Ryan, and Linette Hawkins, "Toward a Theory of Social Work Expertise," *British Journal of Social Work* 27 (1997): 407.

10 Carol Gilligan, *In a Different Voice: Psychological Theory and Women's Development* (Cambridge, MA: Harvard University Press, 1982).

11 Aida Hurtado, *The Colour of Privilege: Three Blasphemies on Race and Feminism* (Ann Arbor, MI: University of Michigan Press, 1996).

12 Donna Baines, "Feminist Social Work in the Inner City: The Challenges of Race, Class, and Gender," *Affilia* 12.3 (1997): 297–317.

13 Mary Bricker-Jenkins, "Hidden Treasures: Unlocking Strengths in the Public Social Services," in *The Strengths Perspective in Social Work Practice*, 2nd ed., ed. Dennis Saleeby (New York: Longman, 1997) 138.

14 Paul H. Ephross and Michael Reisch, "The Ideology of Some Social Work Texts," *Social Service Review* (June 1982): 273.

15 Ephross and Reisch, "The Ideology of Some Social Work Texts" 280.

16 John Coates, "Ideology and Education for Social Work Practice," *Journal of Progressive Human Services* 3.2 (1992): 15–30.

17 John Horton, "Order and Conflict Theories of Social Problems as Competing Ideologies," *The American Journal of Sociology* 71.6 (May 1966): 701–13.

18 See, e.g., Gibson Burrell and Gareth Morgan, *Sociological Paradigms and Organizational Analysis* (London: Heinemann Educational Books, 1979); Ben Carniol, "Clash of Ideologies in Social Work Education," *Canadian Social Work Review* (1984): 184–99; Colin Whittington and Ray Holland, "A Framework for Theory in Social Work," *Issues in Social Work Education* 5.1 (Summer 1985).

19 Whittington and Holland, "A Framework for Theory" 29.

20 Carl R. Rogers, "The Interpersonal Relationship," in *Interpersonal Helping: Emerging Approaches for Social Work Practice*, ed. Joel Fisher (Springfield, IL: Charles C. Thomas, 1973), 381–91.

21 David Howe in his book *An Introduction to Social Work Theory* (Aldershot, UK: Wildwood House, 1987) provides descriptive names for social workers who situate themselves within each of the quadrants. According to Howe, there are the "Raisers of Consciousness" (radical and feminist approaches), the "Revolutionaries" (Marxist approaches), the "Seekers After Meaning" (client-centred approaches), and the "Fixers" (psycho-social, behavioural, and functional systems approaches).

22 Janis Fook, *Radical Casework: A Theory of Practice* (St. Leonards, NSW: Allen and Unwin, 1993); Thomas Keefe, "Empathy: The Critical Skill," *Social Work* 21.1 (1976): 10–14; Thomas Keefe, "Empathy and Critical Consciousness," *Social Casework* 61.7 (1980): 387–93.

23 Gale Goldberg, "Structural Approach to Practice: A New Model," *Social Work* (March 1974): 150; Ruth R. Middleman and Gale Goldberg, *Social Service Delivery: A Structural*

Approach to Social Work Practice (New York: Columbia University Press, 1974). In 1989 the authors published an updated version of the text.

24 Gale Goldberg Wood and Ruth R. Middleman, *The Structural Approach to Direct Practice in Social Work* (New York: Columbia University Press, 1989) 16.

25 Ruth R. Middleman and Gale Goldberg Wood, "So Much for the Bell Curve: Constructionism, Power/Conflict, and the Structural Approach to Direct Practice in Social Work," in *Revisioning Social Work Education: A Social Constructionist Approach*, ed. Joan Laird (New York: The Haworth Press, 1993) 132; emphasis in original.

26 For a summary of the development of the structural approach, see Lecomte, "Connecting Private Troubles and Public Issues" 31–51; Maurice Moreau, "A Structural Approach to Social Work Practice," *Canadian Journal of Social Work Education* 5.1 (1979): 78–94.

27 Maurice Moreau, "Empowerment through Advocacy and Consciousness-Raising: Implications of a Structural Approach to Social Work," *Journal of Sociology and Social Welfare* 17.2 (June 1990): 53–67.

28 Lecomte, "Connecting Private Troubles and Public Issues."

29 Bob Mullaly, *Structural Social Work: Ideology, Theory, and Practice* (Don Mills, ON: Oxford University Press, 1997) 124.

30 Fook, *Radical Casework* 74–75; emphasis in original. During a sabbatical in Australia Maurice Moreau met Fook.

31 See, e.g., Dennis Saleebey, ed., *The Strengths Perspective in Social Work Practice*, 3rd ed. (Boston: Allyn and Bacon, 2002); Lorraine M. Gutiérrez, Ruth J. Parsons, and Enid Opal Cox, *Empowerment in Social Work Practice: A Sourcebook* (Pacific Grove, CA: Brooks/Cole, 1998); Neil Thompson, *Anti-discriminatory Practice* (London: Macmillan, 1993).

32 Wallace Clement, "Canada's Social Structure: Capital, Labour, and the State, 1930–1980," in *Modern Canada 1930–1980s*, ed. Michael S. Cross and Gregory S. Kealey (Toronto: McClelland and Stewart, 1984) 81–82.

33 The 1993 Canadian Violence Against Women Survey reports that men living in families where the joint income is less than $15,000 and unemployed men had rates of violence twice as high as those in upper income categories and employed men. A discussion of the findings can be found in Holly Johnson, *Dangerous Domains: Violence against Women in Canada* (Scarborough, ON: Nelson, 1996).

34 "The *dialectic* is both a way of thinking and an image of the world. On the one hand, it is a way of thinking that stresses the importance of processes, relations, dynamics, conflicts, and contradictions—a dynamic rather than a static way of thinking about the world. On the other hand, it is a view that the *world* is made up not of static structures but of processes, relationships, dynamics, conflicts, and contradictions." George Ritzer, *Contemporary Sociological Theory*, 2nd ed. (New York: Alfred A. Knopf, 1988) 18; emphasis in original.

35 Jeffry Galper, *Social Work Practice: A Radical Perspective* (Englewood Cliffs, NJ: Prentice-Hall, 1980) 131.

36 Fook, *Radical Casework* 43; emphasis in original.

37 Moreau, "A Structural Approach to Social Work Practice."

38 Maurice Moreau and Sandra Frosst, *Empowerment II: Snapshots of the Structural Approach in Action* (Ottawa: Carleton University Press, 1993) 309.

39 Maurice Moreau, *Empowerment through a Structural Approach to Social Work: A Report from Practice* (Ottawa: Carleton University, 1989); Moreau and Frosst, *Empowerment II*.

Sadly, Maurice died before completion of all the data analysis and the second report was authored by a project committee of colleagues and friends.

40 Moreau and Frosst, *Empowerment II* 60.

41 See Moreau and Frosst, *Empowerment II* 163.

42 When social workers in Labrador refused to implement a policy because it was culturally inappropriate and potentially harmful to the health of the Innu, they lost their jobs. See Colleen Lundy and Larry Gauthier, "Social Work Practice and the Master-Servant Relationship," *The Social Worker* 57.4 (1989): 190–94. This case is also discussed in Chapters 6 and 14.

43 Moreau and Frosst, *Empowerment II* 181.

44 Moreau and Frosst, *Empowerment II* 69.

45 Michele Bourgeon and Nancy Guberman, "How Feminism Can Take the Crazy out of Your Head and Put It Back into Society: The Example of Social Work Practice," in *Limited Edition: Voices of Women, Voices of Feminism*, ed. Geraldine Finn (Halifax: Fernwood, 1993) 301–21.

46 Moreau and Frosst, *Empowerment II* 75.

47 Moreau and Frosst, *Empowerment II* 75.

48 Moreau and Frosst, *Empowerment II* 89–90.

49 Moreau and Frosst, *Empowerment II* 126.

50 Moreau and Frosst, *Empowerment II* 92.

51 Moreau and Frosst, *Empowerment II* 145.

CHAPTER 5

THE IMPORTANCE OF INEQUALITY AND SOCIAL LOCATION

A CRITICAL AWARENESS OF STRUCTURAL INJUSTICE and inequality helps us to understand the concerns of diverse populations and to challenge inequality, exploitation, and discrimination. We begin by examining the multiple social factors that influence individuals on a daily basis. This includes our relationship to those who hold economic and decision-making power, since it shapes how we see ourselves, influences our opportunities, and impacts on the ways in which we relate to others. A progressive structural approach starts with such an awareness.

For example, the "power flower" exercise, originally developed for anti-racist work, is a tool designed to help people determine who they are in relation to those who hold power in this society (see Figure 5.1). It can assist social workers in understanding social relationships.

The core of the flower is segmented with identity markers such as age, sex, social class, religion, language, education, and so on. Participants think of a particular period in their lives and indicate, on the inner petals, those factors that reflect their social identity at that time. This can be done individually or in pairs. The group lists the dominant social identity on the larger petals. They are asked to reflect on where they are in relation to the outer petals, "the dominant group in society that controls the economic, political and social participation of other members of society."[1] This group usually consists of white, male, heterosexual, upper-class, middle-aged, and able-bodied people. The exercise recognizes the complexity of who individuals are and how they may be privileged or disadvantaged relative to others. Participants can also think about what has changed over the years, whether they had difficulty in deciding on some of the identity petals, and how their identity is a social product, influenced

FIGURE 5.1 POWER FLOWER

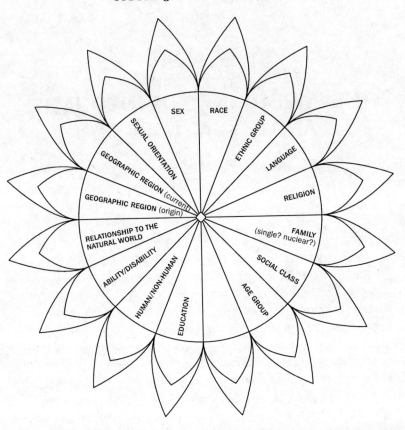

Source: "The power flower" by Margie Bruun-Meyer/Art Work, from *Educating for a Change* by Rick Arnold, Bev Burke, Carl James, D'Arcy Martin, and Barb Thomas (Toronto: Between the Lines, 1991). Reproduced by permission.

by interaction with others. Blank petals encourage people to add another aspect of their identity.

Social relations based on gender, sexual orientation, race/ethnicity, and social class intersect with each other to produce a complex pattern with specific effects influenced by a changing historical, political, and social context. The impact and effects of inequalities are not simply added onto one another but are multiplicative.[2] The concept of intersectionality grew out of Black feminist perspectives and refers to the interlocking, interdependent, and multidimensional nature of one's identity.[3] The 2008 Educational Policy and Accreditation Standards of the Council on Social Work Education make reference to intersectionality:

The dimensions of diversity are understood as the intersectionality of multiple factors including age, class, colour, culture, disability, ethnicity, gender, gender identity and expression, immigration status, political ideology, race, religion, sex, and sexual orientation. Social workers appreciate that, as a consequence of difference, a person's life experiences may include oppression, poverty, marginalization, and alienation as well as privilege, power, and acclaim.[4]

These points of intersection have been described as "a series of tangled knots" where "the tensions pulling on these knots shift and change daily"[5] as social and political conditions change. For example, a Black youth living in Somalia may not experience racism based on the colour of his or her skin, but would do so on relocating to Canada. Similarly after 9/11 and the announcement of the War on Terror, racist attacks and racial profiling increased for those who were, or appeared to be, of Arab origin.

TAKING SOCIAL CLASS INTO ACCOUNT

It is well-established that poverty and inequality impair health and shorten lives. This awareness is not new. Friedrich Engels documented the impact of poverty on people in his book *The Conditions of the Working Class in England in 1844*. Rose and Hatenbuehler integrate the epidemiological approach taken by Engels, apply it to social work, and assert that class "consists of a structurally created, relentless conflict of interests" and that we physiologically embody our class position and the political and economic contexts of our lives.[6] This was demonstrated during the discussion of the social determinants of health in Chapter 2.

Definitions of social class generally fall into two areas: class as stratified by occupation and income, and class as a product of unequal social relations within capitalist societies. It is the latter perspective that usually informs a structural approach to social work.

Wallace Clement regards social classes not as static economic categories but rather as social relationships that are in the process of constant change and that are connected to and affected by other associations.

Not all social relations are class relations, but class affects all social relations; that is, gender, region, ethnicity, and so on are all relational concepts that are affected by class (although class does not determine these relations). This does not mean that gender, regional or ethnic groups are "classes." A key corollary in this argument is that classes never exist in isolation. Conversely, classes are always conditioned by other social relations.[7]

While social classes in traditional Marxist terms are determined by two rela-tions, whether or not one has direct ownership of capital and whether or not one controls the labour of others, advanced capitalism has created intermediary classes. Wallace Clement and John Myles, drawing on empirical data from five advanced capitalist countries, tackle the problem of where to situate those who are in senior management and supervisory positions. They identify four classes of advanced capitalism: the capitalist-executive, old middle, new middle, and working classes. According to them, the two distinguishing factors determining class location are whether or not one controls the means of production and/or the labour of others. Drawing on their research, the class breakdown in Canadian society is illustrated in Table 5.1.[8]

TABLE 5.1 CLASS BREAKDOWN IN CANADIAN SOCIETY

Command Means of Production	Command Labour Power of Others	
	YES	NO
YES	Capitalist-Executive (6.2%)	Old Middle Class (11.3%)
NO	New Middle Class (24.9%)	Working Class (57.6%)

The capitalist-executive class includes those who are self-employed with at least three employees and executives who make decisions about production, budgets, and hiring. The new middle class is composed of those in managerial or administrative positions who oversee the work of others, while the old middle class are self-employed, small business owners with up to two employees. As the illustration indicates, the majority of workers have control over neither the labour power of others nor the means of production; they form the working class.

Clement and Myles offer a clear understanding of the class formation in industrial Western countries and demonstrate how the development of capital impacts on social class itself. Although a new middle class has emerged in the late twentieth century, the majority of workers in Canada continue to comprise the working class.[9] Increasingly, one's social class influences educational oppor-tunities, access to health care, level of health, general social and emotional well-being, and the ability to fully participate in society.

For most people, class position is the least understood factor in their lives and is seldom addressed when identifying social location. Generally, the ten-dency is simply to believe that one belongs to the "middle class" since that includes the notion of having "made it." This is reinforced by the tendency to determine class by income.[10] Those "less fortunate" are commonly referred to as "lower class," "economically disadvantaged," or "poor." The radical and Marxist traditions within social work emphasize class formation and class location as an important factor in understanding the current economic crisis and how it affects growing numbers of people.

But why do so few identify themselves as members of the working class and recognize their potential power? Joanne Naiman reminds us that this omission is intentional—a low degree of class consciousness among the working class is required for the maintenance of any class-based society.[11] We grow up learning very little about the history of working-class contributions to society and resistance against capitalist exploitation and do not find such an analysis in our school books or newspapers or on television.[12] And yet developments such as these have been a powerful force in recent and past worker uprisings. Also, history has shown that social and political change is possible when members of the working class identify their own interests, come together in solidarity, and realize the power they hold in numbers.

RACE, ETHNICITY, AND CULTURAL DIVERSITY

Canada is one of the most culturally diverse countries in the world. The 2006 Canadian Census lists more than 200 ethnic groups, compared to 25 in the 1901 Census, and 11 ethnic origins have passed the 1 million mark, South Asians being the largest group. The visible minority population comprises 16.2 per cent of the population; 75 per cent of immigrants between 2001 and 2006 were visible minorities.[13]

The indigenous peoples of Canada, often referred to as Aboriginal, identify politically as being First Nations, Métis, or Inuit and comprise more than 50 distinct groups, each with its own language. Data from the 2006 Census indicate that Aboriginal people are now over 1 million in number, constituting 3.8 per cent of the population in Canada with 54 per cent living in urban centres.[14]

An understanding of ethnicity, race, and racism is essential if social workers are to develop competence in cross-cultural practice. Providing culturally relevant services is addressed in Chapter 9. Ethnicity refers to social factors that define a group according to some shared experience in regards to language, religion, and/or nationality and ancestry. One's ethnicity "interacts with economics, race, class, religion, politics, geography, the length of time since migration, a group's specific historical experience, and the degree of discrimination it has experienced."[15] At certain times race has been used to classify people hierarchically according to external physical characteristics (such as skin colour, facial features, and hair type), nationality or ethnicity, religion, or language group. The concept of race is an arbitrary social category and has no biological or scientific basis. For example, Vic Satzewich notes that during certain political and historical periods in Canada, immigrants from central, eastern, and southern Europe were seen in racial terms and as inferior to the British and northern Europeans who represented "White Canada."[16] He emphasizes that such prejudice was generally short-lived and ought not minimize the personal and institutional forms of racism experienced by people of colour today.

Race "is a structure rooted in white supremacy, economic exploitation, and social privilege."[17] It has been argued that, although prejudice has existed among peoples throughout history, racism as a systemic practice originated in the development of capitalism and the context of colonial expansion.[18] Freire argues that while "one cannot reduce the analysis of racism to social class, one cannot understand racism fully without a class analysis, for to do one at the expense of the other is to fall prey into a sectarianist position, which is as despicable as the racism that we need to reject."[19] The concept of racial inferiority has been used to justify slavery, seize the lands of Aboriginal peoples, and exploit the labour of particular ethnic and language groups. Peter Li uses the term racialization to highlight the social process by which certain groups are placed in racial categories.[20] These categories are highly problematic for persons whose heritage represents several cultures or who find themselves "between races." Identifying who one is in regards to "race" is fraught with problems since the categories are limited and predetermined.[21]

Norma Akamatsu, a third-generation Japanese American, speaks of her personal experiences as a "checkerboard of disadvantage and privilege." In recalling how she experienced poverty and anti-Japanese stigma during World War II, she remembers an incident that reflects the power and inadequacy of categories based on the concept of race:

> I tell the story of a road trip to the South in 1957, in which my then 11-year-old brother needed to make an emergency bathroom stop. My father pulled up to a roadside diner, where Johnny raced to the rest rooms in the back, only to come careening out front to the car again: "The bathrooms have signs. One says 'White.' The other says 'Colored.' Where am I suppose to go?" And without skipping a beat, my mother told him firmly: "White. White. You go to the White bathroom."[22]

While race is a mythical construct, racism and anti-Semitism are not. Racism is an institutionalized system of economic, political, and ideological relations and practices through which one group exercises power and privilege over other groups. Mike Cole situates racism and racialization in an historical, political, and economic framework in order to account for the various manifestations of racism that accompany changes in the capitalist mode of production in different historical periods.[23] Racist beliefs and actions are not instinctively found in people but are created within social, cultural, and political contexts where the most vulnerable are exploited by the most powerful.

The history of Canada is marked by colonial and capitalist development based on the exploitation of people.[24] Aboriginal people share the longest history of exploitation and forced assimilation in Canada. Over the 500 years of European occupation Aboriginal peoples have had lands expropriated and their languages, customs, and culture erased.[25] Residential schools, to which Aboriginal children were sent, usually far away from their families, and in which they were not allowed to speak their mother tongues, have left a particularly harmful legacy. Not only were they removed from their homelands and forbidden to speak their language, the children were unable to draw on cultural practices and ceremonies for strength and healing because these were against the law.[26]

However, the practice of taking children out of their homes continues, largely due to poverty and inadequate resources in Aboriginal communities. Disturbingly, the number of First Nations children taken into foster care by child welfare agencies has increased 65 per cent in the last decade.[27] Social worker Cindy Blackstock points out that currently the number of First Nations children in apprehension away from their families is three times the peak number that were placed in residential schools. In February 2007 this situation prompted the Assembly of First Nations and the First Nations Child and Family Caring Society of Canada to file a complaint with the Canadian Human Rights Commission, arguing that the unequal benefits for First Nations children was in violation of the Charter of Rights and Freedoms. Blackstock urges social workers "to understand why, despite our good intentions, we are removing more First Nations children from their families than any time in history."[28] She is also passionate regarding attention to a tragic situation in which a First Nations boy, Jordan River Anderson, spent more than two years in a hospital needlessly because provincial and federal governments argued about who should pay for his at-home care. When Jordan died at age five, he had lived all of his life in hospital.[29]

Those who immigrate to Canada and the US encounter similar forms of oppression, exploitation, and inequality. Throughout history, different racial and ethnic groups have struggled to gain basic human rights and civil liberties such as freedom from slavery, the ability to vote in elections, and the maintenance of cultural practices.

People of Jewish origin experience anti-Semitism, hostility expressed through cultural stereotypes, vandalism of synagogues and cemeteries, and hate liter-ature. Historically, Jews in Canada have faced entrance quotas to universities, social exclusion from institutions, and immigration barriers.[30] Irving Abella and Harold Troper, in their book *None is Too Many*, carefully document the extent of anti-Semitism in Canada after World War I and during the 1930s and 1940s when Canada would not open its doors to hundreds of thousands of Jewish people, many of whom faced the Nazi death camps.[31]

The current wave of Islam-bashing and Islamophobia is largely rooted in the fears of terrorism wrought by 9/11 and general misunderstanding of the Muslim religion. Immediately after 9/11, approximately 1,200 people in the US, mainly men, from predominately Muslim countries were placed under "pre-ventive detention," and 82,000 were subjected to special registration. None were found to be connected to terrorism.[32] Nonetheless, social workers have been "ominously silent" in engaging in the impact of the War on Terror on their clients and on their own practice.[33] In 2006 a Gallup poll reported that 39 per cent of Americans supported a requirement for all Muslims, including US citi-zens, to carry special identification.[34] Nine years after 9/11, a public poll indicated that the majority of Canadians did not believe that Muslims share their values.[35] Islamophobia along with anti-immigrant views are spreading in Europe at an alarming rate and prompted one reporter to conclude that "European fascism has returned as mainstream ideology."[36]

In a recent German poll, 55 per cent of the respondents considered Muslim immigrants to be a burden and viewed them as not contributing economically to the country. Of the German population 66 per cent believe that Islam has no place in Germany.[37] When plans were made to build a mosque and Islamic Centre several blocks from Ground Zero in Lower Manhattan, fierce opposition was organized. There was no acknowledgement that Muslims worshipped in a prayer room in the Twin Towers before the attacks and that an estimated 60 Muslims died that day. The threat by fundamentalist Florida Christian preacher Terry Jones to burn the Koran and mount an "International Burn the Koran a Day" movement received international press coverage. One year later Jones organized an "International Judge the Quran Day" and, after a six-hour trial, burned the book, inciting riots in Afghanistan and the deaths of 20 people including seven foreign UN employees.[38]

Because racism is so pervasive and insidious in our society, it is likely that, at times, people will unintentionally express attitudes and act in ways that are racially insensitive.[39] Even social workers, despite the fact that they may be committed to racial justice and equality, may do so. Therefore, part of the strug-gle also involves an openness to feed-back on actions or statements, a willing-ness to acknowledge one's own racial or ethnic insensitivity, and a commitment to personal and political change.[40]

WOMEN'S LONG MARCH TO EQUALITY

Forty years have passed since the Royal Commission on the Status of Women, and, while gains have been made, during the last 15 years women in Canada have felt the impact of neoliberalism and restructuring. According to Shelagh Day, a Canadian expert on human rights, "the neoliberal erosion of the foundations of women's equality—strong social programs and investment in the 'care economy'—is now paired with overt misogyny and hostility to rights of the Harper government."[41]

When feminist activists and 80 foreign aid organizations pressured the Harper government to include abortion in the G20 action plan on child and maternal health, Senator Nancy Ruth created a maelstrom when she told them to "shut the fuck up." For Judy Rebick, a life-long activist and feminist, international solidarity is a central tenet of the women's movement. In her view, Nancy Ruth's "'shut the f… up' was saying loud and clear what governments have been saying for years through funding cuts." Rebick, former president of the National Action Committee on the Status of Women, sees the decline of a militant feminist movement as an outcome of neoliberalism in economics and politics: "Women service groups are under so much pressure to privately raise money to survive that most of them have given up any advocacy function for fear of losing corporate, community, and what's left of government funding."[42]

Since coming into power in 2006 the Harper government has dismantled programs and jeopardized the achievement of women's equality. Cuts to the Department of the Status of Women mean that it can no longer carry out its mandate to promote women's equality or provide research funding to provide documentation for abuses. The Law Commission of Canada and the Court Challenges Program that supported women in taking legal action to advocate for their rights have both been abolished. After the Canadian Labour and Business Centre was closed, funding to the National Association of Women and the Law was also withdrawn, resulting in its closure. Added to this list is the retraction of a signed agreement with the provinces to establish a national system of learning and child care.[43] Accompanying the cuts to women's groups and services have been changes to the funding criteria that prohibit them from engaging in advocacy.

An examination of gender relations in this society highlights the pervasive power men, as a group, have relative to women and the social, political, and economic subordination that women face. Despite the fact that women make up the majority of the population in Canada and throughout the world, they are a minority in positions of decision-making and power. After decades of struggle for equality, women still are not represented in politics in some jurisdictions. In a 2010 report of national parliaments worldwide Canada places 51, with women holding only 22.1 per cent of all parliamentary seats, a significant drop in standing from its standing of 36 in 2002 with 20.6 per cent of the seats in the House of Commons filled by women.[44] The US has also fallen behind, placing 73 with 16.8 per cent of the seats in the House of Representatives held by women. The international data indicate that, as in 2003, women in Western democracies continue to lag behind, while those in developing countries are gaining seats in parliaments.[45] It is encouraging that the 2011 Canadian election resulted in the election of a record number of women. The 41st Parliament has 76 women who make up a quarter of the 308 seats. However, Canada's ranking remains unchanged.[46]

Women continue to earn less than men; are overrepresented among the poor and unemployed; are absent from positions of decision-making, whether in government, business, or organizations; and endure severe forms of violence in their communities, workplaces, and homes. The nature of women's inequality can be understood by examining women's role in the labour force and in the home—women's underpaid and unpaid work.

Women's Work

Women are in the paid labour force in unprecedented numbers; however, wage inequality prevails. For example, in 2008 82 per cent of women in the child-bearing years (age 25 to 44) were in the paid workforce, but women who work full-time, year round, earn only 71 cents for every dollar a man pockets, while it is 63 cents for women in the overall job market. Women are overrepresented in precarious forms of work. They comprise 60 per cent of minimum wage workers, and when unemployed only 39 per cent receive EI benefits, compared to 45 per cent of unemployed men. Many women earn a salary that is below the Statistics Canada LICO poverty line; over four times as many women as men are in part-time permanent jobs and three times as many in part-time tempo-rary jobs.[47]

Despite some progress in entering traditionally male professions, women continue to be concentrated in occupations that are low in pay and prestige. Many women work at part-time, low-paid jobs (McJobs, as they are sometimes called) with little or no possibility of advancement, few employment-related benefits, and little control over their labour. Such work does not offer them independence, nor is it a solution to poverty. In fact, in recent years more and more women are working two or three jobs in order to make ends meet.

As federal and provincial governments cut back on social programs, more and more women and children live in poverty. Since pensions, such as the Canada Pension Plan, are based on one's lifetime earnings, poverty accompanies

FIGURE 5.2 CAPITALISM ALSO DEPENDS ON DOMESTIC LABOUR

CAPTIALISM ALSO DEPENDS ON DOMESTIC LABOUR

Source: Not for Nothing (St. John's, NF: Women's Unemployment Study Group, 1983), 54.

women into retirement. Elderly women who do not have work-related pensions are also likely to find themselves impoverished.

Even though women's participation in the workforce has increased, they continue to do two-thirds of the unpaid work in the household—child care, housekeeping, food purchasing and preparation, care for the ill and elderly family members, and maintenance and repair. In families with children, women spend more than twice as much time on domestic work as men. Among couples without children, women do 60 per cent more of the domestic labour than men.[48] There are few resources to support the family, and the economy depends on women to take on the tasks necessary to ensure the emotional and physical well-being of family members. Women are expected to support and care for family members, providing the services that were previously offered by the state. Therefore, the lack of affordable and quality care for vulnerable family members, and the funding cuts to hospitals and specialized programs for children, persons with disabilities, and the elderly have a greater impact on women.

Women's work within the family is essential in order for the current economic and political system to carry on. Yet, this unpaid domestic work is ignored, unpaid, and undervalued.[49]

Unlearning Sexism

Patriarchy, both a system of social structures and an ideology, supports the exploitation and oppression of women by men in the household and in the public realm. The patriarchal nature of the traditional family is characterized by compulsory heterosexuality, violence against women, and the exploitation of women's labour. Women continue to be portrayed as less capable and intelligent than men, promiscuous, and over-emotional. Since patriarchy, as an ideology, is entrenched in laws, policies, and practices, it becomes internalized by both males and females at a young age. It is not uncommon to find sexist stereotyping and attitudes toward women among professionals, including social workers.

Paulo Freire acknowledged the power of ideology in shaping attitudes and views and spoke of his own struggle to unlearn sexism. Although he was fully committed to women's equality with men, he described his position as a Latin American male influenced by a sexist culture and recognized how he could be progressive in discourse while his actions could be reactionary. Freire realized that his struggle to be non-sexist and to lessen the distance between what he said and what he did required "a progressive obsession."[50] It is not surprising that even men committed to gender equality may at times act in ways that reflect sexist beliefs.

Generally, masculinity—what it means to be a man in our society—is tied to power and aggression and is reproduced and reinforced by men in their day-to-day practices. There is no question that men as a group share greater privileges than women as a group. Although all men benefit from women's oppression, they do so to varying degrees. Also, the problem does not lie solely with men overall—that is too simplistic a position. Working-class men, for instance, are frequently engaged in exhausting and dangerous work and are exploited by their employers. Some men (as do women) face increased insecurity in the workforce as they age, if they are unskilled, have a disability, or are a person of colour. Thus, the majority of men may feel that they have little power in their daily lives, and yet they encounter the societal expectation that to be a man is to be powerful, economically and socially. So, along with acknowledging men's structural power and privilege, it is imperative at the same time to understand how male privilege and institutional power is reduced for working-class men, men of colour, men who have a disability, and gay men.

Women's Rights are Human Rights

Although women's rights were enshrined in the UDHR in 1948, many countries often lack the political and cultural will to protect and promote these rights. Women activists argue that the systematic subordination of women is a violation of human rights and hold that the "lack of understanding of women's rights as human rights is reflected in the fact that few governments are committed, in domestic or foreign policy, to women's equality as a basic human right."[51] In 1993, women's rights were highlighted at The World Conference on Human Rights in Vienna, and violence against women was recognized as a human rights issue for the first time.[52]

Violence against women is the most pervasive human rights violation in the world. Women are beaten and raped by acquaintances, strangers, and their intimate partners; they are subjected to harassment, stalking, female genital cutting, and dowry-associated abuse. Men's violence is supported by misogyny and is "aided and abetted by women's inequality—social, political, legal and economic inequality."[53] Evan Stark outlines the devastating impact on women and concludes that men's violence prevents "women from freely developing their personhood, utilizing their capacities, or practicing citizenship."[54] He also argues that drawing on a human rights framework for anti-violence work has the potential of revitalizing antiviolence organizing in the US and jumpstart the "stalled revolution."

Honour-based violence has been noted as a specific form of violence against women; it transcends religion, occurring in Christian, Hindu, and Muslim families. The recent Aqsa Parvez case has been the subject of media coverage and debate around the term "honour killing."[55] Aqsa, a 16-year-old teenager of Pakistani origin, was strangled and murdered by her father in their home in Mississauga, Ontario after defying her family and not wearing a hijab. Unfortunately, violence against women justified by religion or culture has promoted stereotypes of specific communities and fueled Islamophobia. For example, journalist Mary Rogan reports that "it raised the spectre of religious zealotry in the suburbs" and poses the question "Is this the price of multiculturalism?"[56] According to Terman who has studied honour-killing across all cultures and all faiths, the challenge is to address this form of domestic violence "so that the state, justice, and legal systems provide for the specific needs of minority and/or immigrant women without singling them out for racist or xenophobic treatment."[57]

Women's rights have been under attack, and there has been an erosion of gains made. However, a renewed national and global struggle for women's rights is taking place. In 2000 women marched in the World March of Women in 159 countries. They then moved the campaign to the UN Building in New York and organized a Global Rally where women's delegates met with UN Secretary

General Kofi Annan and leaders of the WB and the IMF. In 2006 the Canadian Feminist Alliance for International Action (FAFIA), composed of nationally and regionally based organizations, launched a month-long campaign to draw attention to women's equality and human rights in Canada.[58] FAFIA chose 10 December 2006 to launch the campaign because it is International Human Rights Day and marked the twenty-fifth anniversary date of Canada's ratification of the UN Convention on the Elimination of All Forms of Discrimination against Women (CEDAW). Such collective actions demonstrate women's potential when they come together and hopefully will give further impetus to the women's movement.

SEXUAL DIVERSITY

The lesbian and gay liberation movement, now over 40 years old, has been successful in educating the public and advocating for changes to laws and policies in areas of sexual orientation and concepts of gender identity and gender relations.[59] Same-sex marriage has been legalized and sexual orientation added to the hate propaganda of the Criminal Code in Canada. Despite this progress, heterosexism and homophobia are pervasive and continue to deny gay, lesbian, bisexual, and transgendered persons full participation in society. In order to achieve fundamental social change, Tom Warner, a leading gay activist in Canada, recognizes the importance to gays and lesbians of gaining a positive consciousness of themselves and of actively opposing "the repression of sexuality and combating sexual stereotyping, sexism, heterosexual supremacy, violence, hatred, bigotry, and hypocrisy."[60]

Heterosexism is an ideology that considers heterosexuality as natural and any other form of sexuality and intimate relationship as unnatural. Homophobia is the irrational fear, hatred, and intolerance of gay men and lesbian women based on myths and stereotypes. Heterosexism has the social and institutional power that supports homophobia while enforcing heterosexual superiority.[61] Suzanne Pharr argues that homophobia, heterosexism, and sexism work effectively together to promote and reinforce compulsory heterosexuality, patriarchal power, and the nuclear family.[62] Heterosexuality as a norm is entrenched in laws, social and cultural practices, and educational institutions.

The cost to gay and lesbian persons has been invisibility, an internalization of harmful beliefs, and threats to their personal safety. Homophobia supports vicious attacks against those who are viewed as gay. Along with derogatory names such as "fag" or "dyke," men and women also face violence and literally fear for their lives—and for good reason. Ritch Dowrey, age 62, was celebrating his retirement at a neighbourhood pub in Vancouver when a 37-year-old construction worker, unprovoked, knocked him unconscious with a single punch to the head. Dowrey suffered serious brain damage and will need extended care for the rest of his life. His assailant said that as a "fag" he deserved it.[63] The action was deemed a hate crime, and the perpetrator was sentenced to six years in prison.

Cases such as this and the 1998 brutal killing of 21-year-old Matthew Shepherd—a gay man living in Wyoming, who was kidnapped, severely beaten, tied to a fence, and left to die in the cold—is a message to all gay men, or men who may be seen to be gay, of the potential threat against them. This brutal murder prompted the *Journal of Gay and Lesbian Social Services* to publish a special issue "From Hate Crimes to Human Rights: A Tribute to Matthew Shepard." The guest editors, Mary E. Swigonski, Robin S. Mama, and Kelly Ward, address how homophobic hatred and hate crimes are a violation of human rights experienced by "the community of lesbian, gay, bisexual, transgendered, and two-spirited (LGBT) persons."[64] Despite the evolution of human rights since the 1948 UDHR, gay and lesbian rights do not appear in the common standards of achievement set for all countries.[65]

Social workers, like other helping professionals, have been slow to fully recognize alternative sexual orientations and to provide gay- and lesbian-positive services. For example, the social work literature does not reflect the gay and lesbian experience or struggle. In a recent examination of 12 social work journals, gay and lesbian content not related to HIV/AIDS was found in only 1 per cent of the articles.[66] This in part reflects the degree of heterosexism and homophobia in society in general and within universities in particular. Jane Aronson, a social work professor, notes how lesbian faculty and students are invisible in the university and how living fragmented lives is a stressful "self-alienating and draining process."[67]

One step in developing a gay- and lesbian-positive social work practice is to develop sensitivity regarding sexual orientation and an awareness of how easily homophobia is internalized. Since heterosexism is so prevalent and present in all social structures, including universities and social welfare agencies, it is important that social workers become aware of their own homophobia and heterosexism. Robin D'Angelo developed several questions that are useful in facilitating a process of critical thinking and advancing critical consciousness in this area.[68] The process begins by examining how one was taught to view gay and lesbian persons and heterosexual persons and how one sees societal responses to them either as a group or individually. The exercise demonstrates how society teaches lesbian and gay persons to hate themselves.

Suzanne Pharr suggests an exercise that facilitates gaining awareness of the structural and personal difficulties that arise when one counters the heterosexual norm. The task is to write a letter to someone who you care about and/or who has power over you, telling them you are a lesbian woman or a gay man. An exploration of the fears that might surface will assist in increasing your critical thinking, awareness, and sensitivity to the reality faced by gay and lesbian persons.[69]

PERSONS WITH DISABILITIES

Persons with disabilities often encounter social workers who are ill-informed regarding physical and mental disability and/or who have patronizing attitudes toward persons with disabilities. This situation is compounded by inadequate and inaccessible social services. In 2006 4.4 million (14.3 per cent) persons in Canada reported a disability, marking an increase of 21.2 per cent since 2001.[70] The three most reported disabilities were lack of mobility, pain, and reduced agility.

Those who are restricted from fully participating in society may have sensory or visual and hearing impairments; a hidden disability such as a psychiatric condition, allergies, multiple sclerosis, arthritis, or learning disabilities; or may belong to the smallest but most visible group, the mobility impaired or physically disabled.[71] Disabilities may be present at birth or be acquired by injuries or illness. For social worker Michael Oliver, the definition of disability contains three elements: the presence of impairment, the experience of externally imposed restrictions, and self-identification as a disabled person.[72]

Activists within the disability rights movement have argued that while functioning may be impaired, it is the environmental barriers and social attitudes that are disabling. It is not only the physical disability that impacts on one's quality of life but also the social and economic conditions people with a disability face. Accessible buildings, transportation and services, technical aids, and personal assistance are essential in order for many persons with disabilities to fully participate in society. Unfortunately, the focus on "helping" often occurs out of a sense of charity rather than social equality, with little attention placed on material and social conditions such as discriminatory structures, laws, policy, and attitudes.

People with mental health disabilities or addictions often are excluded from society and face discrimination in areas such as education, health care, employment, and housing. Barbara Hall, Chief Commissioner of the Ontario Human Rights Commission, provides an example of a recent case that came before her. In the end a tribunal "ordered a company to pay a man with bipolar disorder almost $80,000 because it did not make any attempt to accommodate him."[73] Hall believes that this decision, upheld on appeal, now serves as an important benchmark for future employment challenges involving mental illness.

TABLE 5.2 DISABILITY MODELS

The Individual Model	The Social Model
PERSONAL TRAGEDY THEORY	SOCIAL OPPRESSION THEORY
Personal problem	Social problem
Individual treatment	Social action
Medicalization	Self-help
Professional dominance	Individual and collective responsibility
Expertise	Experience
Adjustment	Affirmation
Individual Identity	Collective identity
Prejudice	Discrimination
Attitudes	Behaviour
Care	Rights
Control	Choice
Policy	Politics
Individual adaptation	Social change

Source: Oliver, *Understanding Disability* 34.

Michael Oliver, one of the leading authors on the social model of disability, contrasts it with the predominate individual model prevalent in society (see Table 5.2). "Unlike previous traditional, individual, medical approaches, the social model breaks the causal link between impairment and disability. The 'reality' of impairment is not denied but it is not the cause of disabled people's economic and social disadvantage."[74] His social model of disability places the focus on societal structures and on the material and social conditions that deny people the right to full participation in society, rather than on individual impairment, personal problems, medicalization, and individual treatment. He emphasizes the social construction and politics of disablement and the rights of those who have a disability. Social workers often assist persons with a disabling illness or injury to overcome their denial and anger to adjust to impaired functioning and arrive at a level of acceptance. "Acceptance depends, in part, on one's ability to perceive oneself as competent and whole, despite dramatic changes in the body image."[75] An accessible environment, adequate social programs, and economic security support persons with disabilities to lead active and fulfilling lives.

In regards to mental health, Iain Ferguson outlines how the members of the working class are more likely to experience mental illness and, when they do, to encounter more serious outcomes. He voices skepticism that a postmodern approach would be capable of effectively challenging this material inequality and advocates instead a class-based political response.[76] While Oliver believes that only members of the disability community can define and challenge oppression based on disability, Ferguson suggests that alliances based on class can best mount a challenge to the material inequalities and stigma encountered by people with disabilities.

The disabled people's movement has been instrumental in the development of disability studies as an academic discipline. However, Oliver and Colin Barnes, two of the important figures in this development, see the impact as only marginal and stress the urgency for proactive strategies for greater inclusion.[77]

THE IMPACT OF INEQUALITY AND DISCRIMINATION

The situation for all disadvantaged and oppressed groups has deteriorated with the neoliberal agenda. The devastating toll of inequality and the vulnerability of those living on the margins are reflected in the social determinants of health, summarized in Chapter 2. Aboriginal status was one of the 14 social determinants of health, and Aboriginal people have high rates of major depression (18 per cent), alcohol overuse (27 per cent), experiences of child sexual abuse (34 per cent), and suicide rates, which are five to six times higher than the non-Aboriginal population. The abysmal economic and social conditions of Aboriginal peoples is highlighted by the fact that when considered by the UN Human Development Index (life expectancy, education, and economic well-being), the Aboriginal population ranks 33 among nations while Canada has a rank of eight.[78]

Unequal relations of power result in the exclusion of certain groups who have limited access to social, cultural, and economic resources, namely, Aboriginal peoples, recent immigrants, women, and people with disabilities. Social exclusion has a dramatic impact on overall health as well as creating a sense of powerlessness, hopelessness, and depression, which in turn fosters further marginalization.[79]

Along with hardship due to the erosion of social programs, the current economic situation fosters discrimination such as racism, homophobia, sexism, and poor-bashing. Targeted groups also face discrimination when looking for work or housing and experience humiliation, harassment, high levels of unemployment, and brutality by the police. A report commissioned by the City of Toronto indicates that Black immigrants face rates of poverty as high as 40 per cent compared to 10 per cent for white immigrants.[80]

The personal costs are immense. The systematic racism and assimilation process that has devastated the lives of Aboriginal peoples is well-documented in the 1997 *Final Report* on the Royal Commission on Aboriginal Peoples.[81] In Cornel West's view, the pervasive racism in the history of Black Americans has created an intense sense of worthlessness and hopelessness, what he has termed nihilism or "the lived *experience of coping with a life of horrifying meaningless-ness, and hopelessness, and (most important) lovelessness*" that results in "a numbing detachment from others and a self-destructive disposition toward the world."[82]

Since the attitudes and beliefs that are dominant in society reflect the expe-riences of those who are privileged and in positions of decision-making, mem-bers of equity-seeking groups often experience life as living in two worlds. In 1903 W.E.B. DuBois, a Black scholar, referred to this as double consciousness, a sense of always looking through the eyes of others to measure oneself. The result, for DuBois, was a feeling of "two souls, two thoughts, two unreconciled strivings."[83] The experience of living and walking in "two worlds" can be com-pounded for those who identify themselves as a member of more than one dis-enfranchised group; for instance, gay Aboriginal men identify themselves as "two-spirited." They often face homophobia in their Aboriginal communities and racism in the gay community.

Those who live in the margins and who encounter racism, sexism, homo-phobia, and stereotypes of mental and physical disability on a daily basis can begin to internalize these messages. If they internalize society's view of them as "other" or "less than," it can be easy to begin to believe that there is something wrong with them, resulting in feelings of inadequacy and/or self-blame. This price of acceptance into the centre is often a denial of who one is. Terry Tafoya likens the denial of part of ourselves as amputation. People are told "to amputate a part of themselves to be able to fit something that's rigid and not built for them in the first place. Amputate your sexuality, amputate your gender, ampu-tate your language, your spirituality" are some of the messages.[84] Tafoya believes that people may overuse drugs and alcohol to numb the pain of amputation and that the healing process involves reclaiming wholeness.

ADDRESSING INJUSTICE

While there have been important achievements, injustice and inequality continue in personal practices, policies, and law. According to the Code of Ethics of the Canadian Association of Social Workers, social workers are to up - hold the right of people to have access to resources to meet basic needs and to advocate for fair and equitable access to public services and benefits (See Appendix B, Value 2: Pursuit of Social Justice, p. 305). Clearly, needed changes cannot come about without a radical restructuring of society and elimination of class exploitation.

Anne Bishop makes the point that social class is different from other forms of oppression such as racism and sexism because while other forms of oppression help keep the hierarchy in place, class *is* that hierarchy.[85] For Bishop, class struggle becomes part of the struggle against racism, sexism, and discrimination based on disability or sexual orientation because social class cuts across all other forms of oppression. For example, financial security mediates the degree of hardship faced by persons with disabilities because it provides increased access to resources, privileges, and opportunities.

However, members of equity-seeking groups do not often include a class analysis in their struggle for change. Addressing the issue of racial identity politics, Manning Marable comments on the absence of class awareness among members in racial minority groups as well as recognition of interests in common.[86] The absence of a class analysis was one of the obstacles in the work of the Ontario Anti-Racism Secretariat from 1992 to 1996. A critical account of the Secretariat reports that, although it was set up under the social democratic government of the New Democratic Party, most of those working within it had ties to centrist or right-wing parties and that "virtually every senior bureaucrat dedicated to anti-racism harboured a deep distrust of class politics and any analysis of institutions as capitalist institutions."[87]

Acknowledging the role of social class does not imply that there is a "hierarchy of oppressions" or that other factors are not equally important. While Allahar and Coté, in their book *Richer and Poorer*, acknowledge the role and centrality of social class in ending all forms of inequality and exploitation, they caution that this view does not imply that race, gender, and age are less real or less important than class. Because of the intersections and interlocking nature of inequality, challenging one form of oppression requires working to end all forms. The struggle to eliminate injustice and all forms of inequality is part of the struggle to transform the existing social and economic institutions of society. Whatever our starting point of critique and analysis of existing injustices, be it race, gender, disability, or sexual orientation, social class remains an important factor. The next chapter examines the legal and ethical context of social work practice.

NOTES

1 Carl E. James, *Perspectives on Racism and the Human Services Sector: A Case for Change* (Toronto: University of Toronto Press, 1996) 19.

2 Patricia Hill-Collins, *Black Feminist Thought: Knowledge, Consciousness, and the Politics of Empowerment* (London: Unwin Hyman, 1990).

3 Gita Mehrotra, "Toward a Continuum of Intersectionality Theorizing for Feminist Social Work Scholarship," *Affilia* 25.4 (2010): 417–30.

4 The Council on Social Work Education, *Educational Policy and Accreditation Standards* (Alexandria, VA: CSWE, 2008) 5.

5 Minelle K. Mahtani, "Polarity versus Plurality," *Canadian Women's Studies* 14.2 (1994): 16.

6 Stephen M. Rose and Stephanie Hatzenbuehler, "Embodying Social Class: The Link between Poverty, Income Inequality and Health," *International Social Work* 52.4 (2009): 460.

7 Wallace Clement, *The Challenge of Class Analysis* (Ottawa: Carleton University Press, 1988) 26.

8 Wallace Clement and John Myles, *Relations of Ruling: Class and Gender in Postindustrial Societies* (Montreal: McGill-Queen's University Press, 1994). Table 5.1 is a combination of two tables found on pages 16 and 19 of this text.

9 I use the term "working class" to refer to waged workers and "middle class" to mean salaried managers and professionals.

10 For example, a process currently identifies all families with incomes of between $35,000 and $69,000 as middle class. *Globe and Mail*, "Canadian Family Income Slips over Past Decade," 27 January 2000: A6.

11 Naiman, *How Societies Work*.

12 It was not until I was in my late twenties that I developed a consciousness of and pride in my working-class background. I began to fully realize the exploitative nature of a grandfather's death in a mine accident at age 34 and the struggle of miners, including my father, for a living wage and safe working conditions. I grew up in mining communities and knew the frequency of "accidents" and the vulnerability of the miners and their families to the "boom and bust" nature of the mining industry.

13 Statistics Canada, Census 2996, http://www.statcan.gc.ca/daily-quotidien/080402/dqo 80402a-eng.htm.

14 Statistics Canada, "Aboriginal Peoples in Canada in 2006: Inuit, Métis and First Nations," Census 2006. http://www12.statcan.ca/english/census06/analysis/aboriginal/children .cfm.

15 Monica McGoldrick and Joe Giordano, "Overview: Ethnicity and Family Therapy," in *Ethnicity and Family Therapy*, 2nd ed., eds. Monica McGoldrick, Joe Giordano, and John K. Pearce (New York: The Guilford Press, 1996) 2.

16 Vic Satzewich, "Race, Racism, and Racialization: Contested Concepts," in *Racism and Social Inequality in Canada*, ed. Vic Satzewich (Toronto: Thompson Educational, 1998) 25–45.

17 Manning Marable, "History and Black Consciousness: The Political Culture of Black America," *Monthly Review* (July–August 1995): 72.

18 James Boggs, *Racism and the Class Struggle: Further Pages from a Black Worker's Notebook* (New York: Monthly Review Press 1970) 136. Boggs reminds us that, although racial prejudice has a long history, the current systemic oppression of one race by another followed the emergence of capitalism 400 years ago. See also Louise Derman-Sparks and Carol Brunson Phillips, *Teaching/Learning Anti-Racism: A Developmental Approach* (New York: Teachers College Press, 1997) 13.

19 Paulo Freire and Donaldo Macedo, *Ideology Matters* (Boulder, CO: Rowman and Littlefield, 2011). This is also mentioned in Freire, *Pedagogy of the Oppressed* 15.

20 Peter Li, *Race and Ethnic Relations in Canada* (Toronto: Oxford Press, 1990).

21 Didi Khayatt, "The Boundaries of Identity at the Intersection of Race, Class, and Gender," *Canadian Women's Studies* 14.2 (1994): 7.

22 Norma Akamatsu, "The Talking Oppression Blues," in *Revisioning Family Therapy: Race,*

Culture, and Gender in Clinical Practice, ed. Monica McGoldrick (New York: The Guilford Press, 1998) 139.

23 Mike Cole, *Critical Race Theory and Education: A Marxist Response* (New York: Palgrave MacMillan/St. Martin's Press, 2009).

24 The importance of acquiring an historical perspective is emphasized by Constance Backhouse in her book, *Colour-Coded: A Legal History of Racism in Canada 1900–1950* (Toronto: University of Toronto Press, 1999). She comments that: "Canadian history is rooted in racial distinctions, assumptions, laws, and activities, however fictional the concept of 'race' may be. To fail to scrutinize the records of our past to identify deeply implanted tenets of racist ideology and practice is to acquiesce in the popular misconception that depicts our country as largely innocent of systemic racial exploitation. Nothing could be more patently erroneous" (7).

25 In the case of the Beothuk people of Newfoundland, an entire nation was eradicated.

26 Marie Wadden, *Where the Pavement Ends* (Vancouver: Douglas and McIntrye, 2008).

27 CBC News, "Foster Care System Needs Improvement: Prentice," 6 February 2007, http://www.cbc.ca/canada/north/story/2007/02/06/foster-care.html.

28 Cindy Blackstock, "Reconciliation Means Not Saying Sorry Twice: Lessons from Child Welfare in Canada," in *From Truth to Reconciliation: Transforming the Legacy of Residential Schools*, ed. Marlene Brant Costellano, Linda Archibald, and Mike DeGagne (Ottawa: Aboriginal Healing Foundation, 2008) 173. In 2006 a court-ordered settlement, the Indian Residential Schools Settlement, was supported by the legal representatives of survivors, churches, and the federal government. A component of the settlement was the establishment of the Truth and Reconciliation Commission. In June 2009, the Honourable Justice Murray Sinclair was appointed Chair of the Commission and given a five-year mandate.

29 Cindy Blackstock, "Leaders in the Social Work Community 2008," *OASW Newsmagazine* 34.3 (June 2010): 1–3.

30 Nora Gold, "Putting Anti-Semitism on the Anti-Racism Agenda in North American Schools of Social Work," *Journal of Social Work Education* 32.1 (Winter 1996): 77–89.

31 Irving Abella and Harold Troper, *None is Too Many: Canada and the Jews of Europe 1933–1948* (Toronto: Lester and Orpen Dennys, 1983). One of the most astonishing accounts is the "Voyage of the Damned." The *St. Louis*, a luxury liner, left Hamburg with 907 German Jewish passengers on 15 May 1939 in a desperate attempt to escape the Nazis. When refused entry to Cuba (despite having obtained entrance visas prior to leaving), the ship made unsuccessful attempts to enter Argentina, Uruguay, Paraguay, Panama, and the US. Canada, their last hope, also denied them entry, and "the Jews of the *St. Louis* headed back to Europe, where many would die in the gas chambers and crematoria of the Third Reich" (64).

32 Gary Younge, "Islamophobia, European Style," *The Nation* 291.15 (11 October 2010): 10.

33 Surinder Guru, "Social Work and the 'War on Terror,'" *British Journal of Social Work* 40 (2010): 272–89.

34 Younge, "Islamophobia."

35 Elizabeth Thompson, "Majority of Canadians Say Muslims Don't Share Their Values," *Ottawa Citizen*, 11 September 2010: A3.

36 Younge, "Islamophobia."

37 Bogan Pancevski, "Germany Turning against Muslims," *Ottawa Citizen*, 11 October 2010: A9.

38 See e.g., http://www.huffingtonpost.com/2011/04/02/obama-afghanistan-quran-burning-un-workers-killed_n_844046.html?view=print.

39 Kenneth V. Hardy and Tracy A. Laszloffy, "The Dynamics of a Pro-Racist Ideology: Implications for Family Therapists," in *Revisioning Family Therapy: Race, Culture, and Gender in Clinical Practice*, ed. Monica McGoldrick (New York: The Guilford Press, 1998): 118–28.

40 In 1983 I was involved in a coalition for racial equality in the US South and helped organize community responses to local incidences of racial discrimination and exploitation. After several months, a tension was evident in the meetings, and finally several Black members came forward with their concerns. Despite the fact that three-quarters of the coalition members were from the Black community, our regular meeting place was always in a part of the city recognized as "white." Further, all spokespeople to the media had been "white," as was the chair of the meetings. There was a period of silence, and then one by one we responded, acknowledging our blindness and beginning to change the practices of the coalition. Our work together was strengthened, and we continued to pursue social action strategies. We also organized a bus to the Twentieth Anniversary March on Washington for Jobs, Peace, and Freedom held on 27 August 1983.

41 Shelagh Day, "Cutbacks Leave Poorest Women Trapped in 'Vicious Circle,'" *CCPA Monitor* 17.3 (July/August 2010): 2.

42 Judy Rebick, "New, Stronger Feminism to Renew Fight for Social Justice," *CCPA Monitor* 17.3 (July/August 2010): 11.

43 Monica Townson, *Women's Poverty and the Recession* (Ottawa: Canadian Centre for Policy Alternatives, September 2009).

44 The data are compiled by the Inter Parliamentary Union on the basis of information provided by national parliaments. Inter Parliamentary Union, "Women in National Parliaments," 1 March 2002 and 31 July 2010.

45 *Globe and Mail*, "Female, Seeking Public Office? Better Try Sweden," 7 March 2003: A7.

46 See e.g., http://www.womensviewsonnews.org/2011/05/record-number-of-women-in-canadian-parliament/.

47 Townson, *Women's Poverty*.

48 See also Kevin McQuillan and Marilyn Belle, "Who Does What? Gender and the Division of Labour in Canadian Households," in *Social Inequality in Canada: Patterns, Problems and Policies*, ed. James Curtis, Edward Grabb, and Neil Guppy (Scarborough, ON: Prentice-Hall, 1999) 186–98.

49 Johanna Brenner, *Women and the Politics of Class* (New York: Monthly Review Press, 2000).

50 Freire, "A Critical Understanding of Social Work."

51 Charlotte Bunch, "Transforming Human Rights from a Feminist Perspective," in *Women's Rights: Human Rights*, ed. Julie Peters and Andrea Wolpe (New York: Routledge, 1995) 12.

52 See, e.g., World Conference on Human Rights, *Vienna Declaration and Program Action*, Vienna (1993); Fourth World Conference on Women, Beijing (1995); *Beijing Declaration and Platform* and its follow-up, *Beijing Plus 5* (2000). Documents can be found at WHO, "Health and Human Rights," http://www.who.int/hhr/readings/conference/en/.

53 Elizabeth Sheehy, "Misogyny is Abetted by Women's Inequality," in *Speaking Truth to Power*, ed. Trish Hennessy and Ed Finn (Ottawa: Centre for Social Policy Alternatives, 2010) 107–10.

54 Evan Stark, *Coercive Control: How Men Entrap Women in Personal Life* (New York: Oxford University Press, 2007) 4.

55 Rochelle L. Terman, "To Specify or Single Out: Should We Use the Term 'Honor Killing,'" *Muslim World Journal of Human Rights* 7.1 (2010): 1–39; *Ottawa Citizen*, "A Matter of Honour," 17 June 2010: A3; Mary Rogan, "Girl, Interrupted," *Toronto Life* (December 2008), http://www.torontolife.com/features/girl-interrupted.

56 Rogan, "Girl, Interrupted."

57 Terman, "To Specify or Single Out" 7.

58 FAFIA, "Join the December 10th Campaign for Women's Equality and Human Rights in Canada," http://www.fafia-afai.org/en/node/381.

59 In June 1969, police raided a known gay bar in the Stonewall Inn, 53 Christopher Street, New York City. The riots that ensued sparked the start of the gay liberation movement. While the early movement primarily comprised gay men, lesbian women, and bisexual persons, transgendered and transsexual persons have been recognized more recently. Transgendered persons are distinct from those who are gay or lesbian. While being gay or lesbian refers to one's sexual orientation and an emotional and sexual attraction for someone of the same sex, a transgendered person is defined by their gender identity, the belief about who they are as a person. The gender identity of transsexuals does not match their anatomical sex at birth, and they often undergo sexual-reassignment surgery when adults. See, e.g., Mary Coombs, "Transgenderism and Sexual Orientation: More Than a Marriage of Convenience?," in *Queer Families: Queer Politics*, ed. Mary Bernstein and Renate Reimann (New York: Columbia University Press, 2001) 397–419.

60 Tom Warner, *Never Going Back: A History of Queer Activism in Canada* (Toronto: University of Toronto Press, 2002) 8.

61 Robin DiAngelo, "Heterosexism: Addressing Internalized Dominance," *Journal of Progressive Human Services* 8.1 (1997): 5–21.

62 Suzanne Pharr, *Homophobia: A Weapon of Sexism* (Little Rock, AR: Chardon Press, 1988).

63 Rob Mickleburgh, "Vancouver Gay Bashing Ruled a Hate Crime," *Globe and Mail*, 9 November 2010: A7.

64 Mary E. Swigonski, Robin S. Mama, and Kelly Ward, "Introduction," *Journal of Gay and Lesbian Social Services* 13.1/2 (2001): 1–6.

65 Janice Wood Wetzel, "Human Rights in the 20th Century: Weren't Gays and Lesbians Human?," *Journal of Gay and Lesbian Social Services* 13.1/2 (2002): 15–45.

66 Rebecca Van Voorhis and Marion Wagner, "Coverage of Gay and Lesbian Subject Matter in Social Work Journals," *Journal of Social Work Education* 37.1 (Winter 2001): 147–59.

67 Jane Aronson, "Lesbians in Social Work Education: Processes and Puzzles in Claiming Visibility," *Journal of Progressive Human Services* 6.1 (1995): 14.

68 DiAngelo, "Heterosexism."

69 Pharr, *Homophobia* 42.

70 Disability Statistics Canada, http://www.disabled-world.com/disability/statistics/disability-statistics-canada.php.

71 See Joan Meister, "Keynote Address: The More We Get Together," in *The More We Get Together*, ed. Houston Stewart, Beth Percival, and Elizabeth R. Epperley (Charlottetown, PEI: CRIAW and Gynergy Books, 1992), 11–18.

72 Michael Oliver, *Understanding Disability: From Theory to Practice* (New York: St. Martin's Press, 1996).

73 Barbara Hall, "Guest Editorial: Mental Health and Human Rights," *Network* 26.1 (Spring 2010): 3.

74 Michael Oliver and Colin Barnes, "Disability Studies, Disabled People and the Struggle for Inclusion," *British Journal of Sociology of Education* 31.5 (September 2010): 547.

75 Marlene Cooper, "Life-Threatening Disability in Adolescence: Adjusting to a Limited Future," *Clinical Social Work Journal* 22.4 (1994): 435.

76 Iain Ferguson, "Identity Politics or Class Struggle? The Case of the Mental Health Users' Movement," in *Class Struggle and Social Welfare*, ed. Michael Lavalette and Gerry Mooney (London: Routledge, 2000) 228–49.

77 Oliver and Barnes, "Disability Studies, Disabled People and the Struggle for Inclusion."

78 Mikkonen and Raphael, *Social Determinants of Health* 42.

79 Mikkonen and Raphael, *Social Determinants of Health* 32–33.

80 *Toronto Star*, 25 July 2000: A20.

81 Royal Commission on Aboriginal Peoples, *Final Report*, http://www.parl.gc.ca/Content /LOP/researchpublications/prb9924-e.htm.

82 Cornel West, *Race Matters* (New York: Vintage Books, 1994) 22–23; emphasis in original.

83 W.E.B. DuBois, *The Soul of Black Folks* (New York: Bantam Books, 1989) 3. The book was originally published in 1903.

84 Terry Tafoya, "Finding Harmony: Balancing Traditional Values with Western Science in Therapy," *Canadian Journal of Native Education* 21 (1995): 27.

85 Anne Bishop, *Becoming an Ally: Breaking the Cycle of Oppression* (Halifax: Fernwood, 1994).

86 Manning Marable, "Beyond Racial Identity Politics: Towards a Liberation Theory for Multicultural Democracy," *Race and Class* 35.1 (July–September 1993): 113–30.

87 Stefano Harney, "Anti-racism, Ontario Style," *Race and Class* 37.3 (1996): 37.

88 Anton L. Allahar and James E. Coté, *Richer and Poorer* (Toronto: Lorimer, 1998).

CHAPTER 6

LEGAL AND ETHICAL SOCIAL WORK PRACTICE

SITUATION #1

A 16-year-old girl was released from hospital after a suicide attempt. She agreed to weekly sessions with a social worker and was aware of her right to confidentiality as well as its limits regarding suicidal and homicidal thoughts. After about two months of counselling, she announced that three days earlier she had taken a kitchen knife and cut herself twice on the arm. Although the cuts were severe enough to bleed, she did not require medical attention. In fact, no one else was aware of the injury. She adamantly denied wanting to end her life, saying she cut herself because she was angry and did not know what else to do. During the session she denied any suicidal ideation but could not guarantee that she would not cut herself again. She refused to tell her parents about the self-harm and warned the social worker "you can't tell them either."[1]

SITUATION #2

Joe is a social worker in an anonymous HIV-testing clinic. Susan, a 24-year-old married woman, tested HIV positive. Joe encouraged Susan to inform her husband Frank of her positive status and to abstain from un- safe sex practices until she had discussed her health with him. Two weeks later, Susan returned to see Joe. She was distraught and confused. She told Joe that she had been having unprotected intercourse with her husband so that he would not suspect anything was wrong. She still had not found the courage to tell Frank about her status for fear of losing him. Joe is unclear how to proceed in his role. He could take more time to work with Susan and encourage her to disclose her HIV status to her husband, but he is also concerned about warning Frank so that he can protect himself.[2]

SITUATION #3

The District Manager of Social Services in a remote Aboriginal community receives a government directive instructing him to implement a policy and deduct 20 per cent for "board and lodging" from social assistance recipients if they have someone living with them who has earnings, pensions, or other allowances. Members in the community are suffering from poverty and a chronic shortage of housing, and at this time there is also an outbreak of tuberculosis. The culture values sharing, and families who have some room welcome those who are in need of housing. No "rent" is charged; instead, "lodgers" help with chores and contribute toward their food. The concept of "boarder' is unknown in the communal culture of the people. The manager believes that implementing the policy would create even further hardship for the community, as well as being culturally irrelevant.[3]

SOCIAL WORKERS REGULARLY ENCOUNTER ethical dilemmas in the context of their daily practice. They are expected to assess competing ethical principles and arrive at an informed decision. The decision-making process takes place in a changing and challenging legal environment and is guided by the profession's code of ethics, as well as laws, social policy legislation, and the policies of the agency. This chapter outlines the central ethical and legal responsibilities facing social workers and gives some direction about responding to difficult situations.

SOCIAL WORK CODE OF ETHICS

Both the CASW in Canada and the NASW in the US have codes of ethics that identify the core values, ethical principles, and standards that are to guide the practice of its members.[4] Many US state licensing boards and each provincial regulatory body have adopted variations of the NASW and CASW Codes of Ethics respectively.[5] Neither association has the legal authority to suspend or remove a social worker's right to practice since such action is situated with the licensing and regulatory bodies.[6] It is useful for practitioners to be aware of various formulations of ethical practice. It is for this reason that reference will be made to both the CASW and NASW Codes of Ethics.

It is important that codes of ethics be regularly debated, assessed, and revised in order to respond to emerging ethical concerns and to better reflect the practice of social work.[7] The current NASW Code of Ethics was approved in 1996 and revised in 1999 (see http://www.socialworkers.org/pubs/code/default .asp), and the CASW Code of Ethics was revised in 2005 (Appendix B). A 33-page document, *Guidelines for Ethical Practice*, serves as a companion to the CASW Code of Ethics (Appendix C).[8] While the codes of ethics of the two professional associations have common ethical standards for social work practice, they differ in the degree of development and detail and in how they are organized.

The NASW Code of Ethics is organized into six ethical standards: social workers' ethical responsibilities to clients, to colleagues, in practice settings, as professionals, to the profession, and to broader society. The CASW Code of Ethics is organized into six core social work values which, if breached, may result in disciplinary action: respect for inherent dignity and worth of persons, pursuit of social justice, service to humanity, integrity of professional practice, confidentiality in professional practice, and competence in professional practice. While the CASW Code of Ethics includes reference to human rights and care for the natural environment and sustainability, it is weak in the area of social action and international concerns. The NASW Code of Ethics places emphasis on respect for ethnic diversity in the US and globally and on promoting social justice and social change. However, what is missing from both national codes of ethics is the role of social workers in promoting peace.[9]

The revised CASW Code of Ethics has been criticized for lacking the clarity and specificity of its predecessor. Bob Mullaly also voiced concern that it is less progressive since it "reflects a 'liberal humanist' approach to social work that seeks to comfort victims of social problems, rather than a critical approach that seeks fundamental social change (i.e. transformation)." Along with a weak view of social justice, he points out that the Code lacks a philosophic statement or vision (unlike the 1996 Code), that the client is no longer the primary professional obligation, that it promotes the fallacy of equal opportunity and impartiality, and that it makes reference to the acknowledgement of diversity rather than a stronger statement of promotion.[10] Yet, the Code is now more explicit on attention to human rights and the obligation of social workers to "uphold human rights of individuals and groups as expressed in the Canadian Charter of Rights and Freedoms (1982) and the United Nations Universal Declaration of Human Rights (1948)."[11]

When conflicts of interest and ethical dilemmas arise, the social worker is expected to act in a manner consistent with ethical principles and standards as outlined in codes of ethics. However, codes of ethics have been criticized for their level of abstraction, which diminishes their usefulness in guiding ethical concerns.[12] Also, in both codes, categories tend to overlap and do not easily match the ethical dilemmas many social workers encounter. It has been suggested that a more useful alternative would be to organize standards around the major conflicts they face.[13] These factors limit the accessibility and usefulness of the codes of ethics in the decision-making process.

MALPRACTICE

Social workers can be subject to discipline if their behaviour or actions do not meet the standards of care, that is, the ethical duties and obligations listed in the Code of Ethics. Malpractice is considered to be a form of negligence that not only violates the standards of practice but also results in some form of injury to a client. Negligence can include behaviours that result in "assault, deceit, fraudulent misrepresentations, defamation of character, breach of contract, violation of human rights, malicious prosecution, false imprisonment or criminal conviction."[14]

Frederic Reamer, one of the leading social work scholars writing in the area of ethics, holds that four conditions must be satisfied to support a claim of malpractice: (1) evidence that the social worker owed a duty to the client (i.e., the duty not to engage in a sexual relationship with the client); (2) the social worker was derelict in that duty; (3) the client suffered some sort of harm or injury; and (4) the harm or injury was the direct result of the social worker's breach of duty.[15]

According to Solomon, claims against social workers have risen markedly in recent years.[16] Social workers are more likely to be involved in a civil rather than a criminal suit, and the majority of civil cases involve tort law. Usually, social workers are held liable in tort law for "intentional, wrongful neglect or otherwise blameworthy conduct."[17] Although there is little written regarding the malpractice cases involving social work, within the current climate of litigation there has been a growing interest in ethical standards and responsibilities among social workers.

THE PROCESS OF ETHICAL DECISION-MAKING

Since ethical dilemmas are often complex, the social work code of ethics is viewed as a necessary but insufficient tool for ethical decision-making.[18] These situations require a careful process of analysis that combines ethical, legal, and clinical concerns and that considers the social and cultural context. In the event of a conflict or dilemma, the following steps are recommended for arriving at an ethical and accountable resolution:[19]

1. Recognize the ethical issue and/or dilemma.
2. Examine the influence of professional, personal, client, and agency values.
3. Identify and rank the conflicting social work values and standards.
4. Identify individuals, groups, and organizations likely to be impacted by the ethical decision; determine who is most at risk.
5. Consider specific information regarding the issue. This may involve an examination of the case file and worker's case notes and/or interviews with relevant parties.
6. Examine differing courses of action and the participants involved in each and weigh the risks and benefits for each.
7. Consult with colleagues and other appropriate staff.
8. Consider other factors such as human rights, relevant laws, social policies, and agency policies.
9. Decide on an action plan.
10. Implement, monitor, and evaluate the outcome.

While social work codes of ethics offer the minimum standards of practice expected of a social worker, agency policy may state additional expectations that may conflict with these codes. For example, an agency may have a policy opposing dual relationships (worker and client) of any form, whereas social work codes of ethics are concerned about whether or not the relationship is potentially exploitative and harmful to the client. In most cases the guidelines in both the agency and the code of ethics are more general than specific and must take into account the context of the situation.

In a study of one agency, Amy Rossiter and her colleagues found that social workers hesitated to disclose uncertainty regarding situations of an ethical nature in their workplace because they feared that their actions would be viewed negatively by a supervisor and their professional judgement placed under question. They also commented on the lack of supervision or opportunities to process complex situations.[20] Social workers in non-unionized agencies are particularly vulnerable to unfair responses by management. Agencies have the obligation to provide social workers with the opportunity to openly discuss occurrences that raise ethical concerns. This includes adequate and regular supervision and an open, non-judgemental process for ethical decision-making. The establishment of an ethics committee to serve as a consultative body when ethical concerns arise would normalize and facilitate the examination of situations of ethical uncertainty in social work practice.

INFORMED CONSENT[21]

Valid, informed, and voluntary consent by a client is essential prior to initiating any social work intervention. Social workers are generally governed by the common law principles of consent unless they are employed in an area under statutory regulation. The consent must include information about the service being rendered and issues regarding record keeping, as well as limits to confidentiality and disclosure. Under common law, consent is only valid if the person is legally competent and is able to understand the information and the nature of the intervention to be provided. For this reason, a person who is severely intoxicated or drugged may not be competent to provide an informed consent. It is particularly important to obtain consent for counselling with clients who are high risk and/or presenting problems in sensitive areas. In these cases the consent ought to have specific and sufficient detail regarding the risks of the proposed intervention. In situations where the social worker and client do not speak a common language, an interpreter should be used in order to ensure comprehension.

While in most cases the consent will be obtained in writing, implied consent or oral consent is sufficient in social work contact of an informal nature such as meeting with youth who come to a drop-in centre. Whether or not the consent is written, it is important that the social worker discuss the limits to confidentiality and the fact that consent may be withdrawn by the client at any time. In emergency situations professionals are authorized to provide services without consent.

While there is no requirement of age to determine competency under common law, there are age-of-consent provisions set by legislation. For example, in Ontario social workers who are employed in agencies funded by the Ministry of Community and Social Services are governed by the Child and Family Services Act, which holds that a child who is 16 years or older may consent to any service, and children 12 or over may provide their own consent to a counselling service without parental approval or even knowledge. If the child is 12 but under the age of 16, the social worker is obligated to *suggest* the involvement of the parents. In regards to residential care programs and intrusive procedures and the administration of psychotropic medication, the consent of the parent or guardian is required for a child who is under the age of 16. This consent may be provided by the Children's Aid Society (CAS) if the child is in custody. For social workers employed in the educational system, the Education Act stipulates that the consent of parents is necessary for personality or intelligence testing on students who are below the age of 18. Also, parents are notified of a student's suspension or infraction of rules. In the event of divorce, the parent who has custody is the one who has the right to make decisions on behalf of the child, while the parent who has access is only authorized to be informed about the situation.

In the case of young children or adults who are not capable of making a decision regarding their own personal care, the social worker relies on an appropriate third party who will act in the best interests of the client. In Canada the Substitute Decisions Act authorizes a substitute decision-maker to provide consent: "A person is incapable of personal care if the person is not able to understand information that is relevant to making a decision concerning his or her own health care, nutrition, shelter, clothing, hygiene or safety, or is not able to appreciate the reasonable foreseeable consequences of a decision or lack of decision."[22]

CONFIDENTIALITY

Social workers and other helping professionals are obligated to not willingly disclose information obtained from a client in confidence. When a person ceases to become a client, the social worker is still professionally obliged to maintain the same confidentiality.

Usually disclosure can only take place with the client's permission or if the law requires it. Also, it is not considered a breach of confidentiality if a social worker discloses information to others when she believes that a client is a danger to him or herself or to someone else. For instance, it is not only mandatory but required by law to report child abuse.

A discussion about confidentiality and its limits should take place early in the social work relationship, since the social worker is not able to guarantee that everything the client says will be held in confidence. The social worker can say something like this:

Normally, what you say or do is held in confidence. This means that I will not discuss your situation with anyone except workers in this agency unless I have your permission to do so. However, there are some exceptions. If you mention, or I suspect, that you or a family member have abused or neglected a child, I must report this to the Children's Aid Society. If possible, I would assist you in making the report yourself. If you say or do something that raises concern for your safety or the safety of another person, I have the responsibility of notifying the person at risk or other appropriate individuals or agencies. Also, in the case of a subpoena, your file becomes the property of the court.

Additional limits to confidentiality might include the file being used in agency research activities or file audits. In both these cases files should not be removed from the site, and a method to protect client confidentiality, such as the use of pseudonyms or initials, ought to be in place.

It is useful for the social worker to anticipate which agencies or professionals may be important in the context of the service to the client and to obtain a release of information from the client. For example, if a social worker is providing drug treatment services to a woman and is also aware that the CAS is involved with the family, a sharing of information would be beneficial in order to coordinate resources and determine progress. The participation agreement or consent in some programs such as those for abusive men may contain additional limitations on confidentiality. For example, men mandated by the court are notified that their probation officers will be contacted regarding their attendance, participation, and progress. Similarly, in some programs, partners of the men have access to information about their attendance, general participation, and/or dismissal from the program, as well as the right to be notified if there is a concern for their safety.[23]

It is important to be vigilant regarding confidentiality. This involves not mentioning names or discussing someone's situation in public places. While it can be tempting to discuss a client's situation with a colleague in the cafeteria or on a bus ride home, it is a breach of confidentiality. Even though the social worker may not mention a client's full name, the circumstances and details may be overheard by others and linked to the client.

Technological innovations—computers, electronic mail, web sites, and answering and facsimile machines in the workplace—create additional possibilities for breaching confidentiality. A client may consent to disclosure of information to another agency, but faxing documents is a breach of confidentiality since a fax is visible to other workers, visitors, and clerical and maintenance staff while it is sitting in the machine waiting to be picked up. Faxes may be lost, and emails circulated beyond the person to whom they are addressed. Care is also required when leaving telephone messages on an answering machine in order to ensure that the message left will be heard only by the intended recipient. Moreover, the social worker should retrieve telephone and electronic messages in private. Computer screens ought to be hidden from public view in the reception area or the social work office, and access to electronic files should be restricted and secured with a password.

It is a good policy not to bring files home. Once they are removed from the agency, there is the possibility of misplacement or loss. Leaving files on buses, in taxis, or on the dining room table in view of others is a breach of confidentiality. Also, files should not be left on top of a desk as other clients may glance at the name or other staff may read through them.

At times social workers from different agencies may share the same client and may telephone each other to ask for information. Without the client's permission, each social worker is ethically bound not even to acknowledge that the person is a client, let alone disclose details about the case. Maintaining confidentiality becomes a particular challenge in settings such as a school where social workers are often approached by parents, teachers, and other school personnel for information regarding the student. There are some who strongly argue that all information should be kept in confidence (except, of course, when there is a threat of harm to the client or others) unless permission is obtained from the student.[24] This position is viewed as "too absolute" by others. Sidney Kardon, a school social worker, questions leaving parents and teachers "out of the loop" and asks "do we withhold information from a warm, affectionate teacher that a sexually abused child may become uncomfortable when touched?… Or perhaps one of my students tells me he is using drugs regularly. Do I withhold this information from his parents?"[25]

Let us consider Situation #1: a 16-year-old girl, with a history of a recent suicide attempt, discloses that she has been cutting her arm and does not want her parents notified. Here, the adolescent's right to confidentiality conflicts with the parents' right to information regarding their child. Applewhite and Joseph begin the assessment by drawing on what is known about acts of self-harm and argue that the act in this situation is one of self-harm and not suicidal behaviour. They also emphasize the importance of confidentiality for trust and the development of a relationship with adolescents. They conclude:

> From a practice perspective, keeping the adolescent's confidentiality helps to maintain the therapeutic relationship, fostering an environment in which work can continue to eliminate self-harming behavior. However, there is a chance that this behavior will continue. But since the client is an adolescent and not clearly incompetent, she should be able to choose her own behavior.[26]

DUTY TO WARN

Social workers have a duty to warn to protect others from potential harm. Based on the premise that public safety overrides the right to individual privacy, the landmark case *Tarasoff v. Board of Regents of the University of California* (1976) set the precedent of duty-to-warn over confidentiality. In this case Prosenjit Poddar informed his therapist, psychologist Dr. Moore, that he was planning to kill an unnamed woman (who was easily identified as Tatiana Tarasoff) when she returned from her vacation. Dr. Moore notified the campus police first by telephone and then in a follow-up letter. Although the police took Poddar into custody, they released him because he appeared rational and promised not to harm the woman. No one notified Tarasoff or her family. Two months later Poddar killed her. Tarasoff's parents sued the Board of Regents, the campus police, Dr. Moore, and his supervisor and won the case based on the court's decision that failure to warn the victim was irresponsible.[27]

A similar situation occurred in Connecticut. A third-year psychiatric resident disclosed to his psychiatrist, who was also a faculty member, that he was a pedophile. Four months after the disclosure, the resident sexually assaulted a 10-year-old boy. The question to be decided is whether or not the resident posed a threat to others that warranted disclosure by his psychiatrist.[28]

Consider Situation #2 in which the social worker faces two ethical principles that are in conflict. The balance between confidentiality and the privacy rights of an HIV-positive client against the duty to warn a partner of imminent harm is debated among social workers and other professionals. Social workers who support maintaining the right of the client to confidentiality may base their decision on the belief that ongoing education can take place in the context of a helping relationship and that clients may be encouraged to voluntarily inform their partners. Further, a breach of confidentiality about clients with HIV may jeopardize their employment and possibilities of securing insurance and housing.[29] On the other hand, a decision to warn the partner may be based on public health policy and the need to protect others from possible infection. A social worker may consider partner notification once he or she has exhausted all options to convince the client to disclose, when unprotected behaviour occurs on a regular basis, and when the threat of transmission of HIV is imminent and the victim is identifiable.[30] After weighing the risks and consequences of such situations, Reamer and Gelman argue that the duty to protect a life takes precedence over the right to confidentiality and privacy.[31] This position is now supported by law, and persons who knowingly engage in unprotected behaviour are charged.

DUTY TO REPORT

There are also situations in which social workers, fearing for the safety of their clients, have a duty to report to another agency. In the case of children under 16 both members of the public and professionals, who have reasonable belief that a child is or may be in need of protection, have an obligation to make a report to the CAS.[32] A social worker must call the CAS directly; it is not sufficient to merely inform a supervisor in the agency. A professional who neglects to report is guilty of an offence, punishable by a fine.

BOUNDARY ISSUES AND DUAL RELATIONSHIPS

Dual relationships occur when social workers enter into more than one form of relationship with clients. For example, a social worker who has a therapeutic relationship with a client may also become a friend, team-mate, intimate partner, or business associate. While social workers often share friendly moments with clients, the development of a friendship raises concerns regarding potential harm to the client.

Both the CASW and NASW Codes of Ethics address the issue of client contact outside the professional relationship. While they state that it is an ethical violation to have a sexual relationship and/or exploit a client in any way, they do not explicitly indicate that all dual relationships ought to be avoided or are necessarily harmful. The CASW Code of Ethics stipulates that a social worker is not to exploit the relationship with a client for personal benefit, gain, or gratification. Examples of exploitation include initiating a sexual relationship with a client or with a student assigned to the social worker, or entering into a business relationship by borrowing from or loaning money to a client.[33] The NASW Code of Ethics defines dual relationships and recognizes that in some cases they are unavoidable:

> Social workers should not engage in dual or multiple relationships with clients or former clients in which there is risk of exploitation or potential harm to the client. In instances when dual or multiple relationships are unavoidable, social workers should take steps to protect clients and are responsible for setting clear, appropriate, and culturally sensitive boundaries. (Dual or multiple relationships occur when social workers relate to clients in more than one relationship, whether professional, social, or business. Dual or multiple relationships can occur simultaneously or consecutively.)[34]

These "tangled relationships," as Frederic Reamer has called them, have the potential to harm others and pose risks to social workers themselves.[35] They are more likely to occur in small geographic communities, or when a social worker belongs to an identity-based community such as the disability or the gay/lesbian community. In these settings social workers and their clients may attend the same social events, share mutual friends, and have membership in common health, religious, or cultural venues.

Increasingly, professionals are pointing out that non-sexual dual relationships are not necessarily unethical or will lead to exploitation or harm to the client, and they distinguish between "boundary violations" and "boundary crossings." Psychologist Ofer Zur identifies boundary violations as occurring when a therapist's relationship with the client is exploitative and harmful, such as typically occurs in sexual relationships, while boundary crossings include activities with the client such as going for a hike, exchanging inexpensive gifts or non-sexual embraces, sending cards, watching a client perform in a show, and accepting an invitation to attend a client's wedding or graduation. The key is that these decisions are made with the client's well-being in mind. Zur points out that not all such boundary crossings constitute dual relationships and may be an extension of the therapeutic relationship. He also argues that the prohibition of dual relationships may infringe on people's rights of freedom of association.[36]

Similarly, Karl Tomm, a family therapist, stresses that, while dual relationships can introduce complexity, they are not inherently harmful. On the contrary, he argues, "the additional human connectedness through a dual relationship is far more likely to be affirming, reassuring, and enhancing, than exploitative. To discourage all dual relationships in the field is to promote an artificial professional cleavage in the natural *pattern that connects* us as human beings."[37] Feminist therapist Miriam Greenspan holds that the emphasis on maintaining boundaries in therapeutic relationships is based on a male distance model where "distance is enshrined" and "connection is seen as inherently tainted and untrustwothy."[38]

Reamer cautions about the possibility of social workers meeting their own emotional needs in dual relationships and gives the following example:

A social worker in a public child welfare agency was responsible for licensing foster homes. The social worker, who was recently divorced, became friendly with a couple who had applied to be foster parents. The social worker also became involved in the foster parents' church. The social worker, who approved the couple's application and was responsible for monitoring foster home placements in their home, moved with her son into a trailer on the foster parents' large farm.[39]

In this case, the dual relationship of friend and social worker is likely to interfere with the supervision of the foster home placement and may place the child at risk. Not all situations are so clearly identified as problematic.

However, in northern Canadian communities dual relationships may be considered as "ubiquitous and inevitable." Halverson and Browntree explain how in the north the limit to formal resources and the client's need for help within these limited resources can contribute to social work practice. The variability of practice concerns facing one social worker in a small community has raised unique difficulties and raised the reality that "a worker may have little choice but either to deny service to a client or to negotiate the difficulties of a dual relationship."[40]

When a dual relationship is being contemplated, the social worker should examine the situation from the perspective of the client and assess potential harm. Gottlieb has developed a model that contains three dimensions to be explored in such situations: the extent and nature of the power of the social worker in relation to the client, the duration of services, and the clarity of termination and the likelihood of further professional contact.[41] He suggests that the three dimensions be examined within a five step process: 1) assess the current relationship; 2) assess the contemplated relationship; 3) examine both relationships for role incompatibility; 4) obtain a consultation with a colleague; and 5) discuss the dilemma with the client. Using this assessment process, the client in the following situation appears to be at a low risk for potential harm in the event that the social worker decided to accept the invitation:

> A single female social worker who works in an emergency room provides support to a single male whose father has suddenly died. After the initial contact and the provision of some bereavement counselling, he is better able to cope with the loss and does not see the need to continue. Three months later, they meet at a ski lodge and discover that they enjoy each other's company and have a lot in common. On the following weekend, he asks her to go skiing.

Here the therapeutic relationship is focused on a brief, situational problem that has been resolved. For this reason, it is likely that the power differential between the social worker and client is minimal; the power of the social worker tends to be greater in long-term, therapy-oriented relationships. In this case the therapeutic relationship has been terminated, but, although it seems unlikely that services will be needed, that possibility always exists. There does not appear to be role incompatibility since there are few expectations remaining in the woman's role as social worker and the power differential between the two is minimal.

It is useful to discuss dual relationships with a colleague or supervisor. When the possibility of conflict between differing relationships arises, the social worker should discuss the dilemma with the client as well.

GUIDELINES FOR RECORD KEEPING

Social workers have a legal and ethical responsibility to maintain an accurate record of their contact with clients. The social work record is a measure of professional and organizational effectiveness. In most cases a file will be maintained on each person coming to the agency, with variations in the recording requirements and expectations. Although the file is the property of the agency, the social worker has a legal and ethical obligation to allow the client reasonable access to it. Usually this access is supervised by the practitioner.

The record is important in coordinating services and keeping track of referral sources. Also, when workers become ill or leave their position, thorough note-taking will ensure that important information is not lost when another worker takes over so that there is as little disruption as possible. Further, file records are a useful source of data for program evaluation, advocacy for specific social concerns, and supervision.

Records are shaped by agency guidelines and expectations. The client's file usually contains signed consent and release of information forms; an intake form; a complete social history and assessment; a client contract or action plan; progress notes or case-notes (from individual, family, or group sessions); and a summary of involvement, which includes the focus of the work, the number of sessions, an evaluation of the goals set, and the reason for ending the service. In recording a group session a summary of the focus of the group and some specific information about the client's participation will usually suffice. Social workers ought also to document meetings and communications they have with their supervisor and/or other professionals and/or family members regarding the client.

The notes should be descriptive and provide details on what the client said or did, as well as the client's feelings. Objective information, such as a description of behaviour and the inclusion of direct quotes, is particularly important when reporting alcohol or drug use or other activities that may have illegal connotations. Care ought to be taken to accurately document the situation, commenting on the client's strengths and resources, as well as the difficulties and limitations the client may face. The record should be completed as soon after the intervention as possible while specific details are fresh. Assessments and progress notes ought to provide concrete information based on the social worker's observations and obtained from the client or others. Sufficient information is needed to outline clearly the presenting concerns, the actions of the social worker, and the practice intervention. Extensive documentation is particularly important in situations of high risk. All notes, whether hand written or entered into a computer should be signed by the practitioner providing the service. Any correction or alteration to the record should be done by leaving the original legible with a line drawn through it and the correction initialed, signed, and dated. Computer notes are considered more reliable if "dated, secure, permanent and unalterable without detection."[42]

The social worker must document with the view that the record may one day be subpoenaed in court: a complete and detailed record will assist the social worker's testimony. The documentation will create the impression of the social worker as a practitioner and as a credible witness. The general court position is that if an event or statement is not recorded in the case record, it did not occur.

> A practitioner's credibility will greatly be influenced by the state of the record. If the record is accurate, objective and complete, the social worker will probably be perceived as organized, methodical and conscientious. Conversely, a sloppy record creates the impression of a social worker who is careless and unconcerned about the client's well-being, whether or not this is actually the case.[43]

For example, when Angie Martin, a Toronto CAS social worker, was charged with criminal negligence when infant Jordan Heikamp died, her case notes were used as evidence during the proceedings and the coroner's inquest.[44] In some situations—i.e., sexual assault cases—documentation found in records may be used against the victim by defence lawyers to discredit her. It is for this reason that workers in sexual assault and rape crisis centres often oppose the release of records of sexual assault survivors.

Agencies usually have policies, often called critical incidents, about the documentation of unusual occurrences and high-risk situations. Examples include situations when a client has been violent, threatening, or suicidal; the client has been threatened or assaulted; or the client reports witnessing child neglect and/or abuse. Critical incidents are documented immediately and reported to a supervisor.

The common practice for social workers is to maintain only one record on each client. However, Solomon indicates that unless a statute or contract directs social workers, nothing prevents them from keeping a private record of their practice with a client. These private records must be consistent with the true records, be kept in a secure location, and may also be subpoenaed under court order.[45] Notes should not be destroyed or altered to avoid court access. Such an action could result in a dismissal of charges against an accused and/or charges against the social worker for the obstruction of justice.[46]

In the context of reduced funding to agencies and growing social work caseloads, social workers are finding that they have little time to keep up their records. The situation is compounded by reduced clerical support, the introduction of detailed assessments, and computerization with its expectation of more documentation. In her research Jill Doner Kagle found that 78 per cent of social workers surveyed reported that they did not have enough time for record keeping or that the requirements for documentation were unrealistic. Further, she found that computerization actually increased the time social workers were expected to spend on record keeping.[47] For example, in Ontario in 2002, there has been a 100 per cent increase in children brought into care by the CAS, with the result that workers spend 70 per cent of their work time on documentation, recording, legal paperwork, and report writing, leaving only 30 per cent of their time for providing front-line services.[48] This is an example of how government decisions and policies may not be compatible with social work ethical standards and make it difficult for social workers to provide accountable and ethical services.

ETHICAL RESPONSIBILITIES TO THE WORKPLACE

Social workers have an ethical obligation to advocate for workplace conditions and policies that contribute to the well-being of the client. The NASW Code of Ethics under a section "Commitment to Employers" directs social workers "to improve employing agencies' policies and procedures and the efficiency and effectiveness of their services" (3.09.b) and that they "should not allow an employing organization's policies, procedures, regulations, or administrative order to interfere with their ethical practice of social work" (3.09.d).

The revised CASW Code of Ethics is not explicit in this area; however, some direction is given in the *Guidelines for Ethical Practice*:

> Social workers appropriately challenge and work to improve policies, procedures, practices and service provisions that:
> • are not in the best interests of the clients;
> • are inequitable;
> • are in any way oppressive, disempowering or culturally inappropriate; and
> • demonstrate discrimination (4.1.4).[49]

However, what is a social worker's recourse in the event that her responsibility to the workplace comes in direct conflict with her obligation to the client? How might she "appropriately" challenge policy or practices? There is no articulation of strategies to ensure ethical practice.

Social workers in the military, particularly when in combat, face specific ethical challenges. They are practicing in often dangerous conditions and "perform the balancing act of trying to meet the needs of the military member clients while continuing to meet the greater needs of the combat mission they are assigned to support. Issues concerning privacy, boundaries, and limited resources are not uncommon in the severe conditions in which deployed military social workers practice."[50]

Malcolm Payne voices the concern that social workers are becoming "more subject to the authority of employers rather than being directly accountable to clients for their decisions."[51] While both the NASW and CASW Codes of Ethics recognize this possibility, neither offer specific guidance to support the social worker in directly challenging the conditions in the workplace.

In Situation #3, the social worker was fired for ignoring a government directive, although he appears to have acted in accordance with the Code of Ethics that dictated his first responsibility was to the Innu community he served. The manager's notification to his employer of the harmful impact of the policy on the community was dismissed, despite supporting documentation from a noted physician and other professionals in the community. Social worker Peter Bown argued that he was forced to "make a choice to enforce a social assistance regulation which was implemented without regard to the particular culture in which I work or to choose what is my moral responsibility and follow the ethics of the social work profession to which I aspire."[52] He was referring to the 1984 Code of Ethics' section on "Responsibilities to the Workplace," which states that when the position of an employer is in conflict with the social worker's obligations to the client that a social worker is to "subordinate the employer's interest to the interests of the client" and that "it may be necessary in extreme circumstances for the social worker to resign from the employment."[53] While the provincial social work association actively supported the social worker in this case, the national association was silent. All attempts at mobilizing a community response were unsuccessful in reversing the government decision and in averting the serious issue facing the Aboriginal community. Bown took his case to the Supreme Court of Newfoundland where the government position was upheld. His appeal was dismissed on the grounds that his "breach of duty was a fundamental breach of *the master-servant relationship*."[54] The rights of the Innu people were deemed "not relevant to the issue."[55]

What recourse does a social worker have in situations where social policies are unjust and come in conflict with the goals and ethical standards of the profession? There is the possibility of mobilizing for collective action, of which the professional association would hopefully be a part. Several other options are possible. The social worker could bend the rules and err on the side of generosity, since rules and policies often have some leeway and flexibility in implementation. The social worker could also assist the client in an appeals process. Although not always effective, as Situation #3 demonstrates, the social worker could mobilize other agencies and organizations to pressure for policy changes.

For example, when the Ontario government set up "welfare snitch" phone lines in the province in order to encourage the public to monitor persons receiving social welfare, a coalition of social workers successfully organized to close down the line in Sudbury District.[56] None of these strategies are likely supported by the current Codes of Ethics.

Situations such as this may become more prevalent and more acute as the reduced funding to social programs and policy changes place the social worker in the position of policing those who rely on dwindling resources. Governments increasingly espouse the view that social welfare recipients take advantage of social welfare provisions and implement punitive measures for those suspected of infractions.

ETHICAL RESPONSIBILITIES FOR
SOCIAL CHANGE AND SOCIAL JUSTICE

While the social work codes of ethics are a contradictory blend of conservative and liberal elements, they do emphasize the social worker's ethical responsibility for social change and the promotion of social justice. The NASW Code says that social workers "should advocate for living conditions conducive to the fulfillment of basic human needs and should promote social, economic, political, and cultural values and institutions that are compatible with the realization of social justice" (6.01). The NASW Code is also explicit regarding the social worker's role in social and political action: "Social workers should engage in social and political action that seeks to ensure that all people have equal access to the resources, employment, services, and opportunities they require to meet their basic human needs and to develop fully" (6.04a). Social workers are also expected to "act to prevent and eliminate domination of, exploitation of, and discrimination against any person, group, or class on the basis of race, ethnicity, national origin, color, sex, sexual orientation, age, marital status, political belief, religion, or mental or physical disability (6.04d). Similarly, the CASW Code says that social workers "uphold the right of people to have access to resources to meet basic human needs." Social workers advocate for equal treatment and protection under the law and challenge injustices, especially injustices that affect the vulnerable and disadvantaged. Social workers promote social development and environmental management in the interests of all people (Appendix B, Value 2: Pursuit of Social Justice, p. 305).

Although codes of ethics also apply to social work relationships in the re-search process, there has been little attention paid to this. In regards to evaluation research, Stanley Witkin urges us to expand our understanding of accountability to include a response to injustice:

Some alternative ways to measure accountability might include the extent to which one's practice challenges existing forms of oppression within the social order, treats clients with dignity and respect (for example, by validating their life experiences, honoring their language, and working with them as collaborators), uses a strengths rather than a pathology perspective... engages in emancipating practices (for example, by helping clients see themselves within a broader historical and social context, helping them identify options to change that context, and facilitate action towards those changes), and is grounded in fundamental human rights.[57]

While social work codes of ethics clearly state that social workers have a responsibility to social change and social justice, there is little guidance on how this responsibility is to be put into operation, nor is there support to do so. Situation #3 is clearly one of injustice. In cases such as this how are social workers to balance their responsibility to their employer with that for social justice? Merely reporting an injustice to the manager and the professional association is not actively addressing the injustice.

In order to establish social justice and human rights as foundational principles for social work theory and practice and as ethical standards, intense discussion is needed regarding the concepts and how social workers are to meet their obligation to social justice and social change.

NOTES

1 Adapted from Larry W. Applewhite and M. Vincentia Joseph, "Confidentiality: Issues in Working with Self-harming Adolescents," *Child and Adolescent Social Work Journal* 11.4 (August 1994): 280.

2 Adapted from Sharon Taylor, Keith Brownlee, and Kim Mauro-Hopkins, "Confidentiality versus the Duty to Protect," *The Social Worker* 64.4 (Winter 1996): 9.

3 Lundy and Gauthier, "Social Work Practice and the Master-Servant Relationship" 190–94.

4 The CASW acknowledges the NASW for permission to use sections of the NASW Code of Ethics in the development of the 2005 Code of Ethics and *Guidelines for Ethical Practice*.

5 The US National Association of Black Social Workers has a Code of Ethics, a one-page statement of guiding principles, that state commitment to and protection of the Black community. See its web site, http://www.nabsw.org/mserver/CodeofEthics.aspx.

6 Information about the 10 provincial regulatory bodies can be found on the CASW web site: http://www.casw-acts.ca.

7 Frederic Reamer outlines the changes in the NASW Code of Ethics over the years in his *Ethical Standards in Social Work: A Critical Review of the NASW Code of Ethics* (Washington, DC: NASW Press, 1998). The 1997 Code of Ethics is almost twice as long as the one accepted in 1979.

8 Canadian Association of Social Workers (CASW), *Guidelines for Ethical Practice* (Ottawa: CASW, 2005).

9 Lundy and van Wormer, "Social and Economic Justice."

10 Mullaly, *The New Structural Social Work* 51–52.

11 Canadian Association of Social Workers (CASW), *Social Work Code of Ethics* (Ottawa: CASW, 2005) 4.

12 Reamer, *Ethical Standards in Social Work*; David Watson, ed., *A Code of Ethics for Social Work: The Second Step* (London: Routledge and Kegan Paul, 1985).

13 Sophie Freud and Stefan Krug, "Beyond the Code of Ethics, Part 1: Complexities of Ethical Decision-Making in Social Work Practice," *Families in Society: The Journal of Contemporary Human Services* 83.5/6 (2002): 474–82.

14 CASW, *Social Work Code of Ethics* 5.

15 Frederic G. Reamer, *Ethics Education in Social Work* (Alexandria, VA: Council on Social Work Education, 2001) 122.

16 R. Solomon, *A Legal Guide for Social Workers*, 2nd ed. (Toronto: Ontario Association of Social Workers and Family Service Ontario, 2009).

17 Solomon, *A Legal Guide for Social Workers* 8.

18 Freud and Krug, "Beyond the Code of Ethics, Part 1."

19 Adapted from Frederic G. Reamer, *Social Work Values and Ethics*, 2nd ed. (New York: Columbia University Press, 1999) 76–77; E. Congress, "What Social Workers Should Know about Ethics Understanding and Resolving Practice Dilemmas," *Advances in Social Work* 1.1 (2000): 1–25; E. Congress, "Teaching Social Work Values, Ethics and Human Rights," in *Social Work: Making a World of Difference*, ed. Nigel Hall (n.p.: IFSW and FAFO, 2006) 71–87.

20 A. Rossiter, Richard Walsh Boweres, and Isaac Prilleltensky, "Learning from Broken Rules: Individualism, Bureaucracy and Ethics," *Ethics and Behaviour* 6.4 (1996): 307–20.

21 The principles of and laws guiding consent for this section are summarized from Solomon, *A Legal Guide for Social Workers* Chapter 2.

22 *Substitute Decisions Act*, 1992, c. 30, s. 45.

23 See, for example, Ontario Ministry of the Solicitor General and Correctional Services, "Implementation of the 'Interim Accountability and Accessibility Requirements for Male Batterer Programs'" (Toronto: Ministry of the Solicitor General and Correctional Services, March 1994). For the US, see Juliet Austin and Juergen Dankwort, "A Review of Standards for Batterer Intervention Programs," http://www.vawnet.org/Assoc_Files_vAW net/AR_standards.pdf.

24 Sandra Kopels, "Confidentiality and the School Social Worker," *Social Work in Education* 14.4 (October 1992): 203–04.

25 Sidney Kardon, "Confidentiality: A Different Perspective," *Social Work in Education* 15.4 (October 1993): 249.

26 Applewhite and Joseph, "Confidentiality" 289.

27 The information on the case was summarized from Frederic G. Reamer, *Social Work Malpractice and Liability: Strategies for Prevention* (New York: Columbia University Press, 1994).

28 Frank Bruni, "Child Psychiatrist and Pedophile," *The New York Times*, 19 April 1998: 35, 40.

29 C.D. Kain, "To Breach or Not to Breach: Is That the Question? A Response to Gray and Harding," *Journal of Counseling and Development* 66.5 (1988): 224–25.

30 A.K. Harding, L.A. Gray, and M. Neal, "Confidentiality Limits with Clients Who Have HIV: A Review of Ethical and Legal Guidelines and Professional Policies," *Journal of Counseling*

and Development 71.3 (1993): 297–305; Jill Donner Kagle and Sandra Kopels, "Confidentiality after Tarasoff," *Health and Social Work* 193 (1994): 217–22.

31 F. Reamer and S.R. Gelman, "Is *Tarasoff* Relevant in AIDS-Related Cases?," in *Controversial Issues in Social Work*, ed. E. Gambrill and R. Pruger (Boston: Allyn and Bacon, 1997) 342–55.

32 In Ontario this is required under the *Child and Family Services Act*.

33 CASW Code of Ethics, Limits on Professional Relationship 4.0: 13.

34 NASW Code of Ethics, Ethical Standard 1.06c: 6.

35 Frederic G. Reamer, *Tangled Relationships: Managing Boundary Issues in the Human Services* (New York: Columbia University Press, 2001) 194.

36 Ofer Zur, "Guidelines for Non-Sexual Dual Relationships in Psychotherapy," http://drzur .com/dualrelationships.html; see also Arnold Lazarus and Ofer Zur, eds., *Dual Relationships and Psychotherapy* (New York: Springer, 2002).

37 Karl Tomm, "The Ethics of Dual Relationships," in *Dual Relationships and Psychotherapy*, ed. A. Lazarus and O. Zur (New York: Springer, 2002) 33; emphasis in original.

38 Miriam Greenspan, "Out of Bounds," in *Dual Relationships and Psychotherapy*, ed. A. Lazarus and O. Zur (New York: Springer, 2002) 427.

39 Reamer, *Tangled Relationships* 15.

40 Glenn Halverson and Keith Brownlee, "Managing Ethical Considerations around Dual Relationships in Small Rural and Remote Canadian Communities," *International Social Work* 53.2 (2010): 247–60.

41 M.C. Gottlieb, "Avoiding Dual Relationships: A Decision-making Model," *Psychotherapy* 30.1 (1993): 41–48; also http://kspope.com/dual/gottlieb.php.

42 Solomon, *A Legal Guide for Social Workers* 63.

43 Solomon, *A Legal Guide for Social Workers* 56.

44 In the spring of 1997 Jordan Heikamp, 4 pounds, 6 ounces, was born to a 19-year-old single woman. Thirty-five days later he died of starvation while living with his mother at a shelter for Aboriginal women and under the supervision of the Toronto Catholic Children's Aid Society. He was 4 pounds, 2 ounces. Both his mother, Renee Heikamp, and the social worker, Angie Martin, were charged with criminal negligence causing death. The case was dropped due to insufficient evidence. On 11 April 2001 the Ontario coroner's jury ruled that his death was homicide; however, no one was prosecuted.

45 Solomon, *A Legal Guide for Social Workers* 63.

46 Cheryl Regehr and Karima Kanani, *Essential Law for Social Work Practice in Canada* (Don Mills, ON: Oxford University Press, 2006).

47 Jill Donner Kagle, "Record Keeping in the 1990s," *Social Work* 38.2 (March 1993): 190–96.

48 *Globe and Mail*, "Child Welfare Time Lost on Paperwork, Report Says," 25 February 2002: A1.

49 CASW, *Guidelines for Ethical Practice* 4.1.4: 16; emphasis added.

50 Catherine A. Simmons and Joan R. Rycraft, "Ethical Challenges of Military Social Workers Serving in Combat Zone," *Social Work* 55.1 (January 2010): 9.

51 Malcolm Payne, "The Code of Ethics, the Social Work Manager and the Organization," in *A Code of Ethics for Social Work: The Second Step*, ed. David Watson (London: Routledge and Kegan Paul, 1985) 104.

52 Peter Bown to William Cook, letter, 14 February 1984. Also see Lundy and Gauthier, "Social Work Practice and the Master-Servant Relationship" 190–94.

53 Canadian Association of Social Workers, *Code of Ethics* (Ottawa: CASW, 1983): Section 8.2.

54 Newfoundland Court of Appeal, *Bown vs. Newfoundland*, in *Nfld. and P.E.I. Reports*, Maritime Law Book 54 (1985): 259; emphasis added.

55 Judgement of J. Noel on 27 April 1984, filed to the Newfoundland Court of Appeal on 29 June 1984.

56 Marge Reitsma-Street and Jennifer Keck, "The Abolition of a Welfare Snitch Line," *The Social Worker* 64.3 (Fall 1996): 35–66.

57 Stanley Witkin, "If Empirical Practice is the Answer Then What is the Question?," *Social Work Research* 20.2 (June 1996): 73.

PART TWO

PRACTICE WITHIN A STRUCTURAL CONTEXT

CHAPTER 7

THE HELPING PROCESS: ASSESSMENT AND INTERVENTION

SOCIAL WORKERS PRACTICE in varied and diverse settings such as family agencies, hospitals, prisons, schools, group homes, shelters, and community centres. Regardless of the practice setting, the social worker engages in a helping process with individuals and their families and, in most cases, assesses the situation, resources, and support networks; negotiates a plan of action or therapeutic contract; and offers support in the work ahead.

AGENCY CONTEXT

Whatever the practice context, it is essential that the setting be accessible with enough space to offer privacy and a certain degree of comfort. An inviting and inclusive atmosphere can be created in an agency by providing coffee, tea, or water; arranging comfortable chairs in conversational settings; decorating the space with plants and pictures; and offering information on community resources in various languages. For example, placing a rainbow flag in an agency window and arranging a display of pamphlets, magazines, newspapers, and notices that address concerns of gay men and lesbian women communicates that gay and lesbian persons are welcome and that culturally sensitive services are located there. Similarly, an assortment of toys, books, and drawing supplies will help keep a small child entertained and be welcomed by parents looking for help.

Individuals and families approach social work agencies when they do not have the personal or material resources to adequately respond to difficulties on their own or when they are legally mandated or directed to seek professional assistance. They do not make a decision to seek help easily and often are tense and apprehensive on arrival at the agency. Asking for assistance and revealing intimate and personal information to a complete stranger is intimidating and difficult for most people. Therefore, since the receptionist is the first contact for individuals and their families, he or she ought to be welcoming and respectful.

PERSONAL AND POLITICAL TUNING-IN

Tuning-in is a preparation process by which the social worker gets in touch with personal biases, feelings, and concerns regarding the person(s) and problem situation. William Schwartz introduced the term "tuning in" as an approach for developing preparatory empathy.[1] Anticipation of how the interview may unfold can prepare the social worker to be a more sensitive listener and effective practitioner.

The effectiveness of the tuning-in process and the intervention that follows will be enhanced by a general understanding and knowledge of a person's experiences as they relate to ethnic/cultural background and customs, geographical setting(s), and the person's overall social and economic position in society. Faith Nolan emphasizes the importance of such an understanding in her song "If you don't know my people, you don't know me."[2]

For example, when providing help to an Aboriginal person, it is important to have a general knowledge about the history of Aboriginal people in Canada, the effects of colonization, and the ongoing struggle to reclaim languages and culture. If a social worker is about to see a Somali family recently arrived in Canada, the tuning-in process may include thinking about the traumatic conditions under which many people fled Somalia and the difficulty in adapting to a new culture and country, one that at times may not be very welcoming.

Helping is not a neutral act. Social workers, like other professionals, have likely developed biases and internalized the dominant messages embedded in the institutional fabric of our society. If social workers do not challenge the existing social structures and exploitative social relations, they implicitly support and maintain them. In cases of woman abuse the concept of neutrality clouds the fact that abusive men frequently deny and/or minimize the forms of control they exert over their partners and poses the risk that the social worker will collude with the man in implicating the woman in her own battering.[3]

During the tuning-in process, social workers reflect on their own assumptions, values, professional skills and experience, and on personal factors such as ethnicity/race, gender, sexual orientation, and age. Reflecting on the differences and commonalities between oneself and the person one is about to see prepares one to effectively respond to possible difficulties and to build a connection. For example, while some people may feel more comfortable initially with a social worker who shares a similar culture and background, they may also feel anxious about disclosing personal information to someone from the same cultural community.

Individuals and families may seek assistance with varying degrees of ambivalence. "A part of the person is always reaching out for growth and change," explains Lawrence Shulman, "but another part is pulling back and holding onto what is comfortable and known."[4] While people want to move ahead to confront difficulties and to make changes in their lives, they may be reluctant to discuss the details of situations that they find painful. They may be embarrassed and not know even how to begin explaining their situation to a stranger and may be fearful that the social worker may not understand them and will blame them for their difficulties. It is likely that these doubts and fears may be more prevalent among members of marginalized groups who have experienced alienating circumstances.

THE HELPING RELATIONSHIP

All social work helping takes place in the context of a therapeutic relationship between the social worker and the client. The social worker who is most likely to develop a positive relationship is one who is "respectful, attentive, interested, caring, trustworthy, friendly, genuine, unpretentious, sympathetic, warm, concerned, empathetic, accepting, compassionate, understanding, supportive, reassuring, patient, comforting, solicitous."[5] Shulman stresses the importance of authenticity and being a real person. "As we demonstrate to our clients our humanness, vulnerability, willingness to risk, spontaneity, honesty, and our lack of defensiveness (or defensiveness for which we later apologize), we will be modeling the very behaviours we hope to see in our clients."[6] These qualities contribute to an effective working alliance in which the client has the opportunity to explore the issues that are of concern and to receive support and resources to make the necessary changes.[7]

The first few minutes of the initial meeting are very important ones in the development of the relationship. During the greeting and introductions, clients will be closely observing to see whether or not the social worker is someone whom they can trust to help them. Therefore, rather than wait for the person or family to be ushered into the office by a secretary, it is preferable that social workers go to the waiting area, introduce themselves, warmly greet clients, and invite them in. The social worker who is seeing a family can begin by connecting with each person, finding out their names and what they would like to be called, and taking time to learn the correct pronunciation.

The client/worker relationship is unequal since social workers practice from a position that carries legal as well as professional influence, authority, and power. People are coming in search of help and, in order to be considered eligible for much-needed resources, must disclose personal information and open their lives to the scrutiny of the social worker and the state. A social worker's position constantly signals that he or she is the expert with power to deny resources and make judgements. At times, however, the client's situation requires that the social worker take on control functions and make decisions that are counter to what the client wants but are in the best interests of more vulnerable members of the family and/or the wider community.

The goal is to create a relationship based on dialogue and in which the helping relationship is demystified, the social worker's power is diminished, and the client's power is increased. Using a first name, soliciting and respecting the client's views, providing information, and working in partnership by involving the person in the decision-making can all assist in reducing, as much as possible, the social worker's power.

CLARIFYING THE SOCIAL WORK ROLE AND THE PROCESS OF THE INTERVIEW

Usually in the first interview, after the introduction, a social worker informs the client about the agency and what can be expected from the service provided: "Before I begin to hear from you about your concerns, I would like to take some time to discuss the agency, how we work, and what you can expect from us." The social worker then describes his or her role in the agency and, if appropriate, provides information about the agency, the resources available, and the client's rights and entitlements. This is particularly important when working with people who are newcomers to Canada and who may not be accustomed to seeking help outside the family for personal issues. Clients ought to be informed about the records that will be kept on the service provided and the access that they will have to their files. An opportunity for questions should be provided, and the use of jargon and complex terminology avoided.

The service contract is the initial agreement that clarifies the agency's obligation and the relationship of the client with the agency. The client is told about the length of each appointment, the fees for service, and the agency's hours and relevant policies. The service contract is usually completed at the time of intake or prior to the first interview.[8] The limits to confidentiality must be discussed with the client early in the interview (see Chapter 6).

Once these preliminary matters are discussed, the process of assessment begins. The social worker begins with a short summary of what is known about the situation and invites the person to begin to talk about why he or she is seeking help at this time. The social worker may say something like, "The intake worker has indicated that you have come for some help to cope with a recent divorce. Where would you like to begin?" Or, if meeting with a couple or family, the social worker could say "Who would like to begin?" A more thorough discussion of social work practice with couples and families takes place in Chapter 11.

The Assessment

The primary task of the first interview is to become familiar with the situation facing the person or family and to initiate a problem-solving process. The social work assessment begins during the first few minutes of contact and may take place on the phone, face-to-face during a scheduled appointment, or during a crisis situation; it can take from 15 minutes to more than an hour. The assessment process will vary depending on the practice setting and whether the social worker is meeting with one person, a couple, or a family.

The social worker provides an opportunity for the person to tell his or her story in order to gain an understanding of the situation and difficulties, as well as the person's resources and strengths. The social worker has the responsibility for respectfully guiding the interview and maintaining a focus on the purpose, whether it is to explore a young person's difficulty with drug overuse or to assess the ability of an elderly person to live independently. Individuals often find that it is difficult to invite a complete stranger to listen to the private and personal details of their lives. The interview belongs to the one receiving the help, not to the one giving it, and it is important that social workers "begin where the client is" and respond to the client's concerns. While this seems obvious, in his research Lawrence Shulman found that workers related to client's concerns only 60 per cent of the time.[9]

Although assessments may vary depending on the practice setting, there are a number of tools that are useful in gathering information and in situating the person and his or her concerns. While an assessment tends to take place at the beginning of the process, in fact it continues throughout. The process of helping consists of assessment and action, action and reflection, and again assessment. While there is a tendency to focus on gaining a history of "the problem" during the assessment phase, it is equally important to identify strengths and focus on solutions, those which have been successful in the past and those that might be possible in the future. A social worker's analysis of the difficulties facing clients guides both the assessment and the intervention. How a social worker views the situation is reflected in the questions he or she poses and the direction the interview takes. At some point while seeing an individual, the social worker may suggest that friends or family members be included. This is usually the case when the difficulty and/or solution involves others.

During the assessment, the social worker gains entry into the lives of troubled individuals and families. We all have intimate knowledge of at least one family, that is, the family or families in which we have lived or are currently living. One of the best ways to begin to understand family structure and family functioning in light of social, political, and economic conditions is for social workers to spend some time reflecting on their own families or a family grouping with which they are intimately acquainted. This process of examining their own family can prepare them to understand individuals and families who will come to them for help (see Appendix D).

Human Needs and Human Rights

Often the difficulties that individuals and families are experiencing are related to basic human needs: *material needs* for food, clothing, and shelter; *social and psychological needs*, such as loving and respectful social relationships, a sense of belonging and acceptance, and a sense of self-worth; *productive needs*, such as meaningful work and opportunities to contribute to society; *safety needs*, which include living without fear for one's life and a high degree of uncertainty; and *self-actualization needs*, which involve developing one's potential.[10] These needs are interrelated and connected. In Canada a family that lacks the "basic needs" (food, shelter, and clothing) is considered to be living in poverty.[11]

However, attention to human needs without also considering human rights is a shortcoming in social work approaches.[12] Both David Gil and Stanley Witkin refer to the 1948 UDHR, which includes social, political, and economic rights. A discussion of human rights situates human needs within a political context. According to the UDHR, "Everyone has a right to a standard of living adequate for the health and well-being of himself and his family, including food, clothing, housing, and medical care and necessary social services, and the right to security in the event of unemployment, sickness, disability, widowhood, old age or other lack of livelihood in circumstances beyond his control."[13] An understanding of poverty that holds that people have a *right* to food, clothing, and shelter has a different connotation than one that states that people *need* food, clothing, and shelter. Reference to need implies that people are somewhat responsible for their own situation and places them in a situation of asking for help. However, when we speak of rights, we begin to see the injustice inherent in the conditions facing people who come for help, and, along with providing immediate resources, we are also led to seek a political solution. Human rights and their relevance for social work practice are fully discussed in Chapter 2.

As social workers listen to the accounts of people and their life experiences, they can begin to assess the degree to which their human rights are being violated. The struggle to survive during social and economic crises can have an impact on one's relationships, health, and self-worth. This is demonstrated in the social determinants addressed earlier.

ASSESSMENT FORMAT

Most agencies have a required format for documenting demographic data and conducting an assessment of the presenting concern. Closely adhering to the agency format and asking question after question can appear bureaucratic and intrusive and result in a scripted and mechanical interview. An alternative is for the social worker to become familiar with the areas that are to be covered and to proceed in a more spontaneous and responsive manner. The social worker can notify the client that questions will be asked in different areas in order to understand the situation and that a few notes may be taken during the interview. Although the assessment can vary greatly, information is generally gathered in the following areas.

1. *Presenting concerns*. The social worker begins by gaining an understanding of the reasons the client has come for help at this time. This involves exploring how long the situation has been present and the attempts at solving it. Often such an inquiry highlights the person's strengths and resources and the times when the situation is better or nonexistent.[14]

2. *Family and support network*. Exploration of the client's support network is based on an inclusive definition of the "family." Families differ culturally and ethnically and include same-sex partners, as well as single-parent mothers or fathers who live with or without children. In a client's view the family may include extended family, friends, and any other persons to whom he or she is most closely connected. It is important not to assume that a client is heterosexual because he or she has children. The assessment tools described below (see pp. 159–62) are useful in constructing visual maps of the client's networks and the nature of the relationships.

3. *Immigration/refugee conditions, migration experience, and status*. All families have a cultural heritage and, unless of Aboriginal origin, have a history of immigration to Canada. As noted in Chapter 9 on immigration and refugee settlement, people entering Canada as Convention refugees have left their country of nationality because of fear of persecution for reasons of race, religion, nationality, political opinion, or membership in a particular social group; they are eligible for government assistance upon settlement. These refugees have left war-torn countries and/or are fleeing persecution and

may arrive with a history of torture and trauma and be divided from family members who have relocated to other countries. They may also have family members who remain in the home country or who have been killed.[15]

The immigration category, whether family or economic, provides important information regarding eligible resources and the stability of the person's status. Information regarding when immigration occurred (in past generations or in recent years) and the time, circumstances, and conditions of the client's relocation will help the social worker better understand the situation. Memories, history, and culture influence the daily lives of all family members. Inability to speak either English or French, essential for integration and full functioning in Canadian society, will impede the client from fully participating in daily life. Also, adaptation to a new country and culture is often easier for younger members of the family than the elderly.

4. *Work and education*. A person's education and work experience influences his or her ability to be economically secure, to connect with others, and to contribute to society. Inquire about paid and unpaid work. If the person is employed in the workforce, assess the nature of the work and the working conditions (hours of work, health and safety concerns, whether or not the job is unionized). In the case of unpaid work, explore the demands of domestic work and child and/or elder care. For students, inquire about academic and social performance in school.

5. *Housing/living arrangements*. Inadequate housing conditions can have a negative impact on social relationships, safety, and health. Are the living arrangements adequate, accessible, and affordable for all members of the family?

6. *General physical and emotional health*. At times a person or his or her family members may experience health problems or concerns. Do family members have nourishing food, adequate clothing, and money for medications and other health care costs, and do they live in a healthy environment? Does the client demonstrate any high-risk behaviours such as suicidal thoughts, eating disorders, overuse of alcohol or other drugs, and/or abusive and controlling actions?

7. *Present or previous social work/counselling services*. It is not unusual for someone seeking help to be also receiving related services from another professional. If so, the social worker might suggest that the client consents to the sharing of information when it is necessary and beneficial.

8. *Role of religious beliefs and spirituality*. Religion or spiritual practices may play a central role in a client's life.

9. *Summary*. The summary of the assessment clearly identifies the major areas of concern and recapitulates strengths, concerns, support system, and recommendations/action plan.

ASSESSMENT TOOLS

A number of assessment tools have been developed to assist people in discussing their family relationships, social networks, and major life events. The use of a family tree or genogram, ecological map (eco-map), social network map, and life line are helpful visual tools for assessment and intervention. They also become a valuable component of the client's record and can assist in communicating information to other service providers.

Family Tree/Genogram

The family tree or genogram is an assessment tool that assists in gathering and organizing information about family members. It provides a visual record of both the relationships of current family members who are living together as well as looking back over several generations and major life events such as retirement, immigration, marriages and divorces, and births and deaths. Over the years it has been widely used by practitioners in their work with both individuals and families. While it can be completed by an individual, family members find that documenting their history together is a particularly rewarding exercise.

There are standard symbols that have been used to communicate the social data collected in the genogram (see Figure 7.1). Males are generally indicated by a square and females by a circle, and the birth date, age, occupation, and name of the person are placed in the centre. A straight line connects two people who are a couple. Separation is noted with one slash across the line, divorce by two slashes. Children are placed below their parents according to age with the oldest first. If there is conflict between two members, a squiggly line connects them. The death of a member is indicated with an X through the figure. Dates for life events such as deaths and marriages/partnerships can also be added. The family members who are currently living together are identified by placing a broken line around them.

The genogram can be adapted to best illustrate the complexity and diversity within families and provides a visual understanding of family structure, including alliances and tensions among family members. For example, if there has been illness in the family, the health conditions of family members can be added and will enhance awareness of the stress on the family, as well as the possibilities of common sources for the illness, whether genetic or environmental. The genogram can also emphasize existing and potential resources and the strengths of the family members by shifting attention away from the nature of the current difficulties to an exploration of the possible solutions.[16]

FIGURE 7.1 FAMILY TREE/GENOGRAM

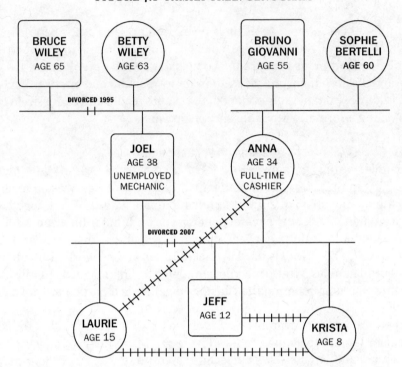

Anna Wiley is the sole parent of three children, ages 15, 12, and 8. She has come to the Family Services Agency to get help with discipline and parenting of her children. The 15-year-old daughter Laurie refuses to listen to her and is influencing her 12-year-old brother Jeff to do the same. Laurie is also overusing alcohol and doing poorly in school. Her 8-year-old daughter Krista is very close to her mother and does not get along with either her brother or her sister.

Eco-map

The eco-map (see Figure 7.2) was developed by Ann Hartman in the late 1970s as a visual tool to situate and record individual and family relationships within a social context.[17] This tool assists social workers during assessment and intervention in exploring how a family is connected to others on a regular basis. The symbols of the genogram are used to depict the immediate family members. The nature of the relationship, whether conflictual and stressful or supportive, is indicated with broken lines or solid lines accordingly.

The completed eco-map provides a snapshot of the family and can have an impact as members see either their isolation and lack of a support network or the family and friendship networks available to them.

FIGURE 7.2 ECO-MAP

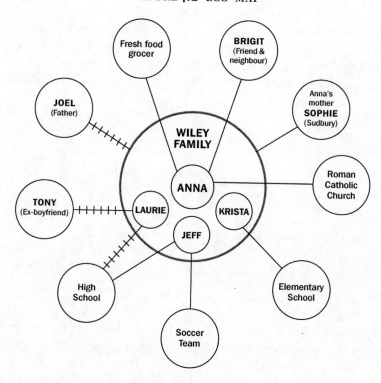

Social Network Map

Similar to the ecological map, the social network map was developed as part of a family support research project in order to collect information on the extent of the person's network, the support provided, and the nature of the relationships.[18] While the eco-map depicts the family's relationships with individuals outside of the family unit, it is often difficult to determine the function of these relationships. The social network map gathers information on members of the person's network in seven areas: (1) those living in the household; (2) other family members and relatives; (3) friends; (4) colleagues from work or school; (5) people from recreational, social, and religious groups/organizations; (6) neighbours; and (7) other social agencies. The length and closeness of these relationships and the degree to which they offer support should also be recorded.

Life Line

A life line records major life events organized chronologically on a horizontal line. This visual tool invites a person or family to explore and assess their situation and to understand how events in their lives have been supportive and/or challenging. The life line in Figure 7.3 illustrates a chronological accounting of major events in the life of a troubled adolescent. Laurie, age 15, was referred to the school social worker by her teacher because she was failing her courses and was angry and aggressive in her interactions with peers. During the first meeting Laurie began talking about how her life "sucks" and that it started falling apart five years ago.

FIGURE 7.3 LIFE LINE

Parents divorce	Mom is Depressed	Moved to Timmins	Mom has new partner	Moved to Ottawa
AGE 10 (1997)	AGE 12 (1999)	AGE 13 (2000)	AGE 14 (2001)	AGE 15 (2002)
Living with Mom	On my own a lot	New school and	Isolated	Anxiety attacks
Limited contact with Dad	Angry outbursts	friends	More alcohol use	Hanging out with rough crowd
	Conflict with Mom	Some alcohol use	Trouble sleeping	
	Grades slipping		Failed grade 8	Bullying

Constructing a life line with Laurie helped both her and the social worker document the major events in her life and quickly highlighted how she had coped with many stressful changes. After her father left and ceased contact and as she and her mother kept moving, Laurie said that she started to shut people out. She found it too painful to get close only to be hurt again. As the interview continued, Laurie also talked about how her use of alcohol had increased and that she had trouble sleeping and was experiencing anxiety attacks. These were all placed on the life line so that the progression could be recorded. It became clear to Laurie that some of her survival strategies were now working against her.

THE CONTRACT

In most helping relationships, a therapeutic contract (see Figure 7.4) is useful in guiding the helping process by identifying realistic and achievable goals. It becomes a working tool that is referred to and changed over the course of the helping relationship. Once the initial assessment is completed, the therapeutic contract or counselling plan is developed to guide the work to follow toward specific concerns and goals.[19] For example, Laurie identified four major concerns on which she wanted to work. While she recognized that her use of alcohol was a problem, she was not prepared to stop completely, since she relied on it to help her sleep and to calm her nerves. The social worker agreed to her plan to cut down and monitor her use. They also discussed whether the inability to accomplish this goal meant that she needed to quit entirely. The social worker and Laurie discussed how the alcohol use was a strategy to respond to her other problems, but that alcohol can also contribute to sleep disturbances, anxiety, and aggressiveness. Laurie also wanted to get closer to her mother and hoped to improve her school performance.

FIGURE 7.4 THE CONTRACT

CONCERN/ PROBLEM	GOALS: What would you like to happen?	THE PLAN: Step/Action	OUTCOME
Overuse of alcohol	Cut down	1. Not drink from Monday–Thursday 2. No more than two drinks at a time 3. Keep a journal	
Not spending time with with mother	Have more time together	1. Plan two activities each weekend 2. Share a meal together each evening	
Trouble sleeping	Sleep at night	1. Walk home from school 2. Go to bed at 10:00 p.m.	
Failing grades	Pass her courses	1. Speak with the teacher 2. Go to all the classes 3. Do homework	

When clients are mandated by law to receive social worker services, the development of the therapeutic contract becomes more difficult. Social workers often are placed in positions of policing and controlling clients in order to protect the most vulnerable members of society or the clients themselves.[20] This is the case for social workers who work with children in need of protection, women who are abused, men who are violent, and clients who are suicidal or homicidal. In such situations the non-negotiable aspects of the contract such as reporting to a probation officer need to be openly discussed.

Scaling questions are useful for evaluating progress and determining outcomes for the agreed-upon goals. For example, the person could be asked to indicate on a scale of zero to ten, where zero is terrible and ten is terrific, how they would rate the progress that they have made on each of their goals. The meaning of the numerical indicator is then explored. What happened or did not happen to produce a three? As a way of building on strengths, the person could be asked what they did to not slide to zero.

ENDING THE INTERVIEW

It is useful to allow from 10 to 15 minutes at the end of the interview for winding down and summarizing the concerns that have been raised, the plan of action, and the next steps. The social worker can alert the client that the interview is coming to the end by saying "In the 15 minutes remaining, I would like to summarize what we have accomplished and where we go from here." This is also a time for both the person and the social worker to reflect on the interview and evaluate the time spent together. At times, a person may disclose a new concern just as the interview is closing. If the social worker determines that it is not an urgent issue, it is still important to validate the concern and place it on the agenda for next time. For example, the following response is appropriate: "You have just raised a very important issue, and we don't have the time to talk about it. I think you have made a good start in raising it now, and we can begin there at the next meeting."

If the initial interview and assessment have been successful, the client ought to leave feeling supported and understood, less overwhelmed, and more hopeful. If this is the case, the helping relationship is off to a good start.

NOTES

1 Lawrence Shulman, *The Skills of Helping*, 3rd ed., 56. Shulman provides a number of examples of tuning-in.
2 Faith Nolan, "Nobody Knows My People," *Africville*, 1986.
3 Deborah McIntyre, "Domestic Violence: A Case of the Disappearing Victim," *Australian Journal of Family Therapy* 5.4 (1984): 253.
4 Shulman, *The Skills of Helping*, 3rd ed., 105.
5 Alfred Kadushin and Goldie Kadushin, *The Social Work Interview: A Guide for Human Service Professionals*, 4th ed. (New York: Columbia University Press, 1997) 103.
6 Shulman, *The Skills of Helping*, 3rd ed., 27.
7 One of the most comprehensive texts on the social work relationship is by Helen Harris Perlman, *Relationship: The Heart of Helping People* (Chicago: University of Chicago Press, 1979).
8 Juliet Cassuto Rothman, *Contracting in Clinical Social Work* (Chicago: Nelson-Hall, 1998).
9 Shulman, *The Skills of Helping*, 3rd ed., 114.

10 Adapted from Chapter 10, "Intermediate Needs," in Len Doyal and Ian Gough's *A Theory of Human Need* (New York: Guilford Press, 1991) 191–221; A. Maslow, *Toward a Psychology of Being* (New York: Van Nostrand, 1962). Maslow's framework for understanding human needs and his five levels of basic human needs required for healthy functioning (physiological, safety, love and belonging, self-esteem, and self-actualization) are well-known to human service workers. Maslow believed that a person's most basic physiological needs had to be met before the others could be fulfilled.

11 Any family spending 56 per cent of gross income on the basic necessities (food, shelter, and clothing) is considered poor. See A. Kazemipur and S.S. Halli, *The New Poverty in Canada: Ethnic Groups and Ghetto Neighbourhoods* (Toronto: Thompson Educational, 2000) 19.

12 Stanley L. Witkin, "Human Rights and Social Work," *Social Work* 43.3 (May 1998): 197–201; David G. Gil, *Confronting Injustice and Oppression: Concepts and Strategies for Social Workers* (New York: Columbia University Press, 1999).

13 UDHR, Article 25.1, Appendix A. The reference only to the male gender reflects the time period in which the document was created.

14 Steve de Shazer et al., "Brief Therapy: Focused Solution Development," *Family Process* 25.2 (1986): 207–21.

15 Convention refugees meet the definition of "refugee" in the UN Convention Relating to the Status of Refugees, which has been incorporated into the Immigration and Refugee Protection Act. See Citizen and Immigration Canada, http://www.cic.gc.ca.

16 Marilyn R. Zide and Susan W. Gray, "The Solutioning Process: Merging the Genogram and the Solution-Focused Model of Practice," *Journal of Family Social Work* 4.1 (2000): 3–19.

17 Ann Hartman, "Diagrammatic Assessment of Family Relations," *Social Casework* (October 1978): 465–76; Ann Hartman and Joan Laird, *Family-Centered Social Work Practice* (New York: The Free Press, 1983). The eco-map is found on page 160.

18 Elizabeth M. Tracy and James K. Whittaker, "The Social Network Map: Assessing Social Support in Clinical Practice," *Families in Society: The Journal of Contemporary Human Services* (October 1990): 461–70.

19 Gilbert Greene, "Using the Written Contract for Evaluating and Enhancing Practice Effectiveness," *Journal of Independent Social Work* 4.2 (1990): 135–55.

20 Wise, "Becoming a Feminist Social Worker" 236–49.

CHAPTER 8

FACILITATING EMPOWERMENT
AND CHANGE

SOCIAL WORKERS ENDEAVOUR TO GUIDE CLIENTS in a helping process that will lead to empowerment and change. As the previous chapters have emphasized, social work practice is informed by ideology, values, and theories and is guided by ethical and legal considerations. In this chapter we focus on a structural approach with its various practice elements and skills that promote individual and social change through a process of empowerment.

Social workers, for the most part, offer help to people who are experiencing a loss of control over their lives, are isolated and marginalized, and often need basic resources. Those coming for help may not have adequate housing or sufficient food and may experience despondency and a loss of dignity as they unsuccessfully search for employment. Others may live in fear and uncertainty as they face violence in their personal lives and/or encounter institutional and personal forms of racism, homophobia, and sexism. There are also those who are coping with physical or mental health concerns.

EMPOWERMENT

Although the term "empowerment" is thought to have been introduced by Barbara Solomon in her 1976 book *Black Empowerment: Social Work in Oppressed Communities*, the concept has a century-long tradition in the field.[1] Currently, the term is widely used and has been incorporated into the lexicon of most practice approaches. At times it is even referred to as a distinct practice approach.[2]

Within a structural approach to social work practice, empowerment is viewed as both a goal and process and has an action component. The concept refers to the act of acquiring a critical awareness of one's situation and an increased capacity to act on that awareness. This process helps a person to gain a greater degree of control over his or her life through personal and social change. The action component is important since awareness on its own without action can leave people feeling despondent.

Power and Powerlessness

Since power is defined as "the capacity to influence the forces that affect one's life space for one's own benefit,"[3] then powerlessness can be understood as the inability to directly influence one's life. Prolonged periods of powerlessness often can result in an oppressed consciousness or a colonization of the mind through which individuals understand themselves and their troubles as those in power define them. If someone is a member of a group that has been historically and/or systematically exploited and discriminated against, there is the possibility that he or she may to varying degrees internalize the damaging messages and in the process feel powerless to change the situation. Sustained feelings of powerlessness, uncertainty, and loss of control over decisions that influence one's life create high levels of damaging stress that impact negatively on mental and physical health. "Chronic stress is expected to increase the rate of premature death directly through the immune and neuroendocrine systems and indirectly through adverse behavioural responses such as smoking, excessive drinking, and violence."[4]

Awareness of the impact that stress can have on an individual can be achieved by remembering a personal experience of powerlessness. For instance, sometimes one can feel that decisions have been made without one's own input, or errors have been made by others that have made one's life difficult, or that a misunderstanding has occurred with no opportunity to offer clarification. One can ask the following questions: "What was I thinking at the time? What was I feeling? What changes in my physical health and general functioning did I notice? What did I do? In what way is this situation of powerlessness structural or social in origin?"

Empowerment can involve both an individual and collective process. Many situations of powerlessness are based on structural problems and require collective solutions to promote social change.[5]

THE CHANGE PROCESS

The anticipated outcome of social work practice, whether with individuals, groups, families, or communities, is positive change. The challenge for social workers is to understand the broader political context and organization of society while responding directly to the immediate concerns and needs of those who seek help. This type of analysis focuses on the socio-economic or structural context of individual problems and the power arrangements and the economic forces in society that create and maintain social conditions that generate stress, illness, deprivation, discrimination, and other forms of individual problems. This means developing an awareness of the ways in which individuals and their families adapt and conform to their social and material conditions, as well as the ways they resist and challenge them.

In order to practice from a social change perspective, social workers must be critical thinkers and engage in exposing the contradictions between how things ought to be and how they are in reality.[6] If social workers fail to see the contradictions within agencies and the welfare state, they may question their abilities and those of the people they are helping.

For example, social workers in a child protection agency who felt that they were not coping adequately with their caseloads requested some skill-based continuing education workshops in order to increase their effectiveness. During the workshops, the social workers were asked to describe the nature of their work and their caseload. This exercise quickly revealed their vast experience and competence and brought into focus the conditions under which they were expected to work. Although they were responsible for an ever-expanding case-load of children and their families, they had few resources since many worked in isolation in remote areas. Not surprisingly, they had come to believe that they were at fault for being unable to cope with these difficult conditions. Through an exchange of information and experience, they gained a critical awareness of the context of their practice and developed both a greater sense of their competencies and an ability to act on their own behalf in order to gain more control of their working conditions.

Critical thinking of this nature contributes to an awareness of the conditions under which we all live day to day and the ways in which personal troubles are connected to broader social forces. As social workers engage in the helping process and utilize a critical analysis they make the connection between the material reality (economic, social, political, legal) and personal reality (self-concept, emotional life, personal troubles) of those seeking assistance (see Figure 8.1).

Central to helping is an understanding of the influence of objective reality and social/economic conditions on one's subjective/emotional reality. Equally important is the role of ideology in shaping the way in which individual and social problems are perceived and defined by society, as discussed in Chapter 3. Also involved is a critical awareness of the role of social work and the delivery of social services and how they are situated within a political context.

FIGURE 8.1 STRUCTURAL APPROACHES TO PRACTICE

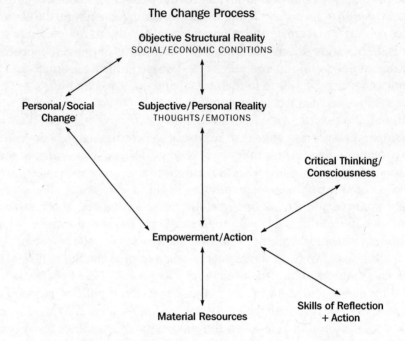

Connecting the Structural and the Personal

There is a direct connection between people's economic and social position in society and their emotional and physical health. Poverty, gender, and racial discrimination contribute to a sense of profound alienation, "a pervasive tendency to feel estranged from—rather than a part of—one's work, other people, the established society, and aspects of oneself."[7] Living with the reality of economic uncertainty produces stress in people's lives. Lillian Rubin, in her study of working-class families, documents how parents struggle to nurture and maintain family members. She found that the lack of both time and money "combine to create families that are both frantic and fragile."[8] While families offer emotional as well as material support to their members, at times they are also the source of tension, stress, violence, and neglect.

It is then reasonable to expect that the degree to which people are exploited and marginalized because of their status in society, based on factors such as social class, race, disability, gender, and sexual orientation, influences the degree of oppression and alienation they experience.

Oppression can be seen as taking two forms, both overlapping in an intricate weave. On the one hand, there's the external oppression of laws, institutions and other social structures that reinforce the principles of inequality—namely that certain people are inferior and therefore deserve less than their "betters." And on the other hand, there's internalized oppression in which we come to believe in our own inferiority, worthlessness and powerlessness, both as individuals and as a group. Whenever we act out negative messages against ourselves and each other, internalized oppression is at work.[9]

How one sees oneself reflected in society, whether in the media or in history books or among professionals such as teachers, doctors, and lawyers, has an impact on one's perceptions of self-worth and ability. Stephen Rose reminds us that oppression is not some distant structure but integral to our social relations with others and is experienced in the activities of daily life.[10]

Whether situational or chronic, a high level of stress impacts negatively on general health and contributes to hypertension, depression, anxiety, and anger. Examining these "symptoms" of anxiety, sadness, and anger by exploring the context of people's lives offers a clearer picture of the situation.

Miriam Greenspan examines how various practice approaches differ in their focus:

> The traditional therapist listens for pathology. The humanist therapist listens for self-awareness. The feminist therapist listens to the connection between the personal and political in women's stories.[11]

If the focus is on psychopathology and weaknesses, the tendency is to decontextualize client concerns and remove them from the social, political, and economic context in which they develop.[12] Central to the change process, as illustrated in Figure 7.1 (p. 160), is the client's empowerment, increased consciousness, and access to resources. As we gain a critical awareness of our situation, and have the necessary resources, we can act to change our circumstances, and, in the course of that activity, we become changed people. Or, as Jeffry Galper said in 1975, "A new society will create new people, but must be brought about by people in the process of becoming new."[13]

Critical Thinking and Consciousness-raising

In his seminal work, *The Pedagogy of the Oppressed*, Paulo Freire introduces scholars and practitioners to the concept of *conscientization*, by which one becomes aware of, and resists, the social, political, and economic conditions that oppress people.[14] Without critical thinking, people often "view social changes or political decisions as somehow mystically removed from their own existence, they frequently turn inward, focusing exclusively on their private lives."[15] Generally, this is reinforced by traditional helping where client problems and behaviour are given diagnostic categories and viewed as pathological.[16] Once behaviour or problems are labeled in a way that emphasizes personal deficiency or malfunction, individuals are "treated" as ill, or less than whole, and can begin to feel unsure of themselves, perhaps assuming total responsibility for their situation. The process of consciousness-raising is fundamental in the work of moving from a position of powerlessness, internalized oppression, and alienation to one of empowerment and individual and social change. If people have internalized a view of themselves as not equal and not worthy, then it is likely that they will assume complete responsibility for the problem situation. Once they have a critical understanding of their situation, they are better able to engage in a process of individual change as well as confront the unjust and alienating circumstances of their lives.[17]

Our consciousness of who we are in relation to others is rooted in the social and material conditions in which we live.[18] Critical consciousness is essentially an educational process that helps individuals to uncover the source of their difficulties within the context of a dialogic relationship and a commitment to both individual and social change.[19] Consciousness-raising involves both reflection on and an understanding of dehumanizing social structures and includes action directed at changing societal conditions. Central to the consciousness-raising process is critical thinking, a way in which individuals situate the circumstances of their lives within the broader social context.[20] Such a process contextualizes the individual's experience and assists in reducing self-blame. Rather than emphasizing only personal and interpersonal dynamics, material conditions and social relations are also considered. It is a process whereby people develop sufficient trust to articulate their views about matters of personal concern, and then, through a dialectic expression of reflection and action, they relate these personal interests to similar concerns of others. The process of uncovering the nature of one's oppression and strengths is believed to increase self-concept and lead to empowerment. An awareness and understanding of daily events is energizing and can lead to organized resistance and social change.

The change and empowerment process, as outlined in this section, includes an education and critical thinking component, the connection of the personal and political, and the mobilization of material and interpersonal resources. Lee Staples adds that "the capacity for effective action is an essential component of any meaningful conceptualization of empowerment."[21]

SKILLS OF REFLECTION AND ACTION

While social workers practicing from a structural approach utilize many of the traditional helping skills, the goals of empowerment and reducing power between the social worker and person coming for help are foremost in their application. What follows are seven key helping skills that facilitate a process of empowerment and the engagement in individual and social change.

1. The Skill of Empathy

The skill of empathy—the ability to feel what the client is going through, to reflect upon the situation, and to communicate that understanding—has long been viewed as essential to the development of a helping relationship and involves both cognitive and emotional responses. It was initially identified with the client-centred counselling of Carl Rogers whose humanistic approach offered an alternative to Freudian psychology. Social workers, too, have recognized the importance of the skill of empathy. Thomas Keefe views it as central to a helping process that is liberating and empowering and believes that "critical consciousness grows from and requires empathy."[22] Recently, the skill of empathy has been extended to include the ability to empathize not only with the person individually but also with the social context of a person's experience. This skill—"social empathy"—was developed by Janis Fook, an Australian social worker, and requires a critical awareness of the social and economic context of a client's problem.[23] For example, in the case of newcomers to Canada, demonstrating knowledge about their country of origin and culture and the general difficulties that occur during the settlement process can offer reassurance that their particular concern is understood.

Empathic responses come most naturally after an expression of feeling or statement of fact. It is important that the social worker listen carefully and hear what the person is saying, asking for clarification and elaboration when necessary. The understanding is then reflected back to the client in brief statements. Often empathic statements begin with "I see that…," "It sounds like…," "You look…," "You sound…," "It's difficult to," and so on.

The following vignette illustrates how one moves from empathy to consciousness-raising.

WOMAN: Mike came home drinking. I was angry and asked him where he had been. We started to argue. He pushed me and I fell over the coffee table, hit my head, and fell to the floor. He was over me, pulling my head up and banging it on the floor… I thought he was going to kill me.

WORKER: How frightening! [*empathic response, calm voice of concern*]

WOMAN: I really should know better than to ask him where he's been when he's drinking.

WORKER: As women we often take responsibility for the actions of others. I think that it is important to remember that no matter what you said or did, he is responsible for his violence.

Here the social worker initially responds with empathy by acknowledging how fearful the woman must have been. In response to the woman's next comment the worker shifts to helping the woman see that she is not to blame for her partner's abuse and thereby begins the process of consciousness-raising. The worker also normalizes the situation by using the phrase "as women we…." This connection also equalizes the power between them and normalizes the client's behaviour. The social worker could also reinforce the idea that the woman has a right to personal safety and could comment on the severity of the situation she has described.

Social workers often find that empathy for those who have harmed another person does not come easily. In these cases it is helpful to empathize with the social and economic context of the person's life and gain an awareness of what the person is going through. The challenge is to communicate empathy while at the same time emphasizing accountability and responsibility.

2. Posing Relevant Questions

The helping process is guided by questions posed by the social worker. The questions assist the client to focus and tell his or her story, to generate important information about the client's situation, and perhaps to influence the client to think about his or her situation in a different way. The choice of questions and tone of voice reflect the social worker's theoretical framework, the assumptions and ideology he or she uses to consider the client's situation. After all, how we understand the problem guides our response, our helping. However, the questions can either facilitate or halt the interview process. For example, if a social worker interviewing a woman who comes to the emergency room because she was raped asks "Why were you out so late?" and "Why did you ask him into your apartment?," the implication is that the woman is to blame for her situation. Such questions will create distance between the social worker and client, as well as be destructive to the helping process. It is preferable to avoid "why" questions because they sound, and often are, judgemental. What follows are some basic guidelines to posing questions that will move the interview along and contribute to an effective empowerment and change process.

While some closed questions may be necessary during the interview, generally open-ended questions generate a more detailed response that includes factual and emotional content. For example, "Is your job stressful?" may solicit a response such as "Yes" or "Isn't everyone's?" On the other hand, the client may respond to "Tell me a bit about the nature of your job—your working conditions," by talking about job hours, shift work, colleagues and boss, stress, and fears about getting laid off in the next downsizing.

It is also important to avoid leading questions such as "You're not married, are you?" Such a question may deter someone from talking about an important relationship that does not have legal sanction. Better questions are "Do you have a partner?" or "Tell me about the people that are most important to you."

Questions that are only problem-focused and aimed at exploring individual deficiencies and limitations can leave the client feeling despair, whereas questions that assist clients in further understanding their situation and their individual and social resources can strengthen and empower them. Paulo Freire believes that people have the right to fully understand their environment—to go beyond "the *common sense* in order to discover the *reason* for the facts."[24] While it is common for people to fully accept their reality as "the way things are," at times they also think critically about their lives. Social workers can facilitate this process by posing critical questions to assist clients in uncovering truths and understanding the sources of their problems. The following situation illustrates a problem-posing question.

> During the Depression years of the 1930s, cookery classes were being organized for women in poor communities in an attempt to help them provide nutritious meals for their families despite their low incomes. One particular evening a group of women were being taught how to make cod's head soup— a cheap and nourishing dish. At the end of the lesson the women were asked if they had any questions. "Just one," said one member of the group, "whilst we're eating the cod's head soup, who's eating the cod?"[25]

The "critical question" posed by the woman in the class reflects honest questioning of the instructions she was receiving—she did not want to know how to do something without also understanding why she must do it in the first place. Her question has the potential of moving the discussion to a deeper level, which may assist in linking poverty to a broader context. A response to the question quickly uncovers structural inequalities and the inequitable distribution of the necessities of life. Such an awareness of the structural context assists both the social worker and the client in avoiding a victim-blaming response.

The Milan Associates, a group of Italian family therapists, base their approach on the concept of "new epistemology," that is, understanding the knowledge and beliefs family members hold rather than analyzing their behaviour.[26] They introduced *circular questioning*, the use of questions that enable families to see their problems differently by highlighting differences among family members and clarifying relationships. For example, take a family in crisis: the father is overusing drugs, and the 17-year-old son wants to leave home, quit school, and find work. The social worker might ask, "Who would miss the son most if he were to leave home"? Or the father might be asked to describe the relationship between his son and daughter or to speculate how an absent member of the family might respond to the question.

Michael White introduced "landscape of action" questions to explore unique outcomes and shift away from "problem-saturated" stories that he believed got people mired in repeating mistakes. For example, he might pose the following series of questions to someone who has just made a change in his or her life: "Just prior to taking this step, did you nearly turn back? If so, how did you stop yourself from doing so? Looking back from this vantage point, what did you notice yourself doing that might have contributed to this achievement?"[27] These questions promote identification of client strengths and strategies.

Similarly, coping questions, popular among solution-focused practitioners, assist clients in exploring the factors that have contributed to a change that they have made.[28] Examples include: "How did you manage to reduce your drug use; what did you do?" or "It is wonderful that you and your daughter are talking more. How did that happen?"

3. Self-Disclosure/Sharing a View

Sharing a personal expression of the social worker's own feelings, ideas, attitudes, and experiences with the client often reduces the power differential and builds a more egalitarian relationship. An essential skill is for social workers to present themselves as real human beings, not clinical, detached, distant professionals. Such involvement and disclosure has been called "unprofessional" by more traditional workers; however, if we do not synthesize "professional" with "personal," spontaneity is lost, and we become robotic in our responses, mechanical social workers who fail to connect on a human level.

It is important to share perceptions without imposing them on the client. The purpose of offering a personal view should be for the benefit of the client, to contribute to problem-solving, empowerment, and lessening the distance between the social worker and the person seeking help. It can improve the client's self-esteem, validate the experience of someone who is seeking help, and/or offer an alternative way of understanding an issue. The focus remains on the client and his or her needs when social workers select what to disclose from their own experience.

In Larry Shulman's research on social work practice "Sharing workers' feelings skills," and the direct expression of the worker's real feelings (anger, fear, love, and ambivalence) were rated the most important. Shulman suggests that this skill "effectively strengthens the working relationship (the process) while contributing important ideas for the client's work (the content)."[29] Self-disclosure can also collectivize dilemmas and foster hope. It is most effective if it is meaningful in both content and context.

4. Reframing/Restorying

Often people are constrained by the beliefs they have or the stories they carry. When someone is in the middle of the forest, only the surrounding trees are visible, not the entire area. Decisions are often made based on limited information and do not provide a complete understanding. Clients may be very hard on themselves for the situations they find themselves in. The social worker can engage the client in a process of re-examination, draw on the client's strengths, and offer another way a situation can be viewed (this is the act of reframing). Suggestions ought to be made tentatively. For example, a social worker might say "Another way of looking at it might be…" or "I see it as…."

The following is an example of reframing adapted from an abused women's group.[30]

> WOMAN: I am as much to blame for the violence. I help cover up for him by lying to his mom about my bruises.
> WORKER: What would happen if you told her the truth?
> WOMAN: He'd get mad at me and beat me up again.
> WORKER: That's right. Your covering up for him was a way to help you survive.

Deconstructing, revisioning, and restorying have a similar outcome. The goal of narrative approaches is to help people become authors of their own stories and to deconstruct and revise old problematic stories. The premise is that people are troubled because "They continue to be constrained by the power of an old story that enabled them to survive what was then a harrowing childhood, but is of no value for adult living…."[31] Stories that are retold in the family often serve to keep the family history alive and speak to the strengths and limitations of the members and their place in the family. Unfortunately, in some cases, these stories are selective and damaging and do not reflect a person's potential.

Another popular technique among narrative therapists is to externalize conversation so that clients are encouraged "to provide an account of how the problem has been affecting their lives and their relationships."[32] In these conversations the problem is viewed as external to the person, not an intrinsic part of his or her identity; in the process, "the problem is to an extent disempowered, as it no longer speaks to persons of the truth about who they are as people, or about the very nature of their relationships."[33] The person is freed from the problem and is able to develop an identity separate from the problem. During this process, it is best if the externalization of the problem is put in the client's own words. For example, a client may refer to depression as "the blue meanies,"[34] waiting for a call as "life glued to the phone," or criminal behaviour as "a career of crime." In some ways externalizing the problem and reframing assist the client to see the problem differently.

Deconstructing is a questioning of assumptions about traditional roles, practices, and beliefs, similar to the consciousness-raising widely used by the women's movement.

5. Identifying Strengths

There is a growing literature on strength-based, solution-focused practice.[35] Identifying strengths and recognizing how people have coped with and survived difficult situations facilitates empowerment and change. In most cases they have done the best they could given the available resources. In the following interview a woman begins by speaking of the years of abuse she endured at the hands of her husband. She speaks of how hard it was to keep going and be a mother to her three children.

> WOMAN: I don't know how I survived. You know, I've never been suicidal even after all I've been through....
>
> WORKER: Well, you're a pretty amazing person to be going through all that and still be functioning and being a good provider for your children. Sounds like you're really there for them.

Later on, the woman wonders if her partner is serious about stopping the abuse. The social worker helps her to rely on her own knowledge.

> WOMAN: I'm battling between whether he's really changing or if he'll be abusive again...like I'm worried and still afraid of him. Like I don't know if I should be scared of him.... I want to find out.
>
> WORKER: What does your gut feeling tell you?
>
> WOMAN: I guess I'm not feeling sure about him.
>
> WORKER: I think if you are feeling unsure, it is important to pay attention to your feelings. You probably are the best person to know. And from what you have said, it sounds like you have recognized some controlling behaviour. Pay attention to things like that. I think it is always important to listen to yourself.

In this situation the social worker links current feelings and behaviour to the immediate context and encourages the woman to allow her own knowledge to guide her. In working with people who have experienced trauma, reach for the strengths that have supported their survival. Dr. Rosemary Meier, a psychiatrist who works with survivors of torture, suggests asking questions such as "Through all this, what sustained you, what kept you going?" or "You've obviously been through something I can hardly imagine, but I hear how you kept going and survived...."[36]

6. Communicating Effectively

Several communication skills are essential to a social worker in the task of helping clients "to tell their story." Listening to someone is an act of respect and acknowledgement and requires time, concentration, and a genuine interest and concern for the teller. Attentiveness and encouragement provide an atmosphere in which someone can feel comfortable expressing thoughts and feelings. Clients frequently have disturbing experiences and gauge the social worker's reaction and responses to what they are saying in order to determine if the social worker is prepared to hear the worst.

Providing an opportunity for people to talk about their situations, responding appropriately, and keeping a focus are the responsibility of the social worker. While there are a number of authors who address interviewing skills, one of the most comprehensive texts is *The Social Work Interview: A Guide for Human Service Professionals* by Alfred Kadushin and Goldie Kadushin. The following skills are among those they recommend in order to be an effective interviewer:

Exploring. As the interview progresses, social workers gather more specific information by exploring and asking for further details. Questions such as "How did you respond?," "And then what happened?," or "What did she say exactly?" move the interview along.

Clarifying. At times social workers will ask for clarification so that they can fully understand the situation. "When you say that she is out late all the time, what do you mean?" Reach for specifics behind the general comments: "Will you say more about that?"

Paraphrasing. When the person has given a detailed account of a situation, it is often useful to capture the main message by paraphrasing what you have just heard, including emotions. "Your son Tom has been getting more and more dependent on pot. It sounds like you are worried about both his drug use and his grades in school." When paraphrasing, it is important that the social worker not impose personal ideas and feelings.

Summarizing. As the interview moves from one area to another, it is useful to summarize before changing focus: "We just discussed the difficulties and stress associated with your job. You have identified how the long hours and unpredictable demands are affecting your health. Now I would like to focus a bit on your family life and relationship with your partner and children."

7. Presenting a Challenge

At times individuals may lack an awareness of the contradictions in their lives and the obstacles in their path to personal change. Challenging ought to take place only in a helping relationship in which the client feels understood and respected and can tolerate some discomfort. Since a challenge can be difficult for someone to hear, be direct, clear, constructive, and caring rather than punitive. Challenging brings the client face-to-face with reality and generally is used when there is a discrepancy between a client's comments and behaviour or what the client is saying and the social worker's perception of the experience: "Oh, I'm fine, just great" (while looking weary and tense). The social worker might respond, "I sense that it has been a difficult week for you."

In this example, a man in group session began to speak in abstract and general terms about why men are abusive. The group leader attempted to get him to focus:

> GROUP LEADER: Can I give you a suggestion: speak of your own experi-
>   ence rather than general information about men.
> GROUP MEMBER: OKAY, I'll shut up if that's what you want.
> GROUP LEADER: Just a minute ... something just happened here. [*Looking
>   at other group members*] Did I ask Joe to shut up?

Challenging comments that assist the person to take a closer look and re-examine beliefs and behaviours can be very effective. While the person may find it difficult to have an action or statement challenged, if done effectively, the result can promote critical awareness and growth. After leaving a group one man said, "I learned the most from what I liked to hear the least."

The empowerment and change process is the core of all social work intervention and is facilitated by a number of essential helping skills. The process that is suggested in this chapter can not only facilitate problem-solving, but also contributes to the development of a critical consciousness and client empowerment.

NOTES

1 Barbara Bryant Solomon, *Black Empowerment: Social Work in Oppressed Communities* (New York: Columbia University Press, 1976). Barbara Levy Simon has documented the history of the empowerment tradition in social work in her book *The Empowerment Tradition in American Social Work: A History* (New York: Columbia University Press, 1994).

2 Stephen M. Rose, "Advocacy/Empowerment: An Approach to Clinical Practice for Social Work," *Journal of Sociology and Social Welfare* 17.2 (1990): 41–51; Ruth J. Parsons, Lorraine

M. Gutiérrez, and Enid Opal Cox, "A Model for Empowerment Practice," in *Empowerment in Social Work Practice: A Sourcebook,* ed. Ruth J. Parsons, Lorraine M. Gutiérrez, and Enid Opal Cox (Pacific Grove, CA: Brooks/Cole, 1998) 3–51; Wes Shera and Lillian M. Wells, *Empowerment Practice in Social Work* (Toronto: Canadian Scholars Press: 1999).

3 Elaine B. Pinderhughes, "Empowerment for Our Clients and for Ourselves," *Social Casework* (June 1983): 332.

4 North York Health Network, *Inequality is Bad for Our Hearts: Why Low Income and Social Exclusion are Major Causes of Heart Disease in Canada* (Toronto: North York Health Network, 2001) 25. The full report can be found at http://action.web.ca/home/narcc/issues .shtml?x=78735&AA_EX_Session=9323d7ca5b2459bc858e0ab5004ef00e.

5 Lee H. Staples, "Powerful Ideas about Empowerment," *Administration in Social Work* 14.2 (1990): 37.

6 Stephen Brookfield, *Developing Critical Thinkers: Challenging Adults to Explore Alternative Ways of Thinking and Acting* (London: Jossey-Bass, 1987).

7 Arthur Maglin, "Alienation and Therapeutic Intervention," *Catalyst* 2 (1978): 70.

8 Lillian B. Rubin, *Families on the Fault Line: America's Working Class Speaks about the Family, the Economy, Race and Ethnicity* (New York: Harper Collins, 1994) 101.

9 Pam Trevithick, "Unconsciousness Raising with Working-class Women," in *In Our Experience: Workshops at the Women's Therapy Centre,* ed. Sue Krzowski and Pat Land (London: Women's Press, 1988) 72.

10 Stephen M. Rose, "Reflections on Empowerment-Based Practice," *Social Work* 45.5 (October 2000): 403–12.

11 Miriam Greenspan, *A New Approach to Women and Therapy,* 2nd ed. (Bradenton, FL: Human Services Institute, 1993) 233.

12 Eleni E. Skodra, "Counselling Immigrant Women: A Feminist Critique of Traditional Therapeutic Approaches and Reevaluation of the Role of Therapist," *Counselling Psychology Quarterly* 2.2 (1989): 185.

13 Galper, *The Politics of Social Service* 185.

14 Freire, *Pedagogy of the Oppressed* 19.

15 Brookfield, *Developing Critical Thinkers* 54.

16 See, e.g., Mary Sykes Wylie, "Diagnosing for Dollars?," *Networker* (May/June 1995): 23–33, 65–69.

17 John F. Longres, "Marxian Theory and Social Work Practice," *Catalyst* 20 (1986): 30.

18 See, e.g., Leonard, *Personality and Ideology.* Peter Leonard places emphasis on the dialectical relationship between consciousness and material existence.

19 Scott Bock, "Conscientization: Paulo Freire and Class-based Practice," *Catalyst* 6 (1980): 5–25.

20 Brookfield, *Developing Critical Thinkers.*

21 Staples, "Powerful Ideas about Empowerment" 38.

22 Thomas Keefe, "Empathy Skill and Critical Consciousness," *Social Casework* (September 1980): 393; Keefe, "Empathy: The Critical Skill."

23 See Fook, *Radical Casework.*

24 Brenda Ball, John Gaventa, John Peters, Myles Horton, and Paulo Freire, *We Make the Road by Walking: Conversation on Education and Social Change* (Philadelphia: Temple University Press, 1990) 157; emphasis in original.

25 Jennie Popay and Yvonne Dhooge, "Unemployment, Cod's Head Soup, and Radical Social

Work," in *Radical Social Work Today*, ed. Mary Langan and Phil Lee (London: Unwin Hyman, 1989) 140.

26 See, e.g., M. Selvini-Palazzoli, L. Boscolo, G. Cecchin, and G. Prata, *Paradox and Counter Paradox* (New York: Jason Aronson, 1978).

27 Michael White, "Deconstruction and Therapy," in *Therapeutic Conversations*, ed. Stephen Gilligan and Resse Price (New York: Norton, 1993) 41.

28 See, e.g., Insoo Berg, *Family-Based Services: A Solution-Focused Approach* (New York: Norton, 1994).

29 Shulman, *The Skills of Helping* 137.

30 Pam A. Brown and Claire E. Dickey, "Facilitating Critical Thinking in an Abused Women's Group," *Proceedings* of the Eleventh Annual Symposium of the Association for the Advancement of Social Work with Groups, Montreal, 26–29 October 1989: 450.

31 Parry and Doan, *Story Re-visions* 40.

32 Michael White, *Re-Authoring Lives: Interviews and Essays* (Adelaide, AUS: Dulwich Centre Publications, 1995) 21.

33 White, *Re-Authoring Lives* 23.

34 Perry and Doan, *Story Re-visions* 87.

35 Steven de Shazer, *Keys to Solution in Brief Therapy* (New York: Norton, 1985); M.D. Selekman, *Solution-Focused Therapy with Children: Harnessing Family Strength for Systemic Change* (New York: Guilford Press, 1997); Berg, *Family Based Services*.

36 Karen Price, ed., "Doing the Right Thing: Suggestions for Non-Medical Caregivers: An Interview with Rosemary Meier," *Community Support for Survivors of Torture: A Manual* (Toronto: Canadian Centre for Victims of Torture, n.d.) 82.

CHAPTER 9

IMMIGRANT AND REFUGEE SETTLEMENT: CULTURALLY SENSITIVE PRACTICE

ANADA IS ONE OF THE MOST DIVERSE and multicultural countries in the world. Within the next 25 years the ethnocultural diversity of the Canadian population is projected to undergo a significant increase, especially within certain census metropolitan areas.[1] By 2031 three Canadians in ten may be a member of a visible minority group. More than 71 per cent will live in Toronto, Vancouver, and Montreal, and in cities such as Toronto and Vancouver three persons in five will belong to a visible minority group. South Asians and Chinese will continue to be the largest visible minority group; however, the greatest increase will be in the Arab and West Asian populations. Canada's Arab population is projected to reach between 806,000 and 1.1 million in 2031 (up from 276,000 in 2006) and the West Asian population between 457,000 and 592,000 (up from 164,000 in 2006). Accordingly, the number of people having a non-Christian religion will more than double by 2031, and of this one person in two will be Muslim. Fewer than two Canadians in three will be Christian compared to three in four in 2006 and nine in ten in 1981.

Currently within Canada there are more than 200 different ethnic groups and 16.2 per cent (over five million) of residents are considered visible minorities.[2] Newcomers to Canada are either economic and family class immigrants, refugees, or undocumented immigrants. Canada has projected to accept 240,000–265,000 migrants in 2010 in the economic, family, and humanitarian (protected persons/refugees) immigration categories. Jason Kenney, Minister of Citizenship, Immigration, and Multiculturalism, announced that there will be a greater emphasis on economic recovery and that Canada will welcome more economic immigrants.[3] Among the permanent residents, the economic class (business and skilled worker immigrants) has been the largest group entering Canada, followed by the family class (family reunification), and humanitarian class (protected persons, including government-assisted and privately sponsored refugees). Among temporary residents are migrant workers, international students, and those who left their country of origin and on arrival in Canada apply to be recognized as refugees. They are often referred to as "asylum seekers." Of the 192,281 temporary residents entering Canada in 2008, 79,528 were foreign workers.[4] Many of these temporary workers have been recruited on behalf of businesses to work at minimum wage or less without access to any benefits. At one time, the arrival of newcomers to Canada was viewed as nation-building; it has now also become part of the labour pool and profit-making source for transnational companies.

The US is experiencing the largest wave of immigration since 1920. However, for the first time in 2010 illegal immigrants outnumbered the legal ones at 11.2 million.[5] Nearly one in five Americans are either immigrants (36.7 million people, 12 per cent of the population) or were born in the US to at least one immigrant parent (33 million, 11 per cent of the population).[6] One in seven marriages is now interracial or interethnic.[7]

Regardless of the category of entry, refugees and immigrants face tremendous challenges when arriving in Canada and the US. Social workers are integral in the process of settlement and the integration of newcomers. This chapter focuses on sensitive and effective social work responses to refugees and immigrants, outlines the immigration and refugee process, summarizes concerns of newcomers, and addresses cultural and spiritual diversity and culturally relevant practice.

SOCIAL WORK AND SETTLEMENT

In the early years of the last century, social workers were active in the settlement movement and in assisting those they referred to as "neighbours in need." In her book on social work and immigrant and refugee settlement, Kathleen Valtonen considers social work as "a singular vehicle for carrying out critical human service interventions for the well-being and welfare of this client constituency of 'newcomers' or 'newer citizens.'"[8]

Working with populations whose language and culture are different poses a particular challenge for social workers. The 2010 special issue of the CASW journal *Canadian Social Work* contains an excellent collection of articles on policy and settlement practice with immigrants and refugees. However, despite the profession's long history in the settlement movement, there is some indication that current social workers are not well-prepared to address the differing needs and concerns of newcomers to Canada. Miu Chung Yan and Sherman

Chan conducted a survey of 218 social workers in British Columbia to determine their readiness to serve newcomers effectively and conclude that "no, we are not ready—not yet." Surprisingly, only five of the 218 social worker respondents worked in immigrant settlement and related services. Social workers identified a need to gain awareness of "the unique situation of newcomers in terms of Canadian immigration policy, the migration process of individuals, the personal and structural challenges and conditions of migrants as well as the existing settlement programs and services along with their limitations."[9]

For Mary Nash, grounding in community work, along with cultural competence, is essential for social workers involved with settlement. She elaborates on what is needed:

> Effective settlement workers will have a critical analysis of the social structures and political pressures, international as well as local, which lead to both voluntary and forced migration and eventual settlement. This, together with knowledge of human rights and social justice issues, provides a foundation on which to build the necessary community work skills for appropriate intervention in this complex field.[10]

THE IMMIGRATION AND REFUGEE PROCESS

Human rights and international contexts influence not only migration but also immigration and refugee policy. In order to be effective practitioners social workers require an awareness of immigration and refugee law and the application process.[11] Migration, whether voluntary or forced, often is in response to international conflict, civil war, national disasters (earthquakes and tsunamis), and economic or environmental crises. At the end of 2009, 43.3 million people were forcibly displaced worldwide, the highest since the mid-1990s. Approximately 6.6 million people were stateless, although unofficial estimates place the number at 12 million.[12]

The 1951 Refugee Convention defines a refugee (referred to as a Convention refugee) as

> Any person who ... owing to a well-founded fear of being persecuted for reasons of race, religion, nationality, membership of a particular social group or political opinion, is outside the country of his nationality and is unable, or owing to such fear, is unwilling to avail himself protection of that country; or who, not having a nationality and being outside the country of his former habitual residence as a result of such events, is unable or, owing to such fear, is unwilling to return to it.[13]

As a signatory to the Refugee Convention, Canada is legally obligated to consider asylum seekers who apply from within the country. Valtonen emphasizes that "refugee protection is a human rights issue. The violation of human rights occurring and perpetrated during periods of repression, internal conflict and wars gives rise to forced migration and refugee situations."[14]

Categories of Immigration/Refugee Status

It is important for social workers to know whether or not a person entered Canada as a refugee or an immigrant, the refugee/immigration status, and where he or she is in the refugee/immigration acceptance process. Individuals apply for admission into Canada as a permanent resident under three categories: Family Class, Economic Class, and Refugees. In 2008 among those arriving permanently 63.9 per cent were economic immigrants, 22.5 per cent family class, and 9.3 per cent refugees.[15]

Convention Refugees

According to Canada's 2002 Immigration and Refugee Protection Act, people applying from outside Canada fall under the Refugee and Humanitarian Resettlement Program, while those applying from within Canada as refugee claimants ("asylum seekers") are considered under the In-Canada Refugee Protection Process.[16]

Refugees selected overseas are either government-assisted refugees (GARS) referred by the UNHCR and supported by the federally funded Resettlement Assistance Program (RAP) or privately sponsored refugees (PSRS) sponsored and supported by voluntary groups such as churches. GARS are provided with income support for one year, airport reception, temporary housing, and an orientation to life in Canada. The Interim Federal Health Program (IFH) provides emergency health insurance to both GAR and PSR refugees in provinces (British Columbia, Ontario, Quebec, and PEI) where there is a three-month period before eligibility for provincial health care. Language classes are offered under the Language Instruction for Newcomers to Canada (LINC) program.[17]

Historically, the political and economic context has shaped Canada's response to those entering the country. The financial crisis and the focus on terrorism have contributed to an anti-immigration sentiment among many citizens. Coverage of the recent arrival of 492 Tamils in British Columbia via Thailand on the MV Sun Sea is a case in point; arriving as asylum seekers by ship raised concerns about "jumping the queue" and not having legitimate reasons for coming to Canada. Their national origin and motives and possible connection to "terrorism" likely had an impact on the processing of their files.[18]

There is ample evidence that the Canadian media "was heavily biased in its reporting, racializing and criminalizing the migrants."[19]

In response the government pushed through the controversial Bill C-11; if it goes through Senate it would change the refugee system policy that deals with those who arrive in large numbers and "abuse the system." The commitment of the federal government to the settlement of newcomers comes further under question after the announcement of funding cuts totaling $53 million. The much needed services of immigration and settlement agencies, particularly in Ontario, British Columbia, and Nova Scotia, will be reduced at a time when they are needed the most.[20]

Immigrants

An eligible Canadian citizen or permanent resident who is 18 years or older can sponsor a person under Family Class who lives outside Canada or who is a partner living in Canada. The applicant must be related to the sponsor as a partner, parents or grandparents, child (dependent or adopted), or an orphaned child under 18 who is related. Other relatives may be sponsored if there are no other sponsorship options in Canada or elsewhere. Once status as an immigrant has been approved, the person becomes a permanent resident and can live and work in Canada. The sponsor is responsible for the support of the individual. Economic Class immigrants gain entry either as skilled workers, investors, or self-employed individuals.

In order to provide culturally sensitive services to immigrants and refugees, social worker practitioners ought to have some knowledge of their culture and the history of their country; the reasons for leaving and their migration experiences; where the individual/family is in the process of immigration and integration; and their settlement experience in Canada, including the presence of financial, physical, and mental health concerns.

ARRIVAL, SETTLEMENT, AND INTEGRATION

The migration experience varies for each individual and depends on pre-migration hardship and the migration journey. Newcomers who come as economic immigrants have employment opportunities and are often joining family members or friends. On the other hand, refugees may be forced to migrate due to fear of persecution. On arrival in a host country, all immigrants and refugees begin a new life and the process of adaptation to a foreign culture and climate. But the migration journey between those two realities can be long and traumatic, and may involve an extended period in an overcrowded refugee camp in a third country. They may have witnessed or been victims of political violence and torture including the assassination, disappearance, or imprisonment of family members and the destruction of their homes and belongings. People often arrive without birth certificates, educational documents, or passports.

Migration for both immigrants and refugees frequently involves a major disruption in their lives such as separation from family and friends and loss of status and identity. These factors can have a profound impact on both children and adult family members. Combined with the stress of settlement, newcomers may require special services along with social and material resources.

"Integration is understood as the situation in which the settling persons can participate fully in the economic, social, cultural and political life of a society, while also being able to retain their own identity."[21] Finding gainful employment, a place to live, and adaptation to one's new country are signs of successful settlement and transition. Both refugees and immigrants must navigate the policies of social service and immigration bureaucracies and the day-to-day challenges of transportation, shopping, and banking. Without comprehension in either English or French, they are unable to read classified advertisements, negotiate rental agreements, and access needed services. Because of the lack of affordable housing, newcomers often are forced to live in substandard apartments. Refugees, who seek asylum on arrival, face a longer integration process due to the uncertainty as far as their residency status is concerned and whether or not they are considered to be a refugee under convention standards.

Landed immigrants and resettled refugees are able to work when they arrive. However, refugee claimants (asylum seekers) and those whose refugee claim has been accepted by the Immigration and Refugee Board must apply for a one-year authorization, a long and bureaucratic process.[22] Many refugees and immigrants arrive with a university degree; however, too often they face unemployment or underemployment and are forced to work in an area outside their expertise. Unemployment rates for recent immigrants are almost twice as high as those for Canadian-born workers (12.1 per cent versus 6.7 per cent).[23] The barriers to obtaining employment include a lack of language proficiency, nonrecognition of foreign credentials, and the lack of Canadian experience. Asylum seekers (or refugee claimants) are issued a social insurance number that begins with a "9" indicating a temporary residence in Canada, and this may deter employers from hiring them.[24] This situation contributes to high rates of low income, three times higher than the Canadian-born population despite the fact that the percentage of recent immigrants with a university degree is twice as high.[25]

An Unwelcoming Environment

While immigrants and refugees may arrive with psychological concerns, the impact of racism, discrimination, and poverty on arrival in Canada may further traumatize them. Martha Ocampo, Co-Director of Across Boundaries, Ethno-racial Mental Health Centre in Toronto, commented that "The mental health system recognizes the need to address post-traumatic syndrome, but fails to recognize that, until racism is addressed, which is the trauma refugees and new immigrants experience on a daily basis, such an approach will be ineffective."[26] Newcomers face racism all too often.

There has been heated debate in the Western world, including Canada and most notably in Quebec, on the accommodation of minority and cultural practices. The Quebec provincial government established the Boucher-Taylor Commission (2007–08) to study the situation. Gada Mahrouse examined the citizens' forums it organized, the Commission's final report *Building the Future: A Time for Reconciliation*, and the media response. She concludes that "the Commission ended up reinforcing the racialized hierarchies and exclusions that it wanted to address." This was evident in the forums that "followed a pattern in which minorities and immigrants were always on the defensive, having to justify their presence, and commitment to Quebec values, while French-Canadian Quebecers were in a position of granting validation and approval, in effect acting like judges of what was tolerable and what was not."[27] Intolerance to diverse cultural practices and their accommodation creates additional barriers for newcomers integrating into Canadian society. It also speaks to assimilation versus acculturation as a goal. Assimilation is embracing the culture of your new country and moving away from your original cultural identity, while acculturation is the process of adapting and adjusting to the new country, without disbanding your own.[28]

Health Concerns

Overall, immigrants and refugees, on arrival in Canada, are healthier than the Canadian-born population. However, their health deteriorates over time, often due to poverty, marginalization, and isolation.[29] In particular, refugees and immigrants with low-income and language levels, especially women, are at risk of health concerns.[30] Many encounter racism as they search for housing, employment, or access to services. As mentioned earlier, this unwelcoming climate contributes to despair and depression. The impact of social exclusion, whether it is the denial of social goods or exclusion from production, creates living conditions that endanger health.[31]

Almost all refugees have experienced some mental health difficulties such as depression, anxiety, sleeping difficulties, suicidal thoughts, and the overuse of alcohol and drugs.[32] Researchers who completed a meta-analysis of 20 surveys representing close to 7,000 refugees in seven Western countries conclude that about one in ten adult refugees has post-traumatic stress disorder; one in 20 has a major depression, while one in 25 has a generalized anxiety disorder.[33]

All too often the tendency is to assess and respond to such situations by looking through a Western lens and drawing on prevalent theories and practices. Nancy Farwell, a social worker who has done extensive research on mental health and war trauma, points out that "the intra-psychic post-traumatic stress disorder framework may be too narrow for conceptualizing war trauma, which is essentially psychosocial in nature, and deeply contextualized in a community's socio-economic and political realities of conflict and its aftermath."[34] Most refugees and torture survivors come from collective cultures, and since they are likely to have experienced personal and collective identity traumas—as in the case of ethnic persecution—healing is often best within a group context.[35] In collective societies, individual identity and psychological well-being is closely linked to the extended family, larger clan, and social and material conditions. Therefore healing from war trauma may best take place collectively, drawing on families, community elders, or religious leaders as an important source of support.

CULTURAL DIVERSITY AND RELEVANT PRACTICE RESPONSES

All social work practice is cross-cultural, and as social workers we all want to be effective in helping people from different cultures while being sensitive to cultural differences. Culture develops in an historical, social, and geographical context, and is the product of a dynamic ongoing process in the lives of people.

Cultural diversity is concerned with honoring difference in values, beliefs, and meaning systems based on ethnicity, religion, occupation, political ideology, or other value-based and meaning-imparting contexts. Immigrants and refugees represent many nations, ethnicities and religions. They bring with them many complex and diverse values in relation to gender, parenting, and religious practices that provide crucial psychological and practical resources.[36]

Social work practice, in order to be culturally relevant, requires attention to "the practices, beliefs, aspirations and culture of individuals, families, groups, communities and nations" and to "the spirit, the values, the philosophies, the ethics, and the hope and ideals of those with whom social workers work and, at the same time to social workers' own values."[37] Central to this process is an appreciation of other cultures, acknowledgement of the importance of cultural differences, and an awareness of personal biases and prejudices. It is suggested that without a cross-cultural understanding we are likely to base our knowledge on stereotypes and neglect to identify diversity within the unfamiliar culture.[38]

Cultural Competency

There has been much attention placed on the term "cultural competency" in the social work literature with little agreement of what it means. In 2001 the NASW approved standards of cultural competence, and in 2003 the CSWE endorsed them. In 2007 the NASW published indicators for their achievement.[39] The NASW defines cultural competence as "the process by which individuals and systems respond respectfully and effectively to people of all cultures, languages, classes, races, ethnic backgrounds, religions, and other diversity factors in a manner that recognizes, affirms, and values the worth of individuals, families, and communities and protects and preserves the dignity of each ... [and a] set of congruent behaviors, attitudes, and policies that come together in a system, agency, or professionals to work effectively in cross-cultural situations."[40]

Others suggest that cultural competence in social work practice "is never fully achieved, but is a lifelong process for social workers, who always encounter diverse clients and new situations."[41] In a study of practitioners Kwong found that, along with problem-solving, "employing clinical knowledge and skills and inserting the cultural elements that apply to different ethnic groups constitute the basis for the fundamental process of cultural competency."[42] Self-awareness and openness to other cultures is essential.[43]

In regards to cultural competence with Aboriginal clients, Weaver noted that knowledge is required in four primary areas: 1) diversity, 2) history, 3) culture, and 4) contemporary realities.[44] These areas also have high relevance for practice with immigrant and refugee populations. Ruby Chau, Sam Yu, and Cam Tran, who advocate a "diversity-based approach," place emphasis on "the fluid nature of culture, the diversity in cultural groups and the impact on inegalitarian and racists power relations on their life."[45] For social work practice with African Canadians, Wanda Bernard and Veronica Marsman draw on Africentric theory and practice that "emphasizes an African world-view that includes harmony, collectivity, and non-materialistic qualities of people; holds a holistic conception of people; connects people culturally, historically, and with community; views the experiences of African people as key movers of their own liberation; is rooted in the African value system; fosters and develops a collective consciousness; and analyzes context and systemic realities."[46]

However, cultural competence is a complicated concept in a multicultural world.[47] Questions have been raised regarding the conceptual framework underlying cultural competence as a practice and whether or not such a goal of competency is achievable.[48] Gordon Pon suggests that cultural competency "promotes an obsolete view of culture and is a form of a new racism" by "otherizing non-whites by deploying modernist and absolutist views of culture, while not using racist language."[49] One of his major criticisms is that the concept of competency assumes a knowable set of attributes represented in a certain culture and disregards the history of racism in Canada. Johnson and Munch agree that the conceptual underpinnings of cultural competence is flawed and argue that "informed social work practice requires knowledge in substantive areas that include racism, structural inequalities, and health disparities."[50] They caution that applying generalized knowledge about cultures to all clients may contribute to stereotyping and therefore disregard uniqueness and individual differences based on factors such as class, gender, and sexual orientation. Frank Kortman explains that it is a static notion of culture as a fixed entity that tends to stereotype groups of people; he argues for a dynamic view where culture is an ongoing process, constantly developing in interaction with the environment and other aspects of one's identity.[51]

Putting aside the debate over the meaning of cultural competence and its formulation, the importance of connecting with persons from varied cultural backgrounds and providing culturally relevant services remains a priority for social work practitioners. Two texts by Canadian authors provide detailed information about the history, backgrounds, and cultures of specific groups of people and suggest practice responses without engaging in stereotyping.[52] This involves the recognition of diversity within countries. While people from a specific culture may share a history, beliefs, and values, they can differ when it comes to social class, political ideology, rural or urban origins, and religion.

Settlement workers, in order to provide effective services, require a critical analysis of the social structures and the political pressures, international as well as local, which lead to migration and eventual settlement.[53] This combines with knowledge of human rights and social justice issues to provide a foundation on which to place direct practice skills and approaches.

The development of a helping relationship where trust can flourish is essential. This requires an awareness of the history of and conditions in the country of origin, understanding of the role of culture and religion and spirituality in the person's life, the pre-migration experience, the migration journey, and the settlement challenges. Supportive listening, attention to practical concerns, and advocacy create the basis for responding to the concerns of most people, and an emphasis on a problem-solving approach is viewed to be more helpful than an emotion-focused approach.[54] Rather than psychological counselling, immigrants and refugees may benefit more from reassurance, practical and financial assistance such as employment, negotiating banking and transportation, and finding adequate housing.

Talk therapies and disclosing personal information to a stranger is not done in many cultures. For those who have experienced trauma, the trauma story needs time to emerge and should not be pursued. A trusting relationship is imperative in order to effectively respond to the distress that disclosure may produce. Clients may report anxiety, somatic symptoms, and flashbacks or grief in response to loss. However, not every symptom warrants treatment and "there is a risk of pathologizing and medicalizing an otherwise normal human response to extreme adversity...."[55] It has also been found that a person may respond to a crisis in three different ways: as a threat, as a loss, or as a challenge.[56] A focus on the inherent strength, resiliency, and resourcefulness of immigrant populations, as well as their material, social, and personal concerns, will contribute to empowerment.[57]

A youth-led, community-based participatory action research project directed at addressing the violence among the Oromo young people in Toronto provides an excellent example of an empowering process in which youth viewed a crisis in the community as a challenge, identified their own needs, and developed their own strategies for change. In the findings alienation was a common theme, and it was closely connected to four forms of invisible violence:

> a) the violence of dislocation and the ensuing alienation from the homeland and its socio-cultural resources; b) the violence of poverty and racism and the ensuing alienation from mainstream Canada and its multicultural global community; c) intergenerational violence and the ensuing alienation from families and communities; d) intra-generational violence and the ensuing alienation from peers; and intra-personal violence and the consequent alienation of youth from their own sense of self.[58]

The community healing was youth-driven and focused on addressing the alienation in all of its facets; it thereby helped integrate youth into their families, community, and peer group. Central to the healing was an understanding of how the young Oromo and their families had fled violence and persecution in Ethiopia and the trauma that they experienced. The findings have relevance for other newcomers to Canada.

THE ROLE OF SPIRITUALITY AND RELIGION

Social work has its origins in church-based social welfare and gradually became secularized as the state assumed the role of social protector. As outlined in Chapter 3, during these early years, the radical social gospellers led the struggle to eliminate class exploitation. Since secularization of social work, perhaps liberation theology was the first to reintroduce and incorporate religion in social work. The writings of Paulo Friere and Gustavo Gutiérrez with their emphasis on spiritual as well as social, political, and economic liberation have informed social work approaches. Liberation theology served as "a catalyst, as a salient ideology and a practical methodology for many grassroots workers, community organizers, educators, health care professionals, church workers, social workers and others concerned with human empowerment." It stressed liberation from all forms of oppression "social, economic, political, racial, sexual, environmental, military and religious."[59]

Even though the radical nature of liberation theology is not evident in the practice of many religions today, there are those who believe in the potential of religions to contribute to social change. Knitter quotes Marx: "Religion is the sigh of the oppressed creature, the heart of a heartless world ... the spirit of a spiritless situation. It is the opium of the people." While he acknowledges that it can be and has been escapist opium, Knitter suggests that "it can also be revolutionary dynamite. It can be as Marx suspected, 'the spirit' that works to deal with and overcome 'a spiritless situation.'"[60]

Along with being multiracial and multiethnic, the US and Canada are also multireligious. While there are clients who are agnostics or atheists, social workers need to be ready to consider the relevance of a client's religion and/or spirituality.[61] The task is complex: there are 19 major world religions subdivided into 270 large religious groups.[62]

As far as religions, Islam has been misinterpreted and harshly judged by the media. After 9/11 there was a rise in Islamophobia and racist attitudes and fears regarding Muslims in both Canada and the US. Muslims are now victims of racial profiling, unwarranted arrests, and imprisonments. Seldom is it acknowledged that Christian, Jewish, and Islamic religions have the same roots and share more similarities than differences.[63] While attention is placed on Muslim fundamentalism, there is less focus on the parallel rise in Christian, Jewish, and Hindu fundamentalisms. Haroon Siddiqui, columnist at the *Toronto Star*, reminds us that the main problems facing Muslims are not religious, but rather "they are geopolitical, economic and social—problems that have caused widespread Muslim despair and in some cases, militancy, both of which are expressed in the religious terminology that Muslim masses relate to." This reality is not discussed in the press and the "ongoing inhumane treatment and deaths of hundreds of thousands of Muslims in the Israeli Occupied Territories, Chechnya, Kashmir, Iraq and Afghanistan are not worthy of political or editorial outrage."[64]

David Hodge points out that Muslims are one of the most misunderstood populations in the US and offers one of the first contributions in the social work literature on the beliefs, practices, and values guiding those who practice Islam. He provides a useful summary of the tenets of Islam and the diversity within the Muslim population and refutes many stereotypes presented in the press. Community is a fundamental value, and Hodge explains how "Muslims tend to emphasize benevolence, care for others, cooperation between individuals, empathy, equality and justice between people, the importance of social support, and positive human relatedness."[65] Other social work contributions to working with Muslim clients includes the first textbook dedicated solely to spiritually and culturally sensitive social work among Muslim families who have settled in Europe.[66] For Muslim clients diversity is also based "on geographic background, level of acculturation in North America, and Sunni versus Shi'a versus Ismaili traditions along with differences in religiosity, socio-economic status, gender, and other social constructs that intersect with faith."[67]

National surveys indicate that people in the US are among the most religious in the world, while Europeans, Australians, and Canadians are more secular. Eighty-five per cent of Americans reported that religion was important in their lives compared to 17 per cent of Canadians.[68] However, if someone states that they are not religious, it does not mean that they are not spiritual. The centrality of religion and/or spirituality in a person's life will vary.

In recent years, there has been increasing attention to the importance of spirituality and a spiritually sensitive social work practice, often as part of cultural competence.[69] The religious congregation contributes to refugee integration and resettlement. Along with sponsorship and offering sanctuary when needed, churches provide concrete settlement services and a close network of supportive relationships.[70] Spiritual competence is an ongoing process that includes an awareness of one's own spiritual world-view and values, understanding the spiritual world-view of clients, and effectively incorporating this awareness in practice responses.[71]

Spirituality, according to Canda and Furman, refers "to a universal quality of human beings and their cultures related to the quest for meaning, purpose, morality, transcendence, well-being, and profound relationships with ourselves, others, and ultimate reality."[72] Canda, one of the pioneers in the inclusion of spirituality in social work practice, views it as an essential process of human life development and the search for meaning and purpose.[73] For Canda, transpersonal experiences are diverse and "may be related to God, Brahman, Buddha nature, cosmic consciousness and connections with ancestors, spirit powers of nature, angels, and demons."[74] In his view, spirituality includes and transcends religion and, along with theistic, may be non-theistic, or animistic.

The inclusion of spirituality in social work includes such diverse practices as "holistic bio-psych-social-spiritual assessment; religious community mutual supports; prayer; meditation; dream reflection; spiritual journaling; subtle energy work; rituals; utilizing spiritually based helpers and healers—including

clergy, monks, shamans, through referral and collaboration; and other complementary and alternative therapies."[75] However, it is unclear how a social
worker would actually incorporate and evaluate the effectiveness of such practices. Compared to liberation theology, the emphasis in spirituality has been
more toward the individual subjective experience. The inclusion of the body-
mind-spirit connection has been combined with the holistic system of thought
of Eastern philosophies such as Taoism (Daoism) and Buddhism.[76] However,
these approaches, as described by Canda above, for the most part disregard an
analysis of the structural conditions that may be contributing to personal stress
and hardship. This is in contrast to liberation theology and Paulo Friere's focus
on the economic, social, and political conditions that oppress people, as discussed in Chapter 8.

Indigenous communities in Canada and the US draw on spirituality, medicines, and ceremonies that have historically been part of their well-being and
healing. Michael Hart views spirituality as distinct from religion and describes
it as "a defining feature of Indigenous ways of life and concerns the relationships
between people and the land and their surrounding environment as well as
between one another and the self. Spirituality is central to an Aboriginal
approach to helping and all aspects of Indigenous life."[77]

Despite the recent attention to religion, research indicates that social workers
are disproportionately secular and hold non-theistic, personally constructed
world-views.[78] Social workers who have no religious affiliation may identify
themselves as atheists or humanists. In a comparative survey of social workers
in New Zealand and Britain, Stirling and colleagues found that social workers
in both countries were cautious about incorporating religion and spirituality
in practice and felt ill-equipped to do so. New Zealand social workers had a
higher appreciation of spirituality, likely a result of the importance of spirituality
for the indigenous population.[79] Other than including a respect for and appreciation of spiritual diversity and its importance in the lives of clients, more
research is needed about what social workers actually do in regards to spirituality
when working with clients.

Increasingly, social workers will be assisting newcomers to Canada and
expected to be prepared to effectively respond to complex settlement concerns.
In order to do so, they need to prepare to respond with knowledge of refugee
and immigrant categories and culturally sensitive practices as they assess the
structural factors that influence the quality of life of their clients.

NOTES

1 Statistics Canada, *Projections of the Diversity of the Canadian Population 2006–2031*
(2010), http://www.statcan.gc.ca/pub/91-551-x/91-551-x2010001-eng.pdf.

2 Brodie Fenlon, "Canada's Visible Minorities Top Five Million," *The Globe and Mail*, 2 April 2008, http://license.icopyright.net/user/viewFreeUse.act?fuid=MTQyMjQ1NDQ %3D.

3 Citizen and Immigration Canada, "Government of Canada Will Welcome More Economic Immigrants in 2010," News Release (26 June 2010), http://www.cic.gc.ca/english/department /media/releases/2010/2010-06-26.asp.

4 Citizen and Immigration Canada, "Facts and Figures 2009—Immigration Overview: Permanent and Temporary Residents," http://www.cic.gc.ca/english/resources/statistics /facts2009.

5 *New York Times*, "Immigration and Emigration," 29 September 2011, http://topics.nytimes .com/top/reference/timestopics/subjects/i/immigration-and-emigration/index.html.

6 Sam Roberts, "1 in 5 Americans Have Close Ties Elsewhere," *New York Times*, 19 October 2010, http://www.nytimes.com/2010/10/20/us/20brfs-1IN5AMERICAN_BRF.html.

7 Susan Saulny, "Race Remixed; In a Multiracial Nation, Many Ways to Tally," *New York Times*, 10 February 2011, http://query.nytimes.com/gst/fullpage.html?res=9E01E5DA1E3BF 933A25751C0A9679D8B63&pagewanted=all.

8 Kathleen Valtonen, *Social Work and Migration: Immigrant and Refugee Settlement and Integration* (Surrey, UK: Ashgate, 2008) 15.

9 Miu Chung Yan and Serman Chan, "Are Social Workers Ready to Work with Newcomers?," *Canadian Social Work* 12.1 (2010): 22.

10 Mary Nash, "Responding to Settlement Needs: Migrants and Refugees and Community Development," *Social Work Theories in Action*, ed. Mary Nash, Robyn Munford, and Kieran O'Donoghue (London: Jessica Kingsley, 2005) 140.

11 See, e.g., Cheryl Regehr and Karima Kanani, "Chapter 8: Immigration and Refugee Law," in *Essential Law for Social Work Practice in Canada* (Don Mills, ON: Oxford University Press, 2006).

12 UNHCR, "Number of Forcibly Displaced Rises to 43.3 Million Last Year, the Highest Level Since mid-1990s" (15 June 2010), http://www.unhcr.org/print/4c176c969.html.

13 United Nations, Refugee Convention (1951), http://www.unhcr.se/SE/Protect_refugees /pdf/magaine.pdf.

14 Valtonen, *Social Work and Migration* 23.

15 Citizenship and Immigration Canada, "Facts and Figures 2009"; Citizen and Immigration Canada, "Facts and Figures 2008."

16 Natalie A. Chambers and Soma Ganesan, "Refugees in Canada," in *Cross Cultural Caring*, 2nd ed., ed. Nancy Waxler-Morrison, Joan M. Anderson, Elizabeth Richardson, and Natalie A. Chambers (Vancouver: University of British Columbia Press, 2005) 289–321.

17 Soojin Yu, Estelle Ouelette, and Angelun Warmington, "Refugee Integration in Canada: A Survey of Empirical Evidence and Existing Services," *Refuge* 24.2 (2007): 17–34.

18 As of January 2010, 225 of the 380 men and 57 of the 63 woman were released; however, the releases were stayed due to the government appealing the decision. Forty-nine children remain detained with their parents. There are also concerns that other members of the Tamil minority will seek asylum in Canada. Their plight and fear of persecution and torture if they return to their homeland appears lost in the discussions. See *Ottawa Citizen*, "Canada New Base of Tamil Tigers," 18 January 2011: A1 and A2.

19 Ashley Bradimore and Harald Bauer, *Mystery Ships and Risky Boat People: Tamil Refugee Migration in the Newsprint Media*, Working Paper Series (Vancouver: Metropolis British Columbia Centre of Excellence for Research on Immigration and Diversity, January 2011) 10; also at http://riim.metropolis.net/wp_2011.html.

20 Jennifer Pagliaro and Jill Mahoney, "Ontario Loses as Immigration Funds Shifted," *Globe and Mail*, 24 December 2010: A3. It is estimated that the cuts to Ontario alone will be more than $43 million.

21 Valtonen, *Social Work and Migration* 62.

22 Chambers and Ganesan, "Refugees in Canada."

23 Mikkonen and Raphael, *Social Determinants of Health* 32.

24 Chambers and Ganesan, "Refugees in Canada."

25 Statistics Canada, "Educational Portrait of Canada," Census 2006 (March 2008), http://www12.statcan.ca/census-recensement/2006/as-sa/97-560/index-eng.cfm?CFID=3697050&CFTOKEN=14405636.

26 Senate Standing Committee on Social Affairs, Science and Technology, *Out of the Shadows at Last: Transforming Mental Health, Mental Illness, and Addiction Services in Canada* (Ottawa: Statistics Canada, May 2006) 48.

27 Gada Mahrouse, "'Reasonable Accommodation' in Quebec: The Limits of Participation and Dialogue," *Race and Class* 52.1 (2010): 85 and 89.

28 Alean Al-Krenawi and John R. Graham, "Social Work Practice with Canadians of Arab Background: Insight into Direct Practice," in *Multicultural Social Work in Canada*, ed. Alean Al-Krenawi and John R. Graham (Don Mills, ON: Oxford University Press, 2003) 174–201.

29 Raymond C.Y. Chung and Maria Lo, "Mental Health and Migration: Journey to Promote Mental Health," *INSCAN* 23.4 (2010): 7–9.

30 Kevin Pottie, Peter Tugwell, J. Freightner, Vivian Welch, Christine Grenaway, H. Swinkels, Meb Rashid, Lavanya Narasiah, Lawrence Kirmayer, Erin Ueffing, and N. MacDonald, "Summary of Clinical Preventative Care Recommendations for Newly Arriving Immigrants and Refugees to Canada," Canadian Collaboration for Immigrant and Refugee Health, *CMAJ* (2010): 1–12, http://www.cmaj.ca/content/early/2010/06/07/cmaj.090313.full.pdf+html.

31 Mikkonen and Raphael, *Social Determinants of Health* 32.

32 Chambers and Ganesan, "Refugees in Canada."

33 Mina Fazel, Jeremy Wheeler, and John Danesh, "Prevalence of Serious Mental Disorder in 7000 Refugees in Western Countries: A Systematic Review," *The Lancet* 35 (9 April 2005): 1309–14.

34 Nancy Farwell, "In War's Wake," *International Journal of Mental Health* 32.4 (Winter 2003–04): 21.

35 Ibrahim A. Kira, Asha Ahmed, Vanessa Mahmoud, and Fatima Wassim, "Group Therapy Model for Refugee and Torture Survivors," *Torture* 20.2 (2010): 108–13.

36 Celia Falicov, "Working with Transnational Immigrants: Expanding Meanings of Family, Community, and Culture," *Family Process* 46.2 (2007): 166.

37 Centre for Human Rights, *Human Rights and Social Work*.

38 Peter Magnus, "Preparation for Social Work Students to do Cross-cultural Clinical Practice," *International Social Work* 52.3 (2009): 377.

39 National Association of Social Workers, "Cultural Competence in Social Work Profession," in *Social Work Speak: NASW Policy Statements* 2000–2003, 5th ed. (Washington, DC: NASW, 2000); National Association of Social Workers, *Indicators for the Achievement of the NASW Standards for Cultural Competence in Social Work Practice* (Washington, DC: NASW, 2007), cited in Clara Simmons, Leticia Diaz, Vivian Jackson, and Rita Takahashi, "NASW Cultural Competence Indicators: A New Tool for the Social Work Profession," *Journal of Ethnic and Cultural Diversity in Social Work* 17.1 (2008): 4–20.

40 Paula Allen-Meares, "Cultural Competence: An Ethical Requirement," *Journal of Ethnic and Cultural Diversity in Social Work* 16.3/4 (2007): 87–88.

41 Simmons et al., "NASW Cultural Competence Indicators" 9.

42 Miu Ha Kwong, "Applying Cultural Competency in Clinical Practice: Findings from Multicultural Experts' Experience," *Journal of Ethnic and Cultural Diversity in Social Work* 18 (2009): 159.

43 M.C. Yan and Y.R. Wong, "Rethinking Self-awareness in Cultural Competence: Toward a Dialogic Self in Cross-cultural Social Work," *Families in Society* 86 (2005): 181–88.

44 Hilary N. Weaver, "Social Work through an Indigenous Lens: Reflections on the State of our Profession," in *Social Work: Making a World of Difference*, ed. Nigel Hall (n.p.: IFSW and FAFO, 2006) 37–51.

45 Ruby C.M. Chau, Sam W.K. Yu, and Cam T.L. Tran, "The Diversity Based Approach to Culturally Sensitive Practices," *International Social Work* 54.1 (2011): 21.

46 Wanda Bernard and Veronica Marsman, "The Association of Black Social Workers (ABSW): A Model of Empowerment Practice," in *Structural Social Work in Action*, ed. Steven F. Hick, Heather I. Peters, Tammy Corner, and Tracy London (Toronto: Canadian Scholar's Press, 2010) 193. See also David Este and Wanda Bernard, "Social Work Practice with African Canadians: An Examination of the African Nova Scotian Community," in *Multicultural Social Work in Canada*, ed. Alean Al-Krenawi and John R. Graham (Don Mills, ON: Oxford University Press, 2003) 306–37.

47 Kwong, "Applying Cultural Competency in Clinical Practice" 164.

48 Emily Rian and David R. Hodge, "Developing Cultural Competency with Mandaean Clients: Synchronizing Practice with the Light World," *International Social Work* 53.4 (2010): 542–55.

49 Gordon Pon, "Cultural Competency as a New Racism: An Ontology of Forgetting," *Journal of Progressive Human Services* 20.1 (2009): 60.

50 Yvonne M. Johnson and Shari Munch, "Fundamental Contradictions in Cultural Competence," *Social Work* 54.3 (July 2009): 229.

51 Frank Kortman, "Transcultural Psychiatry: From Practice to Theory," *Transcultural Psychiatry* 47.2 (2010): 203–23.

52 Nancy Waxler-Morrison, Joan M. Anderson, Elizabeth Richardson, and Natalie A. Chambers, eds., *Cross Cultural Caring*, 2nd ed. (Vancouver: University of British Columbia Press, 2005); Alean Al-Krenawi and John R. Graham, eds., *Multicultural Social Work in Canada* (Don Mills, ON: Oxford University Press, 2003).

53 Nash, "Responding to Settlement Needs."

54 Tom Craig, Peter Jaujua, and Nasir Warfa, "Mental Healthcare Needs of Refugees," *Psychiatry* 5.11 (2006): 405–08.

55 Craig, Jaujua, and Warfa, " Mental Healthcare Needs of Refugees" 407.

56 Christina Hoff Sommers and Sally Satel, *One Nation under Therapy* (New York: St. Martin's Press, 2005).

57 Izumi Sakamoto, "A Critical Examination of Immigrant Acculturation: Toward and Anti-oppressive Social Work Model with Immigrant Adults in a Pluralistic Society," *British Journal of Social Work* 37 (2007): 515–35.

58 Martha Kuwee Kumsa, "Wounds of the Gut, Wounds of the Soul": Youth Violence and Community Healing among the Oromos in Toronto," *Canadian Social Work* 12.1 (2010): 124.

59 Estalla Norwood Evans, "Liberation Theology, Empowerment Theory and Social Work Practice with the Oppressed," *International Social Work* 35.2 (1992): 135–36, 139.

60 Paul F. Knitter, "Social Work and Religious Diversity: Problems and Possibilities," *Journal of Religion and Spirituality in Social Work* 29 (2010): 269.

61 Knitter, "Social Work and Religious Diversity" 256–70.

62 Zulema E. Suarez and Edith A Lewis, "Spirituality and Culturally Diverse Families: The Intersection of Culture, Religion, and Spirituality," in *Multicultural Perspectives in Working with Families*, 2nd ed., ed. Elaine P. Congress and Manny J. Gonzales (New York: Springer, 2005) 425–41.

63 Saxby Pridmore and Mohamed Iqbal Pasha, "Psychiatry and Islam," *Australasian Psychiatry* 12.4 (2004): 380–85.

64 Haroon Siddiqui, *Being Muslim* (Toronto: House of Anansi Press, 2006) 27–28.

65 David R. Hodge, "Social Work and the House of Islam: Orienting Practitioners to the Beliefs and Values of Muslims in the United States," *Social Work* 50.2 (April 2005): 165.

66 Sara Ashencaen, Fatima Husain, and Basia Spalek, *Islam and Social Work: Debating Values, Transforming Practice* (Bristol, UK: The Policy Press, 2008).

67 John R. Graham, Cathryn Bradshaw, and Jennifer L. Trew, "Cultural Considerations for Social Service Agencies Working with Muslim Clients," *Social Work* 55.4 (October 2010): 337.

68 Froma Walsh, "Spiritual Diversity: Multifaith Perspectives in Family Therapy," *Family Process* 49.3 (2010): 330–48.

69 See for example the Directory of International Contacts and Social Work and Spiritual Diversity at http://www.socwel.ku.edu/canda. As early as 1990 The National Society for Spirituality and Social Work was founded in the US, and the first international conference of the Society took place in 2000. In 2002 the Canadian Society for Spirituality and Social Work was formed with John Coates as Director.

70 Nicole Ives and Jill Witmer Sinha, "The Religious Congregation as Partner in Refugee Settlement," *Canadian Social Work* 12.1 (2010): 210–17.

71 David R. Hodge and Suzanne Bushfield, "Developing Spiritual Competence in Practice," *Journal of Ethnic and Cultural Diversity in Social Work* 15.3/4 (2006): 101–27.

72 Edward R. Canda and Leola Dyrud Furman, *Spiritual Diversity in Social Work Practice: The Heart of Helping*, 2nd ed. (New York: Oxford University Press, 2010).

73 Edward R. Canda, "Spiritually Sensitive Social Work: An Overview of American and International Trends," Plenary Address to the International Conference on Social Work and Counseling Practice, City University of Hong Kong, China, (2009) 1–19.

74 Edward R. Canda, "Spiritual Connection in Social Work: Boundary Violations and Creating Common Ground," Key Note Address to the First North American Conference on Spirituality and Social Work, Renison College, University of Waterloo, Waterloo, Ontario (25–27 May 2006) 25.

75 Canda, "Spiritual Connection in Social Work" 40.

76 Mo Yee Lee, Siu-Man Ng, Pamela Pui Yu Leung, and Cecilia Lai Wan Chan, *Integrative Body-Mind-Spirit Social Work* (New York: Oxford University Press, 2009); Steven F. Hick, ed., *Mindfulness and Social Work* (Chicago: Lyceum, 2009).

77 Michael Anthony Hart, "Critical Reflections on an Aboriginal Approach to Helping," in *Indigenous Social Work around the World: Toward Culturally Relevant Education and Practice*, ed. Mel Gray, John Coates, and Michael Yellow Bird (Burlington, VT: Ashgate, 2008) 136.

78 Hodge and Bushfield, "Developing Spiritual Competence in Practice."

79 Blair Stirling, Leola Dyrud Furman, Perry W. Benson, Edward R. Canda, and Cordelia Grimwood, "A Comparative Survey of Aotearoa New Zealand and UK Social Workers on the Role of Religion and Spirituality in Practice," *British Journal of Social Work* 40 (2010): 602–21.

CHAPTER 10

SOCIAL WORK PRACTICE IN MENTAL HEALTH

OCIAL WORK IS A KEY PROFESSION in the delivery of services concerning mental health and addictions. Whether social workers are situated in hospitals, seniors' homes, community centres, or family or youth service agencies, they will be helping people with complex mental health and addiction problems. While for most people these concerns will be alleviated by short-term counselling, others may involve more extensive care and a referral to a psychiatrist. In order to provide effective and relevant help it is essential that social workers are aware of the impact of stress on a person's mental health and have a basic knowledge of the general diagnostic categories, psychopharmacology, and practice responses. Equally important is an awareness of the limitations and critiques of the psychiatric approach to restoring mental well-being. This chapter focuses on mental health concerns within a structural context, includes an examination of major conditions and pharmaceutical treatment, and offers some thoughts on social work responses.

UNDERSTANDING THE STRESS/DISEASE CONNECTION

Harsh material and social living conditions and conflictual relationships are known to contribute to high levels of stress. Stress in turn has a close connection to mental and physical health. Research indicates that there are three factors that universally lead to stress: uncertainty, the lack of information, and loss of control. While most stress is thought to be emotional, the impact is also physical. Dr. Gabor Maté, a Vancouver-based physician, in his book *When the Body Says No: The Hidden Cost of Stress*, explains that stress has three components. The first is the event, physical or emotional, that the body interprets as threatening—the stress stimulus or stressor. The second is the "processing system"—the nervous system, in particular the brain—that interprets the meaning of the stressor. Finally there is the stress response, the physiological and behavioural reactions to the perceived threat.[1] Stress can be the result of severe deprivation of basic human needs; interpersonal conflict in the home, workplace, or community; loss of employment; death of a loved one; or chronic illness.

The impact of prolonged stress on the body's hormonal, immune, and digestive system is well-documented. For example, in depressed people the adrenal gland secretes higher doses of cortisol that can contribute to gastric ulcers. Elevated adrenal levels raise the blood pressure and damage the heart. Chronic stress inhibits the immune system, making a person more susceptible to acute and chronic disease. All too often, those under duress turn to non-healthy coping mechanisms. Maté explains how adverse childhood experiences, such as conflict, violence and/or addiction in the home, or the stress of poverty, place a child at risk of turning to drug addiction. The likelihood is dramatic; a child with six such adverse childhood experiences has an astounding 4,600 per cent increase (or 46-fold) in the risk of turning to injection drugs.[2]

Stress is prevalent in society and is closely connected to one's employment status. Countless men and women faced not only job loss but no prospects for work after the massive Deep Horizon oil spill in the Gulf of Mexico on 20 April 2010, one of the worst environmental disasters in the US, whose destruction is extending to other states and perhaps other nearby nations. A social worker reports that the biggest source of stress for her clients so far is the uncertainty about how much oil will end up in the Gulf and how much damage will be done to the fishery and other wildlife. The livelihood of the coastal population is jeopardized, and fishermen walk around aimless. Adam, a 53-year-old life-long resident of Louisiana who worked on a shrimp boat exclaimed with rising anger, "I got no clue what I am going to do with the rest of my life, and they want to give me a $250 cheque? A kick in the ass, and get the hell out of here? And they (messed) up my waters?" Concern regarding the increasing widespread despair is warranted. After the 1989 Exxon Valdez oil spill in Alaska there was an increase in suicides, violence in the home, and the overuse of alcohol.[3]

Closer to home, workers at INCO in Sudbury, Ontario, now owned by the Brazilian multinational company Vale SA, recently signed a contract after the longest strike in the company's history. For close to a year the workers stood up against a global entity in an attempt to prevent the rollback of previous gains already fought for and won (see the discussion in Chapter 1, p. 19). During labour disputes and strikes, the stress of lost income and the struggle to protect one's rights are felt by the whole family.

The centrality of employment cannot be underestimated. Job loss produces both uncertainty and a loss of control of one's life. Employment not only provides an income but also a sense of purpose and an identity. Mikkonen and Raphael consider the impact of not working and conclude that "Unemployment frequently leads to material and social deprivation, psychological stress, and the adoption of health-threatening coping behaviours."[4] These behaviours include physical and mental health problems, such as depression, alcohol and other drug overuse, anxiety, and increased suicide rates.

Aside from employment, research indicates that the experience of racism can result in anxiety, depression, lowered self-esteem, and a negative identity—all of which have an impact on mental health.[5] The exploration of the context of a person's life and their day-to-day experiences is vital in understanding the role of stress in producing and maintaining symptoms categorized as mental illness. This includes an awareness of the influence of the social determinants of health on one's health as outlined in Chapter 2.

MENTAL HEALTH CONCERNS

In a recent report, the WHO estimates that one in four people globally will experience mental health concerns in their lifetime. The report provides evidence that poor mental health is both a cause and a consequence of poverty, limited opportunities for education, gender inequality, and violence.[6] Persons with mental health concerns are a vulnerable group and often experience stigmatization, social exclusion, ongoing insecurity, and deprivation. Attention to mental health is one of the most neglected issues in achieving the UN Millennium Development Goals.

In 2006 The Senate Standing Committee on Social Affairs, Science and Technology released their report *Out of the Shadows*, the summary of a comprehensive exploration of mental health, mental illness, and addiction services in Canada. More than 2,000 submissions provide a snapshot of both the hardship people experience as well as their resilience and fortitude.[7]

The numbers alone are striking: an estimated 15 per cent (1.2 million) of Canadian children and youth are living with anxiety, attention deficit disorder, depression, or addictions; 20 per cent of seniors are living with mental illness, and 80 to 90 per cent of those living in nursing homes have mental illness or some form of cognitive impairment. Findings indicate that medication alone is not as successful as a combination of psychotherapy and medication.

Regrettably social workers, despite their active role, often are not considered to be key professionals in the area of mental health. Ann-Marie O'Brien and Kimberly Calderwood examined the findings of a survey of 339 mental health social workers in Ontario and conclude that "despite social workers' apparent contribution, significant challenges keep social work practice in the shadows of other mental health professionals."[8] They point out that since the regulation of social workers in Ontario falls under the provincial Ministry of Community and Social Services and not the Ministry of Health and Long-term Care that oversees the Regulated Health Professions Act, social workers are not recognized as regulated health professionals. Yet social workers are found at all levels of health care provision. Of the survey respondents, 20 per cent worked in in-patient settings, 28 per cent in out-patient settings, while 31 per cent were in community-based programs. Social workers' primary role is to provide assessment and referral, counselling, crisis intervention, discharge planning, and advocacy. Cheryl Regehr and Graham Glancy's recent book *Mental Health Social Work Practice in Canada* is comprehensive in its coverage of social work practice in the field of mental health.[9]

THE DIAGNOSTIC AND STATISTICAL MANUAL OF MENTAL DISORDERS (DSM)

Social work responses to mental health concerns, whether in community centres, family service agencies, or hospitals, are frequently framed within a medical model. Diagnosis by physicians follows the immensely influential American Psychiatric Association's *Diagnostic and Statistical Manual of Mental Disorders* (4th edition, also known as the DSM-IV-TR, Text Revisions). In 1980 the DSM-III introduced the multiaxial assessment system for understanding individual and social concerns and the classification of symptoms into disorders. The assessment is based on five axes that summarize the issues the client is facing. Axis I indicates clinical problems or disorders such as substance abuse or schizophrenia; Axis II summarizes any personality disorders/disturbances or mental retardation; Axis III lists clinically relevant general medical conditions; Axis IV addresses psychosocial and social environmental problems such as stress and lack of support or personal resources; and Axis V rates global assessment of functioning (GAF) on a scale of 1 to 10 where 10 indicates the highest functioning.[10] The primary or principal diagnosis is noted, whether in Axis I or II. All diagnoses are indicated with a standard code. While Allen Frances, a renowned US psychiatrist, supports dimensional diagnosis, he points out that rushed clinicians do not take enough time and that Axis V is often ignored.[11]

While acknowledging the limitations of such a prescriptive psychiatric model and a manual such as the DSM, social workers ought to be aware of the diagnostic categories and terminology utilized. The DSM has acquired prominence because it is the key to insurance coverage and reimbursement by private, provincial, and state programs. Still, the medical model with emphasis on individual deficiency or disease comes in conflict with social work approaches that consider structural factors in the production and maintenance of such concerns. Not surprising, a "pathology-ridden perspective" and the increased medicalization of relatively normal feelings and responses to extreme adversity and life stressors have come under challenge.[12]

The Sickening of Society

As the number of disorders increase and their definitions broaden, there is growing concern that normal behaviour may be too quickly pathologized. Since 1952, when the first DSM was published as a 132-page spiral-bound booklet containing 128 disorders, the current DSM-IV-TR has grown to over 900 pages and lists 365 disorders.[13] Some contend that this is the result of the increasing pathologizing of everyday behaviour and particularly of "those in our society who are powerless or undesirable; this occurs not because of any malicious intent but because of unspoken cultural biases about what should be considered normal and what should be considered disease."[14]

This is particularly worrisome since there is speculation that the fifth edition (DSM-V) will further expand the definitions for current conditions while adding new ones. Dr. Allen Frances, the chair of the task force for the current edition of the DSM, is highly critical of the DSM-V to be released in 2013. He clearly outlines the potential impact, risk, and unintended consequences of the inclusion of many new categories and argues that the result will be "a wholesale imperial medicalization of normality" and a "bonanza for the pharmaceutical industry."[15] This diagnostic inflation and shrinking of the normal will result in a dramatic increase in people diagnosed with a mental disorder and prescribed unnecessary mood-altering drugs. Among those conditions to be added are normal grief, non-suicidal self injury, hoarding disorder, and a series of so-called behavioural addictions to shopping, sex, food, and videogames.[16]

Attention Deficit Disorder (ADD) and Attention Deficit Hyperactivity Disorder (ADHD) are among the most commonly diagnosed disorders in children. In North America diagnosis rates are higher than other Western countries. Approximately 7 to 10 per cent of children are diagnosed with ADHD in Canada, and they are mainly boys who appear to be hyperactive and to have difficulty focusing, the core features of ADHD. In 2009 more than 2 million prescriptions were written for children under 17 with ADHD, 75 per cent for boys, an increase of 43 per cent since 2005. There is growing concern that we are pathologizing childhood, particularly boyhood. Gordon Floyd, CEO of Children's Mental Health in Ontario, voices his concern: "When we see a high energy youngster, we jump to put the label on. An assessment would look much deeper."[17]

Gabor Maté is equally troubled regarding the increase in ADD and the chemical control of children's behaviour. He notes that the 3 million youth in the US that are on stimulant medication and the half-a-million who are on anti-psychotics are exhibiting "the effects of severe stress, increasing stress in our society, on the parenting environment. Not bad parenting. Extremely stressed parenting, because of social and economic conditions." He explains that ADD is a problem of brain development and what is needed is a nurturing environment and non-stressed and emotionally available parents for children so that they can develop those brain circuits.[18] All behaviour is the result of a complex interaction among biological, psychological, social, and material factors.

Change to the DSM and the decisions to include, revise, or eliminate disorders occur within a social and political context and frequently reflect changing societal norms. For example, as a result of the gay liberation movement, homosexuality was eliminated as a disorder in the DSM-III, and this change demonstrated that whether or not a condition is included in the DSM can be based on values and beliefs rather than science.[19] This may also be the case for the current position on transgender. Social workers have been challenging the pathologizing of transgenderism as a gender identity disorder in the DSM.[20]

Post-Traumatic Stress Disorder

Post-traumatic stress disorder (PTSD), a widely used diagnosis, is an example of the impact of expanding the criteria for diagnosis. PTSD, initially called post-Vietnam syndrome, emerged as a result of political mobilization by veterans. In 1970 returning Vietnam veterans were dealing with the impact of witnessing the atrocities of war and lobbied to have their symptoms recognized and compensated. Their experiences resulted in the eventual inclusion of PTSD as a category in the 1980 DSM-III and expanded the diagnosis to include severe accidents, natural disasters, and rape.[21] Sommers and Satel caution that despite all of the revisions and the wide application, the condition is not inevitable following a catastrophic event. They point out that the returning veterans from the Persian Gulf War did not present with the symptoms of PTSD but instead with depression, weight loss, and insomnia, and they attributed these symptoms to exposure to biological and chemical agents.

Over the years, the diagnosis of PTSD has undergone a number of changes: 11 changes in the 1987 DSM-III and 15 changes to the 1994 DSM-IV, all expanding the criteria for diagnosis. In the 1994 DSM hearing about the unexpected death of a loved one or receiving a diagnosis of a fatal disease were added to the range of events qualifying as traumatic.[22] Some disagree with the broader inclusion that now applies to those who experience intimate violence and who witness disastrous events. More and more the price of seeking help is to be labeled with a mental disorder and provided with a pharmaceutical solution. Kutchins and Kirk in their book *Making Us Crazy, DSM: The Psychiatric Bible and the Creation of Mental Disorders* claim that "It is a disservice to victims to give them a diagnosis because they are suffering from the after effects of trauma."[23] Similarly, soldiers returning from combat with a diagnosis of PTSD find that frequently emotions such as anger and frustration are placed in the biopsychosocial realm, not a political one. Still, in the Canadian forces it has become acceptable to have an operational stress injury or PTSD, but it is not acceptable to have ordinary depression.[24]

The current diagnostic criteria for PTSD (code 309.81) as adapted from the 2000 DSM-IV-TR is summarized below:

   A. the exposure to a traumatic event where "the person experienced, witnessed or was confronted with an event or events that involved actual or threatened death or serious injury, or a threat to the physical integrity of self or others" and "the person's response involved intense fear, helplessness, or horror";
   B. the event is "persistently re-experienced" (often dreams, images, thoughts or perceptions) and severe anxiety when reminded of the event;
   C. efforts to avoid activities, place or people that are associated with the event, emotional numbness, social withdrawal, and;
   D. persistent symptoms of increased arousal, hypervigilance, irritability, difficulty sleeping or concentrating.[25]

The duration of the criteria in B, C, and D is more than one month. Along with symptoms, a person must experience incapacitation or intense emotional pain, fear, or helplessness. Delayed onset of symptoms can occur at least six months after the stressful event.

It is widely recognized that there is a high rate of PTSD among refugees since traumatic events such as threatened death or serious injury are common experiences. However, recovery from PTSD may be closely connected to settlement factors. For example, a study of 19 Convention Refugees concluded that a positive outcome for the appearance before the Immigrant and Refugee Board of Canada related to reduced symptoms of PTSD in the claimants.[26]

Since PTSD was added to the DSM in 1980, it has become the standard response to any psychological trauma, and now the diagnosis of PTSD is being widely applied in many situations,[27] including practitioners who provide help to traumatized clients. In a study of secondary traumatic stress among social workers, Bride concludes that 15.2 per cent met the diagnostic criteria for PTSD.[28] There is a growing literature on "vicarious traumatization" of those in the helping professions who work with victims of violence and who have developed symptoms of PTSD as a result.[29]

For many, the diagnostic category has offered legitimacy—"a name"—to the disabling psychological and physical symptoms following traumatic events. The challenge is to be cautious and not assume that all who experience trauma have PTSD.

Considering Gender and Culture

Gai Harrison and Rose Melville point out that the use of standardized classification systems such as the DSM have the potential to over-diagnose people.[30] The over-diagnosis, particularly of both women and persons from minority cultures, demonstrates the limitations of the DSM,[31] and these limitations should not be underestimated.[32]

Feminists have pointed out how the DSM and psychiatric responses can pathologize the experiences of women. Women are twice as likely to be diagnosed with anxiety and depression and nine times as likely as men to develop eating disorders. The concern is that women's responses to social and structural factors in their lives are often interpreted as psychiatric symptoms and treated with pharmaceuticals.[33]

In a book chapter titled "How Feminism Can Take the Crazy out of Your Head and Put it Back in Society: The Example from Social Work Practice," social work authors emphasize that there is a need for long-term and in-depth transformation of the political, economic, and ideological structures that produce gender inequality and impact on the mental health of women.[34] In a similar vein, Helen Levine, a retired social work professor and long-time feminist activist, wrote about her experience of being hospitalized with severe depression:

> As a consumer, in and out of hospital, I was "helped," as were others, to see my problems as individual, pathological, personal and blameworthy. I was not helped—except by other patients, some friends and the women's movement—to see myself as only one of millions of women with similar life stresses and strains that cried out for political as well as personal solutions.[35]

During the mid-1980s when the DSM came up for revision, "masochistic personality disorder" was to be added to apply to someone who remains in an abusive situation despite possible opportunities to leave, such as abused women who often are entrapped physically and psychologically. There was an outcry from women's groups and an insistence that women be part of the committee making the revisions. Judith Herman became a committee member and recalls that the compromise was to change the diagnosis to "self-defeating personality disorder," which was placed in an appendix.[36] Although Levine and Herman wrote about their experiences close to 30 years ago, women still face gender stereotypes in the home, in the workplace, and when accessing health services.

Cultural factors shape our beliefs about mental health concerns and guide our understanding regarding causes and what ought to be done in response. For example, a person who is clinically depressed may report fatigue, headaches, and emptiness, rather than sadness.[37] However, psychopathology should not be automatically presumed if the behaviour of a person deviates considerably from the norm for Western culture. Research suggest that persons of ethno-racial backgrounds have "a culturally informed, *individual* way of understanding mental illness, substance use, and life struggles, as well as a set of culturally specific preferences and styles for remediation and recovery."[38]

Ethan Watters, in *Crazy Like Us: The Globalization of the American Psyche*, draws on comprehensive case studies to document the extent to which Western ideas about mental illness—namely, depression, anorexia, and PTSD—have been transported globally as scientific certainties and, when applied, have discounted indigenous beliefs and practices.[39] He found research that shows that wide application of Western belief about trauma and early intervention may impede the mind's natural healing process. In his case study of Sri Lanka after the 2004 tsunami, he noted that Western trauma counsellors were the first to arrive and immediately began treating the population with the PTSD protocol without considering that, culturally, Sri Lankans may have a fundamentally different reaction to traumatic events nor the possible influence of religious beliefs, traditions, support structures, or past events. As it turns out, despite decades of war and poverty, Sri Lankans are a people of remarkable psychological resilience, and they draw on their ethnocultural beliefs and traditions in times of hardship.

Watters interviewed American psychologist Dr. Gaithri Fernando, a native of Sri Lanka, about her research and found that after traumatic events Sri Lankans are more likely to experience physical symptoms such as aches in the joints or pain in the chest and not symptoms such as the anxiety, fear, and numbing that are part of the PTSD symptomatology. Instead Sri Lankans "tended to see negative consequences of an event like the tsunami in terms of the damage it did to social relationships" and those who suffered the most "had become isolated from their social network and were not fulfilling their role in kinship groups. In short, they conceived of the damage done by the tsunami as occurring not inside their mind, but outside the self, in the social environment."[40]

This example demonstrates how diverse cultures have different interpretations of and reactions to a traumatic event. For example, the meaning that Sri Lankan survivors gave to the traumatic event depended on their religious and traditional ethnocultural beliefs such as the belief in spirits.[41] This led Watters to conclude that "cultural conceptions of the mind remain more intertwined with a variety of religious and cultural beliefs as well as the ecological and social world."[42]

As noted in the previous chapter, Western approaches such as the psychosocial "talking therapies" may not be effective with people from non-Western cultures. Problem-focused, rather than emotional-focused, approaches may have more relevance. An emphasis on practical aspects includes an understanding of pre-migration and post-migration history and the current challenges facing those who have settled in a new country. For many, disclosing personal experiences such as trauma to a stranger is a foreign concept and highlights the importance of building a relationship that will foster the disclosure of such experiences in time.[43]

Not all of the disorders in the DSM are recognized internationally. Eriksen and Kress point out that, according to research, schizophrenia, manic-depressive (bipolar) disorder, major depression, and some anxiety disorders are the only four mental disorders that are found worldwide.[44]

STIGMA

All too often, a psychiatric label leads to stigma and those who have experienced mental illness frequently face discrimination, particularly in areas of employment and housing. Gaps in work history create barriers to future employment and therefore financial stability. Although work is found to be important in recovery, 90 per cent of persons with serious mental illness are unemployed. Due to low income, people often are forced to live in sparsely furnished rooming houses or sub-standard apartments in neighbourhoods of high crime and drug use. They find themselves on the margins of society.

> No one really knows what it is like until they experience living in a dark, damp room with no windows, no refrigerator, no heat and no rights. At the time I felt fortunate just to have a roof over my head and a bed to sleep in. I paid $550 a month for this, a cockroach-, a mouse-infested room with bed springs that scratched my body.[45]

It is not unusual for health professionals and the general public to view individuals with mental illness and addiction in terms of their diagnostic labels. The primacy of the diagnosis is demonstrated by the names of units in some psychiatric hospitals. Increasingly, rather than being distinguished by floor number, units are named the "schizophrenia unit," "mood disorders unit," and so on. Such labeling can contribute to the stigma experienced by many people with mental illness and thereby undermine their quality of life.[46] In 2006, the findings of the Senate Standing Committee on Social Affairs, Science and Technology "confirmed that the social stigma, discrimination, and oppression of persons with mental illness are more damaging than mental illness itself."[47] If people are viewed only as schizophrenics, addicts, or depressives, they lose their identity as artists, performers, carpenters, teachers, as well as partners, fathers, mothers, daughters, and sons.

PSYCHOTROPIC MEDICATIONS

Many of those coming to social workers are likely to have been prescribed psychotropic medications by their physicians. Canadians are among the highest per capita users of psychotropic medicines in the world, the second highest user of sedatives, and fourth highest user of prescription narcotics.[48] Antidepressants, anti-psychotics, and other psychoactive drugs are the second most-prescribed drug class in Canada, second to cardiovascular drugs.[49] While pharmaceuticals can be effective in the reduction of troubling behaviour, regrettably there are situations where these medications are prescribed in response to symptoms that have social underpinnings.

Social workers require a basic knowledge of the specific medications and why they are prescribed, the desired effects, and the most common side-effects. They also ought to have a critical perspective and an awareness of the controversies in their use and their harmful effects. There are five classes of psychotropic medication that are prescribed in response to psychiatric symptoms: antipsychotic, antidepressant, mood stabilizing, anti-anxiety, and psychostimulant drugs.[50] Medications are referred to by either their trade or generic name and both are included in the discussion that follows, with the trade name placed in brackets.

Central Nervous System and Psychopharmacology

Psychotropic medications have a direct effect on the thinking and feelings areas as well as other areas of the brain and the nervous system. All activities depend on a coordinated series of connecting neurons called a pathway. The neuron is responsible for the transmission of signals through the nervous system and relies on neurotransmitters to do so. While some 40 chemical neurotransmitters have been discovered, "the intended benefits of psychotropic drugs are at present generally attributed to only six neurotransmitters: acetylcholine, norepinephrine, dopamine, serotonin, gamma-aminobutyric acid (GABA) and glutamate."[51]

1. Antipsychotic Medications   Antipsychotic medications are prescribed to reduce or stop the symptoms of psychosis such as schizophrenia, including being
out of touch with reality; thought disorders or delusions (false beliefs, thinking
that someone is out to harm one); hallucinations or false perceptions (hearing
voices, seeing or smelling things that are not there); or loose associations (confused or bizarre thoughts).[52] High dopamine levels are linked to psychosis and
schizophrenia, and a number of drugs are designed to reduce these levels.

Typical/conventional antipsychotic medications were developed prior to
the mid-1980s and include chlorpromazine (Thorazine), haloperidol (Haldol),
thioridazine (Mellaril), or trifluoperazine (Stelazine). It is believed that they
block dopamine D2 receptors, some of which are related to neuromuscular
control of some parts of the body.[53]

A lack of sufficient dopamine can cause muscle rigidity, the Parkinsonian
side-effect of typical antipsychotic drugs. These drugs are often referred to as
neuroleptics due to their effect on motor function and side-effects that vary
from significant levels of sedation to extrapyramidal symptoms (EPS) such as
muscle spasms, tremors, restlessness, shuffling gait, and stiffness. These side-
effects can be very disabling and distressing. Anti-Parkinsonian drugs such as
benzotropine (Cogentin) and trihexiphenidyl (Artane) are prescribed to alleviate
symptoms of EPS. A serious long-term adverse effect is Tardive Dyskinesia (TD),
which produces involuntary movements of the extremities and face; there is
no treatment for it.

Atypical/second generation antipsychotic medications include repisperi-
done (Resperdal), olanzapine (Zyprexa), clozapine (Clozaril), and ziprasidone
(Geodon).[54] Atypical antipsychotics, while less likely to cause extrapyramidal
side-effects, tend to produce dizziness, drowsiness, and drooling and to cause
weight gain.

2. Antidepressant Medications   Antidepressant medications are prescribed for
varying levels of depression. There are four different classes of antidepressants:
monoamine oxidase (MAO) inhibitors, cyclic antidepressants, selective serotonin
reuptake inhibitors (SSRIs), and a group of atypical antidepressants.[55] The physician considers the nature and extent of the depression and the client's situation
when choosing a drug. Most medication requires from two to six weeks to take
effect. Serotonin is thought to be deficient when a person is depressed, and its
level is increased by many of the antidepressant drugs.

MAO inhibitors such as isocarboxazid (Marplan), phenylzine (Nardal), and
tanylcypromine (Parnate) stabilize depression by inhibiting MAO in the nervous
system and increasing biogenic amines that are thought to decrease depression.
They are highly effective but not frequently prescribed because dietary restric-

tions are required to avoid a serious adverse reaction (i.e., no caffeinated beverages, aged cheese, chocolate, red wine, or beer) as well as the avoidance of certain drugs (i.e., stimulants, decongestants, fluoxetine, and cocaine).

Cyclic drugs, so named after their chemical structure, include amitriptyline (Elavil), sinequan (Doxipine), and imipramine (Tofranil). They are thought to prevent the reuptake of norepinephrine, serotonin, and dopamine.

SSRIs such as paroxetine (Paxil), fluroxetine (Prozac), or sertraline (Zoloft) block serotonin but generally do not interfere with the actions of norepinephrine. They are relatively new and are well tolerated with few side-effects.

A fourth group of drugs are atypical; for instance, bupropion (Zyban) and venlafaxine (Effexor) target a subset of serotonin receptors and prevent serotonin reuptake, thereby increasing levels.

3. Mood-stabilizing Drugs Mood-stabilizing drugs are prescribed for disorders such as bipolar disorder. Due to chemical imbalances in the nervous system, typically a person diagnosed with bipolar disorder experiences one or more major periods of depression accompanied by one or more manic episodes. Lithium carbonate is the primary drug prescribed. While its exact effect is unclear, it is thought that it stabilizes electrolyte imbalances in the cell membrane and reduces both sensitivity in dopamine receptors and the cellular enzymes that produce dopamine. A steady blood level is required, and therefore close monitoring is needed.

4. Anti-anxiety Medications Benzodiazepines, including diazepam (Valium), clonazepam (Klonopin), and alprazolam (Xanax), are among the most prescribed anti-anxiety medications. They cause the GABA neurotransmitter to effectively bind at its receptor site.

5. Psychostimulants Ironically, stimulants—i.e., methylphenidate (Ritalin), pemoline (Betanam), and dextroamphetamine (Dexadrine)—are used in the treatment of ADHD. Their exact action is not known, but the drugs do release dopamine, norepinephrine, and serotonin, thereby regulating impulsivity.

MEDICATION MANAGEMENT

It is imperative that social workers understand the intended effects of psychotropic drugs as well as any harmful side-effects. Social workers are involved in medication management by encouraging compliance, identifying troubling side-effects, and, when necessary, advocating on behalf of a client for medication reassessment.[56] Giving people information about their condition can improve compliance with medication. Precise prescribing of medication can provide enormous benefits. The right medication and dosage can contribute to "improved attention and socialization and decreased anger" and thereby facilitate "increased self-esteem, improved conversational skills, decreased impulsiveness and self-preoccupied egocentricity...."[57]

Frequently, social workers will refer someone to a physician for assessment and possible medication. When doing so, it has been suggested that the social worker's response include the following:

1. Establishing and maintaining collaborative relationships with prescribers;
2. Sharing up-to-date information about psychiatric medications with clients and families;
3. Helping clients and families understand and manage the meaning of medications;
4. Preparing clients and families for the actual medication evaluation and anticipating issues that might emerge;
5. Following up on the results of the referral;
6. Managing legal and ethical concerns.[58]

A CASE FROM PRACTICE: PETER FROM SUDAN[59]

The following situation highlights the complexities of providing mental health services to immigrants and refugees. Yohannes Drar, a former refugee from Eritrea, has worked as a psychiatric social worker for over 20 years. He emphasizes that knowledge of the historical background, including migration history, is essential to respond effectively to the mental health concerns of refugees and new immigrants.[60] Also important is the realization that human behaviour is influenced by psychological, physical, social, cultural, and spiritual factors.

Context

"The Republic of Sudan, along with Djibouti, Somalia, Eritrea, and Ethiopia, is in The Horn of Africa, a region that has been in constant social, political, economic, cultural and religious crisis, and has been ruled by different op - pressive regimes and dictatorships."[61] Since its independence in 1956, Sudan, the largest country in Africa, has been in constant armed conflict and civil war between the southern Sudanese population and the ruling dominant Muslim and Arab north. As a result, many Sudanese have left their country to settle in Canada.

Background

Peter is a 21-year-old, tall, Black, Christian man, originally from southern Sudan. His parents divorced when he was six. Due to ongoing civil war, his mother immigrated to Toronto when he was eight. Peter remained in a refugee camp in Uganda under the care of his grandmother. Subsequently, his mother remarried and sponsored him to come to Canada at age ten. After his arrival, he had to adjust to a life that included a new step-father and two younger step-brothers.

Shortly after his relocation to Canada, Peter began fighting, stealing, and running away from home. He was physically disciplined by his step-father, and the CAS became involved. Consequently, he was placed in group homes and foster homes until he was 17. Other than occasional contact with his mother, he was alone with no other family support. His adjustment to Canada became increasingly difficult, and he began using cannabis, alcohol, and cocaine to cope. In order to support his drug use, he began to engage in criminal activities and was eventually charged with robbery and theft.

At the time of his arrest, he was homeless and experiencing auditory hallucinations and paranoia. After spending several months in prison, he was admitted to a psychiatric hospital where he underwent a forensic assessment. He was diagnosed with schizophrenia and polysubstance use. He was found criminally responsible and fit to stand trial. His case was presented to the Immigration Enforcement Office regarding possible deportation back to Sudan based on his criminal involvement.

Following the forensic assessment, Peter was admitted to a psychiatric unit. During the course of his admission, a treatment plan of psychiatric medications was implemented. He was placed on the long-acting conventional antipsychotic flupenthixol decanoate (Fluxannol), 60 mg every two weeks by intra-muscular injection, and a second generation antipsychotic olanzapine (Zydis, Zyprexa), 30 mg daily. Side-effects for the former may include EPS and TD, but there is less weight gain while side-effects for the latter include weight gain.[62]

Social Work Assessment and Plan

Peter experienced war, separation from his family, and life in refugee camps in Uganda. Cultural and political conditions of the area have significantly impacted his life and his mental well-being. He also endured the stress of family instability, migration, and settlement in a new country. The social worker, in collaboration with a multidisciplinary team, collected all information required to complete the psychosocial assessment as well as to formulate a "person-centred" response and prepare a plan for discharge. The general process for assessment outlined in Chapter 7 proved useful here.

An understanding of schizophrenia, as well as hallucinations and delusions, guide a social worker's response. Factors in the family or wider community may play a part in the onset and course of psychoses. Psychologist Peter Chadwick's own psychotic experience informs his response to persons who exhibit hallucinations and delusions. He explains that "delusional reinterpretations of one's life and one's place and function in the world can often conceal and protect against unbearable intrapsychic anguish."[63] He also cautions that one should not pathologize all a person's statements because some so-called delusional beliefs have been found to be true or partly true.

Engagement/Developing a Relationship

It can be difficult to engage a person in conversation while they are hearing voices and are suspicious. Cognitive behavioural treatment based on cognitive theory has been successfully used with people diagnosed with schizophrenia.[64] Aaron Beck and his colleagues provide a comprehensive understanding of schizophrenia that incorporates elements of cognitive and neurobiological science and the use of cognitive therapy through which the person is assisted to gain awareness about the link between thoughts, feelings, and behaviour. Part of the process includes metathinking, that is thinking about one's thoughts (or delusions). Virginia Lafond explains that metathinking is "standing back from ourselves in order to get a different view of our perceptions and to explore other possible ways of thinking about one's situation."[65] Moreover, "The cognitive-behavioral approach maintains an interest in both the form *and* content of delusional beliefs. The content of delusions is assumed to represent the person's attempts to make sense of some prior experiences."[66]

The cognitive approach weakens delusional beliefs by exploring alternative explanations that could have produced the delusional thoughts. Auditory hallucinations can be explored by asking open-ended questions about frequency and description. For example, are they male or female voices, warning or threatening messages, and how often and when (i.e., stressful events) do they occur?[67]

Peter was initially hesitant to engage, but during the course of his admission the social worker was able to establish rapport and a strong therapeutic alliance. This became easier as the medication took effect and suppressed the voices. Peter was eventually able to speak about his childhood, family members, and life in the camps. Brief supportive counselling was provided. Eventually Peter was able to engage in group work, attending several substance use support and education groups. Engaging in small talk can be therapeutic since it links a person back to everyday life. Often getting out of the office and taking a walk on the grounds can offer a normalizing experience and further develop the helping relationship.

During this time it was important for Peter to focus his energies on his present and immediate needs, and so he was unable to fully address past issues and traumas. This coping strategy is common among refugees and was respected by the social worker who recognized that trauma work often occurs long after a client has settled into their new community. The social worker provided the following:

1. *Legal supports/resources:* The social worker briefly educated Peter regarding his legal rights and available supports. He was connected with an immigration and refugee lawyer via the local Legal Aid office. The lawyer was able to present Peter's case to the Immigration and Refugee Review Board, which resulted in a plan aimed at keeping him in Canada. This plan was achieved by accessing safe and supportive housing as well as community case management support services. Peter was placed on a Community Treatment Order (CTO) with the conditions that he adhere to the treatment plan or return to the hospital.[68]

2. *Finances:* Peter initially had no income or financial supports. While he was in hospital, the social worker completed an application for him for the Ontario Disability Support Program. Peter was accepted into the benefit program.

3. *Housing:* Peter required stable housing in order to continue with his goals. With support from the social worker, he was able to move to a supportive residential setting.

4. *Family and spiritual reconnection:* With social work support, Peter was reconnected with his mother and siblings. He was also able to attend church with his Sudanese community members. This gave him social connectedness, support, and a sense of belonging.

This case illustrates a variety of social work interventions including advocacy, counselling, and discharge planning that utilizes an approach relevant to the immigrant and refugee experience.

DRUG OVERUSE AND ADDICTION

The overuse of substances often overlaps with other mental health concerns. Research indicates that 30 per cent of those diagnosed with a mental illness will also have a substance abuse problem in their lifetime, while 37 per cent of those who overuse alcohol and 53 per cent of those who abuse drugs will also develop mental illness.[69] The vast majority of people who become addicted use legally available substances.

Mood altering drugs are very effective in making unbearable situations more tolerable and distant. Whether legal substances such as alcohol, tobacco, and prescription drugs or illicit substances such as cannabis, heroin, cocaine, or the array of pharmaceuticals, such as Oxycontin, that find their way onto the street, they offer an escape from extreme stress or boredom and offer meaning to the lives of many. In some cases self-medicating helps someone to survive adversity.

Bruce Alexander in his book *The Globalization of Addiction: A Study of Poverty of the Spirit* points out that addiction is a way of adapting to sustained dislocation within a free-market society, that is, capitalism. The dislocation or alienation from traditions and cultures halts "psychological integration," which is based on active participation in society and a sense of belonging and contributing—an essential human need. Addiction, whether for days or years, helps people survive during unbearable dislocation.[70] This may have been the situation in the case of Peter, discussed earlier.

Maté explains that "Addiction is any repeated behaviour, substance-related or not, in which a person feels compelled to persist, regardless of its negative impact on his life and the lives of others…. Compulsion, impaired control, persistence, irritability, relapse and craving—these are the hallmarks of addiction—any addiction."[71] Addiction involves a complex interaction between people's neurological and emotional mechanisms and their environment. According to Maté, three factors need to be present for addiction to take place—a susceptible host, an addictive drug, and stress.

Contrary to the disease model that underpins most treatment programs for alcohol and drug overuse, there is no gene for addiction. What is referred to as addiction is the response of complex neurological and emotional mechanisms produced by the body, "the key organizers and motivators of human life and behaviour"—the dopamine system, the self-regulation system, and the opioid attachment/reward system.[72]

The opioid system's messengers to the brain are endorphins, important regulators of the autonomic nervous system. They are powerful soothers of physical and emotional pain, creating parent-infant bonds, maintaining social relationships, and producing intense feelings of pleasure. Endorphins are the brain's own painkillers and bear resemblance to morphine and other opiates that fit into the brain's endorphin receptors.

Endorphins influence the experience of key emotions in human life. Oxytocin, a "love hormone," increases the sensitivity of the brain's opioid system to endorphins and promotes physical and emotional nurturing and connectedness. Maté explains how attachment is a drive for emotional and physical closeness with others and that "when endorphins lock into opiate receptors, they trigger the chemistry of love and connection, helping us to be the social creatures that we are."[73] When the activity of the opioid system is diminished, we are more likely to turn to taking drugs to feel good.

Dopamine is the neurotransmitter responsible for an area of the mid-brain, the ventral tegmental apparatus that produces feelings of elation, desire, or craving. All mood altering substances raise dopamine levels, and events associated with use—people, places, and situations—trigger dopamine release. The dopamine system reinforces patterns of all addictive substances, including alcohol, cocaine, nicotine, and cannabis. Chronic use reduces the number of dopamine receptors so that the addicted person in desperation increases their use.

Both opioid and dopamine circuitry are components of the limbic system that processes emotions such as pleasure, love, joy, anger, fear, and pain. They regulate two responses that are central to human life—attachment and aversion—moving us toward experiences that are nurturing and away from those that are threatening. Both are central to developing healthy relationships.

Scientific evidence shows that drug addiction can lead to changes in the part of the brain responsible for decision-making. This damage to the self-regulation circuits influences the degree to which an addicted person can choose to stop using substances. This fact is rarely acknowledged, and people who continue drinking or taking drugs are often harshly judged and blamed for their situation. However, Maté points out that due to neuroplasticity and positive attachment in relationships, this condition can be overcome.[74]

Harm reduction aims to reduce the impact of substance use without insisting on abstinence. Harm reduction activities include needle exchange programs and supervised injection facilities (SIF). Although internationally there are more than 65 SIF, Vancouver has the only medical SIF in North America. Recent research on the reduction of overdose mortality rates before and after the opening of the Vancouver site found that it has decreased by 35 per cent.[75]

Another harm reduction strategy is the controlled provision of alcohol in homeless shelters to ensure that people are using safer forms of alcohol than Lysol, hair spray, mouthwash, or rubbing alcohol—all cheap and readily available. The evaluation of an Ottawa shelter program that offers the homeless a glass of wine every hour with progressive dilution found that those residents who stuck with it used fewer social and medical resources such as jails, emergency wards, ambulances, and hospitals. They were also likely to enter a treatment program.[76]

Unfortunately, we are quick to stereotype those who struggle with substance abuse as people who only care about getting high. Maté, reflecting on his work on the east side of Vancouver with severely addicted individuals, counters this view and speaks of the "grace" that he and others witness in neighbourhoods where people are struggling to survive: "…we who have the privilege of working down here: the courage, the human connection, the tenacious struggle for existence and even for dignity. The misery is extraordinary in the drug gulag, but so is the humanity."[77]

LOSS

Loss is all around us. On the news are pictures of the devastation and casualties of armed conflict and war, tragic accidents, job lay-offs, or natural disasters such as earthquakes and hurricanes. Chronic unresolved grief is a major factor in the lives of many refugees and immigrants who have experienced separation from family members, loss of homes, and loss of dreams. Other personal tragedies and losses include the illness and death of loved ones. Virginia Lafond, in her ground-breaking book *Grieving Mental Illness: A Guide for Patients and Their Caregivers*, examines the process of grieving for those who have a mental illness experience. In her work as a mental health social worker, she began to understand "that grief, with its attendant feelings of doubt, sadness, anger, guilt, fear, and shame, is an inevitable partner to mental illness."[78]

Coping with personal losses—whether a job, health, friend, loved one, or companion animal—can produce stress and have a serious physical or psychological impact on one's health and functioning. Grief is an intense emotional response and a normal reaction to loss. The process and duration of grieving will vary for each person, depending on their emotional state, culture, and social and structural context.

Grief and mourning differ for everyone and are complicated processes. Common emotional reactions are numbness, intense sadness and despair, anger, confusion, and denial. However, there can be cultural differences in the outward expression of grief such as crying. The Mandaeans, a minority in Iraq, may withhold tears because of their belief that crying after the death of a loved one will adversely affect the journey of their departed soul to the Light World.[79]

Dr. Elizabeth Kubler-Ross defined five stages of grief—denial, anger, bargaining, depression, and acceptance. She never intended the steps to be a linear timeline for grief or that everyone would go through each stage. They are useful steps to help identify and name one's place in the grieving process.[80] When grieving, a person may experience a loss of appetite, reduced energy, insomnia, and/or vague physical symptoms. These are normal reactions. Prolonged grief, accompanied by a loss of interest in all activities, hopelessness, and thoughts of wanting to die, can become debilitating and may suggest a clinical depression.

We all face grief at one time or another. Losing a life partner can be overwhelming and shake the foundations of a life. It is important to recognize not only the immense impact and challenge ahead but also acknowledge the healing power of grieving.

With the power of grief comes much of the fruits of our grief and grieving. We may still be in the beginning of our grief, and yet, it winds its way from the feelings of anticipating loss to the beginnings of reinvolvement. It completes an intense cycle of emotional upheaval. It doesn't mean we forget; it doesn't mean we are not revisited with pain and loss. It does mean we have experienced life to its fullest, complete with the cycle of birth and death. We have survived loss. We are allowing the power of grief and grieving to help us to heal and to live with the one that we have lost.[81]

NOTES

1 Gabor Maté, *When the Body Says No: The Cost of Hidden Stress* (Toronto: Alfred A. Knopf, 2003) 31.

2 Gabor Maté, "When the Body Says No: Understanding the Stress-Disease Connection," an interview with Amy Goodman, *Democracy Now!* (15 February 2010), http://www.demo cracynow.org/2010/2/15/dr_gabor_mat_when_the_body.

3 *Ottawa Citizen*, "Where Do I Go from Here? It is Heartbreaking Baby," 26 June 2010: A14.

4 Mikkonen and Raphael, *Social Determinants of Health* 17.

5 Uppala Chandrasekera, "Multiple Identities, Multiple Barriers," *Network* 26.1 (2010): 5–8.

6 WHO, "UN (DESA) — WHO Policy Analysis" 16 September 2010, http://www.who.int/mental _health/policy/mhtargeting/en/print.html.

7 Senate Standing Committee, *Out of the Shadows at Last.*

8 Anne-Marie O'Brien and Kimberly A. Calderwood, "Living in the Shadows: A Canadian Experience of Mental Health Social Work," *Social Work in Mental Health* 8 (2010): 319.

9 Cheryl Regehr and Graham Glancy, *Mental Health Social Work Practice in Canada* (Don Mills, ON: Oxford University Press, 2010).

10 American Psychiatric Association, *Diagnostic and Statistical Manual of Mental Disorders,* 4th ed. Text Revision (Washington, DC: APA, 2000): 27–34.

11 Allen Frances, "A Warning Sign on the Road to DSM-V: Beware of the Unintended Consequences," *Psychiatric Times* 26.8 (26 June 2009): 1–6, http://www.psychiatrictimes.com /print/article/10168/1425378?printable=true.

12 Denise Dreikosen, "Radical Social Work: A Call to Link Arms," *Journal of Progressive Human Services* 20 (2009): 107–09.

13 Sharon Kirkey, "The Sickening of Society," *Ottawa Citizen,* 26 April 2010: A1 and A4; American Psychiatric Association, *Diagnostic and Statistical Manual of Mental Disorders.*

14 Herb Kutchins and Stuart A. Kirk, *Making Us Crazy, DSM: The Psychiatric Bible and the Creation of Mental Disorders* (New York: The Free Press, 1997) 16.

15 Frances, "A Warning Sign on the Road to DSM-V" 3. Allen Frances was also interviewed by Anna Marie Tremonte on CBC Radio, "The Current," 11 April 2011.

16 See, e.g., the American Psychiatric Association web site for the DSM-V development at http://www.dsm5.org/Pages/Default.aspx.

17 Carolyn Abraham, "2 Million Prescriptions for Attention Deficit Disorder Written for Kids," *Globe and Mail*, 19 October 2010: A13. The article is subtitled: "A jump of 43%. About 75% of them for boys. Are we medicating a disorder or treating boyhood itself as a disease?"

18 Gabor Maté, "Dr. Maté on the Stress-Disease Connection, Addiction, Attention Deficit Disorder and the Destruction of American Childhood," *Democracy Now!* (24 December 2010): 5, http://www.democracynow.org/2010/12/24/dr_gabor_mat_on_the_stress.

19 Kutchins and Kirk, *Making Us Crazy, DSM*.

20 Julie L. Nagoshi and Stephanie Brzuzy, "Transgender Theory: Embodying Research and Practice," *Affilia* 25.4 (2010): 431–43.

21 Sommers and Satel, *One Nation under Therapy*.

22 Sommers and Satel, *One Nation under Therapy*.

23 Kutchins and Kirk, *Making Us Crazy, DSM* 125.

24 Senate Standing Committee, *Out of the Shadows at Last*.

25 American Psychiatric Association, *Diagnostic and Statistical Manual of Mental Disorders* 467–68.

26 Rebecca Meghan Davis and Henry Davis, "PTSD Symptom Change in Refugees," *Torture* 16.1 (2006): 10–19.

27 While the diagnosis of PTSD has helped in the understanding of some conditions, there is concern that it may be applied too widely. In 1992 Judith Herman, in her seminal book *Trauma and Recovery*, discusses the limitations of the diagnosis of PTSD for responding to people who experience prolonged and repeated trauma and exploitation such as hostages and survivors of domestic abuse and childhood physical or sexual abuse. According to Herman, their symptoms are complex and include alterations in identity and in the perception of the perpetrator. See Judith Herman, *Trauma and Recovery* (New York: Basic Books, 1992).

28 Brian E. Bride, "Prevalence of Secondary Traumatic Stress among Social Workers," *Social Work* 52.1 (January 2007): 63–69.

29 Christine Pross, "Burnout, Vicarious Traumatization and its Prevention," *Torture* 16.1 (2006): 1–9.

30 Gai Harrison and Rose Melville, *Rethinking Social Work in a Global World* (New York: Palgrave MacMillan, 2010).

31 Karen Eriksen and Victoria E. Kress, *Beyond the DSM Story: Ethical Quandaries, Challenges, and Best Practices* (Thousand Oaks, CA: Sage, 2005).

32 The inaccuracy of diagnosing was demonstrated in a classic article by US researcher David Rosenhan. In 1973, he conducted a controversial study where eight pseudo-patients gained entry to 12 different hospitals with symptoms that were "existential in nature." Once admitted, the symptoms stopped, and they resumed their healthy normal behaviour. All but one was diagnosed as schizophrenic and prescribed a regime of drugs; all were discharged with the diagnosis of "schizophrenia in remission." While in hospital, all of their behaviours were viewed through their diagnosis. Rosenhan concluded that we cannot distinguish the sane from the insane in hospitals and that diagnoses are not often useful or reliable. See David L. Rosenhan, "On Being Sane in Insane Places," *Science* New Series 179.4070 (19 January 1973): 250–58.

33 Eriksen and Kress, *Beyond the DSM Story*.

34 Bourgon and Guberman, "How Feminism Can Take the Crazy out of Your Head."

35 Levine, "The Personal is Political" 187.

36 Herman, *Trauma and Recovery*.

37 R.J. Castillo, *Culture and Mental Illness* (Pacific Grove, CA: Brooks/Cole, 1997).

38 Elizabeth Carpenter-Song, Edward Chu, Robert E. Drake, Meika Ritsems, Beverly Smith, and Hoyt Alverson, "Ethno-Cultural Variations in the Experience and Meaning of Mental Illness and Treatment: Implications for Access and Utilization," *Transcultural Psychiatry* 47.2 (2010): 224–51, quote p. 246; emphasis in the original.

39 Ethan Watters, *Crazy Like Us: The Globalization of the American Psyche* (New York: Free Press, 2010).

40 Watters, *Crazy Like Us* 91.

41 Gaithri A. Fernando, "Interventions for Survivors of the Tsunami Disaster: Report from Sri Lanka," *Journal of Traumatic Stress* 18.3 (June 2005): 267–68.

42 Watters, *Crazy Like Us* 255.

43 Craig, Jajua, and Warfa, "Mental Healthcare Needs of Refugees."

44 Eriksen and Kress, *Beyond the DSM Story*.

45 Senate Standing Committee, *Out of the Shadows at Last* Section 1.4.1.

46 Patrick W. Corrigan, "How Clinical Diagnosis Might Exacerbate the Stigma of Mental Illness," *Social Work* 52.1 (January 2007): 31–39.

47 Senate Standing Committee, *Out of the Shadows at Last*.

48 J. Rehm and J. Weekes, "Abuse of Controlled Prescription Drugs," in *Substance Abuse in Canada: Current Challenges and Choices* (Ottawa: Canadian Centre on Substance Abuse), http://www.ccsa.ca (2005): 31–37.

49 Sharon Kirkey, "Psychiatric Drugs Carry Serious Physical Risks, Researchers Find," *Ottawa Citizen*, 15 June 2010: A5.

50 Kia J. Bentley and Joseph Walsh, *The Social Worker and Psychotropic Medication*, 3rd ed. (Belmont, CA: Brooks/Cole, 2006).

51 Bentley and Walsh, *The Social Worker and Psychotropic Medication* 60.

52 Bentley and Walsh, *The Social Worker and Psychotropic Medication*.

53 Regehr and Glancy, *Mental Health Social Work Practice in Canada*.

54 Regehr and Glancy, *Mental Health Social Work Practice in Canada*.

55 Bentley and Walsh, *The Social Worker and Psychotropic Medication*.

56 Bentley and Walsh, *The Social Worker and Psychotropic Medication*.

57 Peter K. Chadwick, *Schizophrenia: The Positive Perspective: In Search of Dignity for Schizophrenic People* (London: Routledge, 1997) 53.

58 Kia J. Bentley, Joseph Walsh, and Rosemary Farmer, "Referring Clients for Psychiatric Medication: Best Practices for Social Workers," *Best Practices in Mental Health* 1.1 (Winter 2005): 61.

59 Yohannes Drar generously provided this case from his practice as a social worker in mental health. The name and other identifying information has been changed in order to ensure confidentiality.

60 Yohannes F. Drar, "Mental Health Social Work Practice with Refugees from the Horn of Africa: A Personal Experience," Eastern Branch, Ontario Association of Social Workers *Bulletin* 36.2 (Summer 2010): 12.

61 Drar, "Mental Health Social Work Practice" 12; Robert O. Collins, *A History of Modern Sudan* (Cambridge: Cambridge University Press, 2008).

62 Regehr and Glancy, *Mental Health Social Work Practice in Canada* 138–39.

63 Chadwick, *Schizophrenia* 17.

64 Regehr and Glancy, *Mental Health Social Work Practice in Canada*; Aaron T. Beck, Neil A. Rector, Neal Stolar, and Paul Grant, *Schizophrenia: Cognitive Theory, Research and Therapy* (New York: The Guilford Press, 2009).

65 Virginia Lafond, "The Grief of Mental Illness: Context for the Cognitive Therapy of Schiz-

ophrenia," in *Cognitive Psychotherapy of Psychotic and Personality Disorders*, ed. Carlo Perris and Patrick D. McGorry (New York: John Wiley and Sons, 1998) 237–56.

66 Larry Davidson, Stacey Lambert, and Thomas H. McGlashan, "Pychotherapeutic and Cognitive-behavioral Treatments for Schizophrenia: Developing a Disorder-specific Form of Psychotherapy for Persons with Psychosis," in *Cognitive Psychotherapy of Psychotic and Personality Disorders: Handbook of Theory and Practice*, ed. Carlo Perris and Patrick D. McGorry (New York: John Wiley and Sons, 1998) 8; emphasis in the original.

67 Beck et al., *Schizophrenia*.

68 A CTO permits someone to agree to a community-based treatment plan rather than hospitalization.

69 Senate Standing Committee, *Out of the Shadows at Last*.

70 Alexander, *The Globalization of Addiction*.

71 Gabor Maté, *In the Realm of Hungry Ghosts: Close Encounters with Addiction* (Toronto: Vintage Canada, 2009) 128–29.

72 Maté, *In the Realm of Hungry Ghosts* 150.

73 Maté, *In the Realm of Hungry Ghosts* 154.

74 Regarding the brain's neuroplasticity, see N. Doidge, *The Brain that Changes Itself* (New York: Penguin 2007).

75 Brandon D.L. Marshall, M-J Milloy, Evan Wood, Julio S.G. Montaner, and Thomas Kerr, "Reduction in Overdose Mortality after the Opening of North America's First Medically Supervised Safe Injecting Facility: A Retrospective Population-based Study," *The Lancet*, Early Online Publication (18 April 2011), doi:10.1016/S0140-6736(10)62353-7, http://www.the lancet.com/journals/lancet/article/PIIS0140-6736%2810%2962353-7/fulltext.

76 Alderson-Gill & Associates Consulting Inc., "Evaluation Prepared for the National Homeless Initiative: Shepherds of Good Hope, Harm Reduction Program, Ottawa, Ontario" (2002), www.homelessness.gc.ca/projects/casestudies/docs/ottawa/shepherds_e.pdf. Reported in the Senate Standing Committee, *Out of the Shadows at Last*.

77 Maté, *In the Realm of Hungry Ghosts* 85.

78 Virginia Lafond, *Grieving Mental Illness: A Guide for Patients and Their Caregivers*, 2nd ed. (Toronto: University of Toronto Press, 2002) xi.

79 Rian and Hodge, "Developing Cultural Competency with Mandaean Clients."

80 Elizabeth Kubler-Ross and David Kessler, *On Grief and Grieving* (New York: Scribner, 2005).

81 Kubler-Ross and Kessler, *On Grief and Grieving* 231.

CHAPTER 11

SUPPORTING FAMILIES AND COUPLES

Families shape, and are shaped by, the communities and societies in which they are imbedded.[1]

ORE THAN EIGHT IN TEN PEOPLE IN CANADA live in families, and 84 per cent of these are couple families, married or common-law. The nuclear family is now a minority that represents only 39 per cent of families. Surveys indicate that same-sex couples comprise less than 1 per cent of all couple families.[2] Families are diverse in their make-up and may be one parent or multigenerational or may be described as adoptive, foster, or blended. Some who live in supportive collectives consider the other members as family.

At any one time, families are faced with health crises, losses, conflict, and financial hardship. Life is particularly stressful for the working poor and families living in poverty. During the economic recession, a number of individuals lost their jobs, had salary cuts, exhausted their savings, and lost their retirement and benefit plans. They and their families now face the devastating stress that accompanies uncertainty. Financial stress and disagreements about money and how to manage can become a source of conflict between couples. As well, families may be responding to a myriad of concerns beyond the economic realm.

In such situations, all too often the result is to blame those closest to one, engage in angry outbursts, and create a situation in the home that impacts on all family members. This may be the reality for many families who come to social workers for help. Four in ten marriages now end in divorce with most occurring in the third or fourth years of marriage. This chapter offers an overview of the impact of social and economic conditions on couples and families as well as approaches to support them when they face difficult situations.

THE IMPORTANCE OF HEALTHY RELATIONSHIPS

Close relationships are vital to surviving difficult times such as the current economic depression, health crises, and resettlement after migration. At times we meet individuals who are exposed to tremendous challenges and hardship and yet manage to recover and thrive. Nurturing relationships among family members are critical to emotional and physical health. It has been shown that a close and available caregiver, particularly during the first year of a child's life, and the presence of alternative caregivers such as grandparents and neighbours, provide support for children during difficult times and contribute to resiliency.[3]

In earlier chapters we mentioned some of the neurological and emotional factors that are active within each of us as we respond to life's experiences. In a similar fashion Sue Johnson draws on research that demonstrates how the quality of our relationships with loved ones significantly impacts on our physical health: it affects our blood pressure, our immune system functioning, and the production of stress hormones.[4] When we are hostile and fight with those closest to us, our wounds heal slower, and if we are emotionally isolated, we are twice as likely to suffer a heart attack or stroke. In fact, isolation has been found to be more dangerous to our physical health than smoking or a lack of exercise. Coming close to those we love, or even thinking about them, releases oxytocin, considered to be a "love hormone," and promotes our connection to others whether they are partners or children. Oxytocin reduces the hormones that produce stress and generates a sense of contentment. A close and loving relationship can act as a buffer against the stress and uncertainty facing many couples.

The support of family and friends provides the strength and fosters the resilience needed to survive difficult times. However, for others the pressures facing a family can be enormous and erode relationships. Close to 25 per cent of adults report that most of their days are extremely stressful. Along with the conflicting demands of work and family responsibilities, the reasons that couples grow apart vary from developing different values and interests to the presence of intimate violence, infidelity, or alcohol and other drug overuse.[5] Social and economic crises can also have an impact on one's relationships, health, and self-worth.

WORKING WITH FAMILIES

Families are situated within a community and a culture and have a history that goes back generations. Our family of origin and past generations are always with us. As social workers, it is therefore important to see that the family may extend beyond those members who come to a family session or who are living together.

Migration always involves separation. Refugees or new immigrants often maintain close relationships with family members who are left behind in the country of origin or who have settled in other countries. Celia Falicov explains how migration can affect the next generation and points out that "Symptoms precipitated or aggravated by the process of migration, such as depression, anxiety, psychosomatic illnesses, addictions, or behavioral problems, can appear in any of the family members in any location at any time: the departure, at a later time, at the time of a life cycle event (physical illness, divorce, death), or at a time of a reunion among separated members as reported or observed in clients seeking help in clinical settings."[6] She therefore emphasizes the importance of understanding how problems arise in social settings, not simply in intrapsychic life. This understanding of the role of the social context in shaping behaviour must also acknowledge how gender inequality and sex roles disadvantage women.

Family life is like an iceberg. More is concealed than revealed to family members or the social worker. Families will come to you in crisis, and it takes great courage to open up about one's family to a stranger. All family members are capable of growth and change, and acceptance and empathy provide an environment where risks can take place. The responses of family members are basically reasonable and adaptive if understood within a context. Therefore, it is essential to get an understanding of how family members organize their daily lives based on the material and social resources that are available to them.

Virginia Satir, a social worker and family therapist, emphasized the importance of communication in influencing and resolving family difficulties. Her "growth model," influenced by humanistic psychology and the work of Fritz Perls, Carl Rogers, and Eric Berne, avoids labelling and diagnostic categories. Rather than pathology Satir saw potential and possibilities. She viewed parents as "people-makers" and viewed troubled families as producing troubled people. She influenced many social workers during the 1970s, including Maurice Moreau, and her work continues to inform practice with families today. Satir proposed four areas of difficulties that can be experienced by troubled families, areas that can be related to their basic human needs and rights:

1. *Communication*. How do family members communicate with each other? How do they discuss differences and express anger, affection, joy, and sadness? How are decisions made? How do they let each other know that they care?
2. *Links to and place in society*. How are family members connected to other people, institutions, and material resources? What is their social and economic position in society, their social class, ethnic background, and experiences of discrimination?
3. *Rules*. Within families there are expectations of behaviour. What are the family rules? Who makes them? Who enforces them? What happens when a member acts outside of the expectations? Identify rules that enforce inequality within the family.
4. *Self-worth*. How do family members think about themselves? What are their feelings of self-worth?

Satir believed that any behaviour at a moment in time reflects the interaction of a person's self-worth, the relationship with others, and his/her position in the situation.[7] Take time to reflect on your own family and consider these four areas as you respond to the questions in the guide provided (Appendix D).

All communication is learned, and communication is viewed as the largest single factor affecting our health and determining the kinds of relationships we make with others. When there was stress in relationships, Satir observed that people handled it in five ways—placating (being apologetic, agreeable no matter what), blaming (responding as if the problem is someone else's), being overly reasonable (responding logically without feeling as if the stress/threat was harmless), being distracting and irrelevant (ignoring the threat), or being congruent (appropriate response where feelings and behaviours are in proportion to the stress). It was the latter that Satir fostered in her work with families.

Ethnicity and cultural practices inform the behavioural expectations of family members. Culture may provide a source of strength and connection to a community while at the same time foster gender inequality within the family.[8] The challenge for the social worker is to identify this tension and to engage family members to determine possible responses while attending to safety of the members. Culture ought never to be used as a reason for abuse to take place within a family.

Starting Out with the Family

Disclosing one's family difficulties to a stranger is difficult, particularly for those from cultures where counselling is a foreign concept. As social workers, it is an honour to enter into a family and to be trusted with the intimate details about the lives of its members. During the first interview, the tasks of the social worker are to assess the situation, recruit and engage all family members, motivate them to participate in the current and future sessions, and perhaps to contract to make some changes. The assessment skills outlined in Chapter 7 are applicable here. Each family member will be wondering what kind of a person you are, whether you will understand their experiences in the family, and if you will take sides.

Begin by welcoming the family into your office or a larger meeting room and invite them to choose a seat among those placed in a circle. Introduce yourself by commenting on your role in the agency and your expertise. Acknowledge that it is difficult to open up about one's family to a stranger. However, their willingness to come tells you that there is motivation to invest some time in solving the situation. Invite the family members to introduce themselves and make a connection with each one. In the case of children it is often useful to ask about age and/or grade in school. If a child is wearing a t-shirt printed with a message, you could comment, "Looks like you're a hockey player? What position do you play?"

Often it is useful to ask how everyone found out about the meeting and what they were told about it. The responses will reflect the level of communication in the family. It also gives you an opportunity to clarify your role and to emphasize that you are not a judge but more like a detective as you aim to gather information and work with the family to solve the problem. Let them know that you need their help to get all the information possible and that you will work together to identify and address the concerns.

Family members will usually have different views of "the problem." Begin with the person who precipitated the initial contact and arranged the appointment. Ask what is this person's view of the problem? Who else in the family is concerned about the problem and what are their views? After going around to all family members, it is often useful to explore the differing views. Create an environment where it is safe to express different perspectives and feelings. As you proceed with the family session, you will be modeling effective communication. Ask family members to speak directly to each other rather than talking through you.

As family members begin to participate, observe communication and interaction patterns. Behaviour in a family session may be indicative of behaviour at home. At the same time take every opportunity to identify strengths and successes in responding to past and present concerns. Also identify current and potential resources that support the family. Foster agency by asking family members about their hopes for change. While listening to the problems, also listen for the strengths in family members.

Communication break-down is often based on false assumptions and mis-understandings. We are often quick to respond to a comment without fully understanding what is meant by it. Misunderstandings that occur between client and social worker during a helping situation can halt progress. Ask for clarification to ensure that you understand and interpret the information correctly and incorporate an ethnic/cultural sensitive approach.

Family genograms, eco-maps, and time lines are useful visual aids in identifying the family in context and to gain an understanding of their daily lives and the material and social resources available to them (see Chapter 7). Genograms portray families over generations while an eco-map situates them in their current social context. Since the eco-map and genogram do not address the role of culture in the family, Elaine Congress introduced the culturagram as an assessment tool to assist addressing this limitation. Similar to an eco-map in design, the culturagram examines ten areas: reasons for relocation; legal status; time in the community; language spoken in the home and community; health beliefs; crises; holidays and special events celebrated; connection with cultural and religious institutions; values regarding education and work; and values about the family structure including power, hierarchy, rules, and boundaries.[9]

Different cultures have beliefs about illness and what ought to be done as far as intervention. However, health beliefs and traditional healing practices can often be misunderstood by health care professionals. Nancy Waxler-Morrison and Joan M. Anderson recount the experience of a social worker in western Canada who was contacted to assess the possibility of child abuse in a Vietnamese family. While examining a two-year-old child who was brought in by his parents, the physician noticed bruises on his back. During the social work home visit the mother explained the source of the bruising—she had tried to cure the child by "spooning," a treatment used in Vietnam, that involved pressing a silver spoon up and down the child's back.[10] An awareness of such cultural and spiritual practices enhance the social work response.

Both the genogram and the eco-map have been adapted to explore spirituality and religion in families. Hodge introduced a spiritual eco-map as an assessment tool to understand the family's level of religious/spiritual beliefs and their involvement in faith communities.[11] Similarly, the spiritual genogram explores how religious and spiritual history, and traditions, beliefs, and practices impact on current concerns of couples and families.[12]

ATTACHMENT THEORY

There is a growing recognition of the relevance of attachment theory in understanding individual and family relationships. It is natural to seek love and connection from others and this "love sustains us and offers a safe haven or a secure base from which to explore the world."[13] John Bowlby, a British child psychiatrist, and Mary Ainsworth, his research assistant, observed that the quality of the connection to loved ones is central to the development of the personality and how an individual learns to connect with others. We cannot thrive without an attachment relationship that meets our human need for belonging. Safe and secure attachment in relationships remains important throughout our lives, although it is particularly critical in a child's first year of life.

The three environmental conditions that are essential to optimal development of the brain are nutrition, physical security, and consistent emotional nurturing "by at least one reliably available, protective, psychologically present and reasonably non-stressed adult."[14] A primary caregiver's body language, tension, and tone of voice are communicated to the child. It is through secure attachment with a psychologically and physically present caregiver that children have their basic needs—comfort, security, food, and shelter—met.

While the term bonding happens in the mind of the caregiver, attachment develops between two people who are in a caring relationship.[15] Instead of using words for those who are closely connected that imply a negative relationship such as "codependent" or "enmeshed" or "fused," Bowlby spoke of "effective dependency" to refer to people who are very close.

Attachment theory has come under criticism for its early assumption that child rearing should be the sole responsibility of women and for how it continues to shape common understanding of what constitutes good mothering.[16] This is reflected in the most recent version of the DSM-IV-TR where insecure attachment underlies a number of the disorders.[17] It is also important to consider the crosscultural application of attachment theory in cultures where there is an emphasis on collective care. The attachment patterns of children in diverse families such as those with gay or lesbian parents must also be considered.[18]

Drawing on attachment theory, a family assessment would consider the nature of all relationships. Specific questions ought to elicit a history of the nurturing close relationships within and outside the family, the presence of abuse in the family, and any exposure to trauma.[19]

CASE EXAMPLE:
A FAMILY IN ONTARIO

You are a social worker in an Ottawa community centre that provides services to homeless families who are currently living in motels while searching for housing. Joan Nelson calls you to ask for your assistance. She is a single mother with two children, her partner Dan, the father of her children, is in jail. The family has been living in a motel for five weeks since they were evicted from their apartment for failure to pay the rent. She sounds exhausted, frustrated, and overwhelmed. She is concerned about her two sons Sean (age 10) and Justin (age 8). She speaks about Sean as being a very responsible child but fears that he is bottling up a lot of emotions. Apparently Justin has been sent home from school several times this week. Joan says that Justin feels that he doesn't fit into the school, other students tease him, and now he wants to stay home instead. She is particularly worried because he seems so sad and has mentioned that he might as well die. From the brief phone call, you get the sense that Joan is trying very hard to care for all family members and to find an apartment. At the end of the call she mentions that she is in early recovery from drug use and doesn't ever want to return to that life.

You decide to meet with Joan, Sean, and Justin as a family. At the first meeting the family members were very easy to engage and you find out the following:

1. Joan is relieved to talk to someone. She has been trying to provide for the family. She stopped using drugs nine months ago but fears and feels guilty that her years of using may have caused problems for the family. She feels overwhelmed with the current situation and wonders how she will be able to keep going. Her mother is dead, and her father lives in Sudbury. Her father refused to have any contact with her 12 years ago because she started living with Dan who is from Trinidad. She and Dan were both using drugs for a couple of years, and then six months ago he was sent to prison for aggravated assault of another man and possession of cocaine. She misses him a lot and hasn't been able to see him because she has no transportation to Kingston where he is in the penitentiary. She is waiting for the day that he is out of prison and they can make a new start. Until then she wonders how she can keep it all together.

2. Sean hopes that you will be able to help the family. He worries about his mother and tries to keep the stress down in her life by doing many chores such as shopping and cooking. He remembers when she was using drugs and how scary it was for him. He misses his father a lot and wants to see him. Sean likes school and wants to learn and get ahead. He has tried to make some friends in the new school, but other students seem to avoid him. He feels very alone and begins to cry.

3. Justin was very worried about seeing you because he thought that the meeting was about him not doing well in school. He wants to participate and belong, but nothing seems to be working. He finds the motel very crowded, and the other children in school tease him saying that he "smells funny." At school he finds it difficult to concentrate and listen.

How would you respond to each family member as they disclosed their concerns? As they talk, you observe their closeness and caring. Joan is very attentive and affectionate with the boys, and they in turn look to her for support and reassurance.

The Nelsons are one of many families in Canada who are unable to afford high rent while on a meagre social welfare allowance. What is your initial understanding/assessment of the situation? What are the strengths/limitations of each family member? How will this initial information help guide your response in the first and future family sessions? To what resources can you gain access to assist this family?

WORKING WITH COUPLES

Throughout life we generally seek and form meaningful and close relationships. Unfortunately incidents such as intimate violence, affairs, and withdrawal of support during crises leave partners feeling hurt, angry, betrayed, violated, and vulnerable. Other couples face financial or health difficulties or other stressful situations. Couples who seek help for relationship issues have often pushed each other away as they attempt to deal with such difficulties. "When partners feel abandoned or invalidated, their trust in their partners' reliability and supportiveness is shattered, they feel betrayed and this has a deleterious effect on the relationship bond and leaves partners with unresolved hurt and anger."[20] Men who adhere to the norms of traditional masculinity have been identified as having difficulty with emotional intimacy and expressiveness, and this may pose additional challenges in couple work.[21] While practice with couples is informed by assessment and the helping skills discussed in previous chapters, some specific approaches have been developed to assist in relationship building.

Emotionally Focused Therapy

Emotionally focused therapy (EFT) has been successful in addressing unresolved emotions, de-escalating conflict, and strengthening relationships. Developed by Sue Johnson, a professor at the University of Ottawa, as a means of helping couples, the approach has become widely used.[22] EFT integrates humanistic and family system approaches and is rooted in attachment theory; research has shown that it significantly improves relationships.[23] EFT is a nonpathologizing approach and is based on the assumption that emotion is central in our interaction with loved ones. Woolley and Johnson contend that "It is the music of the dance between intimates" and "working with emotion is most often the best, most efficient, and often the only way to transform close relationships."[24]

EFT is therefore aimed at encouraging emotional responsiveness, and Johnson has outlined three necessary components in supporting and caring relationships.

1. *Accessibility:* Can I reach you? This means staying open to partners even when feeling insecure and having doubts.
2. *Responsiveness:* Can I rely on you to respond to me emotionally? It means accepting and placing priority on the emotional signals that a partner conveys and sending clear signals of caring when a partner needs them. Sensitive responsiveness always touches us emotionally and calms us at a physical level.
3. *Engagement:* "Do I know that you value me and will stay close?"[25]

Woolley and Johnson maintain that "secure couple relationships involve powerful emotional bonds where each partner is accessible and responsive to the needs of the other."[26] During times of vulnerability and uncertainty, it is important to be able to reach out to a partner and know that they will be there for comfort and support. Attachment theory is believed to be a factor that contributes to intimate violence and offers one explanation of why women who have been abused stay with their partners despite opportunities for leaving.[27] While this may contribute to our understanding, we must not lose sight of the social and political context of intimate violence, that is, patriarchy and the beliefs that men have about women and relationships as well as women's inequality and their lack of opportunities to leave and live independently.

A partner's unavailability, infidelity, and violence, referred to as attachment injuries, create stress in the relationship and impact on attachment.[28] However, regretfully, based on a national survey of 620 couple therapists, researchers found that the majority do not routinely screen couples for domestic violence and concluded that domestic violence may be under-identified.[29]

Prior to beginning couple work, in order to determine which couples can safely enter couple counselling, each couple ought to be interviewed followed by separate interviews with each partner. It is important to assess couples to ensure that there is no ongoing violence, affairs, or substance overuse. If there is ongoing violation of trust, such as violence or infidelity, working with the couple is not recommended.

The material from individual interviews ought to be held in confidence unless the person chooses to disclose in the couple session.[30] Michelle Bograd and Fernando Mederos, who have had extensive experience in the area of intimate violence, suggest the following goals for the individual assessment interview to rule out violence:

1. to learn whether there is any violence between the couple;
2. to ascertain the nature, frequency, severity, and physical consequences of the physical aggression;
3. to elicit detailed behavioral descriptions describing the sequence of events in context;
4. to understand the intended function of violence and its impact;
5. to evaluate the degree of fear and intimidation present;
6. to determine whether there is a broad pattern of coercion and domination, including psychological abuse and marital rape;
7. to lay the ground work for an informed decision about the advisability of continued couples work.[31]

Along with incurring physical injuries, those who experience intimate partner violence are at great risk for depression, anxiety, and PTSD.[32] If intimate violence is identified, the perpetrator must be held accountable, and the victim must be protected.

In the case of couples where there are currently no situations of betrayal or violation of trust, they should be assessed to determine the degree of the attachment injury that has resulted and proceed with EFT with a focus on full resolution. In cases such as these several specific steps are identified and inform how the session unfolds: the injured partner speaks about the injury and its impact; the impact is connected to emotions and attachment fears; the other partner acknowledges his or her partner's pain and discomfort and communicates empathy; the injured partner is able to ask for caring; and partners experience a bonding that results in a more secure, safe, and connected relationship.[33]

For couples who have identified difficulties in the relationship, Johnson asks what they see as the basic problem in their relationship and what the solution might be. It is important to connect with each member of the couple and to establish trust so that they feel supported and understood and will risk being vulnerable. The work also involves basic helping skills of empathy, reflecting, validating, and reframing.

The process of change involves a three-stage process of "identifying the negative cycles of interaction, accessing the emotions that are both a response to and organizers of these cycles, and reprocessing these emotions to create new responses that shape secure bonding events and new cycles of trust and security."[34] The first stage is de-escalation and involves assisting the couple to stop attacking, criticizing, and fighting. Often the couple is caught in the ineffective communication patterns outlined by Satir where one partner pursues, blames, criticizes, and coerces while the other withdraws, placates, and is defensive. This dance then takes on a life of its own, and the cycle of "demon dialogues" is identified as the enemy, not each other. This is similar to Michael White's externalization of the problem.[35] The second stage involves the expression of need and wants, changing interactional patterns, and creating new cycles of trust and caring. The third stage of consolidation and integration involves helping the couple to find new solutions to old problems and to integrate new cycles of communication into their day-to-day lives.

Social work intervention with families and couples has the possibility of enriching relationships and transforming lives. Central to this process is respect for families, affirmation of their culture, and the provision of community resources.

NOTES

1 Vanier Institute of the Family, *Families Count: Profiling Canada's Families* (Ottawa: The Vanier Institute of the Family, 2010) xi.

2 Vanier Institute of the Family, *Families Count.*

3 Carl F. Rak and Lewis E. Patterson, "Promoting Resilience in At-Risk Children," *Journal of Counseling and Development* 74 (March/April 1996): 368–72.

4 Sue Johnson, *Hold Me Tight: Seven Conversations for a Lifetime of Love* (New York: Little, Brown and Company, 2008).

5 Vanier Institute of the Family, *Families Count.*

6 Falicov, "Working with Transnational Immigrants: Expanding Meanings of Family, Community, and Culture." *Family Process* 46.2 (2007): 157–71.

7 Virginia Satir, *Peoplemaking* (Palo Alto, CA: Science and Behaviour Books, 1972).

8 Laura A. Bryan, "Neither Mask nor Mirror: One Therapist's Journal to Ethically Integrate Feminist Family Therapy and Multiculturalism," *Journal of Feminist Family Therapy* 12.2/3 (2011): 105–21.

9 Elaine P. Congress and Winnie W. Kung, "Using the Culturagram to Assess and Empower Culturally Diverse Families," in *Multicultural Perspectives in Working with Families*, ed. Elaine P. Congress and Manny J. Gonzalez (New York: Springer, 2005) 3–21.

10 Nancy Waxler-Morrison and Joan M. Anderson, "Introduction: The Need for Culturally Sensitive Health Care, " in *Cross-Cultural Caring*, 2nd ed., ed. Nancy Waxler-Morrison, Joan M. Anderson, Elizabeth Richardson, and Natalie A. Chambers (Vancouver: University of British Columbia Press, 2005) 2–10.

11 David R. Hodge, "Spiritual Eco-maps: A New Diagrammatic Tool for Assessing Marital and Family Spirituality," *Journal of Marital and Family Therapy* 26.2 (April 2000): 217–28.

12 Marsha Wiggins Frame, "The Spiritual Genogram in Family Therapy," *Journal of Marital and Family Therapy* 26.2 (April 2000): 211–16.

13 Brent Bradley and Sue M. Johnson, "EFT: An Integrative Contemporary Approach," in *Handbook of Couples Therapy*, ed. Michele Harway (Hoboken, NJ: John Wiley and Sons, 2005) 183.

14 Maté, *In the Realm of Hungry Ghosts* 185.

15 Sue Watson, "Attachment Theory and Social Work," in *Social Work Theories in Action*, ed. Mary Nash, Robyn Munford, and Kieran O'Donoghue (London: Jessica Kingsley, 2005) 208–22.

16 Lynda R. Ross, "Mom's the Word: Attachment Theory's Role in Defining the 'Good Mother,'" in *Feminist Counselling: Theory, Issues and Practice*, ed. Lynda R. Ross (Toronto: Women's Press, 2010) 51–76.

17 Ross, "Mom's the Word."

18 Nikki Evans and Marie Connolly, "Attachment Issues and Work with Adolescents," in *Social Work Theories in Action*, ed. Mary Nash, Robyn Munford, and Kieran O'Donoghue (London: Jessica Kingsley, 2005) 239–50.

19 Nicola Atwood, "Working with Adults Who are Parenting," in *Social Work Theories in Action*, ed. Mary Nash, Robyn Munford, and Kieran O'Donoghue (London: Jessica Kingsley, 2005) 223–38.

20 Leslie Greenberg, Serine Warwar, and Wanda Malcolm, "Emotion-focused Couples Therapy and the Facilitation of Forgiveness," *Journal of Marital and Family Therapy* 36.1 (January 2010): 28–42.

21 Robert Garfield, "Male Emotional Intimacy: How Therapeutic Men's Groups Can Enhance Couples Therapy," *Family Process* 49.1 (2010): 109–22.

22 Johnson, *Hold Me Tight*.

23 Scott R. Woolley and Susan M. Johnson, "Creating Secure Connections: Emotionally Focused Couples Therapy," in *Handbook of Clinical Family Therapy*, ed. Jay L. Lebow (Hoboken, NJ: John Wiley and Sons, 2005) 384–405.

24 Woolley and Johnson, "Creating Secure Connections" 385.

25 Johnson, *Hold Me Tight*.

26 Woolley and Johnson, "Creating Secure Connections" 386.

27 Watson, "Attachment Theory and Social Work."

28 Mario Mikulincer and Phillip R. Shaver, *Attachment in Adulthood: Structure, Dynamics, and Change* (New York: The Guilford Press, 2007).

29 Rebecca L. Schacht, Sona Dimidjian, William H. George, and Sara B. Berns, "Domestic Violence Assessment Procedures among Couples Therapists," *Journal of Marital and Family Therapy* 35.1 (2009): 47–59.

31 Michelle Bograd and Fernando Mederos, "Battering and Couples Therapy: Universal Screening and Selection of Treatment Modality," *Journal of Marital and Family Therapy* 25.3 (1999): 291–312.

31 Bograd and Mederos, "Battering and Couples Therapy" 298.

32 Sandra M. Stith, Eric E. McCollum, Karen H. Rosen, Lisa D. Locke, and Peter D. Goldberg, "Domestic Violence-Focused Couples Treatment," in *Handbook of Clinical Family Therapy*, ed. Jay L. Lebow (Hoboken, NJ: John Wiley and Sons, 2005) 406–30.

33 Woolley and Johnson, "Creating Secure Connections."

34 Woolley and Johnson, "Creating Secure Connections" 387.

35 White, *Re-Authoring Lives*.

CHAPTER 12

USE OF GROUPS FOR EMPOWERMENT AND SUPPORT

GROUP WORK IS A POWERFUL MEANS FOR OFFERING SUPPORT, increasing awareness, and influencing change. The sense of belonging that develops in groups—the "we're all-in-the-same-boat" phenomenon—can be empowering. Members experience being part of a collectivity and come to realize that others not only share their struggles and experiences but can also offer assistance in finding solutions. As a result, problems become less overwhelming. For those who are isolated, alone, or marginalized, the group can offer a support network and a sense of hope.

Group work may combine the goals of individual change, mutual aid, and social change.[1] (The combination of mutual aid with a community development component is discussed in the next chapter.) It is an effective method for helping people with a variety of concerns, from healing from traumatic situations such as an illness, a death in the family, or physical and sexual assault to addressing problems in professional and personal relationships. An increased awareness of one's situation and access to resources all contribute to problem-solving and empowerment. Group members, once they have gained a sense of competency, begin to make changes in their lives.

The role of the group facilitator is to create a process that encourages members to identify common ground and purpose and to respond to concerns raised in the group. The social worker's understanding of these concerns will be reflected in her responses, the issues she chooses to highlight or to set aside, and the various paths she suggests for resolution. She provides some of the structure and guidelines for the group as well as uses her knowledge and prac - tice skills to situate the personal troubles of individuals within a broader context of social structures and unequal social relations based on class, gender, race/ethnicity, and sexual orientation.

Most people have been part of a group in school, the workplace, or the community. Some may recall a positive experience, while others may remember feeling misunderstood, anxious, and uncomfortable. Simply having people come together does not naturally create a supportive and therapeutic environment. All members entering a group bring with them differing viewpoints, biases, and ideas about the source of their concerns, possible solutions, and ideas about how the group will work. Facilitating a successful group takes careful planning.

PLANNING THE GROUP

Usually the idea for developing a group emerges from a need that has been identified. In some cases an agency has a long-standing mandate and receives funding in specific areas, such as intervention for women who have been sexually abused as children or for men who are perpetrators of violence against their partners.

A social worker may recognize a common concern among those she is seeing on an individual basis and decide to invite them to meet as a group. For example, as a social worker in a community counselling centre, I noticed that several women were coming for help about how to live on their own for the first time in many years. They agreed to meet as a group and were open to inviting others as well. This resulted in an ongoing group for "Women Who are Alone" either by choice or circumstance. Members included women who had been recently widowed or separated. One woman came because her partner was dying and she wanted to prepare for being alone.

Personal Preparation

The social worker does not have to be an all-knowing expert with all the answers. While it is important to be responsive in an authentic way to the experiences being shared by group members, he is not expected to do this flawlessly. Larry Shulman, a seasoned group worker, believes that effective practice is "shortening the time between making and catching a mistake."[2] A belief in, and commit - ment to, the group process, as well as a willingness to risk and admit mistakes and to be fully present for group members are essential qualities for a group leader.

Group members often speak openly about their situation and the social worker's role is to join with them in trying to understand the problems they face and to search for solutions. While professional experience contributes to group work skills, the social worker's personal life experience is also important in responding to group members. "It is important that you acquire knowledge of how groups function, learn the necessary skills and techniques to implement your knowledge in actual group work, and do so in such a way that your techniques become an expression of your personal style and an extension of the unique person you are."[3]

At the time I facilitated the group for women living alone, I myself was a woman living on my own. While this was helpful, it was not necessary. However, in some situations, such identification is important; for instance, a gay or lesbian social worker is best suited to facilitating a group for gay or lesbian persons who are "coming out."

Group Structure

Some groups are closed: all its members come in at the same time and no new members are invited to join. The result is cohesiveness and a sense of safety, and it works well for those who feel particularly vulnerable and are struggling with sensitive concerns—for instance, survivors of violence such as childhood sexual abuse, woman assault, or torture. A fixed membership is also desirable for groups with an educational focus and a structured content delivered over a limited number of weeks. Groups to stop smoking and anger focus groups are examples of the latter.

Closed groups usually have a set time frame (8 to 12 weeks) with a planned agenda. The time boundary creates a sense of urgency and helps members focus quickly and maintain purpose and direction, although its closed nature means that members cannot be replaced if they drop out. In an open group members enter and leave at different times. In residential settings, such as a group home or drug rehabilitation program, whoever is in residence is expected to attend the group.

Some groups for abusive men are open-ended and are up to 24 weeks in length. The content is planned in such a way that no matter when a man enters, he will rotate through all topic areas in the course of the six months. While new members are always being integrated into the group, its strength is in its older members who are there as role models and to challenge and offer feedback. Because many men who have been abusive tend to enter a group full of denial and minimizing the abuse they have done, it is very helpful for them to be challenged by other members.

Open-ended groups offer new members encouragement as they see others who have made important changes leave; some senior group members may achieve a sense of growth and accomplishment. However, for some, entering a pre-existing group may be stressful, and some existing members may resent time taken with a new member. One solution to these problems is to introduce three or four new members at a time so that they feel they belong to a cohort.

The frequency and duration of the group must be decided in advance. Many groups tend to meet weekly for two to three hours. In some residential programs, such as those for alcohol and other drug problems, groups often meet daily. Generally, groups for children are shorter in duration because of their limited attention span.

The size of the group depends on its purpose. Small groups of seven to ten members offer greater opportunity for individual work, while at the same time they have greater expectations for participation. Smaller groups are disadvantaged when members are absent. Large groups of 15 or more work well when the purpose is primarily educational.

While some groups are structured and cover particular content (abused women, drug addiction, or assertiveness training), others are more focused on process and depend on the material that emerges from members. At any rate, groups tend to centre around a common need.

Group Membership

Often groups are organized around a common need or concern. Therefore, it is important to decide on the purpose of the group and on any restrictions on membership; for instance, a group may consist of all women, women over 55 years of age, or lesbian women who are recovering from an addiction. The group may be for male survivors of childhood sexual abuse or for people who are living with HIV disease.

Group members who are diverse in regards to age, social class, gender, race, and ethnicity may have more difficulty coming together. However, sharing a common problem can minimize such differences, and "as a rule of thumb members usually tolerate and use greater diversity when common interests and concerns are expressed intensively."[4] While diversity is expected, it can be difficult if a group member is the only representative of a particular group—the only woman in a group, the only Aboriginal person, or the only gay man.

Once the structure of the group has been put into place, the next task is the recruitment of members. Potential participants ought to have information about the purpose of the group and the expectations for membership so that they can make an informed decision about attending. Members can be recruited from existing caseloads, from the agency as a whole, or from the community. For some groups, members are invited, while for others they are referred or decide on their own to join. Abusive men are frequently mandated by the court to attend.

Often advertising assists with recruitment. For example, a notice announcing a group for men who are partnered with survivors of childhood sexual abuse can be placed on bulletin boards of a family agency. In this way workers within the agency can refer prospective members from their own caseloads. Notices can also be placed in community centre newsletters or posted in the centres themselves. It is important to include all the relevant information so that someone can make an initial contact knowing the purpose of the group, the time and place, and cost if any.

In situations where a particularly isolated population (i.e., sex trade workers, homeless youth at a drop-in) is to be reached, active recruitment might include personal contact. The provision of day care and/or transportation costs insures that low-income women and men will not be excluded.

Meeting individually with each prospective group member before the group starts can be helpful in clarifying both the structure and purpose of the group and expectations of membership. The individual meeting also provides an opportunity to assess the appropriateness and readiness of the person for group membership and whether or not the group will be able to meet his or her needs. During the interview the social worker can begin the therapeutic relationship by identifying the client's concerns, how these concerns have been handled, and what are the goals. Thus, the social worker can address any special needs before the group meets. Pre-group meetings reduce anxiety, enhance participation, and prepare the member for the group.[5]

Limits to confidentiality ought to be clearly stated. It is helpful to have information about the group in writing and to offer information about the group leader(s). Potential members, having gained a sense of the leader's personality and qualifications and the expectations about their participation, are better able to make an informed decision about joining.

In some settings, such as hospitals and residential programs, where everyone in a particular unit/ward will be expected to attend the group, pre-meetings will not be necessary.

Location and Time of the Group

Meeting with people in a familiar and convenient location can encourage participation. The social worker may decide to hold the group in a local community centre or within a major housing development. The building, the group room, and the rest room ought to be wheelchair accessible. The room itself should fit the size of the group, have comfortable chairs that can be placed in a circle, and provide a quiet and private place to meet.

Evening groups are preferable for those who are working during the day, while afternoon groups may suit those who are primary caregivers of school-age children, are unemployed, or who work during the evening or night. If meeting in the evening, women, the elderly, and people with disabilities will appreciate a well-lit parking lot and entrance way and attention to concerns regarding personal safety. The location should be on regular bus routes.

Working with a Co-facilitator

Working with another person in the group, thus sharing responsibility for responding to all issues that may arise, can be a source of support and feedback. Also, co-leadership offers the assurance that groups will not have to be cancelled if one of the group leaders becomes ill; in addition, it provides excellent opportunities for training and skill development for students and volunteers.

Two leaders offer alternate role models for group members. For example, it is recommended that groups for abusive men be co-led by a man and a woman. Co-leaders who differ culturally will be able to offer diverse perspectives and a welcoming environment. Also, when possible, "it is helpful to a minority member to have at least one worker of similar sex and/or ethnicity."[6]

Of course, matching leaders for groups requires some care. Qualities such as mutual respect and trust are important for co-operative work,[7] as are a common theoretical approach to the analysis of problems, approaches to group practice, and leadership styles. While co-facilitators do not need to be identical in their views, it is essential that they are complementary. A group leader who is highly directive and confrontational will not be well-matched with someone who is low-profile and interested in engaging group members.

Group leaders who work well together usually have established an excellent process of communication and clarity regarding the division of responsibilities and roles. It is important that both workers are committed to being involved in the myriad tasks and planning details required to insure a successful group. These include setting up the room, preparing materials, primary facilitating, post-group reflection and feedback, recording group notes, and follow-up of absent members.

Attending to Special Needs

Some members may require assistance in order to be full participants in the group. If using written materials, it is important to be aware of members who are illiterate, have low reading and writing levels, or whose first language is not English or French. On a number of occasions I have had members approach me outside the group, fearful that I will call on them to read something, or ask them to write on a flip chart, or complete written homework.

Written material should be clearly and simply written, and assistance should be provided outside the group to members who require it. Alternately, films can be used to stimulate discussion and provide information. Popular education methods, such as having members draw a picture to describe something and then to speak from their drawing, are very effective.

GETTING STARTED

Everyone participates in the first group session with a degree of dread, as well as a sense of excitement. Members wonder what will be expected of them and who the others are. A minority member may feel particularly vulnerable. It is likely that there will be distrust, defences, and a certain degree of caution. Often group leaders are apprehensive about their ability to facilitate a therapeutic group process. Certain tasks and aims are crucial to set the tone at the first meeting and to insure a sound beginning for the group.

Personal/Political Tuning-In

Before the group meets, the social worker engages in tuning-in to the personalities of the members, to the issue(s) they have in common, and into how group members may be feeling. If it is an ongoing group session, the worker reflects on the members and the previous work that has taken place in the group and identifies possible areas of conflict, hostility, and/or disengagement among members. The tuning-in process heightens responsiveness and can result in increased empathy and more effective intervention.

Introductions

Getting to know each other is the most important goal of the first meeting. It is helpful to have participants put their name on a file card bent in half and placed on the floor in front of each chair. This facilitates a quick learning of names, and the file cards can be retrieved at the end of each group. The group facilitator may decide to be the first to introduce herself and can begin by saying something about who she is professionally, her interest in the group, and how she is feeling at the first session: "I'm Nicole, and I'm a social worker here at the agency. I have been involved in couple groups for the past five years. I've already spoken to all of you, and I am excited that we're finally here as a group."

There are a number of ways in which members can be asked to introduce themselves. In a simple go-around everyone says their name and a little about why they came to the group. Members can also interview and introduce each other. Emphasis can be placed on goals by having each member complete a sentence such as, "What I want most from the group is…" or introduce themselves as the person they want to be when they leave the group. Completing sentences like "A fear I have about being in the group is…" raises concerns early so they can be addressed. If the members are from different geographical areas, a world map can be very useful: each member pins his or her name tag on their country of origin.

Whatever form the introductions take, when everyone has finished, the facilitator's role is to summarize her observations by noting the similarities and the common experiences, anxieties, and difficulties. Such feedback will help begin connecting the group members in developing common ground, and will demonstrate that the worker has been listening.

In open-ended groups, one or two members may be joining when everyone else is already familiar with each other. These new members should be invited to say a few words about why they decided to come to the program and what they hope to get out of it.

Guidelines and Ground Rules

Whether someone is attending group for the first time or has had other group experiences, some basic guidelines for participation and group functioning are essential in assisting members to participate and to enhance feelings of safety and security. Some recommended guidelines include:

1. *Keep names and personal information heard in group confidential.* In the group setting both the social worker and the group members are obligated to honour confidentiality. Generally, group members are told that information shared in the group stays in the group. If members want to speak about their group experience to others, they ought to talk only about what they are learning or the changes they are making. Members often want to know what they should do if they see each other on the street or how the facilitator will respond to them outside the group. While there is no firm protocol, one suggestion is that group members not openly acknowledge each other in the presence of friends, family, employers, etc. This is important for group members who may not wish others to know that they are attending a group and don't want to be placed in the situation of explaining who is greeting them. The facilitator also reminds members of the limits to confidentiality that professionals must follow (as outlined in Chapter 6).

2. *Arrive on time or call if absent.* The expectation that the group will begin on time respects the busy schedules of members and their efforts to attend. At the same time, it is important to understand when members are unavoidably late due to unreliable or missed buses and paid work and domestic responsibilities.

   Group members should be informed that their absence will be noticed and that an explanation will reduce the concern of the group facilitators and members. In some cases there may be a guideline about absences; i.e., after three unexplained absences, a member will be asked to leave the group. Absences due to illness, vacation, and crises in the family ought to be accepted; however, at some point the social worker will have to decide how many absences can be accommodated. The person may be better off rejoining another group at a later time if they cannot attend regularly. At times members will be unable to come to group because they don't have bus fare or resources for child care, and advocacy on the part of the social worker will be necessary.

3. *No eating in the group.* While coffee or juice are often provided during group sessions, eating can be a distraction.

4. *No alcohol or illicit drugs on the day of the group.* The personal work that takes place in group requires the full presence of participants, and the use of substances can cloud perceptions and effect judgement. If the facilitator suspects that someone has arrived at the group under the influence of drugs, the response will vary depending on the situation. If the person has "had a beer," the facilitator can talk to him prior to the group, remind him of the agreement, and continue with the group as usual. If, on the other hand, the group member has had "several beers" and is noticeably affected, the social worker may choose to remind him of the agreement, restrict his group participation to listening, or arrange for him to get safely home. In the case of someone who is attending a group because of a problem with alcohol and has a goal of abstinence, the decision to drink or use other drugs will require special consideration.

It is advisable to explore the possibility of substance use in a non-threatening and supportive manner, preferably in private. The social worker can begin with an observation, posing questions such as "I smell alcohol—have you had a drink before group?" and "You appear very drowsy tonight—is everything okay?" At times the behaviour the social worker observes may be the effects of prescribed drugs such as tranquilizers, antidepressants, or analgesics, and the group member may need encouragement to approach a physician to speak about side-effects.

It is always possible that something else is contributing to the signs of intoxication other than alcohol or other drug use. For example, on one occasion, I observed reddened eyes in a young male group member. Suspecting marijuana use, I commented on this. His response was, "Yeah, I've been hanging drywall all day."

5. *One person speaks at a time.* Group members may need to be reminded not to interrupt when another group member or the group facilitator is talking.

6. *Give feedback to each other; express oneself, one's thoughts and feelings, in a respectful way. Speak directly to the person.* The strength of the group is in the feedback given to one another.

7. *Respect difference and be open to hearing different ideas and views.* Group members represent differing views and cultures and are expected to respond to each other in a respectful manner. As the facilitator and other group members respond to comments in group in a respectful manner, they become models for others.

8. *Do not leave group for unscheduled breaks unless absolutely necessary.* The coming and going of members while the group is meeting is disruptive.

It is helpful to encourage discussion on the guidelines and to ask if there are others that members would like to see. It is useful to record the established guidelines and to provide a copy for all members. At times throughout the course of the group, the guidelines should be revisited and revised as needed.

THE GROUP SESSION

The group leader maintains the focus while facilitating participation, attending to both content (the topic of discussion) and process (responses of group members). The core communication skills, relationship-building, and problem-solving skills discussed in previous chapters are essential to the task. During the initial stages of the group, the social worker strives to connect members and to build cohesion among them.

According to Lawrence Shulman, two themes present in every group to some degree are authority and intimacy.[8] The authority theme refers to the relationship between the social worker, who leads the group, and the group members. Some members who are court-mandated or pressured to attend the group may directly challenge the social worker's authority. For instance, in group work with abusive men, I found that some reacted to the imposed service and the fact that it was delivered by a woman. The intimacy theme reveals itself in the way group members develop relationships with each other and disclose personal details of their lives. As an effective group process is established and group members gain trust and begin working with each other, the facilitator becomes viewed less as an authority.

Group sessions often have an overall structure to them. It can be helpful to have opening and closing rituals. At the beginning of open group sessions, various "housekeeping" tasks take place, such as the introduction of a new member or farewell to an old. The group facilitator may want to check briefly with a member who achieved some progress the previous week or offer some personal reflections.

In highly structured groups centred on a specific topic, the agenda may be prearranged and leader-focused. Such groups offer new information and promote learning. In other groups the focus emerges from the members themselves, often prompted by a question such as "Who needs some time tonight?" Members, knowing that they will have an opportunity to speak up in the group, come prepared to work on their issues. Two or three members may raise their hands, thus giving the session structure. Instead of a show of hands, members as they arrive write their names and the amount of time they need for discussion on a flip chart. The list, reviewed at the start of group and changes made if necessary, can be part of the agenda for the evening. Once feedback and some closure has come to one member's concern, the social worker moves on to the second person who wanted some time by saying "Is it okay if we move on to Marie now?"

Helping Members Tell Their Story

The group facilitator has two clients, the group member who is raising a concern and the remaining group members.[9] While the focus may be on one member and his or her issue, the facilitator observes other members and attempts to include them in the process to discover common ground. Questions such as "Has anyone else shared Bob's fear of being on his own after many years of marriage?" or "Who else has difficulty expressing their feelings?" invites others to connect with these experiences. Often group members are very unfocused and go on at great length. The social worker must listen carefully during these situations. She can then pose questions for clarification or offer a succinct summary in order to assist the group member to focus. Careful listening also communicates that the group member's story is important.

At times members can begin to talk about other people in their life and how they have to change. For example, it is common for men who have been abusive to focus on what their partner said or did, not on their own actions. Redirecting attention to how the actions of others affected them or to how they responded can be helpful and emphasize that the group can help only the group member, not friends and family.

Use of Contracts

The contract offers a focus and purpose for attending the group and contains goals for personal change, actions that will meet those goals, and the outcomes of these efforts. Effective contract goals are specific and stated in terms that can be assessed and that are achievable. For example, the action plan below records the goals, actions, and outcomes of a group member in a program for abusive men.

FIGURE 12.1 ACTION PLAN

I am in the New Men program to make some positive changes in my life. There are specific behaviours and attitudes that I want to change so that I stop my abuse and begin to respect and support my partner. I want a relationship based on equality.

		ACTION PLAN	
Date	Behaviour / Attitude (What I want to change)	Action (What will I do)	Outcome (The results)

The goals and outcomes of group members can be reviewed on a regular basis in the group.

Use of Homework

Assigning a structured activity to be completed in between group sessions assists members to continue to work on the agreed-upon goals. Expectations for homework are an integral component of re-education programs for abusive men. One assignment is to log any abusive behaviour (the Abuse Log); this helps the men to identify and to examine their controlling actions and to realize that they occur in a context, are connected to beliefs, and are purposeful. The Abuse Log below was adapted from the one initially developed in the Duluth program and is designed to assist men in the development of critical thinking. The Log helps men to examine their own violence and guides them through a process of naming the problem, critically reflecting on the impact on others, and taking action to change.[10] This counters the common view that men abuse because they lose control and shows instead that abuse is based on an intention to gain control—to stop their partner from saying something or doing something.

The journal is another useful tool sometimes recommended to group members as a way to develop self-awareness.

Giving Feedback

The feedback that members give each other is a vital aspect of helping in groups. The following guidelines are useful to assist group members in giving feedback:

1. *Use "I" statements:* "I think you …"
2. *Be specific:* "When you … it reminded me of …"
3. *Be tentative:* "I have a hunch …"; "I'm wondering if …"
4. *Connect to personal experience:* "When I first came to the group I felt the same way."

FIGURE 12.2 ABUSE LOG

NAME _____

DATE _____

ABUSE LOG

1. **The situation:** A brief description of the incident that I responded to in an abusive way.

2. **My feelings:** What I felt.

3. **My actions:** A description of what I did, what I said, my facial expressions and tone of voice.

4. **My intent:** What did I want to happen.

5. **My self talk:** What I was saying to myself just before and during my actions.

6. **My beliefs that support my actions.**

7. **The effects of my actions on:**
   a) my partner
   b) others, including children
   c) myself.

8. **What I can do differently:** It would have been better if I...

If the feedback is challenging, a group member may begin to deflect what is being said and counter each point. Instead of listening, he may be actively constructing a response. In this case it is helpful to ask the member to listen silently while a number of people give feedback. Then ask him what he has heard and what has been helpful.

Use of Structured Activities

There is often a tendency when first starting out to highly structure the group and control the content. This offers a sense of security to a new group leader. However, with experience, the social worker soon discovers that much of the material comes from the group. Nevertheless, structured exercises can be very useful in assisting group members to express themselves. All participation in such activities ought to be voluntary. Members should have the option of passing or declining.

1. *The check-in.* A common practice in working with groups is to begin with a "check-in," a go-around in which each member summarizes the week or speaks about their current feelings. In working with men who are abusive,

one of the objectives is to increase their sensitivity and understanding toward partners. Thus, George checks in as his partner Alice and speaks about how it was living with George in the past week. The group leader and the members then have an opportunity to ask Alice questions. This manner of checking tends to elicit far more information and also provides men with an increased awareness about their partners' lives.[11]

Sometimes the go-around is done by passing a "talking stick" or an object such as a seashell or stone. Only the person who holds the object can speak. When that person is finished speaking, she passes it to the one next to her. The passing continues until no one has any more to say, and the object completes the talking circle without anyone saying anything.

2. *Role plays*. At times the social worker will invite a group member to role play. This is particularly important when a member is facing a difficult situation and would benefit from a practice session. A woman who wishes to talk to her 15-year-old daughter about expectations for curfew and household responsibilities and the consequences for not complying is very hesitant to do so because in previous attempts the daughter has been hostile and left the room. The group leader asks group members how they would respond to such a situation and then invites the woman to play out one of these suggestions; another member is asked to volunteer to play the role of the daughter. After the role play, the group leader asks both the "mother" and "daughter" what they learned from the exercise and asks group members for their feedback.

Critical Thinking and Problem-posing

Critical thinking is central to consciousness-raising as individuals place the events of their lives within a social, political, and economic context and identify ways that they can work to change that context.[12] Rather than emphasizing personal and interpersonal dynamics only, material conditions and social relations are also considered. This process of consciousness-raising helps clients to move from a position of powerlessness, internalized oppression, and alienation to one of empowerment and liberation. The assumption is that once clients reach a critical understanding of their situation, they are able to more effectively engage in personal change as well as confront inadequate social and economic conditions.

In the group process, the group facilitator asks a number of questions of group members, some of which elicit more information than others. For example, open-ended questions generate a richer response than closed questions. Questions can also help a group member reach for deeper meaning and understanding.

Problem-posing is an approach that structures dialogue and advances critical thinking in a group process.[13] Introduced by Freire, problem-posing has been adapted to the university classroom, including schools of social work[14] and ESL classes in North America.[15] The dialogical approach invites group members to enter the process of learning "not by acquiring facts, but by constructing their reality in social exchange with others."[16] For example, many abusive men are aware of the "facts" of abuse and read newspaper accounts about the prevalence of male violence in intimate relationships, but they have seldom considered or connected their own thoughts and actions to these events.

In groups for abusive men, the use of codification or codes help to stimulate problem-posing, structure and focus the discussion, and assist men in examining their beliefs and feelings about their violence. A code is a depiction of reality, a physical representation of an issue, concept, or theme that has emerged from the group. Codes can take the form of video vignettes, photographs, poems, drawings, comics, newspaper clippings, or a song. In groups for men who are abusive, the code externalizes actions of abuse so that they can be examined and connected to personal experiences.

The video vignettes and power and control wheel, developed by the Duluth program and now used in countries around the world, are the result of women coming together in focus groups and speaking of their experiences of violence.[17] By portraying several minutes in a relationship when a man is abusive, each vignette focuses and grounds the work of the group.

In order to move the discussion of a code to critical analysis and action, Wallerstein suggests using the following process:

1. Describe what you see.
2. Define the problem(s).
3. Share similar experiences.
4. Question why there is a problem.
5. Strategize what you can do about the problem.[18]

This process examines situations that directly impact on the lives of the members; it may lead to consciousness-raising and personal and social action. The abuse logs described earlier reflect a similar questioning process.

In my own groups, I have suggested that members draw a picture of a situation in which they used violence. Many of these pictures portray the man as larger than everyone else and holding his fist in the air; his partner has a look of horror and pain; and there are often children hovering in the background. This has proved to be a particularly moving experience for men as they describe their picture to the group.

Ending the Session

The group facilitator must set aside time to bring the session to a close and the work of the group together by pointing out connections among the issues discussed and identifying issues for the following sessions. A final go-around to all group members creates closure. For example, a group for abusive men could close with a round of commitments: the men identify something they will put into practice, some action they will take in the week to come toward their goal of equality with their partner. Occasionally, an issue may arise during the go-around that appears to be something on which one member needs to work; that member is encouraged to take group time in the following week for the issue.

CHALLENGES IN GROUP WORK

Lack of Participation

There are many reasons why someone may not fully participate in group. A member may be reluctant to talk about a part of her life that is very painful and/or that she may feel guilt or shame about. While a part of her may want to move ahead, another part may fear change. She may fear being rejected or misunderstood or may think that the social worker and other members have nothing of importance to contribute. In the case of mandated group attendance, group members may be angry and thus take the only control over the process they believe they have: "You can force me to be here, but you can't make me listen." Another reason for a member's silence could be cultural differences and/or language difficulties. It may take some members longer to trust the group because of some past vulnerability. Fully acknowledging a problem in group means doing something about it.

Instead of pressuring quiet members to talk about a particular problem, it is often helpful to ask them to talk about what makes it difficult to share. Regular go-arounds in which all members are given an opportunity to say a few words are helpful in assisting those who tend to be quiet.

In a group for abused women, a member talks about wanting to leave her husband but feeling frightened and insecure about being alone with two children. In order to draw out other members the social worker might respond, "It's very difficult thinking of being on your own, yet you're feeling very unsafe living with your husband. Who can relate to what Elaine is saying?" It is important to collectivize the work—to search out a common ground between the individual and the group as a whole—without denying the uniqueness of the member's problem. Moving around the circle to scan members' faces and reactions will give the facilitator a sense of how the members are responding.

Another strategy to draw out quiet members is to recognize their nonverbal communication and invite them to comment. If one member nods her head while another speaks, the facilitator could say, "Nora, you seem to be connecting to what Connie said," thus linking the experience of members together.

Promoting Co-operation

It is common for group members to be reluctant to acknowledge difficult situations in order to begin the process of change. At times members enter the group against their will. When the service is imposed, the social worker may find that the group members may defy guidelines, challenge the leadership, and refuse to participate. This is a common occurrence in groups for men who are abusive, where the men are there involuntarily as the result of legal or non-legal pressure to attend, or are court-mandated, or partner-mandated. Men's reluctance to participate in this case may be termed "resistance," and the frustrated facilitator may demand participation, impose group content, and engage in harsh confrontation. Such a response shows disrespect, violates the dignity of group members, and may encourage others to rally in support of the member(s) under attack. In this situation a more effective response is to recognize that the member is more than the abuse that he has done and to engage him as a whole person. While men are held responsible for their actions and their violence, they should not be viewed "as demonic beings out to inflict pain and suffering but as people who are acting from a set of beliefs that are harmful and make stable and loving relationships impossible."[19]

Diversity and Conflict

At times actions of group members will reflect their prejudice and beliefs regarding gender, ethnicity, sexual orientation, and social class. Sandra Butler and Claire Wintram discuss this in their book *Feminist Groupwork*:

> J, for example, had ended a lesbian relationship and was now caring for her elderly father at home. After several months of hearing other women in the group talk about their heterosexual partners and their child-rearing practices, she suddenly shouted out that she was sick of women making heterosexist assumptions about the "normality" of sexual relations with men, that she felt excluded, and that it was further assumed that choosing to have a child-free life made her incomplete. For months she had felt marginalized and oppressed by other women because of inferences with which she was surrounded.[20]

It appears that the group leaders had been unaware of the degree to which this woman felt alienated and alone. Since this had gone on for "several months," it is possible that the leaders too are practicing with a heterosexual bias. In responding to this woman's outburst it would be critical for the group leaders to acknowledge what she has said and to join with the other women as they begin to address their exclusion of her experience.

The following is an excerpt from Ellen Pence and Michael Paymar's book *Education Groups for Men Who Batter* and shows how a facilitator can respond to racist language:

BILL: She's going out with this gook.

FACILITATOR: Why do you use the term "gook"?

BILL: It's a term for Vietnamese—you know, I think of them as gooks. You would too if you'd been to Nam.

FACILITATOR: Bill, let's finish what we were talking about, then I want to go back to this discussion about Vietnamese as gooks. OK?

BILL: Yeah, anyway, she's going out with this Vietnamese guy...

After the discussion on why Bill was following his ex-wife, the facilitator turned to the use of the term "gook."

FACILITATOR: I want to talk a few minutes about the words that we use for people based on their race, like the word "gook" or the terms used in World War II for Japanese people, and look at why it's important to objectify the enemy in war and how and why we do that in civilian life too.[21]

The response of the group leader in this situation is respectful: he acknowledges what he has heard, flags it for later, and continues with the situation the member has started to talk about. Later he gets back to the comment and invites group members to think critically about what to many may seem as everyday thinking.

GROUP CLOSURE

Whether the entire group is coming to an end or an individual is leaving an open group, the social worker should mention the ending at least two weeks before. It is not unusual for participants to want to disregard or deny their leaving. Generally, we have not learned to say good-byes very easily and often find it easier to just slip out the back door. The group leader can provide a model for ending relationships.

The last group meeting should provide an opportunity for members to express their feelings and thoughts about the group experience and their time together. Facilitating a "talking circle," as described above (see p. 252), offers an opportunity for all to fully contribute and creates a symbolic closing.

Comments from members inevitably are a combination of humour, memories of high points in the group, and moving accounts of the impact of the group on their lives and the changes they have made. In one group I facilitated, a member said, "I have been in Canada for 12 years, and this group is the first time I have socialized with Canadians, and now I know that I can do that." Members also express sadness to see the group end and resolve to keep in touch and to continue with the changes they have made.

NOTES

1 Marcia Cohen and Audrey Mullender, "The Personal is Political: Exploring the Group Work Continuum from Individual to Social Change Goals," *Social Work with Groups* 22.1 (1999): 13–31.

2 Lawrence Shulman, "Group Work Method," in *Mutual Aid Groups and the Life Cycle*, ed. Alex Gitterman and Lawrence Shulman (Itasca, IL: F.E. Peacock, 1986) 25.

3 Gerald Corey, Marianne Scheider Corey, Patrick Callanan, and J. Michael Russell, *Group Techniques*, 2nd ed. (Pacific Grove, CA: Brooks/Cole, 1992) 12.

4 Alex Gitterman, "Developing a New Group Service: Strategies and Skills," in *Mutual Aid Groups and the Life Cycle*, ed. Alex Gitterman and Lawrence Shulman (Itasca IL: F.E. Peacock, 1986): 53–71.

5 Hannah Patricia, "Preparing Members for the Expectations of Social Work with Groups: An Approach to the Preparatory Interview," *Social Work with Groups* 22.4 (2000): 51–66.

6 Allan Brown and Tara Mistry, "Group Work with Mixed Membership Groups: Issues of Race and Gender," *Social Work with Groups* 17.3 (1994) 14.

7 Marianne Schneider Corey and Gerald Corey, *Group Process and Practice*, 4th ed. (Belmont, CA: Brooks/Cole, 1992).

8 Shulman, "Group Work Method."

9 Shulman, *Skills of Helping Individuals, Families and Groups.*

10 The Duluth program spearheaded education groups for abusive men and introduced the use of tools such as the abuse log, now adapted in programs around the world. See, e.g., Ellen Pence and Michael Paymar, *Education Groups for Men Who Batter: The Duluth Model* (New York: Springer, 1993). The version included in this chapter was created with colleagues while I was facilitating groups in the New Directions program for abused men in Ottawa, Canada.

11 This exercise was developed by Mark Holmes, Coordinator of the New Directions Program in Ottawa, Canada.

12 Freire, *Pedagogy of the Oppressed.*

13 Ira Shor, "Education is Politics: Paulo Freire's Critical Pedagogy," in *Paulo Freire: A Critical Encounter*, ed. Peter McLaren and Peter Leonard (London: Routledge, 1993) 25–35; Ira Shor, *Empowering Education: Critical Teaching for Social Change* (Chicago: University of Chicago Press, 1992).

14 Bonnie Burstow, "Freirian Codifications and Social Work Education," *Journal of Social Work Education* 272 (1991): 196–207.

15 Nina Wallerstein, "Problem-Posing Education: Freire's Method for Transformation," *Freire for the Classroom*, ed. Ira Shor (Portsmouth, MA: Boynton Cook/Heinemann, 1987) 33–44.

16 Wallerstein "Problem-Posing Education" 34.

17 Fernando Mederos, "Batterer Intervention Programs: Past and Future Prospects," in *Coordinated Community Response to Domestic Violence: Lessons from the Duluth Model*, ed. Melanie F. Shepherd and Ellen L. Pence (Newbury Park, CA: Sage, 1998) 127–50.

18 Wallerstein, "Problem-Posing Education" 38.

19 Mederos, "Batterer Intervention Programs" 132.

20 Sandra Butler and Claire Wintram, *Feminist Groupwork* (Newbury Park, CA: Sage, 1992) 76.

21 Pence and Paymar, *Education Groups for Men Who Batter* 82.

CHAPTER 13

COMMUNITY-BASED SOCIAL WORK PRACTICE

THE SOCIAL WORK PROFESSION HAS A LONG HISTORY of working within communities to create social, economic, and political changes. Although community work was widely practiced by social workers in the settlement houses during the early part of the last century, it was not acknowledged as a primary area of social work practice by university schools of social work until the 1930s. This is not surprising because of the emphasis at the time on individual problems and advancing the theory and practice of casework. Another factor contributing to the lack of recognition of community practice was the early tension between professionalization and social and political activism. However, the high levels of unemployment and poverty during the Great Depression years drew attention to the importance of community-based social work practice. The social movements of the 1960s contributed to a redefinition of community work with a focus on creating community-based services and the inclusion of a social action component.[1]

This chapter provides an overview of social work practice in communities and suggests strategies for joining with community members to strengthen and restore their communities. Most social workers, regardless of where they work, extend their practice into communities. For example, those who offer agency-based services to individuals, families, or groups also identify areas of concern for which a community-based solution is needed. Others who are employed in community-based programs, such as community health centres, neighbourhood community centres, and shelters, work with community members to identify resources and needs and organize to change the conditions that produce social inequalities and injustices.

The relevance and importance of community practice during times of economic hardship, poverty, homelessness, and unemployment cannot be overstated. Currently, as federal and provincial governments privatize services and shift the responsibility for social welfare provision to municipalities, more and more pressure has been placed on local communities to provide for their members. Decreasing employment and family incomes have resulted in growing numbers of impoverished families and have intensified the social needs, social divisions, and conflict in communities. The result has been a particularly high concentration of poverty in neighbourhoods with a large percentage of people of visible minority origins.[2] In such neighbourhoods, or ghettos as Kazemipur and Halli refer to them, poor families have a connection only to other poor families and end up separated from society generally. In their analysis of the situation Kazemipur and Halli report that this over-representation is due to ethnic poverty, the kinds of jobs that are available to these residents, and residential segregation.

Within this context a revitalization and rethinking of community-based social work practice is taking place. It has even been suggested that the very survival of social work requires a reclaiming of community practice.[3] "The challenge for the social work profession is to respond to these changing conditions in ways that are proactive, advocate for vulnerable populations, and emphasize and expand skills in community-focused practice that connect empowerment strategies with social and economic development."[4] Community practice is a political undertaking, essential to achieving social justice and social change.

APPROACHES TO COMMUNITY-BASED PRACTICE

A number of models have been proposed for social work community organizing activities. The three forms of community development proposed by Jack Rothman over 30 years ago—locality development, social planning, and social action—still capture the specific social work practice activities in the community today.[5] Rothman suggested that community practice involves mixed models and a combination of these three strategies:[6]

1. *Locality development.* The primary method used in settlement houses focuses on building community capacity: members of a defined locality or neighbourhood are supported in identifying problems and/or common concerns and discovering solutions. Capacity building as a goal involves increasing community resources, increasing member involvement and local leadership, and enhancing community functioning. Neighbourhood-based services improve accessibility and solve transportation difficulties. They are also likely to offer culturally relevant and appropriate services in a number of languages or through translation.

2. *Social planning.* Social planning councils and task forces place emphasis on specific tasks and goals for information-gathering, analysis, and the identification of solutions. The outcome might be a brief to the municipal government on concerns such as homelessness, illicit drug use, or hate crimes.

3. *Social action.* The organized resistance and response of community members intend to force concessions and achieve institutional and structural social change in policies or laws and power distribution. When the source of community concerns is situated within unequal power relations and unequal material conditions, social action is a necessary part of social work practice. The social action approach, according to Rothman, requires that the social worker act as an advocate and activist with "a disadvantaged segment of the population that needs to be organized, perhaps in alliances with others, in order to make demands on the larger community for increased resources or treatment more in accordance with social justice or democracy."[7] Such activity can lead to the development of alternative services as well as program and policy changes.

Elements of Rothman's models are evident in current social work practices in the community such as "community organizing," "community development," "community action," "building community capacity," and "restoring communities." While the language has changed, the actual practices reflect his original formulation. For example, community development, as defined by Felix Rivera and John Erlich, combines locality development and social action and refers to "efforts to mobilize people who are directly affected by a community condition (that is, the 'victims,' the unaffiliated, the unorganized, and the nonparticipating) into groups and organizations to enable them to take action on the social problems and issues that concern them."[8] However, Rivera and Erlich are critical of Rothman's models because they do not acknowledge the racial, ethnic, and cultural diversity of community members and the role of religion, language, and kinship patterns in community building. For Weil, community practice involves development, organizing, planning, and implementing social change strategies.[9]

Robyn Munford and Wheturangi Walsh-Tapiata speak to the bicultural context of community development in New Zealand, and the importance of working from peoples' own definitions of the issues in order to insure that the local and indigenous knowledge of communities guides the practice. In their view community workers assist groups who have become marginalized and excluded from participation "to achieve positive changes that will enhance their daily lived experiences in all domains (social, political, cultural, economic etc.)."[10] In order to facilitate positive social change, it is necessary that the community worker understand how structures and policies can be challenged and transformed.

In their book *Community Action*, Lamoureux et al. emphasize the importance of mobilizing community members and suggest that the process of community organizing:

1. brings together people who directly or indirectly have common interests;
2. utilizes a democratic process for decision-making and participation;
3. engages in an educational process that builds on existing knowledge and skills of members;
4. brings about "change, to reduce or eliminate exploitation, oppression and alienation."[11]

A feminist understanding of community work has further transformed community practice. Women's organizing expresses their standpoint and grows out of specific issues that are impacting their lives. While working toward empowerment through consciousness-raising, such organizing concentrates on bridging differences and building solidarity. Marilyn Callahan describes feminist community organizing as including all of the traditional activities; however, she finds that what distinguishes feminist community organizing from other approaches is the inclusion of gender analysis, alongside that of class and race and its commitment to helping women to identify their needs and to organize for solutions in their communities.[12] Most social workers who are working with communities would concur that structural inequalities are best addressed at a collective rather than an individual level.

ASSESSMENT AND STRATEGIES FOR CHANGE

Often the term "community" refers to residents in a geographic area, including their diversity and subgenres. There are also communities of individuals who have common interests based on culture, ethnicity, disability, sexual orientation, or gender. For the most part, community practice and organizing takes place in neighbourhoods that include "a majority of workers, welfare recipients, the unemployed, the elderly, and the young, and a minority of petty bourgeois, which includes artist and organizers."[13] These communities may have fewer resources and greater social concerns, little space or opportunity to come together to create and sustain a sense of community, and serious environmental pollution.

Entering the Community

Researching the community is an essential component of community work and prepares the social worker for the process ahead.[14] If a social worker does not live in the community, the first task is to learn about its history and geographic boundaries; the diversity among its residents; their strengths; the available social, educational, and health resources; and local primary industries and employers. The depth of the social worker's knowledge and sensitivity will influence the working relationship that follows. All communities have specific problems and conflicts as well as strengths, resources, and existing leaders. The social worker generally begins by identifying these community leaders and connecting with local organizations. Recognition of current strategies and programs established by committed community workers and agencies will facilitate the full and meaningful participation of members and relevant community strategies.

Since geographic communities are not homogeneous, members are diverse based on their identification with ethnicity/race, age, gender, sexual orientation, and/or ability. When working in ethnically mixed communities, the uniqueness of diverse groups and the economic and political realities in each community must be taken into account. The relationship of the specific community with the wider community and the political and economic factors that are impacting on its members is another consideration. For example, after 9/11, there has been an increase in racism against persons of Arab and Muslim backgrounds in both Canada and the US. Discrimination against and injustice experienced by specific groups in society generally thus may be reflected in the smaller community.

Identifying Concerns/Needs and Social Action

The common goal of community approaches is to work collectively and engage members of the community in the task of identifying concerns or needs and in improving social, political, and economic conditions. This practice facilitates communication among members, enhances knowledge and skills, contributes to improved individual and community functioning, and fosters empowerment through consciousness-raising. Through effective participation and control of the process and decision-making, social relationships and organizational structures in the community are strengthened. Particular attention is placed on creating bridges among diverse ethnic groups, fostering positive relationships, and engaging members who have systematically been disadvantaged.

Community organizer Joan Kuyek, in her book *Fighting for Hope: Organizing to Realize Our Dreams*, suggests an exercise called "community mapping" to assist members in the assessment of their community.[15] In the exercise, the social worker provides pencils, crayons, or markers and a piece of paper for each participant and divides people into groups of four to five members. Each participant is asked to draw a picture of their community, including the geographic area, friends, workplace, or organizations. Then the members come together as a larger group and discuss the major concerns facing their communities, their strengths and sources of hope, as well as the limitations and sources of despair. The social worker can assist community members to compile a list of concerns and prioritize them, identify goals and resources, and create a plan of action.

Community activists in Toronto also suggest an educational process as a means to strengthen the ability of community members to identify concerns and to engage in collective struggle toward social change. The popular education tool called the "spiral model" is an action and reflection model that guides the process of social action (Figure 13.1).

The beginning point is the concrete experiences and past actions of the concerned community members; from these, a problem, need, or identified injustice may emerge. The members begin to reflect on their experiences, to identify patterns in what they have reported, and to discern commonalities and differences. New information and theory builds on the experiences and helps to explain them, leading to further debate and discussion. The members apply what they have learned in order to develop a strategy, a plan of action based on their knowledge and experience. Finally, the plan is implemented, and a process of praxis—reflection, action, and reflection—takes place. Strategies may be revised and members may move through the cycle again.

Bernard Wohl offers the following example of the spiral model and education process. A youth group in a New York settlement house organized a social action project called the "Nike 'Give-Back' Campaign."[16] It began with a discussion among the members about how brand name sneakers, particularly Nike, are coveted but too expensive for them and many other poor young people. Working with staff, the young people researched the corporate exploitation of workers and the high price of the sneakers in the US and wrote letters to the company's president and to Michael Jordan, the basketball star who endorsed the product. When they did not receive adequate answers to their questions, they began to organize a "sneaker give-back" action. They were able to mobilize youth from 11 other settlement houses to travel by bus to Niketown in New York City to demonstrate and give back bags of worn Nike sneakers. In the process they increased their understanding of the globalization of poverty and social injustice, developed organizing skills, and gained a realization of their collective capacity to carry out a plan of action.

Mutual aid groups often have a community development component and follow a process similar to the spiral model, as evident in this experience of the

FIGURE 13.1 THE SPIRAL MODEL OF COMMUNITY ACTION

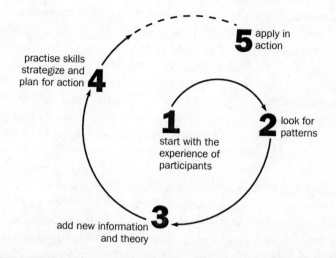

Sources: "The spiral model of community action" by Margie Bruun-Meyer/Art Work, from *Educating for a Change* by Rick Arnold, Bev Burke, Carl James, D'Arcy Martin, and Barb Thomas (Toronto: Between the Lines, 1991). Reproduced by permission.

Canadian Centre for Victims and Torture.[17] One young Muslim woman disclosed to a worker that she had been raped while in a Somali prison and was ashamed to tell anyone. She experienced serious physical trauma not only from the rape but from earlier ritual female genital mutilation. Workers soon became aware of other women with similar experiences who shared a profound sense of physical, psychological, and social isolation. A weekly mutual aid group was formed to help these women make new friends connected by these common experiences. The women quickly identified basic survival needs—housing, food, clothing, job and English language training, and their rights as refugees—as their primary concerns. At the time Metro Toronto Housing Authority had refused to accept applications from refugees for subsidized housing. The women decided to form a Somali Women's Advocacy Group and successfully challenged the housing policy under the Canadian Human Rights Code. The direct involvement of the women and their collective action demonstrated their potential and prepared them for more involvement.

Community Functioning

Communities differ in their level of functioning, their resources, and their strengths. Therefore, a community assessment inevitably leads to identifying needs and issues and questioning why the disparities exist in the first place.

The promotion of critical thinking assists members in gaining an understanding of the inequities facing them.

The task of the social worker is to engage community members in order to advance the goal of enhancing overall community functioning in economic terms (work and income) and in areas such as mutual support. Members of the community must be able to find assistance in extreme circumstances or emergencies; this requires a process for communication among members and between them and the wider community. Through such communication, a forum for expressing ideas and concerns develops.[18] Building capacity in communities in this way helps members to take control of their communities, establishes local leadership, and lays the groundwork for much-needed community resources.

One example of a community-driven and controlled community centre that has enhanced community functioning is the Debra Dynes Family House in Ottawa.[19] The Family House, directed by social worker Barbara Carroll, is situated in one of the town houses in a low-income social housing neighbourhood of 800 people living in 183 homes. The highly diverse community population consists of families from 25 nations, many of whom are recent immigrants and refugees who have arrived in Canada from war-torn countries. The Family House is the centre of the community and provides a food bank, educational programs such as English as a second language and sewing classes, day care services and an after-school program for children, access to computers and the Internet, support for job hunting, and a drop-in area to socialize and connect with others. People are often isolated from their extended families and benefit greatly from organized community support. In communities such as this social work practice is based on capacity-enhancement and the recognition that there are personal and social resources in the community. Such an approach strengthens and unifies communities, particularly those that consist of groups from different ethnic and cultural backgrounds.[20]

Community gardens are another example of addressing locally defined problems, strengthening mutual support, and promoting participation from a cross-section of the community. The garden itself provides food and many learning opportunities. Coordination and co-operation are needed to make decisions regarding the space, preparation of the soil, planning the garden itself, the ongoing upkeep, and the harvest. It can become a focal point of the community and a source of pride as a vacant lot or unkempt field is transformed into a productive space. The garden is perceived as a safe and neutral place in which to interact. Research has demonstrated the importance of gardening in "revitalizing and strengthening neighborhoods, including reclaiming devastated urban areas and fostering neighborhood social ties and interaction, neighborhood pride, community involvement, political activism, and feelings of safety and adjustment."[21]

Murals generate a sense of community pride and can also serve as a strategy for conveying a message. Posters, banners, and buttons all educate and mobilize community members around an issue. In Ottawa in the 1970s a group of activists living in a low-income community produced a button that said "Pierre Trudeau [the prime minister at the time] lives in public housing" in order to dispel the myth that only they were receiving direct support from the government.

EMPOWERMENT THROUGH PARTICIPATION

Community members gain the most for their communities when they participate in decision-making at all levels of the process of organizing. Table 13.1, adapted from the work of George Brager and Harry Specht, demonstrates the differing degrees of community participation in various organizing strategies.

TABLE 13.1 DEGREES OF PARTICIPATION OF COMMUNITY MEMBERS

Degree of Participation	Organizing Strategy
None	Community not informed
Receives information	Present a completed plan to community members with expectation of compliance
Is consulted	Present a completed plan and asks for support
Offer advice	Present a plan and invite feed-back/contributions
Some decision-making	Identify and present a problem to the community and request decisions be made in a number of defined areas
Has control	Assist the community in identifying the problem and generating solutions/goals and a means to meet them

Source: adapted from Brager and Specht, Community Organizing 39.

In any form of community practice, there is the danger of community members losing their voice as community practitioners take the lead and neglect to involve them in the process. In her discussion of feminist organizing Joanna Brenner points out that feminist activists have shifted from organizing to advocacy and that there has been "a displacement of goals in which feminists aim to get something from the state for women rather than to encourage the self organization of women."[22]

If the goal is to work in partnership with community members to achieve a better functioning community, as is argued here, emphasis must be placed on the knowledge and skills of community members, as well as on their full participation in decision-making both in their communities and in society generally. While advocacy may continue to be a social work activity, it should not occur without a community organizing component and community involvement. In this way the process of community change is not imposed from the outside but created, owned, and controlled by the community members. Otherwise, community members become passive recipients of service rather than actors in the change process.

As members participate in the act of acquiring resources for themselves and their community, they also become empowered and have improved functioning. Si Kahn reminds us that the process and content of our organizing activities very much influence the outcome:

> Through the organizing process, people are supposed to become empowered. Because knowledge is power (and because lack of knowledge is in and of itself disempowering), people also need to become knowledgeable. They need new information, and new interpretations of old information, along with the tools to acquire and interpret information in the future. But they need to learn all this in ways that are themselves empowering. If the content of what they learn is contradicted by the way(s) in which they learn it, the organizing and empowerment process undercuts itself and dies.[23]

Through direct involvement to bring about change, community members gain awareness of their existing and potential resources and strengths and, in the process, become empowered to act on their own behalf.

At times grassroots community responses to problems are both initiated and controlled by community members. For example, in Harlem a mutual support approach to communal living was organized by drug users themselves in order to provide services to both those who are active drug users and those who have stopped and are in recovery. "Stand Up Harlem" has around 30 people living and working out of three houses. They work in partnership with those who are experiencing drug-related harm, homelessness, hunger, and ill health and offer them a meal, shower, clean clothes, and a safe environment. By providing a place where survival needs can be met, the staff support people in their choices while opening up other options to drug use. As "Stand Up Harlem" demonstrates: "What works for many is a community-based response that provides social networks, services, and medical intervention that allow individuals to make choices and to reclaim their lives."[24]

Dave Backwith and Greg Mantle turn to the Cuban community-oriented social work (COSW) model in which social workers are considered to be the "army of the healers of the soul" because of their close relationship and commitment to families in the communities in which they work. They are proactive in their approach, going out and meeting people block by block, learning about the issues, and working collectively in order to change them.[25] On one visit to Cuba, I was scheduled to meet with some social work students in Santiago; however, due to a campaign to prevent dengue fever, they were in the communities going door to door educating families. Such a proactive approach and level of participation is reflective of Cuban culture, but it can inform practice in the Western context.

Canadian social workers Purnima George and Sara Marlowe provide an example of structural social work in action and a social action community practice in India. The focus of the project was working with a grassroots organization to improve conditions for Dalits (untouchables) and poor-caste Hindus in Marthwada, India. The success of the project is astounding in that untouchability has been abolished in over 200 villages—the result of the simultaneous use of social care and social change and planting seeds of transformation.[26]

ART AND PERFORMANCE IN THE DISABILITY COMMUNITY

In an innovative community outreach program, Alan Shain, a social worker, disability activist, and performer, has brought the art of dance to the disability community by integrating their issues into a community development framework.[27] In the context of a graduate field placement at The Ottawa School of Dance, Shain was co-creator and co-facilitator of creative movement programs for people with disabilities. External funding for the project ensured that community programs could be offered for a reduced fee at the school itself, as well as on site in group homes, community organizations, and day programs. Information packages were developed and sent to organizations of people with disabilities, and the mail-out was followed with emails and telephone calls. This outreach strategy generated considerable interest within the community. A planned event to spotlight the new program drew over 100 people and showcased a performance by two dancers with disability from Toronto. Shain contacted the media, issued press releases, and offered interviews. The active and well-planned outreach component successfully captured the attention of the community.

Weekly workshops involved improvisation exercises with live music accompaniment and explored different techniques to link music, space, anatomy, and energy to dance. Shain describes how he used movement and dance as a source of creative expression:

Dance therapy focuses on unlocking individual emotions. While this was partly what our workshops involved, we were also working on building concrete skills in using dance as artistic expression that sometimes involved analysis/commentary on the part of the participants. We were also developing participants' skills in using dance as a way of working with others and of working within a larger group context.[28]

Using the concepts of community and isolation to create a dance piece, Shain incorporated the meaning these concepts had for group members and developed a series of movements to express what these concepts meant to the participants. "In practice," Shain explains, "I learned how to use movement and dance to bring out people's own ideas about the world around them."

The challenge is to make dance and creative movement relevant to the lives of people with disability. This requires adapting exercises and techniques to allow people to explore movement on their own terms. But this initiative is not merely about adapting techniques. Participants will be creating new dance and new ways of moving. These workshops will be changing the meaning of dance itself.[29]

On a personal level, participants reported improved balance, coordination, and fitness as well as increased confidence. In turn social work practice is advanced, and the art of dance is being enriched and transformed.

FIGHTING FOR SOCIAL JUSTICE

Community-based social work practice cannot be separated from the political context and, at times, is controversial. On occasion community members will decide that they have "had enough" and that an organized protest or mass defiance is the only avenue open to them. "Disruptive dissensus," as Richard Cloward and Frances Fox Piven refer to it, is a mass action that is often unlawful and institutionally disruptive;[30] disruptive protests, such as strikes, pickets, and civil disobedience, have been effective strategies to communicate concerns and gain concessions throughout the history of community organizing in Canada and the US. Cloward and Piven note that in the US substantial gains, preceded by disruptive protest, were made in labour rights, social welfare legislation, and civil rights during the periods of 1933–37 and 1963–67. They conclude that "poor people's organizations have a dependent, even parasitical relation to the very disruptive protest that they disparage; they form and thrive during periods when there is a surge of political energy from the bottom, only to wither and disappear when the energy subsides."[31] The organizing efforts of social workers therefore are influenced by the political climate and the readiness of citizens to act on their own behalf.

Social workers have fought for both a community service and their own employment. For instance, in 1990 the already meagerly funded Women's Program of the Canadian Secretary of State was targeted for cuts in funding to women's publications and 80 women's centres across the country. This prompted an organized resistance from women, particularly centre workers and grassroots activists. That spring, women in St. John's, Halifax, and Vancouver occupied Secretary of State offices to protest the elimination of operational funding to women's centres. While police removed women in Halifax and Vancouver within a few hours, the St. John's occupation lasted five days and received solid support from the wider community. The resistance resulted in a reinstatement of funding to all the centres.

Increasingly, social workers are realizing the importance of coalition and social movement building in order to gain a more powerful base and a greater voice. Coalitions are able to quickly mobilize large numbers of people for marches and advocacy campaigns. In recent years anti-poverty activists have been most active and visible. The Ontario Common Front (OCF) was formed to mount a militant resistance against the attack on poor people that accompanied the Progressive Conservative government's drastic dismantling of social programs and reduction of social assistance. The Ontario Coalition Against Poverty (OCAP), a province-wide alliance of anti-poverty activists and advocates for the poor actively opposes evictions and police mistreatment of the homeless. In June 2000 an OCAP protest at the Ontario Legislature in opposition to the government's policies and against the growing crisis in homelessness and poverty drew 1,500 marchers, including a delegation of poor and homeless people. Police in riot garb and on horseback charged the crowds and a melee ensued. Dozens of charges were laid, and three OCAP leaders were given particularly serious charges. The activists believe that these actions are intended to intimidate those who are part of an effective protest.[32] Similarly, in the US, the Coalition on Human Needs is an active anti-poverty coalition of national and grassroots organizations, including the NASW.[33]

While some social workers do become involved in disruptive dissensus, others may feel more comfortable in exerting pressure on decision-makers through other tactics such as organizing petitions, leafleting, and letter-writing. Whether situated in family agencies, schools, hospitals, or community centres, when social workers focus on the community, they become aware of the strengths and resilience of community members and the difficulties facing them on a daily basis. Community work inevitably includes strategies to promote social change and social justice.

NOTES

1 George Brager and Harry Specht, *Community Organizing* (New York: Columbia University Press, 1973).

2 Kazemipur and Halli, *The New Poverty in Canada.*

3 Ken Barter, "Reclaiming Community: Shaping the Social Work Agenda," *Canadian Social Work* 2.2 (Fall 2000): 6–18.

4 Marie O. Weil, "Community Building: Building Community Practice," *Social Work* 41.5 (September 1996): 481.

5 Jack Rothman, "Three Models of Community Practice," in *Strategies of Community Organization*, 2nd ed., ed. Fred Cox et al. (Itasca, IL: F.E. Peacock, 1974) 22–39.

6 Jack Rothman, "Approaches to Community Intervention," in *Strategies of Community Intervention*, 5th ed., ed. J. Rothman, J.L. Erlichs, and J.E. Tropman, with F.M. Cox (Itasca, IL: F.E. Peacock, 1995) 26–63. Cited in Weil, "Community Building" 491.

7 J. Rothman, "Three Models of Community Practice" 24.

8 Felix G. Rivera and John L. Erlich, "A Time of Fear; A Time of Hope," in *Community Organizing in a Diverse Society*, 3rd ed., ed. Felix G. Rivera and John L. Erlich (Toronto: Allyn and Bacon, 1998) 3.

9 M. Weil, *The Handbook of Community Practice* (Thousand Oaks, CA: Sage, 2005).

10 Robyn Munford and Wheturangi Walsh-Tapiata, "Community Development: Principles in Practice," in *Social Work Theories in Action*, ed. Mary Nash, Robyn Munford and Kieran O'Donoghue (London: Jessica Kingsley, 2005) 98.

11 Henri Lamoureux, Robert Mayer, and Jean Panet-Raymond, *Community Action* (Montreal: Black Rose Books, 1989) 7.

12 Marilyn Callahan, "Feminist Community Organizing in Canada," in *Community Organizing*, ed. Brian Wharf and Michael Clague (Don Mills, ON: Oxford University Press, 1997) 183.

13 Lamoureux et al., *Community Action* 30.

14 Lamoureux et al., *Community Action* 62.

15 Joan Newman Kuyek, *Fighting for Hope: Organizing to Realize Our Dreams* (Montreal: Black Rose Books, 1990) 82.

16 Bernard J. Wohl, "The Power of Group Work with Youth: Creating Activists of the Future," *Social Work with Groups* 22.4 (2000): 3–13.

17 Jill Blakeney, Fadumo Jama Dirie, and Mary Ann MacRae, "Empowering Traumatized Somali Women: A Support Group Model for Helping Survivors to Cope," in *Community Support for Survivors of Torture*, ed. Karen Price (Toronto: Canadian Centre for Victims of Torture, n.d.) 50–58.

18 Antonia Pantoja and Wilhelmina Perry, "Community Development and Restoration: A Perspective and Case Study," in *Community Organizing in a Diverse Society*, ed. Felix G. Rivera and John L. Erlich (Toronto: Allyn and Bacon, 1998) 220–42.

19 For a detailed report on activities, see *Ottawa Citizen*, "Humble Computer Station Links Global Village," 16 October 2001: 13.

20 Melvin Degado, *Community Social Work Practice in an Urban Context: The Potential of a Capacity-Enhancement Perspective* (New York: Oxford University Press, 2000).

21 Mary Ohmer, Pamela Meadowcroft, Kate Freed, and Erica Lewis, "Community Gardening and Community Development: Individual, Social and Community Benefits of a Community Conservation Program," *Journal of Community Practice* 17 (2009): 378.

22 Brenner, *Women and the Politics of Class* 262.

23 Si Kahn, "Leadership: Realizing Concepts through Creative Process," in *Community Practice: Models in Action*, ed. Marie Weil (Binghamton, NY: The Haworth Press, 1997) 110.

24 Kelly McGowan and Nancy McKenzie, "A Community Response to the Needs of Drug Users, Stand Up Harlem," *Health/PAC Bulletin* (Winter 1993): 13.

25 Dave Backwith and Greg Mantle, "Inequalities in Health and Community-oriented Social Work: Lessons from Cuba," *International Social Work* 52.4 (2009): 507.

26 Purnima George and Sara Marlowe, "Structural Social Work in Action: Experiences from Rural India," *Journal of Progressive Human Services* 16.1 (2005): 5–24.

27 Alan Shain is committed to the power of performance in transforming the social experience of disability. Through his company, Smashing Stereotypes Productions, he performs across Canada and around the world at festivals and comedy clubs, as well as for schools and community events. He can be reached at alanshain@yahoo.ca.

28 Alan Shain, personal interview, 1 April 2003.

29 *Dance Network News* 9.35 (Winter–Spring 2002) 4.

30 Richard A. Cloward and Frances Fox Piven, "Disruptive Dissensus: People and Power in the Industrial Age," *Reflections on Community Organization: Enduring Themes and Critical Issues*, ed. Jack Rothman (Itasca, IL: F.E. Peacock, 1999) 165–93.

31 Cloward and Piven, "Disruptive Dissensus" 188–89.

32 E.g., see Bryan Palmer, "Repression and Dissent: The OCAP Trials," *Canadian Dimension* (May/June 2003), http://www.canadiandimension.mb.ca.

33 Coalition on Human Needs, http://www.chn.org/humanneeds/.

CHAPTER 14

THE WORKPLACE, PROFESSIONAL ASSOCIATIONS, AND UNION MEMBERSHIP

So what has CASW contributed to social work in Canada? The simplest answer is that it has created the profession. That is not to say that it created social work, but the early pioneers of the CASW worked tirelessly to develop and promote an indigenous social work profession in Canada.[1]

T HESE ARE DIFFICULT TIMES not only for those who seek help from beleaguered social agencies, but also for those who work in these agencies. The global economic crisis, funding cuts, and expanding caseloads mean that social workers are experiencing tremendous stress both from the nature of people's social and personal problems, inadequate resources, and the structure of social welfare delivery, and from the tension between their role as social workers and the mandate of the agency and the needs of the client. This chapter examines the working conditions of social workers, the current challenges, and the role of professional associations and unions in advancing social work practice.

THE WORKPLACE

Along with the declining commitment by governments to the welfare state that has resulted in dwindling resources, social workers face increased bureaucratization of the workplace, greater control from funding sources, and lack of autonomy and consequently reduced ability to make decisions that directly affect policy and practice. They witness the impact on people of inadequate social welfare programs and suffer a greater feeling of helplessness and frustration. Those who work with victims of torture and of physical and sexual violence may begin to experience symptoms of trauma themselves, such as emotional numbing, sleep disturbances, and fear for their own safety and the safety of family members.[2]

Worsening economic and social conditions, compounded with the absence of workplace autonomy and organizational support, contribute to burnout and impact negatively on the physical and mental well-being of social workers. A survey by the Canadian Union of Public Employees (CUPE) found that an increase in workload among Ontario social service workers in Development Services, Worker's Compensation, and Children's Aid Societies has an alarming impact on their well-being. Of the social service workers who responded, 87 per cent reported an increase in work-load with a negative toll on their overall health (Figure 14.1). Of the survey respondents, 50 per cent reported that their physicians also suggested that their symptoms were connected to their work. Social workers also deal with actions that pose a threat to their personal safety. Close to three-quarters (71 per cent) of the workers said that they were subjected to physical assaults, verbal abuse, or threats at work, and 50 per cent of the CAS workers were threatened with assault by a client. Acts of violence against social workers are often perpetrated by clients who are in desperate situations, who have exhausted all possibilities, who feel powerless, and who are reduced to vicious expressions of legitimate rage. There is no evidence that this situation has changed in the ten years since the survey.

FIGURE 14.1 IMPACT ON WORKERS' HEALTH

- 94% reported feeling run down
- 89% reported having headaches
- 87% reported feeling exhausted
- 86% reported muscle or joint pain
- 84% reported sleeping difficulties
- 80% reported anxiety
- 65% reported change in appetite
- 60% reported indigestion

Source: CUPE, *Overloaded and Underfire.*

Although social welfare agencies operate under a clear mandate, they often fall short of meeting their objectives. For example, Children's Aid Societies are mandated to protect children who are being abused and/or neglected, but funding levels prohibit the agencies from hiring a sufficient number of social workers to meet the demands for service. At the same time as social welfare services are cut, and the cost of housing and food rise, more and more parents find the struggle to provide adequate care to their children a more onerous one. In 2001 the Ottawa CAS reported a 20 per cent increase in caseload over a two-month period, far exceeding the existing resources.[3] As a result, 400 reports of abuse or neglect were waiting for investigation, potentially placing children in jeopardy. Such situations create anxiety among social workers, in part because they are aware of the possibility of being blamed and charged in the event of traumatic occurrences among children on their caseload. A study to establish US child welfare worker caseloads found that the average worker had been assigned twice as many as the recommended 16 to 17 per month.[4] The authors of that study refer to the recommendations of the Council on Accreditation, an international independent accrediting body for public and private social agencies, which suggests that 15 active investigations along with 15 to 30 open cases is the optimal caseload for child protection.

Tragic outcomes such as the Ontario case of Jordan Heikamp, a 37-day infant who starved to death at a women's shelter in Toronto, are on every child protection worker's mind. Although both Jordan's mother and the social worker were charged initially, these charges were dropped at the inquiry as the judge, lawyers, and CUPE attributed the baby's death to an inadequate social service system.[5] However, press coverage of the case denigrated the social worker and called into question the profession's educational standards by suggesting that a province-wide public review of social work education in Ontario ought to be conducted.[6] The media coverage prompted the Ontario Association of Social Workers (OASW) to release an "opinion article" on 26 March 2001, speaking out against the vilification of the social worker and the profession by the media.[7]

As more and more families are marginalized, child protection workers face heartbreaking situations where children and their parents are increasingly at risk. The coroner's inquest into the death of Diane Anderson, age 35, and two of her five children in a fire reveals a woman who reached out for help on several occasions as she became unable to care for herself and her family. Diane lived in a Toronto Community Housing project in a "cockroach-infested, too small and decaying townhouse."[8] The complex was considered too dangerous for welfare case workers to visit.[9] Her life began falling apart when her fiancé was shot to death in front of her 10-year-old son. Then the couple's baby was delivered stillborn on the day of his funeral. Afterwards, she called the police on several occasions pleading for help: "I've lost my fiancé and I had a child on the way and I lost my baby. And everything has been going downhill and I am—

I just—I don't feel like I'm, I'm, I can't, I can't cope. I can't, I can't cope anymore." A report was made to the Toronto CAS; however, the referral was "lost" and never assigned to a worker. After 19 months and drinking more heavily, she fell asleep while her smallest two boys played with a lighter and the townhouse went up in flames. Reporting on the tragedy, Christie Blatchford exclaimed, "If only the world had tried as hard to save her as she tried to save herself."[10]

Child protection workers, in particular, are expected to assume the contradictory and difficult roles of both compassionate individuals concerned mostly with social care and agency bureaucrats who must enforce rules and take on the function of social control. For example, in their work, they offer support to families while, at the same time, they use their authority to monitor and police parents and make decisions regarding children. A social worker interviewed by CUPE offers a list of the changing working conditions and policies in child welfare that make the work more difficult and stressful: "Over the last four or five years in child welfare, things are in a constant state of change—new legislation, changes in job expectations, new paperwork formats, increased reliance on computer technology. Staff shortages, lack of resources for referring clients, changes in client procedures, significant delays in matters moving through court process, reduced availability of at-school programs for children with special needs—The list is endless."[11] A workload study of CAS workers in Ontario found that 70 per cent of workers' time is spent on paperwork, leaving a mere 30 per cent for the children and families they are mandated to help.[12] A child protection worker interviewed by the author summed up the difficulties of working under these kind of conditions by stating, "When you go home, you have this pain in your stomach."

ORGANIZATIONAL ANALYSIS

One of the first tasks of social workers is to gain familiarity with the stated goals of the agency in which they work and to understand the policy and procedures that are in place to meet these goals. Much of this information is available in annual reports, staff manuals, and agency web sites, as well as being imparted by the agency to workers on the job. As social workers familiarize themselves with an agency's structure, programs, and policies, they invariably gain an understanding of the contradictions and conflicts within it. An organizational analysis, argues Joan Arches, assists social workers in understanding burnout as a public issue rather than as a private trouble due to individual deficiency. In a study of social workers Arches found that the only statistically significant contributors to burnout were bureaucratization, control from funding sources, and lack of autonomy in the workplace. In particular, social workers reported conflict between the policies of the organization and the professional judge-ments of agency employees. Arches emphasizes the importance of conducting an organizational analysis of workplace stress and to develop strategies for responding to it. She guides social workers in assessing sources of organizational conflict by examining four areas: (1) decision-making and the degree of input employees have in decisions that impact on their work; (2) the labour process itself, including the assignment of caseload and the determination of activities and tasks; (3) bureaucratization of the workplace; and (4) the connection between private individual issues and collective public issues and the isolation and powerlessness experienced by employees. All areas are important in under-standing the current context of cuts to programs and restructuring of services. The following questions will guide an assessment of agency bureaucratization and capture the workplace reality experienced by many social workers:

1. Are there too many rules and/or too long a chain of command to permit working in a way that feels clinically correct?
2. Do you feel that you cannot always carry out the professionally best type of intervention because of organizational constraints?
3. Do you often experience ethical dilemmas between agency policy and your professional judgement?
4. Are you spending too much time on paperwork? Does it help the client or others working with the client?
5. Are you encouraged or discouraged by supervisors/administrators from making changes in the way work is carried out?
6. Have you seriously discussed these concerns with others in your work-place, union, or professional organization? What other individuals and groups might be most receptive?[13]

Increased bureaucratization, whether imposed by agency administration or government policy, has a profound effect on the autonomy of social workers and their ability to be both ethical and caring in their practice. The majority of social workers must complete a daily log of their activities and account for their hours at work. This documentation informs staffing decisions.

As suggested above, there are many challenges for social workers as needed welfare programs and resources are reduced. One of these is the difficulty of advancing a critical perspective without becoming isolated within one's agency. Colleagues and supervisors are more likely to respect a differing view, critique, or suggestion if they see the social worker as a valued member of the agency, a person who has demonstrated competence and commitment. However, gaining this acceptance often means tacitly accepting or not criticizing agency goals and practices. This is particularly true in the case of social work managers who are placed in the position of enforcing agency policy.

Social workers face a growing pressure and increasing dilemma as they experience the tension between practicing in an ethical and competent manner and implementing policies and program regulations in the context of program cutbacks and mean-spirited governments; sometimes, they decide that they cannot ethically follow agency or state directives. Using a fair degree of latitude in the interpretation of rules and regulations allows them to err on the side of generosity and maximize resources for the client. However, social workers who take a stand for their clients in opposition to the agency and employer often face dismissal.[14] As was discussed in Situation #3 in Chapter 6, a social worker manager and three workers refused to implement a provincial policy on the grounds that it was culturally inappropriate to the Aboriginal community they were serving, potentially harmful, and counter to the social work ethics of practice at the time, which directed the social worker to "subordinate the employer's interests to the interests of the client."[15] They were dismissed by the employer and subsequently pursued legal action. The Supreme Court of Newfoundland supported the actions of the government. One of the social workers appealed, only to find the appeal dismissed by the Newfoundland Court of Appeal on the grounds that his "breach of duty was a fundamental breach of the master-servant relationship."[16] The concerns of the Innu population were "not relevant" to the case. Despite the potential seriousness of the ethical dilemma between policy and their professional judgement, neither the national office of CASW nor the union advocated on behalf of these workers.

THE PROFESSIONALIZATION AND REGULATION OF SOCIAL WORK

In the early years, one of the central tasks for social work was to gain recognition as a profession by establishing educational programs, a theoretical and practice base, a professional association, and a code of ethics. The purpose of the CASW, formed in 1926, was "to bring together professional social workers for such cooperative effort as may enable them more effectively to carry out their ideals of service to the community."[17] The activities of the association included the promotion of professional standards, development of educational programs, public recognition of the profession, the production of an official publication, a professional employment service, participation at the international level, and research.

Branches were soon formed in provinces and regions. Initially they reported directly to the national office but gradually became autonomous organizations. In 1975 CASW became a national association by gathering these provincial associations under a federated structure.[18] In 2010 CASW was the voice for close to 18,000 social work members in Canada. However, gradually the national voice and profile of social work is being weakened by the withdrawal of member organizations and the growing prominence of the Canadian Council of Social Work Regulators, formed in 2010.

In August 31, 2003, the Ordre professionnel des travailleurs sociaux du Québec (OPTSQ) withdrew from CASW for budgetary reasons. At 5,841 members, the OPTSQ had the largest membership among the provincial/territorial associations.[19] The loss of the representation and practice contributions from them has created a void in the profession of social work in Canada. Unexpectedly, in the fall of 2010, the Alberta College of Social Workers (ACSW) gave notice of leaving the federation and the OASW gave notice of withdrawal for a one-year period. As of 2010, the ACSW has 6,307 members and the OASW 3,812 members, comprising over 50 per cent of the national membership. On 31 March 2011 both OASW and ACSW withdrew from CASW. Since CASW relies on membership fees for its revenue, it now faces a serious challenge.

The decision by both the boards of OASW and ACSW to leave a national association with an 84-year-old history, without consulting with their members, is unconscionable. The repercussions are immense; the decision reflects a narrow view of the profession and excludes a national and international presence. Fortunately there is a mobilization of members in both provinces who are opposed to this direction.

It comes as no surprise that there are dissenting views among some provincial members regarding CASW's governance, mandate, and fee structure. It is for these reasons that in 2009 CASW, in partnership with the member organizations, initiated an organizational review and obtained the services of a consulting group AGORA to assist with the process. A comprehensive report *Together... An Operational Review of the Canadian Association of Social Workers* was distributed widely and a subcommittee formed to develop an action plan with a time-line. Changes have already been made to the development of an equitable fee structure, and the fees of both ACSW and OASW were reduced by over 20 per cent.[20] The decisions of the two provincial organizations are perplexing and troubling given the consultative process and agreed changes on the restructuring of CASW. Jake Kuiken, former president of ACSW, is critical of the fee argument as a reason for withdrawing from CASW. He points out that, in the case of ACSW, the provincial association instituted a fee increase of $50 in 2010 resulting in a projected savings of $250,000. Along with estimated savings from withdrawing from CASW that places revenues of close to $450,000 with no apparent plans that have been shared with the membership on how to best use them.[21]

CASW has consistently offered a social work voice in response to national and international concerns. When the federal government announced a $53 million cut from national settlement funding on 23 December 2009, the following day the national office issued a statement on behalf of the 18,500 social workers associated with the organization and appealing the government to reverse the decision and restore the funding. Although Ontario is hardest hit by the cuts, the OASW has been silent on the issue.

The fracturing of the profession comes at a time when neoliberal globalization is impacting on the day-to-day struggles of working people and determining the availability of social welfare programs. More than ever, a strong national voice and international solidarity with colleagues around the world are critical to our own relevance and growth.

Social Work Regulation

All provinces in Canada and all states in the US legally regulate the social work profession. Along with protecting the title "social worker" to gain public legitimacy, professional regulation is viewed as a way of protecting the public from incompetent practitioners by providing a structure to police those who call themselves social workers. It is also recognized that a consequence of giving the social work occupation credential is "to benefit the profession by limiting its practice to those who can establish their qualifications, thus providing a mechanism for professional identity and public recognition, social prestige, and financial rewards."[22] The nature of the regulation of the profession differs across the provinces and states.[23]

All the regulated provinces have an academic requirement and title protection as the basic control over who can use the title social worker. One exception is Manitoba where registration is voluntary, and, although the title "registered social worker" is protected, the term "social worker" is not. However, the protection of title loses meaning when the decision regarding who qualifies as a social worker is at the discretion of the regulatory body. For example, the Ontario College of Social Workers and Social Service Workers allows the granting of the title Registered Social Worker to someone who has no social work education while prohibiting a person with a Masters of Social Work from calling themselves a social worker unless they are registered with the college.

All provincial associations have responsibility for the regulation of social work practice, except for Ontario, British Columbia, and Prince Edward Island, where a college separate from the association has been formed. Member organizations that have a dual function are "indicating that regulatory matters consume the highest percentage of time, resources and activities."[24]

The proportion of social workers who belong to the association is considerably higher in those provinces where the association also regulates practice. For example, almost 100 per cent of social workers in Newfoundland, Nova Scotia, and New Brunswick belong to their provincial associations, whereas in Ontario only 25 per cent do.[25] In Ontario membership in the Ontario College of Social Workers and Social Service Workers costs $270, and the membership in the Ontario Association of Social Workers is also $270. In the case of economic hardship social workers are likely to give priority to the former since they must belong to it in order to use the title "social worker" and secure employment.

Provincial regulatory bodies have formed a national association, the Canadian Council of Social Work Regulators. All are members of the US-based Association of Social Work Boards (ASWB), the North American association whose mission is to support social work regulatory bodies both in Canada and the US.[26] Its emphasis is on enhancing the public and professional understanding of the value, competency, and accountability of regulated social workers. In May 2008 the Ontario College of Social Workers and Social Service Workers became a member, and shortly after Newfoundland and Labrador became the last Canadian province to join the ASWB.

The Canadian Council of Social Work Regulators will soon be releasing a competency-based framework for overseeing the practice of its members. The AIT, a component of NAFTA, SPP, and the Trade, Investment and Labour Mobility Agreement (TILMA), requires worker mobility within and between the signatory countries and therefore that competencies be identified. Ken Collier explains that with these developments "the flexibility and discretion that characterized Social Work is stifled, to be replaced by competencies and skills that increasingly resemble standardized machinery parts, transferable to any part of the country, representing the assumption that exercise of these skills and competencies supposes a guarantee of service quality."[27] This will also include a standardized exam for all social workers applying for regulation; schools of social work will need to shape their curriculum to prepare their students. These developments will have an immense impact on social work education and practice and contribute to a conservative trend within the profession.

The Struggle for Regulation in Ontario

All provinces in Canada, except Ontario, had introduced regulatory legislation for social workers by 1966. It wasn't until 1998 that efforts by the OASW (previously the Ontario Association of Professional Social Workers) and the Ontario College of Certified Social Workers (OCCSW) resulted in the government's Bill 76 to regulate the profession.[28] That it took well over 15 years of active lobbying reflects the opposing visions of social work and the diverse views of the role and practice of social work that have divided the profession itself as well as public and government attitudes toward it. The debate that ensued highlights the tension between professionalization and social action and the direction of the profession.

While the OCCSW, formed in 1982, provided for voluntary certification, others argued that statutory legislation was needed to protect "clients of social workers in Ontario in respect to cases of alleged professional incompetence or misconduct."[29] Project Legislation, as it was named, consumed much of the energy and finances of both the members of the association and college in order to lobby the members of the Ontario Legislature, the media, senior bureaucrats of other professional associations, and the public. The decision to keep the college independent of the association had grave implications for the latter. "While the profession in Ontario may be capable of supporting two independent organizations, the viability of both may be endangered as they compete for members and resources. The future viability of OASW has significant implications for the support of CASW and consequently for the social work profession in Canada."[30] Those opposed to the legislation were not only concerned with the possible demise of the national voice provided by CASW since OASW represented 40 per cent of national membership but also took exception to the assumption that there was widespread malpractice by social workers and a need for a policing mechanism monitored by the state.

The central argument of those advocating for a legislated regulatory framework for social work was the need to protect the public from incompetent social workers. In support of this position Shannon McCorquodale offered a summary of the kinds of complaints received by social work regulatory bodies across Canada that have presumably placed clients at risk. Included were a number of problems such as errors in judgement, incorrect assessments, mis-diagnosis, and employing inappropriate treatment.[31]

Many of the examples provided by McCorquodale inevitably raise questions about how workplace and working conditions impact on the delivery of services in an ethical and accountable manner. For instance, given the current conditions for child protection workers discussed earlier, it is imperative that social workers not have to carry full responsibility in situations where factors in their workplace are beyond their control. In most of these examples of "incompetent practice," the social and economic context has been stripped away. Ben Carniol and Brigitte Kitchen agree that there is a crisis in the social services but argue that it is not a crisis caused by social work incompetence:

Rather, it is a crisis of underfunding and of structures which perpetuate inequalities. It is a crisis experienced daily by social service clients who are not provided the means by which to escape poverty. As a consequence, child poverty, homelessness and hunger escalate to scandalous levels, even within prosperous Ontario.[32]

Harm to clients most likely results from punitive social policies and inadequate social welfare programs rather than from unethical social workers. Thus, an examination of the ethical practice of social workers cannot be separated from their working conditions. It has been my experience that social workers are extremely committed and work long hours in order to meet the needs of their clients. Judith Globerman, in her review of the literature, discovered little support for the premise that legislation protects the public and reduces unethical practice.[33] On the contrary, she found reports of a growing gap between the profession and clients, with less accountability to the public, more emphasis on self-interests, and a move away from social problems.

Some argue that the less visible agenda of government regulation is the pursuit of power, autonomy, and control by the established professions. Magali Sarafatti Larson in her study of professions examines how occupations organize as professions in order to attain power in the market. She defines professionalization as "the process by which producers of special services sought to constitute *and control* a market for their expertise. Because marketable expertise is a crucial element in the structure of modern equality, professionalization appears *also* as a collective assertion of social status and as a collective process of upward mobility."[34] Both regulation and licensing reflect authority and community sanctions, two of the attributes of a profession.[35] Paul Wilding argues that "professions are occupational groups that have been taken over by the state or have forged an alliance with it."[36]

The Social Work and Social Service Worker Act of Ontario (1998) marked a social work alliance with the Progressive Conservative government at the time. The Act, developed by the government, gives widespread power to the Minister of Community Services who controls and directs the regulatory body, the College of Social Workers and Social Service Workers, which is governed by a Council of 21 people, with equal representation from social workers, social service workers, and members of the public appointed by the government. The minister has the power to review the activities of the Council and require it to provide reports and information, or do anything that the minister believes necessary or advisable to carry out the objectives of the College; in addition, under section 36 of the Act, the minister may require the Council to make, amend, or revoke a regulation. Ironically, the government in power at the time was the same government that drastically cut social welfare programs, introduced workfare, passed anti-labour legislation, closed hospitals, and stopped building subsidized housing in the province. By dividing the college from the association and by legislating government influence on the college Council, social work practice in Ontario has been compromised. In particular, there is the danger of a weakened provincial association and the development of clinical social work practice at the expense of social action. The membership in the Ontario provincial association has declined—at 3,812, it now represents 21 per cent of the national membership, down from 40 per cent prior to regulation.

There are growing concerns that the preoccupation with status and social work professionalism has been pursued at the expense of social action and fighting social injustice.[37] In my view this has been intensified with social work regulation. While all professional associations and most schools of social work espouse a human rights/social justice orientation, the reality in practice is far different. David Wagner suggests that such a position requires a radical approach to social work and comments that "I have to say that I have met many more radical poor people, carpenters, farmers, gardeners, park rangers, and even sanitation workers than radical social workers."[38] It is not sufficient to invoke social work's history of advocacy and social action; as social workers, we must also reflect it in our practice.

In 1988 Paulo Freire commented on the political nature of social work practice in his address to the IFSW conference:

> ...the social worker, as much as the educator, is not a neutral agent, either in practice or in action. One of the inclinations that we sometimes have—and this is an offence, an illegality, that we imbibe in our technological society—is to think that the social worker is a very specialized person, a technician, who works in a compartmentalized technical area, and who has a sort of protection within this area, a sort of aggregate of rights, as a particular social group, to stand apart from the political battles of society. For me, this is impossible. It is an error. Social workers are compromised if they become convinced that they possess a technical expertise that is more defended than is the work of other workers.[39]

However, if social work practice is political as Freire argues, and if professional associations are to be active in supporting a social change agenda, it is imperative that there be a strong national association. As well, support must be provided to social workers who challenge policies and programs in support of ethical and accountable social work practice. In turn social workers need to support professional associations while working toward change within them. The profession's Code of Ethics provides the broad principles of social work practice; a strong and responsive professional association can offer a national voice for social workers and leadership in meeting the challenges that face the profession.

THE ROLE OF UNIONS

Whether in factory or in social agency, the relationship between employer and employee is precisely the same.[40]

Like all wage earners, social workers are experiencing the impact of restructuring and privatization of services and are fighting against roll-backs in wages and benefits and lay-offs. While exact numbers are not known, it can be expected that the majority of social workers in Canada belong to public-sector unions such as CUPE, the Public Sector Alliance of Canada (PSAC), or the National Union of Public and Government Employees (NUPGE). It is estimated that 25 per cent of social workers in the US labour force are unionized, double the 12.5 per cent for the overall population.[41] However, there is little attention placed on the labour movement in social work curriculum or in social work journals.[42] While professionalism is promoted in social work courses and represented in social work publications, identification as a worker and as a union member is not.

In the first half of the twentieth century, social workers in Canada and the US joined organized labour. In the US between 1931 and 1942 a group of politically progressive social workers organized the Rank and File movement to become part of organized labour. The membership of the movement exceeded that of the national social work association of the time, the American Association of Social Workers. Rank-and-file social workers realized that they needed a collective voice in order to achieve job protection, benefits, and decent working conditions:

Recognized by most historians of social work and social welfare as the most significant radical movement in social work history, rank and file social workers such as [Mary] van Kleeck, Harry Lurie (Director of Jewish Social Research, New York City), Gordon Hamilton (Professor, New York School of Social Work), Eduard Lindeman (Professor, New York School of Social Work), Ewan Clague (Director of Research, Community Council, Philadelphia), Bertha Reynolds (Assistant Director of Social Work, Smith College) and Jacob Fisher (Editor, Social Work Today) helped develop social work's first and most powerful union in its history and forced the profession to examine its relationship with government, organized labour, and its own client base.[43]

The New York branch was the first to define the employer-employee relationship in social work, to fight for collective bargaining, and to organize mass meetings and petitions on various issues.[44] Members were very connected to prominent people on the left both at national and international levels.[45]

In Canada, it was not until the early 1940s that full attention was placed on collective bargaining and the formation of "staff associations." Nonetheless, those who led the movement made the connection between workers in the social welfare arena and workers in factories. It was felt that "Organized labour and organized social work had their origins in identical conditions, but they rose for different reasons and at opposite ends of the economic scale."[46] It was argued that both labour unions and social work emerged in response to the social injustice and inequality that accompanied capitalist industrialization—unions from class conflict, social work from charity. Social work's role in the early days of charity provision was seen as "minor benefits handed down, often through the medium of the church, by those who owned the wealth, to those who had helped create the wealth but who had no part in controlling it."[47] It was argued by some that the emphasis on professionalization, in some ways came in conflict with the principles of unionization. "The concern with status not only prevents *alliances* with other workers or with clients. It also works as a preventive against unity—and the unionization—of professional workers themselves."[48]

There were also opponents. For example, a long-time board member of a number of social welfare agencies in Toronto felt that terms such as "collective bargaining" and "demands of employees" were "red rag words."[49] Others, while not opposed to staff associations, wished to separate social workers from factory workers on the basis that "In Canada, with almost no fee-collecting agencies, social agencies have neither goods nor services to sell. The 'management group' is therefore not in direct competition with 'labour' in the distribution of income."[50] Past worker-management conflicts—such as occurred in 1936 at the Ottawa Welfare Bureau where social workers were blamed for the high cost of relief and 40 female social workers were fired and replaced by a smaller number of men—supported the more radical view.[51]

There has always been reluctance by some social workers to actively support unionism. This position is often based on the view that social workers are "professionals," not "workers." Professionals have the expectation and belief that they are better able to negotiate working conditions and salaries on an individual basis and that the negotiation process will be a fair one. In a study of organized shelters Joan Pennell found that while shelter staff initially joined unions to resolve labour-management conflicts and gain control in the workplace, they also realized the effectiveness of collective bargaining for increasing their wages, benefits, and job security.[52] She also discovered that in some shelters where staff and management were committed to the same organizational goals, consensual bargaining was a possibility and was viewed as a synthesis of the collective manner in which women work and the traditionally male-dominated process within unions.[53] A partnership between management and worker within social agencies can be expected to be an uneasy one at best.

Since the right to strike is fundamental to the bargaining process, unionized social workers usually have the right to strike and withdraw their labour. The strike situation can present a major dilemma for many social workers, who realize that a disruption in services may have negative consequences for their clients and may conflict with professional ethics. Both the CASW Guidelines for Ethical Practice and the NASW Code of Ethics have a section on "Labour-Management Disputes." The CASW guidelines offer no specific guidance for social workers who face the possibility of a strike other than being "guided by the profession's values and principals" (4.2.2).[54] Both CASW and NASW affirm the right of social workers to engage in organized action and acknowledge that in a strike situation there may be differing views within the membership. However, the NASW has acknowledged the importance of collective bargaining by taking a position to oppose any law or policy that prohibits strikes.

No doubt there are conflicting views within the profession over unionization. However, individual social workers have made their pro-union stand very clear. During the regulation process in Ontario, in the consultation paper written by the government, social workers commented on a query regarding labour action: "We expect [that] registered/certified social workers who are members of unions will develop an effective means of both maintaining their direct accountability to those served and their responsibility as a union member."[55]

In a survey of social workers in the US, Alexander et al. conclude that, while unionism and professionalism are viewed as compatible, social workers disapproved of tactics such as strikes and slow downs.[56] This became evident in 1984 when social work staff in hospitals and nursing homes in the US went on a 47-day strike. Within the membership there was "substantial disagreement regarding the congruence and conflict between labor union activities and professional activities and responsibilities by professional social workers in a hospital."[57] Clearly, collective bargaining for unionized social workers is accepted, while use of the ultimate weapon for unions—strikes—is a problem.

While some might question the ethics of strike action for a professional association, Howard Karger, drawing on major schools of ethical theory, concludes that "the morality of action depends on the goodness of consequences.... A short-term strike—which may harm clients for some limited time period—may be justified if it leads eventually to improved care and quality of service."[58] In a study of Canadian social workers, Ernie Lightman found that social workers were more likely to strike to enhance client services than to improve their own wages and benefits. Survey findings report that over three-quarters of the social workers who responded approved going on strike as long as adequate safeguards, such as emergency services, were provided for clients.[59] Social workers in Liverpool, UK, went on strike for three months because of concern regarding the erosion of professional social work (i.e., calls from clients managed by a centralized call centre, infrequent team meetings, pressure to close cases, and social work positions filled with non-professional social workers).[60]

Although the majority of social workers in Canada are members of unions and a substantial number belong to their professional associations, research on the effectiveness of both in contributing to the delivery of ethical, accountable, and effective social work services is needed. The working conditions of social workers are related integrally to the quality of service that they are able to provide. There is evidence that increased workloads and diminished resources impact negatively on both social workers' ability to meet the expectations of their jobs and on the people who are accessing the service. Unions play a critical role in not only protecting job security, wages, and benefits but also in securing workplace conditions, caseloads in particular. Clearly, however, the militancy of unionized social workers and the range of tactics they are willing to use are affected by the position they occupy and the professional ideology and standards to which they adhere.

THE WAY FORWARD: SOCIAL WORK, SOCIAL JUSTICE, AND HUMAN RIGHTS

> The ultimate measure of a man [woman] is not where he [she] stands in moments of comfort and convenience, but where he [she] stands at times of challenge and controversy.[61]

As outlined in Chapter 1, the current context of recession and neoliberalism, with the accompanying erosion of federal support for social welfare, is creating harsh social and economic conditions for citizens, particularly working people. Since the role of a federally funded welfare state is to redistribute resources in favour of the most vulnerable in society, advancing a social justice agenda under current conditions will not be easy. However, it must be done, and social workers must be an integral part of the movement.

For Michael Reisch, "the pursuit of social justice in the twenty-first century requires social workers to acknowledge the political dimensions of all practice and to engage in multifaceted struggles to regain influence within the public arena."[62] Iain Ferguson and Michael Lavalette suggest that what is needed is a "social work of resistance."[63] This includes developing an alliance with service users and engaging with social movements that originate outside social work.

Sam Gindin proposes two essential components of an effective resistance against globalization and imperialism: the ability to have a vision and dream and to work internationally, yet to be rooted locally and nationally. A vision for a just society and the means to get there requires an informed analysis of the political context. For Gindin, our perception of social justice is affected by what we believe is possible:

> Social justice demands reviving the determination to dream. It's not just that dreaming is essential for maintaining any resistance, but because today, if we do not think big—as big as the globalizers themselves think—we will not even win small.[64]

The rich history of social work demonstrates the important position social workers hold within the social welfare arena and the potential the profession has for influence. This is the time for social work to renew its vision and visibility and to become active proponents of social justice. Reisch and Andrews remind us that this requires much more than written statements:

> In today's media-saturated age, it is enough, therefore, to use words like "empowerment," "multiculturalism," "oppression," and "social justice." The test of social work's commitment to its underlying values lies in the will - ingness to struggle on an often mundane, day-to-day basis to translate these values into deeds, as our professional forebears did individually and collectively.[65]

Such an engagement will need to extend beyond the submission of briefs or letters to include advocacy, social action, and participation in collective mobilization.

However, social workers do not agree about the potential of social work, as it stands, to advance social justice. Some argue that the drive for professionalization has been a major obstacle to a progressive practice, while others believe that the two are compatible.[66] Fred Newdom argues that "Professionalization of social work has led to a deification of technique over social justice: a concern for protecting our professional status even at the cost of assigning client concerns a lower priority."[67] Neil Thompson believes the challenge for social work is to develop forms of professionalization based on partnership and a commitment to equality and social justice.[68] Although he does not develop the specific ways that this could occur, the idea is an important one for social workers to collectively pursue. Unfortunately, recent developments in Canada will result in social work becoming a fractured profession.

There are striking similarities between the current period and 1929 and the conditions facing social workers and those that seek their services. During the Great Depression, the harsh realities of capitalism, unemployment, poverty, and homelessness were laid bare, and social workers engaged in social advocacy and social action in order to ensure that people had shelter and food. Today, thousands line up at food banks or shelters and the numbers are increasing at an alarming rate. Due to the scarcity of social housing and the limited number of shelter beds, homeless families are placed in motel rooms that lack cooking facilities.

There is a growing mobilization of people who are challenging the neoliberal agenda and globalization. "Movements made up of workers, peasants, indigenous peoples, environmentalists, intellectuals, students, and others have come together in a broad coalition of forces to oppose corporate globalization that has advanced the interests of the dominant classes in society to profit from exploitation and oppression of the great majority of the people...."[69] Social workers ought to be a part of this mobilization.

While social workers have an ethical responsibility to advancing social justice and social change, leadership, guidance, and support are needed from the professional associations in order to meet this mandate. Now is the time to strengthen social work professional associations and to have both a local and a national voice in response to the crisis in social welfare and the increase in globalization. Social work associations and the trade union movement are both connected internationally. If the social work profession could capture the strengths and potential of both, it could become a vital force in the social justice movement locally, nationally, and internationally.

NOTES

1 Colleen Lundy and Therese Jennissen, "The Shifting Terrain of Social Work," *OASW Eastern Branch Bulletin* 37 (2011): 9.

2 Cheryl Regehr, "Secondary Trauma in Social Workers," *Newsmagazine: Journal of the Ontario Association of Social Workers* 28.3 (2001): 11.

3 Bev Wake, "CAS Workers Warn Child 'Disaster' Awaits," *Ottawa Citizen*, 29 June 2001: A1, 2.

4 Hide Yamatani, Rafael Engel, and Solveig Spjldnes, "Child Welfare Worker Caseload: What's Just Right?," *Social Work* 54.4 (2009): 361–68.

5 Wake, "CAS Workers Warn Child 'Disaster' Awaits."

6 *Ottawa Citizen*, Editorial, 16 April 2001: A2.

7 Brian R. Adams and Joan MacKenzie Davies, Editorial, "Social Work Profession Speaks Out About Press Coverage of Heikamp Inquest," Press Release, 26 March 2001: 2.

8 Christie Blatchford, "CAS Failed to Answer Mother's Cry for Help," *Globe and Mail*, 14 April 2011: A10.

9 Christie Blatchford, "Children Died Where Welfare Workers Feared to Tread," *Globe and Mail*, 2 April 2011: A13.

10 Christie Blatchford, "A Desperate Call, a Lost File, Brought This Woman's Story to its Deadly, Tragic Close," *Globe and Mail*, 16 April 2011: A2.

11 CUPE, *Overloaded and Under Fire*, Report of the Ontario Social Services Work Environment Survey (Ottawa: CUPE, 1999) 5, http://cupe.ca/social-services/ART3ee7744be7311.

12 Wake, "CAS Workers Warn Child 'Disaster' Awaits."

13 Joan L. Arches, "Burnout and Social Action," *Journal of Progressive Human Services* 8.2 (1997): 55.

14 Lundy and Gauthier, "Social Work Practice and the Master-Servant Relationship" 190–94.

15 CASW, Code of Ethics, 1983, Section 8.2. This section of the Code was revised in 1993 to read: "Where a serious ethical conflict continues to exist after the issue has been brought to the attention of the employer, the social worker shall bring the issue to the attention of the Association or regulatory body."

16 Newfoundland Court of Appeal, *Bown vs. Newfoundland*, in *NFLD and PEI Reports, Maritime Law Book* 54 (1985): 259.

17 Maines, "Through the Years in CASW" 2.

18 For a summary, see Juliet Foley, "Professional Associations in Canada," in *Social Work Practice: A Canadian Perspective*, ed. Francis J. Turner (Scarborough, ON: Prentice Hall, 1999) 477–91.

19 Membership figures obtained from France Audet, CASW National Office, 13 June 2001.

20 CASW, Communiqué, "To Members of CASW Member Organizations from CASW Executive," 1 November 2010: 1–2.

21 Jake Kuiken, http://easternoasw.wordpress.com/2010/11/. This is a blog set up by Bill Dare, OASW member, Eastern Branch.

22 Bruce A. Thyer and Marilyn A. Biggerstaff, *Professional Social Work Credentialing and Legal Regulation: A Review of Critical Issues and an Annotated Bibliography* (Springfield, IL: Charles C. Thomas, 1989) 4.

23 For a summary of provincial regulation, see Shannon McCorquodale, "The Role of Regulators in Practice," in *Canadian Social Welfare*, 3rd ed., ed. Joanne C. Turner and Francis J. Turner (Scarborough, ON: Allyn and Bacon, 1995) 462–76. Also see the CASW web site for a complete listing of regulation in all provinces: http://www.casw-acts.ca. In the US the ASWB, an association that coordinates regulation and develops and maintains the licensing examinations for all states except Michigan (which does not use an exam) and California, has a web site at http://www.aswb.org.

24 Letter to Colleen Lundy from Kate Powers, President, OASW, 1 December 2010: 1.

25 Foley, *Understanding Capital* 477–91.

26 See, for example, the ASWB web site, http://www.aswb.org.

27 Ken Collier, letter submitted to the Editor of the ACSW *Advocate*, 25 September 2009. The *Advocate* did not publish it.

2 The Ontario Social Work and Social Services Act can be found at http://www.e-laws.gov.on.ca.

29 Frank Turner, "Legislative Protection against Malpractice," *Canadian Review of Social Policy* 25 (May 1990): 63–64.

30 OAPSW, Strategic Planning Committee, *Interim Report* (Toronto: Ontario Association of Professional Social Workers, September 1987) 3.

31 McCorquodale, "The Role of Regulators in Practice" 472–73.

32 Ben Carniol and Brigitte Kitchen, "OAPSW Proposal is a Disaster and Must be Defeated," *Canadian Review of Social Policy* 25 (May 1990): 62.

33 Judith Globerman, "Regulating Social Work: Illuminating Motives," *Canadian Social Work Review* 9.2 (Summer 1992): 229–43.

34 Magali Sarfatti Larson, *The Rise of Professionalism: A Sociological Analysis* (Berkeley, CA: University of California Press, 1977) xvi; emphasis in original.

35 E. Greenwood, "Attributes of a Profession," *Social Work* 2 (1957): 45–55. Greenwood sug-

gested that there were five attributes of a profession: systematic theory, authority, community sanctions, ethical codes, and a culture.

36 Paul Wilding, *Professional Power and Social Welfare* (London: Routledge and Kegan Paul, 1982) 15.

37 Allison Thompson, "Radical Social Work in These Contemporary Times," *Journal of Progressive Human Services* 20 (2009): 110–11.

38 David Wagner, "Radical Social Work as Conceit," *Journal of Progressive Human Services* 20 (2009): 105.

39 Freire, "A Critical Understanding of Social Work" 5.

40 Ethel Jessel, "Staff Associations," *The Social Worker* 11.4 (May 1943): 20.

41 Jessica Rosenberg and Samuel Rosenberg, "Do Unions Matter? An Examination of the Historical and Contemporary Role of Labor Unions in the Social Work Profession," *Social Work* 51.4 (2006): 295–302.

42 Ben Carniol is one of the few who has contributed to discussions on social work and unions in Canada. See, e.g., Ben Carniol, "Social Work and the Labour Movement," in *Social Work and Social Change in Canada*, ed. Brian Wharf (Toronto: McClelland and Stewart, 1990) 114–43; Ben Carniol, *Case Critical: Challenging Social Work in Canada*, 2nd ed. (Toronto: Between the Lines, 1990).

43 Patrick Selmi and Richard Hunter, "Beyond the Rank and File Movement: Mary van Kleeck and Social Work Radicalism in the Great Depression, 1931–1942," *Journal of Sociology and Social Welfare* 27.2 (June 2001): 76.

44 Jacob Fisher, "The Rank and File Movement 1930–1936," *Social Work Today* 3.5/6 (February 1936), repr. in *Journal of Progressive Human Service* 1.1 (1990): 95–99.

45 For example, Florence Kelly, one of the social work leaders in the labour movement, had a long-standing friendship with Frederick Engels. See Howard Jacob Karger, *Social Work and Labor Unions* (New York: Greenwood Press, 1988).

46 Hazel Wigdor, "Social Work and Trade Unions," *The Social Worker* 12.2 (November 1943): 18.

47 Wigdor, "Social Work and Trade Unions" 18–19.

48 Larson, *The Rise of Professionalism* 236; emphasis in original.

49 Catherine Canfield Elliott, "A Board Member Speaks Out," *The Social Worker* 12.2 (November 1943): 15.

50 Katherine Best, "Another Point of View on Staff Associations," *The Social Worker* 12.2 (November 1943): 16.

51 *The Social Worker*, "What Happened in Ottawa" 5.2 (November 1936): 1–8. Bessie E. Touzel, then supervisor of staff of the Ottawa Public Welfare Board, resigned in protest. "A Social Workers Protest," her address to the Board of Control, and her resignation appear in the same volume.

52 Joan Pennell, "Feminism and Labor Unions: Transforming State Regulation of Women's Programs," *Journal of Progressive Human Services* 6.1 (1995): 45–72.

53 Joan Pennell, "Consensual Bargaining: Labor Negotiations in Battered Women's Programs," *Journal of Progressive Human Services* 1.1 (1990): 59–74.

54 CASW, *Guidelines for Ethical Practice* (Ottawa: CASW, 2005) 17.

55 *Response to the Consultation Paper on Regulation of Social Workers and Other Social Service Practitioners in Ontario*, undated and no indication of authors. The consultation paper was published in 1989.

56 Leslie Alexander, Philip Lichtenberg, and Dennis Brunn, "Social Workers in Unions: A Survey," *Social Work* (May 1980): 216–23.

57 Dena Fisher, "Problems for Social Work in a Strike Situation: Professional, Ethical, and Value Considerations," *Social Work* 32.3 (1987): 252.

58 Karger, *Social Work and Labor Unions* 141.

59 Ernie Lightman, "Social Workers, Strikes, and Service to Clients," *Social Work* 28.2 (March–April 1983): 142–47.

60 Iain Ferguson and Michael Lavalette, "Globalization and Global Justice: Towards a Social Work of Resistance," *International Social Work* 49 (2006): 309–18.

61 Martin Luther King, *The Strength to Love* (New York: Harper Row, 1963) 20.

62 Michael Reisch, "Defining Social Justice in a Socially Unjust World," *Families in Society: The Journal of Contemporary Human Services* 83.4 (2002): 351.

63 Ferguson and Lavalette. "Globalization and Global Justice."

64 Gindin, "Social Justice and Globalization" 2

65 Reisch and Andrews, *The Road Not Taken* 231.

66 See Reisch and Andrews, *The Road Not Taken*, for an excellent discussion on this topic.

67 Fred Newdom, "Progressive and Professional: A Contradiction in Terms?" *BCR Reports* 8.1 (1996): 1.

68 Neil Thompson, "Social Movements, Social Justice and Social Work," *British Journal of Social Work* 32 (2002): 711–22.

69 Berch Berberoglu, "Conclusion: Globalization for a New Century," in *Globalization in the 21st Century*, ed. Berch Berberoglu (New York: Palgrave Macmillan, 2010) 199.

THE UNIVERSAL DECLARATION OF HUMAN RIGHTS

O N DECEMBER 10, 1948 THE GENERAL ASSEMBLY of the United Nations adopted and proclaimed the Universal Declaration of Human Rights, the full text of which appears in the following pages. Following this historic act the Assembly called upon all Member countries to publicize the text of the Declaration and "to cause it to be disseminated, displayed, read and expounded principally in schools and other educational institutions, without distinction based on the political status of countries or territories."

PREAMBLE

WHEREAS recognition of the inherent dignity and of the equal and inalienable rights of all members of the human family is the foundation of freedom, justice and peace in the world,

WHEREAS disregard and contempt for human rights have resulted in barbarous acts which have outraged the conscience of mankind, and the advent of a world in which human beings shall enjoy freedom of speech and belief and freedom from fear and want has been proclaimed as the highest aspiration of the common people,

WHEREAS it is essential, if man is not to be compelled to have recourse, as a last resort, to rebellion against tyranny and oppression, that human rights should be protected by the rule of law,

WHEREAS it is essential to promote the development of friendly relations between nations,

WHEREAS the peoples of the United Nations have in the Charter reaffirmed their faith in fundamental human rights, in the dignity and worth of the human person and in the equal rights of men and women and have determined to promote social progress and better standards of life in larger freedom,

WHEREAS Member States have pledged themselves to achieve, in cooperation with the United Nations, the promotion of universal respect for and observance of human rights and fundamental freedoms,

WHEREAS a common understanding of these rights and freedoms is of the greatest importance for the full realization of this pledge,

Now, THEREFORE the GENERAL ASSEMBLY proclaims THIS UNIVERSAL DECLARATION OF HUMAN RIGHTS as a common standard of achievement for all peoples and all nations, to the end that every individual and every organ of society, keeping this Declaration constantly in mind, shall strive by teaching and education to promote respect for these rights and freedoms and by progressive measures, national and international, to secure their universal and effective recognition and observance, both among the peoples of Member States themselves and among the peoples of territories under their jurisdiction.

Article 1: All human beings are born free and equal in dignity and rights. They are endowed with reason and conscience and should act towards one another in a spirit of brotherhood.

Article 2: Everyone is entitled to all the rights and freedoms set forth in this Declaration, without distinction of any kind, such as race, colour, sex, language, religion, political or other opinion, national or social origin, property, birth or other status. Furthermore, no distinction shall be made on the basis of the political, jurisdictional or international status of the country or territory to which a person belongs, whether it be independent, trust, non-self-governing or under any other limitation of sovereignty.

Article 3: Everyone has the right to life, liberty and security of person.

Article 4: No one shall be held in slavery or servitude; slavery and the slave trade shall be prohibited in all their forms.

Article 5: No one shall be subjected to torture or to cruel, inhuman or degrading treatment or punishment.

Article 6: Everyone has the right to recognition everywhere as a person before the law.

Article 7: All are equal before the law and are entitled without any discrimination to equal protection of the law. All are entitled to equal protection against any discrimination in violation of this Declaration and against any incitement to such discrimination.

Article 8: Everyone has the right to an effective remedy by the competent national tribunals for acts violating the fundamental rights granted him by the constitution or by law.

Article 9: No one shall be subjected to arbitrary arrest, detention or exile.

Article 10: Everyone is entitled in full equality to a fair and public hearing by an independent and impartial tribunal, in the determination of his rights and obligations and of any criminal charge against him.

Article 11: (1) Everyone charged with a penal offence has the right to be presumed innocent until proved guilty according to law in a public trial at which he has had all the guarantees necessary for his defence.

(2) No one shall be held guilty of any penal offence on account of any act or omission which did not constitute a penal offence, under national or international law, at the time when it was committed. Nor shall a heavier penalty be imposed than the one that was applicable at the time the penal offence was committed.

Article 12: No one shall be subjected to arbitrary interference with his privacy, family, home or correspondence, nor to attacks upon his honour and reputation. Everyone has the right to the protection of the law against such interference or attacks.

Article 13: (1) Everyone has the right to freedom of movement and residence within the borders of each state.

(2) Everyone has the right to leave any country, including his own, and to return to his country.

Article 14: (1) Everyone has the right to seek and to enjoy in other countries asylum from persecution.

(2) This right may not be invoked in the case of prosecutions genuinely arising from non-political crimes or from acts contrary to the purposes and principles of the United Nations.

Article 15: (1) Everyone has the right to a nationality.

(2) No one shall be arbitrarily deprived of his nationality nor denied the right to change his nationality.

Article 16: (1) Men and women of full age, without any limitation due to race, nationality or religion, have the right to marry and to found a family. They are entitled to equal rights as to marriage, during marriage and at its dissolution.

(2) Marriage shall be entered into only with the free and full consent of the intending spouses.

(3) The family is the natural and fundamental group unit of society and is entitled to protection by society and the State.

Article 17: (1) Everyone has the right to own property alone as well as in association with others.

(2) No one shall be arbitrarily deprived of his property.

Article 18: Everyone has the right to freedom of thought, conscience and religion; this right includes freedom to change his religion or belief, and freedom, either alone or in community with others and in public or private, to manifest his religion or belief in teaching, practice, worship and observance.

Article 19: Everyone has the right to freedom of opinion and expression; this right includes freedom to hold opinions without interference and to seek, receive and impart information and ideas through any media and regardless of frontiers.

Article 20: (1) Everyone has the right to freedom of peaceful assembly and association.
(2) No one may be compelled to belong to an association.

Article 21: (1) Everyone has the right to take part in the government of his country, directly or through freely chosen representatives.
(2) Everyone has the right of equal access to public service in his country.
(3) The will of the people shall be the basis of the authority of government; this will shall be expressed in periodic and genuine elections which shall be by universal and equal suffrage and shall be held by secret vote or by equivalent free voting procedures.

Article 22: Everyone, as a member of society, has the right to social security and is entitled to realization, through national effort and international co-operation and in accordance with the organization and resources of each State, of the economic, social and cultural rights indispensable for his dignity and the free development of his personality.

Article 23: (1) Everyone has the right to work, to free choice of employment, to just and favourable conditions of work and to protection against unemployment.
(2) Everyone, without any discrimination, has the right to equal pay for equal work.
(3) Everyone who works has the right to just and favourable remuneration ensuring for himself and his family an existence worthy of human dignity, and supplemented, if necessary, by other means of social protection.
(4) Everyone has the right to form and to join trade unions for the protection of his interests.

Article 24: Everyone has the right to rest and leisure, including reasonable limitation of working hours and periodic holidays with pay.

Article 25: (1) Everyone has the right to a standard of living adequate for the health and well-being of himself and of his family, including food, clothing, housing and medical care and necessary social services, and the right to security in the event of unemployment, sickness, disability, widowhood, old age or other lack of livelihood in circumstances beyond his control.
(2) Motherhood and childhood are entitled to special care and assistance.
(3) All children, whether born in or out of wedlock, shall enjoy the same social protection.

Article 26: (1) Everyone has the right to education. Education shall be free, at least in the elementary and fundamental stages. Elementary education shall be compulsory. Technical and professional education shall be made generally available and higher education shall be equally accessible to all on the basis of merit.

(2) Education shall be directed to the full development of the human personality and to the strengthening of respect for human rights and fundamental freedoms. It shall promote understanding, tolerance and friendship among all nations, racial or religious groups, and shall further the activities of the United Nations for the maintenance of peace.

(3) Parents have a prior right to choose the kind of education that shall be given to their children.

Article 27: (1) Everyone has the right freely to participate in the cultural life of the community, to enjoy the arts and to share in scientific advancement and its benefits.

(2) Everyone has the right to the protection of the moral and material interests resulting from any scientific, literary or artistic production of which he is the author.

Article 28: Everyone is entitled to a social and international order in which the rights and freedoms set forth in this Declaration can be fully realized.

Article 29: (1) Everyone has duties to the community in which alone the free and full development of his personality is possible.

(2) In the exercise of his rights and freedoms, everyone shall be subject only to such limitations as are determined by law solely for the purpose of securing due recognition and respect for the rights and freedoms of others and of meeting the just requirements of morality, public order and the general welfare in a democratic society.

(3) These rights and freedoms may in no case be exercised contrary to the purposes and principles of the United Nations.

Article 30: Nothing in this Declaration may be interpreted as implying for any State, group or person any right to engage in any activity or to perform any act aimed at the destruction of any of the rights and freedoms set forth herein.

CANADIAN ASSOCIATION OF SOCIAL WORKERS, CODE OF ETHICS

PURPOSE OF THE CASW CODE OF ETHICS

ETHICAL BEHAVIOUR LIES AT THE CORE OF EVERY PROFESSION. The Canadian Association of Social Workers (CASW) *Code of Ethics* sets forth values and principles to guide social workers' professional conduct. A code of ethics cannot guarantee ethical behaviour. Ethical behaviour comes from a social worker's individual commitment to engage in ethical practice. Both the spirit and the letter of this *Code of Ethics* will guide social workers as they act in good faith and with a genuine desire to make sound judgements.

This *Code of Ethics* is consistent with the International Federation of Social Workers (IFSW) *International Declaration of Ethical Principles of Social Work* (1994, 2004), which requires members of the CASW to uphold the values and principles established by both the CASW and the IFSW. Other individuals, organizations and bodies (such as regulatory boards, professional liability insurance providers, courts of law, boards of directors of organizations employing social workers and government agencies) may also choose to adopt this *Code of Ethics* or use it as a basis for evaluating professional conduct. In Canada, each province and territory is responsible for regulating the professional conduct of social workers to ensure the protection of the public. Social workers are advised to contact the regulatory body in their province or territory to determine whether it has adopted this *Code of Ethics*.[1]

Recognition of Individual and Professional Diversity

The CASW *Code of Ethics* does not provide a set of rules that prescribe how social workers should act in all situations. Further, the *Code of Ethics* does not specify which values and principles are most important and which outweigh others in instances of conflict. Reasonable differences of opinion exist among social workers with respect to which values and principles should be given priority in a particular situation. Further, a social worker's personal values, culture, religious beliefs, practices and/or other important distinctions, such as age, ability, gender or sexual orientation can affect his/her ethical choices. Thus, social workers need to be aware of any conflicts between personal and professional values and deal with them responsibly.

Ethical Behaviour Requires Due Consideration of Issues and Judgement

Social work is a multifaceted profession. As professionals, social workers are educated to exercise judgement in the face of complex and competing interests and claims. Ethical decision-making in a given situation will involve the informed judgement of the individual social worker. Instances may arise when social workers' ethical obligations conflict with agency policies, or relevant laws or regulations. When such conflicts occur, social workers shall make a responsible effort to resolve the conflicts in a manner that is consistent with the values and principles expressed in this *Code of Ethics*. If a reasonable resolution of the conflict does not appear possible, social workers shall seek appropriate consultation before making a decision. This may involve consultation with an ethics committee, a regulatory body, a knowledgeable colleague, supervisor or legal counsel.

PREAMBLE

The social work profession is dedicated to the welfare and self-realization of all people; the development and disciplined use of scientific and professional knowledge; the development of resources and skills to meet individual, group, national and international changing needs and aspirations; and the achievement of social justice for all. The profession has a particular interest in the needs and empowerment of people who are vulnerable, oppressed, and/or living in poverty. Social workers are committed to human rights as enshrined in Canadian law, as well as in international conventions on human rights created or supported by the United Nations.

As professionals in a country that upholds respect for diversity, and in keeping with democratic rights and freedoms, social workers respect the distinct systems of beliefs and lifestyles of individuals, families, groups, communities and nations without prejudice (United Nations Centre for Human Rights, 1992). Specifically, social workers do not tolerate discrimination[2] based on age, abilities, ethnic background, gender, language, marital status, national ancestry, political affiliation, race, religion, sexual orientation or socio-economic status.

CORE SOCIAL WORK VALUES AND PRINCIPLES

Social workers uphold the following core social work values:

Value 1: Respect for Inherent Dignity and Worth of Persons
Value 2: Pursuit of Social Justice
Value 3: Service to Humanity
Value 4: Integrity of Professional Practice
Value 5: Confidentiality in Professional Practice
Value 6: Competence in Professional Practice

The following section describes each of these values and discusses their underlying principles.

Value 1: Respect for the Inherent Dignity and Worth of Persons

Social work is founded on a long-standing commitment to respect the inherent dignity and individual worth of all persons. When required by law to override a client's wishes, social workers take care to use the minimum coercion required. Social workers recognize and respect the diversity of Canadian society, taking into account the breadth of differences that exist among individuals, families, groups and communities. Social workers uphold the human rights of individuals and groups as expressed in the *Canadian Charter of Rights and Freedoms* (1982) and the United Nations *Universal Declaration of Human Rights* (1948).

Principles:

- Social workers respect the unique worth and inherent dignity of all people and uphold human rights.
- Social workers uphold each person's right to self-determination, consistent with that person's capacity and with the rights of others.
- Social workers respect the diversity among individuals in Canadian society and the right of individuals to their unique beliefs consistent with the rights of others.
- Social workers respect the client's right to make choices based on voluntary, informed consent.
- Social workers who have children as clients determine the child's ability to consent and where appropriate, explain to the child and to the child's parents/guardians, the nature of the social worker's relationship to the child.
- Social workers uphold the right of society to impose limitations on the self-determination of individuals, when such limitations protect individuals from self-harm and from harming others.
- Social workers uphold the right of every person to be free from violence and threat of violence.

Value 2: Pursuit of Social Justice

Social workers believe in the obligation of people, individually and collectively, to provide resources, services and opportunities for the overall benefit of humanity and to afford them protection from harm. Social workers promote social fairness and the equitable distribution of resources, and act to reduce barriers and expand choice for all persons, with special regard for those who are marginalized, disadvantaged, vulnerable, and/or have exceptional needs. Social workers oppose prejudice and discrimination against any person or group of persons, on any grounds, and specifically challenge views and actions that stereotype particular persons or groups.

Principles:

- Social workers uphold the right of people to have access to resources to meet basic human needs.
- Social workers advocate for fair and equitable access to public services and benefits.

- Social workers advocate for equal treatment and protection under the law and challenge injustices, especially injustices that affect the vulnerable and disadvantaged.
- Social workers promote social development and environmental management in the interests of all people.

Value 3: Service to Humanity

The social work profession upholds service in the interests of others, consistent with social justice, as a core professional objective. In professional practice, social workers balance individual needs, and rights and freedoms with collective interests in the service of humanity. When acting in a professional capacity, social workers place professional service before personal goals or advantage, and use their power and authority in disciplined and responsible ways that serve society. The social work profession contributes to knowledge and skills that assist in the management of conflicts and the wide-ranging consequences of conflict.

Principles:
- Social workers place the needs of others above self-interest when acting in a professional capacity.
- Social workers strive to use the power and authority vested in them as professionals in responsible ways that serve the needs of clients and the promotion of social justice.
- Social workers promote individual development and pursuit of individual goals, as well as the development of a just society.
- Social workers use their knowledge and skills in bringing about fair resolutions to conflict and in assisting those affected by conflict.

Value 4: Integrity in Professional Practice

Social workers demonstrate respect for the profession's purpose, values and ethical principles relevant to their field of practice. Social workers maintain a high level of professional conduct by acting honestly and responsibly, and promoting the values of the profession. Social workers strive for impartiality in their professional practice, and refrain from imposing their personal values, views and preferences on clients. It is the responsibility of social workers to establish the tenor of their professional relationship with clients, and others to whom they have a professional duty, and to maintain professional boundaries. As individuals, social workers take care in their actions to not bring the reputation of the profession into disrepute. An essential element of integrity in professional practice is ethical accountability based on this *Code of Ethics,* the IFSW *International Declaration of Ethical Principles of Social Work,* and other relevant provincial/territorial standards and guidelines. Where conflicts exist with respect to these sources of ethical guidance, social workers are encouraged to seek advice, including consultation with their regulatory body.

Principles:
- Social workers demonstrate and promote the qualities of honesty, reliability, impartiality and diligence in their professional practice.

- Social workers demonstrate adherence to the values and ethical principles of the profession and promote respect for the profession's values and principles in organizations where they work or with which they have a professional affiliation.
- Social workers establish appropriate boundaries in relationships with clients and ensure that the relationship serves the needs of clients.
- Social workers value openness and transparency in professional practice and avoid relationships where their integrity or impartiality may be compromised, ensuring that should a conflict of interest be unavoidable, the nature of the conflict is fully disclosed.

Value 5: Confidentiality in Professional Practice

A cornerstone of professional social work relationships is confidentiality with respect to all matters associated with professional services to clients. Social workers demonstrate respect for the trust and confidence placed in them by clients, communities and other professionals by protecting the privacy of client information and respecting the client's right to control when or whether this information will be shared with third parties. Social workers only disclose confidential information to other parties (including family members) with the informed consent of clients, clients' legally authorized representatives or when required by law or court order. The general expectation that social workers will keep information confidential does not apply when disclosure is necessary to prevent serious, foreseeable and imminent harm to a client or others. In all instances, social workers disclose the least amount of confidential information necessary to achieve the desired purpose.

Principles:
- Social workers respect the importance of the trust and confidence placed in the professional relationship by clients and members of the public.
- Social workers respect the client's right to confidentiality of information shared in a professional context.
- Social workers only disclose confidential information with the informed consent of the client or permission of client's legal representative.
- Social workers may break confidentiality and communicate client information without permission when required or permitted by relevant laws, court order or this *Code.*
- Social workers demonstrate transparency with respect to limits to confidentiality that apply to their professional practice by clearly communicating these limitations to clients early in their relationship.

Value 6: Competence in Professional Practice

Social workers respect a client's right to competent social worker services. Social workers analyze the nature of social needs and problems, and encourage innovative, effective strategies and techniques to meet both new and existing needs and, where possible, contribute to the knowledge base of the profession. Social workers have a responsibility to maintain professional proficiency, to continually strive to increase their professional knowledge and skills, and to apply new knowledge in practice commensurate with their level of professional education, skill and competency, seeking consultation and supervision as appropriate.

Principles:
- Social workers uphold the right of clients to be offered the highest quality service possible.
- Social workers strive to maintain and increase their professional knowledge and skill.
- Social workers demonstrate due care for client's interests and safety by limiting professional practice to areas of demonstrated competence.
- Social workers contribute to the ongoing development of the profession and its ability to serve humanity, where possible, by participating in the development of current and future social workers and the development of new professional knowledge. Social workers who engage in research minimize risks to participants, ensure informed consent, maintain confidentiality and accurately report the results of their studies.

GLOSSARY

Capacity The ability to understand information relevant to a decision and to appreciate the reasonably foreseeable consequences of choosing to act or not to act. Capacity is specific to each decision and thus a person may be capable of deciding about a place of residence, for example, but not capable with respect to deciding about a treatment. Capacity can change over time (Etchells, Sharpe, Elliot and Singer, 1996).

Recent references in law point to the concept of "a mature minor," which Rozovsky and Rozovsky (1990) define as "… one with capacity to understand the nature and consequences of medical treatment. Such a person has the power to consent to medical treatment and parental consent is not necessary" (p. 55). They quote the comments by The Honorable Justice Lambert in *Van Mol v. Ashmore,* which help clarify common law with respect to a minor's capacity to consent. He states:

> At common law, without reference to statute law, a young person, still a minor, may give, on his or her own behalf, a fully informed consent to medical treatment if he or she has sufficient maturity, intelligence and capacity of understanding what is involved in making informed choices about the proposed medical treatment … Once the capacity to consent has been achieved by the young person reaching sufficient maturity, intelligence and capability of understanding, the discussions about the nature of the treatment, its gravity, the material risks and any special and unusual risks, and the decisions about undergoing treatment, and about the form of the treatment, must all take place with and be made by the young person whose bodily integrity is to be invaded and whose life and health will be affected by the outcome.

Child The *Convention on the Rights of the Child* passed by the United Nations in 1959 and ratified by Canada in 1990, define a child as a person under the age of 18 years unless national law recognizes an earlier age of majority (Alberta Law Reform Institute, 1991). The age of majority differs in provinces and territories in Canada. Under the *Crim-*

inal Code of Canada, the age of consent is held to be over the age of 14 years; age in the context of the criminal code frequently refers to capacity to consent to sexual relations. All jurisdictions in Canada have legislation regarding child protection, which defines the age of a child for the purposes of protection. In Canada, in the absence of provincial or territorial legislation, courts are governed by common law. Social workers are encouraged to maintain current knowledge with respect to legislation on the age of a child, as well as capacity and consent in their jurisdiction.

Client A person, family, group of persons, incorporated body, association or community on whose behalf a social worker provides or agrees to provide a service or to whom the social worker is legally obligated to provide a service. Examples of legal obligation to provide service include a legislated responsibility (such as in child welfare) or a valid court order. In the case of a valid court order, the judge/court is the client and the person(s) who is ordered by the court to participate in assessment is recognized as an involuntary client.

Conduct Unbecoming Behaviour or conduct that does not meet social work standard of care requirements and is, therefore, subject to discipline. In reaching a decision in *Matthews and Board of Directors of Physiotherapy* (1986) 54 O.R. (2d) 375, Saunders J. makes three important statements regarding standards of practice, and by implication, professional codes of ethics:

1. Standards of practice are inherent characteristics of any profession.
2. Standards of practice may be written or unwritten.
3. Some conduct is clearly regarded as misconduct and need not be written down, whereas other conduct may be the subject of dispute within a profession. (See "Standard of Practice.")

Confidentiality A professional value that demands that professionally acquired information be kept private and not shared with third parties unless the client provides informed consent or a professional or legal obligation exists to share such information without client informed consent.

Discrimination Treating people unfavourably or holding negative or prejudicial attitudes based on discernable differences or stereotypes (AASW, 1999).

Informed Consent Voluntary agreement reached by a capable client based on information about foreseeable risks and benefits associated with the agreement (e.g., participation in counselling or agreement to disclose social work report to a third party).

Human Rights The rights of an individual that are considered the basis for freedom and justice, and serve to protect people from discrimination and harassment. Social workers may refer to the *Canadian Charter of Rights and Freedoms* enacted as Schedule B to the *Canada Act* 1982 (U.K.) 1982, c. 11, which came into force on April 17, 1982, as well as the *Universal Declaration of Human Rights* (1948) proclaimed by the United Nations General Assembly December 10, 1948.

Malpractice and Negligence Behaviour that is included in "conduct unbecoming" and

relates to social work practice behaviour within the parameters of the professional relationship that falls below the standard of practice and results in, or aggravation of, injury
to a client. It includes behaviour that results in assault, deceit, fraudulent misrepresentations, defamation of character, breach of contract, violation of human rights, malicious
prosecution, false imprisonment or criminal conviction.

Self-Determination A core social work value that refers to the right to self-direction and
freedom of choice without interference from others. Self-determination is codified in
practice through mechanisms of informed consent. Social workers may be obligated to
limit self-determination when a client lacks capacity or in order to prevent harm (Regehr
and Antle, 1997).

Social Worker A person who is duly registered to practice social work in a province or
territory; or where mandatory registration does not exist, a person with social work education from an institution recognized by the Canadian Association of Schools of Social
Work (CASSW) or an institution from outside of Canada that has been approved by the
CASW, who is practising social work and who voluntarily agrees to be subject to this
Code of Ethics. Note: Social workers living in Quebec and British Columbia, whose social
work education was obtained outside of Canada, follow a separate approval process
within their respective provinces.

Standard of Practice The standard of care ordinarily expected of a competent social
worker. It means that the public is assured that a social worker has the training, the skill
and the diligence to provide them with social work services. Social workers are urged
to refer to standards of practice that have been set by their provincial or territorial regulatory body or relevant professional association (see "Conduct Unbecoming").

Voluntary "In the context of consent, 'voluntariness' refers to a patient's right to make
treatment decisions free of any undue influence, such as ability of others to exert control
over a patient by force, coercion or manipulation.…, The requirement for voluntariness
does not imply that clinicians should refrain from persuading patients to accept advice.
Persuasion involves appealing to the patient's reason in an attempt to convince him or
her of the merits of a recommendation. In attempting to persuade the patient to follow
a particular course of action, the clinician still leaves the patient free to accept or reject
this advice." (Etchells, Sharpe, Dykeman, Meslin and Singer, 1996, p. 1083.)

NOTES

1 To find the IFSW declarations or information about your relevant regulatory body, visit the CASW
web site: http://www.casw-acts.ca.

2 Throughout this document the term "discrimination" refers to treating people unfavourably or
holding negative or prejudicial attitudes based on discernable differences or stereotypes. It does
not refer to the positive intent behind programs, such as affirmative action, where one group
may be given preferential treatment to address inequities created by discrimination.

REFERENCES

AASW. (1999). *AASW code of ethics*. Kingston: Australian Association of Social Workers (AASW).

Alberta Law Reform Institute. (1991). *Status of the child: Revised report* (Report No. 60). Edmonton, Alberta: Law Reform Institute.

BASW. (2002). *BASW: A code of ethics for social workers*. British Association of Social Workers (BASW).

Canadian Charter of Rights and Freedoms Enacted as Schedule B to the *Canada Act* 1982, c.11 (1982). http://laws.justice.gc.ca/en/charter/.

CASW. (1994). *Social Work Code of Ethics*. Ottawa: Canadian Association of Social Workers (CASW).

Criminal Code, R.S., c. C-34, s.1. (1985). http://laws.justice.gc.ca/en/c46/40670.html.

Etchells, E.; G. Sharpe; C. Elliott and P. Singer. (1996). Bioethics for clinicians: 3: Capacity. *Canadian Medical Association Journal*, 155, 657–661.

Etchells, E.; G. Sharpe; M.J. Dykeman and P. Singer. (1996). Bioethics for clinicians: 4: Voluntariness. *Canadian Medical Association Journal*, 155, 1083–1086.

IFSW. (1994). *The ethics of social work: Principles and standards*. Geneva, Switzerland: International Federation of Social Workers (IFSW). (2004). *Ethics in social work: Statement of principles*. Geneva, Switzerland: International Federation of Social Workers (IFSW).

Lens, V. (2000). Protecting the confidentiality of the therapeutic relationship: *Jaffe v. Redmond*. *Social Work*, 45(3), 273–276.

Matthews and Board of Directors of Physiotherapy (1986) 54 O.R. (2d) 375.

NASW. (1999). *Code of Ethics*. Washington: National Association of Social Workers (NASW).

Regehr, C. and B.J. Antle. (1997). Coercive influences: Informed consent and court-mandated social work practice. *Social Work*, 42(3), 300–306.

Rozovsky, L.E. and F.A. Rozovsky. (1990). *The Canadian law of consent to treatment*. Toronto: Butterworths.

United Nations. (1948). *Universal Declaration of Human Rights*. New York: United Nations. http://www.unhchr.ch/udhr/.

United Nations Centre for Human Rights. (1992). Teaching and learning about human rights: A manual for schools of social work and the social work profession (Developed in co-operation with International Federation of Social Workers and International Association of Schools of Social Workers). New York: United Nations.

CANADIAN ASSOCIATION OF SOCIAL WORKERS, GUIDELINES FOR ETHICAL PRACTICE

GUIDELINES FOR ETHICAL PRACTICE

THESE GUIDELINES SERVE as a companion document to the CASW *Code of Ethics* and provide guidance on ethical practice by applying values and principles in the *Code* to common areas of social work practice. While detailed, these guidelines for ethical practice are not intended to be exhaustive, or entirely prescriptive, but rather are intended to provide social workers with greater clarity on how to interpret and apply the ethical values and principles in the *Code*.

The extent to which each guideline is enforceable is a matter of professional judgement. Social workers are encouraged to consult their relevant provincial/territorial regulatory body or professional association for more specific guidance with respect to the application of these ethical guidelines in their own jurisdiction.

CORE SOCIAL WORK VALUES AND PRINCIPLES

Social workers uphold the following core values of the profession as outlined below. For a more detailed description of these values and principles please see the CASW *Code of Ethics* (2005). While all of these values and principles inform social work practice, to facilitate practical application a cross-reference is provided below between values from the *Code* and values from sections in the *Guidelines to Ethical Practice*. The reader is cautioned that this is not an exhaustive cross-reference and is meant only to enhance reader familiarity. The reader may also use the "Index" at the back of this document to help locate relevant sections of the *Guidelines to Ethical Practice*.

Value 1: **Respect for Inherent Dignity and Worth of Persons**
See Section 1, "Ethical Responsibilities to Clients." See also Sections 5.3 and 6.

313

Value 2: Pursuit of Social Justice

See Section 8, "Ethical Responsibilities to Society." See also, Sections 1.4, 1.6, 4.1.3 and 4.2.

Value 3: Service to Humanity

See Section 2, "Ethical Responsibilities in Professional Relationships." See also Sections 3.3, 5.2, 6.4 and 8.

Value 4: Integrity of Professional Practice

See Section 2, "Ethical Responsibilities in Professional Relationships;" Section 3, "Ethical Responsibilities to Colleagues;" Section 4, "Ethical Responsibilities to the Workplace;" and Section 5, "Ethical Responsibilities in Private Practice." See also Sections 1.1 and 7.4.

Value 5: Confidentiality in Professional Practice

See Section 1.5, 1.4, 6.3 and 7.3.2.

Value 6: Competence in Professional Practice

See Section 6, "Ethical Responsibilities in Research" and Section 7, "Ethical Responsibil - ities to the Profession." See also Sections 3.2.1, 3.2.3, 3.4.1, 3.5.1, 3.5.2 and 8.2.5.

1.0 ETHICAL RESPONSIBILITIES TO CLIENTS

1.1 Priority of Clients' Interests

1.1.1 Social workers maintain the best interests of clients as a priority, with due regard to the respective interests of others.

1.1.2 Social workers do not discriminate against any person on the basis of age, abil- ities, ethnic background, gender, language, marital status, national ancestry, political affiliation, race, religion, sexual orientation or socio-economic status.

1.1.3 Social workers collaborate with other professionals and service providers in the interests of clients with the client's knowledge and consent. Social workers recognize the right of client determination in this regard and include clients (or legally mandated client representatives when clients are not capable of giving consent) in such consultations.

1.1.4 Social workers limit their involvement in the personal affairs of clients to matters related to service being provided.

1.1.5 In exceptional circumstances, the priority of clients' interests may be out- weighed by the interests of others, or by legal requirements and conditions. In such situations clients are made aware of the obligations the social worker faces with respect to the interests of others (see section 1.5), unless such disclosure could result in harm to others.

1.1.6 Social workers seek to safeguard the rights and interests of clients who have limited or impaired decision-making capacity when acting on their behalf, and/or when collaborating with others who are acting for the client (see section 1.3).

1.2 Demonstrate Cultural Awareness and Sensitivity

1.2.1 Social workers strive to understand culture and its function in human behaviour and society, recognizing the strengths that exist in all cultures.

1.2.2 Social workers acknowledge the diversity within and among individuals, communities and cultures.

1.2.3 Social workers acknowledge and respect the impact that their own heritage, values, beliefs and preferences can have on their practice and on clients whose background and values may be different from their own.

1.2.4 Social workers seek a working knowledge and understanding of clients' racial and cultural affiliations, identities, values, beliefs and customs.

1.2.5 Where possible, social workers provide or secure social work services in the language chosen by the client. If using an interpreter, when possible, social workers preferentially secure an independent and qualified professional interpreter.

1.3 Promote Client Self-Determination and Informed Consent

1.3.1 Social workers promote the self-determination and autonomy of clients, actively encouraging them to make informed decisions on their own behalf.

1.3.2 Social workers evaluate a client's capacity to give informed consent as early in the relationship as possible.

1.3.3 Social workers who have children as clients determine the child's capacity to consent and explain to the child (where appropriate), and to the child's parents/guardians (where appropriate) the nature of the social worker's relationship to the child and others involved in the child's care (see section 1.5.5 regarding confidentiality).

1.3.4 Social workers, at the earliest opportunity, discuss with clients their rights and responsibilities and provide them with honest and accurate information regarding the following:
- the nature of the social work service being offered;
- the recording of information and who will have access to such information;
- the purpose, nature, extent and known implications of the options open to them;
- the potential risks and benefits of proposed social work interventions;
- their right to obtain a second opinion or to refuse or cease service (recog - nizing the limitations that apply when working with involuntary clients);
- the client's right to view professional records and to seek avenues of complaint; and
- the limitations on professional confidentiality (see section 1.5 regarding confidentiality).

1.3.5 Social workers provide services to clients only on valid informed consent or when required to by legislation or court-ordered (see section 1.4 regarding involuntary clients).

1.3.6 Social workers obtain clients' informed consent before audio taping or video taping clients or permitting observation of services to clients by a third party.

1.4 Responsibilities to Involuntary Clients and Clients Not Capable of Consent

1.4.1 Social workers recognize that in some cases their ability to promote self-determination is limited because clients may not be capable of making their own decisions, are involuntary or because clients' actions pose a serious threat to themselves or others.

1.4.2 Social workers endeavour to minimize the use of compulsion. Any action that violates or diminishes the civil or legal rights of clients is taken only after careful evaluation of the situation (see section 1.6 regarding protection of vulnerable members of society).

1.4.3 When a social worker is court-ordered or agrees to conduct a legally-mandated assessment, the social worker's primary obligation is to the judge or designate. The social worker, however, continues to have professional obligations toward the person being assessed with respect to dignity, openness regarding limits to confidentiality and professional competence.

1.4.4 In all cases where clients' right to self-determination is limited by duty of care (e.g., client intent to self-harm), the law (e.g., child abuse), or court order, social workers assist clients to negotiate and attain as much self-determination as possible. In particular, involuntary clients are made aware of any limitations that apply to their right to refuse services and are advised how information will be shared with other parties.

1.4.5 Social workers, wherever possible or warranted, notify clients regarding decisions made about them, except where there is evidence that this information may bring about, or exacerbate, serious harm to individuals or the public.

1.4.6 In instances when clients lack the capacity to provide informed consent, social workers protect clients' interests by advocating that their interests are represented by an appropriate third party, such as a substitute decision-maker.

1.5 Protect Privacy and Confidentiality

Social workers respect clients' right to privacy. Social workers do not solicit private information from clients unless it is required to provide services or to conduct social work research. Once information is shared or observed in a professional context, standards of confidentiality apply. Social workers protect clients' identity and only disclose confidential information to other parties (including family members) with the informed consent of clients or the clients' legally authorized representatives, or when required by law or court order. This obligation continues indefinitely after the social worker has ceased contact with the client. The general expectation that social workers will keep information confidential does not apply when disclosure is necessary to prevent serious, foreseeable, and imminent harm to a client or others (see section 1.6 regarding protection of vulnerable members of society). In all instances, social workers disclose the least amount of confidential information necessary to achieve the desired purpose.

1.5.1 Social workers discuss with clients the nature of confidentiality and limitations of clients' right to confidentiality at the earliest opportunity in their relationship. Social workers review with clients when disclosure of confidential information may be legally or ethically required. Further discussion of confidentiality may be needed throughout the course of the relationship.

1.5.2   Social workers ascertain and take into account the manner in which individual clients wish confidentiality to apply within their cultural context.

1.5.3   Social workers inform clients, to the extent possible, about the disclosure of confidential information and its potential consequences before the disclosure is made. This applies in all circumstances of disclosure, except when, in the professional judgement of the social worker, sharing this information with the client may bring about, or exacerbate, serious harm to individuals or the public.

1.5.4   When social workers provide services to families, couples, or groups, social workers seek agreement among the parties involved concerning each individual's right to confidentiality and the obligation to preserve the confidentiality of information shared by others. Social workers inform participants in family, couples, or group counselling that social workers cannot guarantee that all participants will honour such agreements.

1.5.5   When social workers provide services to children, they outline for the child and the child's parents (where appropriate) their practices with respect to confidentiality and children. Social workers may wish to reserve the right to disclose some information provided by a young child to parents when such disclosure is in the best interest of the child. This should be declared prior to the first session with a child (see section 1.3.3. regarding consent and capacity).

1.5.6   Social workers take care to not discuss confidential information in public or semi-public areas such as hallways, waiting rooms, elevators, and restaurants.

1.5.7   Social workers take precautions to ensure and maintain the confidentiality of information transmitted to other parties through the use of computers, electronic mail, facsimile machines, telephone answering machines and other electronic technology. Social workers inform clients of the limits to confidentiality that may apply to these forms of communication.

1.5.8   Social workers protect the confidentiality of clients' written and electronic records. Social workers take reasonable steps to ensure that clients' records are stored in a secure location and that clients' records are not available to others who are not authorized to have access (see section 1.6 regarding protection of vulnerable members of society).

1.5.9   Social workers do not disclose identifying information when discussing clients for teaching or training purposes, unless the client has consented to such disclosure.

1.5.10 Social workers do not disclose identifying information when discussing clients with consultants unless the client has provided informed consent or if there is a compelling need for such disclosure. If the agency practices and policies involve routine consultations with a supervisor or professional team, social workers make clients aware of these practices as a limitation to confidentiality.

1.5.11 Social workers protect the confidentiality of deceased clients consistent with the preceding responsibilities.

1.5.12 Social workers take reasonable precautions to protect client confidentiality in the event of the social worker's termination of practice, incapacity, or death.

1.5.13 Social workers take appropriate steps to address a breach of confidentiality should it occur, with due care to the values and principles of the *Code*, the standards of their employer and relevant regulatory body.

1.6 Protection of Vulnerable Members of Society

(See sections 1.3 on informed consent; 1.5 on confidentiality.)

1.6.1 Social workers who have reason to believe a child is being harmed and is in need of protection are obligated, consistent with their provincial/territorial legislation, to report their concerns to the proper authorities.

1.6.2 Social workers who have reason to believe that a client intends to harm another person are obligated to inform both the person who may be at risk (if possible) as well as the police.

1.6.3 Social workers who have reason to believe that a client intends to harm him/herself are expected to exercise professional judgement regarding their need to take action consistent with their provincial/territorial legislation, standards of practice and workplace policies. Social workers may in this instance take action to prevent client self-harm without the informed consent of the client. In deciding whether to break confidentiality, social workers are guided by the imminence of self-harm, the presence of a mental health condition and prevailing professional standards and practices.

1.6.4 Social workers who have reason to believe that an adult client is being abused take action consistent with their provincial/territorial legislation. Only a minority of jurisdictions in Canada have mandatory reporting of abuse of adults.

1.7 Maintenance and Handling of Client Records

Social workers maintain one written record of professional interventions and opinions, with due care to the obligations and standards of their employer and relevant regulatory body. Social workers document information impartially and accurately and with an appreciation that the record may be revealed to clients or disclosed during court proceedings. Social workers are encouraged to take care to

• report only essential and relevant details;
• refrain from using emotive or derogatory language;
• acknowledge the basis of professional opinions;
• protect clients' privacy and that of others involved.

1.7.1 Social workers do not state a professional opinion unless it can be supported by their own assessment or by the documented assessment of another pro - fessional.

1.7.2 Where records are shared across professions or agencies, information is recorded only to the degree that it addresses clients' needs and meets the requirements of an employer or professional standards of practice.

1.7.3 Before using clients' records for any purpose beyond professional services, for example education, social workers obtain the informed consent of clients.

1.7.4 In some circumstances, access to client records may be officially authorized or required by statute. Where consent of clients is not required, social workers attempt to notify clients that such access has been granted, if such notification does not involve a risk to others.

1.7.5 Social workers ensure that clients have reasonable access to official social work records concerning them. However, if there are compelling professional, ethical or legal reasons for refusing access, social workers advise clients of their right to request a review of the decision through organizational or legal channels, e.g., *Access to Information Act* (1983).

1.7.6 Social workers take due care to protect the confidences of others when pro - viding clients with access to records. This may involve masking third party information in the record.

1.7.7 If clients are not satisfied with their records, social workers advise them regarding complaint mechanisms.

1.7.8 Social workers protect clients' records, store them securely and retain them for any required statutory period.

1.7.9 Social workers transfer or dispose of clients' records in a manner that protects clients' confidentiality and is consistent with provincial/territorial statutes governing records and social work regulation. Social workers also ensure that mechanical or electronic records are properly transferred or disposed of.

1.8 Practices for Termination or Interruption of Services

1.8.1 Social workers renegotiate or terminate professional services when these services are no longer required or no longer meet the needs of clients.

1.8.2 Social workers respect the right of voluntary clients to discontinue service, engage another practitioner or seek a second opinion.

1.8.3 Whether the decision to renegotiate or terminate is that of the client or the social worker, social workers (where appropriate) initiate a discussion with the client to appreciate, and if possible, address any difficulties or misunder- standings that may have occurred. If the client desires other professional services, the social worker may assist in referral.

1.8.4 Social workers discuss client's needs, options and preferences before con - tinuing or discontinuing services, or offering to seek transfer or referral.

1.8.5 Social workers at the earliest opportunity inform clients of any factor, condi- tion or pressure that affects their ability to practice adequately and compe- tently.

1.8.6 When obliged to interrupt or terminate a professional relationship, social workers advise clients regarding the discontinuation of service and if possible, ensure their referral to another professional.

2.0 ETHICAL RESPONSIBILITIES IN PROFESSIONAL RELATIONSHIPS

It is the responsibility of the social worker to establish the tenor of their professional relationship with clients and others, and to ensure that the relationship serves the needs of clients, and others to whom there is a professional duty, over the needs of the social worker. In establishing a professional relationship the social worker takes into account relevant contextual issues, such as age, culture and gender of the client, and ensures the dignity, individuality and rights of the person and vulnerable members of society are protected.

2.1 Appropriate Professional Boundaries

2.1.1 Social workers maintain appropriate professional boundaries throughout the course of the professional relationship and after the professional relationship.

2.2 No Exploitation for Personal or Professional Gain

2.2.1 Social workers do not exploit professional relationships for personal benefit, gain or gratification.

2.2.2 Social workers do not take unfair advantage of any professional relationship or exploit others to further their personal, religious, political or business interests.

2.3 Declare Conflicts of Interest

Social workers avoid conflicts of interest that interfere with the exercise of professional discretion and impartial judgement. Social workers inform clients when a real or potential conflict of interest arises, and take reasonable steps to resolve the issue in a manner that makes the clients' interests primary. In some cases, protecting clients' interests may require termination of the professional relationship with proper referral of the client to another professional.

2.3.1 When social workers provide services to two or more people who have a relationship with each other (e.g., couples, family members), social workers clarify with all parties which individuals will be considered clients and the nature of the professional relationship with other involved parties.

2.3.2 Social workers who anticipate a conflict of interest among the individuals receiving services, or who anticipate having to perform a difficult role, clarify with clients their role and responsibilities. (For example, when a social worker is asked to testify in a child custody dispute or divorce proceedings involving clients).

2.3.3 Social workers consider carefully the potential for professional conflicts of interest where close personal relationships exist or where social, business or sexual relationships with colleagues are contemplated or exist.

2.4 Dual and Multiple Relationships

Dual or multiple relationships occur when social workers relate to clients in more than one relationship, whether professional, social or business. Dual or multiple relationships can occur simultaneously or consecutively. While having contact with clients in different life situations is not inherently harmful, it is the responsibility of the social worker to evaluate the nature of the various contacts to determine whether the social worker is in a position of power and/or authority that may unduly and/or negatively affect the decisions and actions of their client. (See section 3.2.3 regarding supervisees, and section 3.3.9 regarding students.)

2.4.1 Social workers take care to evaluate the nature of dual or multiple relationships to ensure that the needs and welfare of their clients are protected.

2.5 Avoid Physical Contact with Clients

2.5.1 Social workers avoid engaging in physical contact with clients when there is a possibility of harm to the client as a result of the contact. Social workers who engage in appropriate physical contact with clients are responsible for setting clear, appropriate and culturally sensitive boundaries to govern such physical contact.

2.6 No Romantic or Sexual Relationships with Clients

2.6.1 Social workers do not engage in romantic relationships, sexual activities or sexual contact with clients, even if such contact is sought by clients.

2.6.2 Social workers who have provided psychotherapy or in-depth counselling do not engage in romantic relationships, sexual activities or sexual contact with former clients. It is the responsibility of the social worker to evaluate the nature of the professional relationship they had with a client and to determine whether the social worker is in a position of power and/or authority that may unduly and/or negatively affect the decisions and actions of their former client.

2.6.3 Social workers do not engage in a romantic relationship, sexual activities or sexual contact with social work students whom they are supervising or teaching. (See Section 3.5 Responsibilities to Students.)

2.7 No Sexual Harassment

Sexual harassment refers to unwelcome sexual comments or lewd statements, unwelcome sexual advances, unwelcome requests for sexual favours or other unwelcome conduct of a sexual nature in circumstances where a reasonable person could anticipate that the person harassed would be offended, humiliated or intimidated.

2.7.1 Social workers do not sexually harass any person.

3.0 ETHICAL RESPONSIBILITIES TO COLLEAGUES

3.1 Respect

Social workers relate to both social work colleagues and colleagues from other disciplines with respect, integrity and courtesy and seek to understand differences in viewpoints and practice.

3.2 Collaboration and Consultation

When collaborating with other professionals, social workers utilize the expertise of other disciplines for the benefit of their clients. Social workers participate in and contribute to decisions that affect the well-being of clients by drawing on the knowledge, values and experiences of the social work profession.

3.2.1 Social workers co-operate with other disciplines to promote and expand ideas, knowledge, theory and skills, experience and opportunities that improve professional expertise and service provision.

3.2.2 Social workers seek the advice and counsel of colleagues whenever such consultation is in the best interests of clients.

3.2.3 Social workers keep themselves informed about colleagues' areas of expertise and competencies. Social workers only consult colleagues who have, in the judgement of the social worker, knowledge, expertise and competence related to the subject of the consultation.

3.2.4 Social workers take responsibility and credit, including authorship credit, only for work they have actually performed and to which they have contributed.

3.2.5 Social workers honestly acknowledge the work and the contributions made by others.

3.3 Management of Disputes

Social workers remain open to constructive comment on their practice or behaviour. Social workers base criticism of colleagues' practice or behaviour on defensible arguments and concern, and deal with differences in ways that uphold the principles of the *Code of Ethics*, the *Guidelines for Ethical Practice* and the honour of the social work profession.

3.3.1 Social workers who have ethical concerns about the actions of a colleague attempt to resolve the disagreement through appropriate channels established by their organization. If the disagreement cannot be resolved, social workers pursue other avenues to address their concerns consistent with client well-being, ethical principles and obligations outlined by their regulatory body.

3.4 Responsibilities in Supervision and Consultation

In addition to the general provisions of the *Code*, social workers in supervisory or consultation roles are guided by the following specific ethical responsibilities.

3.4.1 Social workers who have the necessary knowledge and skill to supervise or consult do so only within their areas of knowledge and competence.

3.4.2 Social workers do not engage in any dual or multiple relationships with supervisees when there is a risk of exploitation of, or potential harm to the supervisee. If questioned, it is the responsibility of the supervisor to demonstrate that any dual or multiple relationship is not exploitative or harmful to the supervisee. (See section 2.4 regarding dual and multiple relationships.)

3.4.3 Social workers evaluate supervisees' performance in a manner that is fair and respectful and consistent with the expectations of the place of employment.

3.5 Responsibilities to Students

In addition to the general provisions of the *Code,* social worker educators and field instructors who supervise students are guided by the following specific ethical responsibilities.

3.5.1 Social workers provide instruction only within their areas of knowledge and competence.

3.5.2 Social workers endeavour to provide instruction based on the most current information and knowledge available in the profession.

3.5.3 Social workers foster in social work students' knowledge and understanding of the social work profession, the *Code of Ethics* and other appropriate sources of ethical practices.

3.5.4 Social workers instruct students to inform clients of their student status.

3.5.5 Social workers inform students of their ethical responsibilities to agencies, supervisors and clients.

3.5.6 Social workers adhere to the principles of privacy and confidentiality in the supervisory relationship, acknowledging with students any limitations early in the professional relationship.

3.5.7 Social workers recognize that their role in supervising students is intended to be educational and work-focused. In the event that a student requests or requires therapy, the instructor refers the student to another competent practitioner.

3.5.8 Social workers evaluate a student's performance in a manner that is fair and respectful and consistent with the expectations of the student's educational institution.

3.5.9 Social workers do not engage in any dual or multiple relationships with students in which there is a risk of exploitation or potential harm to the student. Social work educators and field instructors are responsible for setting clear, appropriate and culturally sensitive boundaries. (See section 2.4 regarding dual and multiple relationships.)

4.0 ETHICAL RESPONSIBILITIES TO THE WORKPLACE

4.1 Professional Practice

4.1.1 Social workers acknowledge and strive to carry out the stated aims and objectives of their employing organization, agency or service contractor, consistent with the requirements of ethical practice.

4.1.2 Social workers work toward the best possible standards of service provision and are accountable for their practice.

4.1.3 Social workers use the organization's resources honestly and only for their intended purpose.

4.1.4 Social workers appropriately challenge and work to improve policies, procedures, practices and service provisions that
- are not in the best interests of clients;
- are inequitable;

- are in any way oppressive, disempowering or culturally inappropriate; and
- demonstrate discrimination.

4.1.5 When policies or procedures of employing bodies contravene professional standards, social workers endeavour to effect change through consultation using appropriate and established organizational channels.

4.1.6 Social workers take all reasonable steps to ensure that employers are aware of their professional ethical obligations and advocate for conditions and policies that reflect ethical professional practices.

4.1.7 Social workers take all reasonable steps to uphold their ethical values, principles and responsibilities even though employers' policies or official orders may not be compatible with its provisions.

4.2 Labour-Management Disputes

4.2.1 Social workers may engage in organized action, including the formation of and participation in labour unions, to improve services to clients and professional wages and working conditions.

4.2.2 The actions of social workers who are involved in labour-management disputes, job actions or labour strikes are guided by the profession's values and principles. Reasonable differences of opinion exist among social workers concerning their primary obligation as professionals during an actual or threatened labour strike or job action. Social workers carefully examine relevant issues and their possible impact on clients before deciding on a course of action.

4.3 Responsibilities of Managers

In addition to the general provisions of the *Code of Ethics* and *Guidelines for Ethical Practice,* social workers in management or similar administrative positions are guided by the following specific ethical responsibilities.

4.3.1 Social workers acquaint organizational administrators with the ethical responsibilities of social workers. Social workers encourage employers to eliminate workplace factors that prohibit or obstruct adherence to ethical practice.

4.3.2 Social workers strive to promote effective teamwork and communication and an efficient and accountable social work service.

4.3.3 Social workers strive to obtain and maintain adequate staff levels and acceptable working conditions.

4.3.4 Social workers strive to facilitate access to appropriate professional consultation or supervision for professional social work practice.

4.3.5 Social workers strive to facilitate access for staff under their direction to ongoing training and professional education, and advocate for adequate resources to meet staff development needs.

4.3.6 Social workers provide or arrange for appropriate debriefing and professional support for staff, especially when they experience difficult or traumatic circumstances.

5.0 ETHICAL RESPONSIBILITIES IN PRIVATE PRACTICE

In addition to the general provisions of the *Code of Ethics* and *Guidelines for Ethical Practice,* social workers in private practice are guided by the following specific ethical responsibilities.

5.1 Insurance Requirements

5.1.1 Social workers maintain adequate malpractice, defamation and liability insurance.

5.2 Avoid and Declare Conflicts of Interest

(See also section 2.3 regarding conflicts of interest.)

5.2.1 Social workers do not solicit clients for their private practice from their colleagues or their place of work, unless there is a request for social workers to do so. (For example, in hard to serve areas, employers may need employees who also have a private practice to provide follow-up services.)

5.2.2 Subject to 5.2.1, social workers may accept clients from their workplace when the workplace does not provide a similar service or in accordance with established workplace guidelines regarding such referrals.

5.3 Responsible Fee Practices

5.3.1 Social workers who enter into a fee for services contract with a client:
- Disclose at the outset of the relationship, the fee schedule for social work services including their expectations and practices with respect to cancellations and unpaid bills.
- Only charge a fee that was disclosed to and agreed upon by the client.
- Charge only for the reasonable hours of client services, research, consultation and administrative work on behalf of a given client.
- Avoid accepting goods or services from clients as payment for professional services. Bartering arrangements, particularly involving services, create the potential for conflicts of interest, exploitation and inappropriate boundaries in social workers' relationships with clients.
- Social workers may participate in bartering when it can be demonstrated that such arrangements are an accepted practice for professionals in the local community, considered to be essential for the provision of services, negotiated without coercion, and entered into for the client's benefit and with the client's informed consent. Social workers who accept goods or services from clients as payment for professional services assume the full burden of demonstrating that this arrangement will not be detrimental to the client and the profession.

5.3.2 Social workers may charge differential fees for services when such a difference in fee is for the benefit of the client and the fee is not discriminatory.

5.3.3 Social workers may charge a rate of interest on delinquent accounts as is

allowed by law. When such interest is being charged, social workers state the
rate of interest on all invoices or bills.

5.3.4 Social workers may pursue civil remedies to ensure payment for services to a
client, where the social worker has advised the client of this possibility at the
outset of the contract. (See section 1.5 regarding confidentiality.)

6.0 ETHICAL RESPONSIBILITIES IN RESEARCH

In addition to the general provisions of the *Code of Ethics* and *Guidelines for Ethical
Practice,* social workers engaged in research are guided by the following ethical responsibilities.

6.1 Responsible Research Practices

6.1.1 Social workers educate themselves, their students and their colleagues about
responsible research practices.

6.1.2 Social workers observe the conventions of ethical scholarly inquiry when engaged in study and research. Social workers utilize only appropriately qualified
personnel (or provide adequate training) to carry out research, paying
particular attention to qualifications required in conducting specialized
techniques.

6.2 Minimize Risks

6.2.1 Social workers place the interests of research participants above the social
worker's personal interests or the interests of the research project.

6.2.2 Social workers consider carefully the possible consequences for individuals
and society before participating in, or engaging in, proposed research and also
when publishing research results.

6.2.3 Social workers submit research proposals to an appropriate independent
scientific and ethical review prior to implementation of the research.

6.2.4 Social workers strive to protect research participants from physical, mental
or emotional discomfort, distress, harm or deprivation.

6.2.5 Social workers take appropriate steps to ensure that research participants have
access to appropriate supportive services.

6.2.6 Social workers ensure that due care has been taken to protect the privacy and
dignity of research participants.

6.3 Informed Consent, Anonymity and Confidentiality

Social workers obtain informed consent to take part in research from either participants
or their legally authorized representatives. In addition, social workers offer children and
others whose ability to provide consent is compromised for any reason, the opportunity
to express their assent or objection to research procedures and give their views due
regard.

6.3.1 Social workers ensure that consent is given voluntarily, without coercion or
inferred disadvantage for refusal to participate. Participants are informed

that they may withdraw from a study at any time without compromising any professional service being offered in the research project or future access to social work services.

6.3.2 Social workers ensure confidentiality of research participants' identity and discuss them only in limited circumstances for professional purposes. It is recommended that any identifying information obtained from or about participants during the research process is treated as confidential and the identity of participants separated from data that is stored, for example, through the use of identification numbers for surveys or similar questionnaires, and pseudonyms in transcripts of qualitative interviews.

6.3.3 Social workers ensure the anonymity of research participants is maintained in subsequent reports about the research.

6.3.4 Social workers store research material securely and for the required period as indicated by relevant research ethics guidelines.

6.4 Avoid Deception

6.4.1 Social workers generally avoid the use of deception in research because of its negative implications for the public trust in the profession.

6.4.2 Social workers only design or conduct research that involves deception or waiver of consent, such as certain forms of naturalistic observation and archival research, when third party review of the research has found it to be justified because of its anticipated scientific, educational, or practice value and when equally effective alternative procedures that do not involve deception or waiver of consent are not feasible.

6.5 Accuracy of Report of Research Findings

6.5.1 Social workers report research results accurately and objectively, acknowledging the contributions of others, and respecting copyright law. In research and scholarly endeavours, credit is taken only for work actually performed.

6.5.2 Where feasible, social workers inform research participants or their legally authorized representatives of research results that are relevant to them.

6.5.3 Where feasible, social workers bring research results that indicate or demonstrate social inequalities or injustices to the attention of the relevant bodies.

7.0 ETHICAL RESPONSIBILITIES TO THE PROFESSION

7.1 Maintain and Enhance Reputation of Profession

7.1.1 Social workers promote excellence in the social work profession. They engage in discussion about and constructive criticism of the profession, its theories, methods and practices.

7.1.2 Social workers uphold the dignity and integrity of the profession and inform their practice from a recognized social work knowledge base.

7.1.3 Social workers cite an educational degree only after it has been conferred by the educational institution.

7.1.4 Social workers do not claim formal social work education in an area of expertise or training solely by attending a lecture, demonstration, conference, workshop or similar teaching presentation.

7.1.5 Social workers uphold provincial and territorial regulations for continuing professional education, where such regulations exist.

7.1.6 Social workers do not make false, misleading or exaggerated claims of efficacy regarding past or anticipated achievements regarding their professional services.

7.1.7 Social workers strive to promote the profession of social work, its processes and outcomes and defend the profession against unjust criticism.

7.1.8 Social workers distinguish between actions and statements made as private citizens and actions and statements made as social workers, recognizing that social workers are obligated to ensure that no outside interest brings the profession into disrepute.

7.2 Address Unethical Practices of Colleagues

7.2.1 Social workers take appropriate action where a breach of professional practice and professional ethics occur, conducting themselves in a manner that is consistent with the *Code of Ethics* and *Guidelines for Ethical Practice*, and standards of their regulatory body.

7.2.2 Social workers who have direct knowledge of a social work colleague's incompetence or impairment in professional practice consult with colleagues about their concerns and when feasible assist colleagues in taking remedial action. Impairment may emanate, for example, from personal problems, psychosocial distress, substance abuse or mental health difficulties.

7.2.3 Social workers who believe that a colleague has not taken adequate steps to address their impairment to professional practice take action through appropriate channels established by employers, regulatory bodies, or other professional organizations.

7.2.4 Social workers do not intervene in the professional relationship of other social workers and clients unless requested to do so by a client and unless convinced that the best interests and well-being of clients requires such intervention.

7.3 Support Regulatory Practices
(in jurisdictions where social work is regulated)

7.3.1 Social workers co-operate with investigations into matters of complaint against themselves or other social workers and the requirements of any associated disciplinary hearings.

7.3.2 Social workers may release confidential information as part of a disciplinary hearing of a social worker when so directed by a tribunal or disciplinary body, taking care to divulge the minimum information required.

7.3.3 Social workers report to the relevant professional body, persons who misrepresent their qualifications as a social worker or their eligibility for regulation or membership in a professional association.

8.0 ETHICAL RESPONSIBILITIES TO SOCIETY

Social workers advocate for change in the best interests of clients and for the overall benefit of society, the environment and the global community. In performing their responsibilities to society, social workers frequently must balance individual rights to self-determination with protection of vulnerable members of society from harm. These dual ethical responsibilities are the hallmark of the social work profession and require well-developed and complex professional skills. When social workers' legal obligations require them to break confidentiality and limit client self-determination they do so with the minimum compulsion required by law and/or the circumstances (see Value 1).

8.1 Source of Information on Social Needs

8.1.1 Social workers identify and interpret the basis and nature of individual, group, community, national and international social problems with the intention of bringing about greater understanding and insight for policy makers and the public.

8.2 Participate in Social Action

8.2.1 Social workers strive to identify, document and advocate for the prevention and elimination of domination or exploitation of, and discrimination against, any person, group, or class on the basis of age, abilities, ethnic background, gender, language, marital status, national ancestry, political affiliation, race, religion, sexual orientation or socio-economic status.

8.2.2 Social workers endeavour to engage in social and/or political action that seeks to ensure that all people have fair access to the resources, services and opportunities they require to meet their basic human needs and to develop fully.

8.2.3 Social workers are aware of the impact of the political arena on practice and strive to advocate for changes in policy and legislation to improve social conditions in order to meet basic human needs and promote social justice.

8.2.4 Social workers endeavour to expand choice and opportunity for all people, with special regard for vulnerable, disadvantaged, oppressed and exploited people and groups.

8.2.5 Social workers strive to promote conditions that encourage respect for cultural and social diversity within Canada and globally. Social workers promote policies and practices that demonstrate respect for difference, support the expansion of cultural knowledge and resources, advocate for programs and institutions that demonstrate cultural competence and promote policies that safeguard the rights of and confirm equity and social justice for all people.

8.3 Encourage Public Participation

8.3.1 Social workers strive to facilitate informed participation by the public in shaping social policies and institutions.

8.4 Assist in Public Emergencies

8.4.1 Social workers provide professional services during public emergencies to the greatest extent possible.

8.5 Advocate for the Environment

8.5.1 Social workers endeavour to advocate for a clean and healthy environment and advocate for the development of environmental strategies consistent with social work principles and practices.

REFLECTING ON
YOUR FAMILY

W E ALL HAVE INTIMATE KNOWLEDGE of at least one family—the family or families in which we have lived or are currently living. One of the best ways to begin to understand family structure and family functioning in light of social, political, and economic conditions is to spend some time reflecting on your own family or a family grouping with which you are intimately acquainted. This process of examining your own family can prepare you to understand families who will come for help.[1]

In the process of reflecting on your family, ask yourself the questions you might ask a client family should you wish to work with them within a structural perspective. The best way to proceed is to select a particular time period when you were growing up and respond to the following family assessment questions.

1. Family Composition and History

- Who are the members of your family?
- Did they change over time—i.e., separation of parents, new partnerships, death, extended family entering or leaving?
- What were the circumstances in which your family immigrated to Canada?
- Were family members separated during immigration to another country?
- In the case of Aboriginal heritage, what was the impact of colonization on your family?
- What is the history of your family and your culture?
- Construct a genogram of your family.

2. Problem Identification

In all families there are usually certain conflicts and tensions among members that develop over time—tensions in regards to ideas, behaviours or feelings, health, financial difficulties, losses, and/or discrimination from outside the family.

- In your family, which family members, if any, identified concerns/problems? To whom was this communicated? If the problem was not identified or communicated to all members of the family, how was it kept from the others?
- Did someone outside of the family (i.e., teachers, neighbours, social agency representatives, important relatives) label anything/anyone a problem?
- To what extent was what was labeled a problem in the family related to: (1) who the family was within the community (i.e., an immigrant family, an Aboriginal family, a family headed by a same-sex couple or a single parent); (2) experiences of racism, heterosexism, sexism, or discrimination based on religion or physical and/or mental ability; (3) who the person was with the problem and how much power he or she had in the family; (4) the family's social class, income, debts, and access to resources.

3. Strengths and Solution Patterns

- Identify the strengths of your family.
- Who in the family usually took the initiative and acted on problem situations? What solutions were proposed by whom?
- How was the situation dealt with when a family member had a problem? Did family members usually turn to people outside the family for help or was the rule to keep family problems inside the family?
- To what extent was the way a problem was to be solved in the family related to the dominant ideas regarding men, women, and children's problem-solving capacities and/or cultural factors within the family?

4. Material Conditions of the Family

How did the family's material conditions influence how members related to each other and participated in the community?

- *Neighbourhood resources:* Did needed resources exist in your neighbourhood— i.e., day care, homemaker service, health care, etc.—and if so were they accessible, affordable, and appropriate?
- *Personal resources:* Could neighbours be counted on for help? In what situations? What kind? If not, why not? What friends and/or relatives could be counted on to help?
- *Home:* What was the quality and quantity of housing space and furnishings? Did your family own their home or rent?
- *Work:* Who in the family does the domestic and/or wage labour? What was the nature of wage labour (monotonous, fast-paced, dangerous, shift work, weekend work)? What were the positions held? Were the jobs permanent or contract? Were they unionized? What were the salaries/benefits?

5. Power and Authority within the Family

- Who made the rules inside the family and who enforced them?
- How did the cultural background of the family contribute to the rules?

- Did gender, age, or ability play a part in differences in the family regarding these messages?
- Who brought in the money and how was it distributed and managed?
- Who pushed their weight around and who didn't?
- Who allied with whom?

6. Communication Patterns within in the Family

What messages were given or rules transmitted regarding:

- How close family members should get to one another and how this closeness should be expressed?
- Asking directly for what you needed or refusing or rejecting what you did not need or want?
- How were family rules communicated, and what happened when they were not followed? How were differences/disagreements discussed?

7. Parental Models

Think about the relationship between the experiences your mother and father had in their own families of origin (what happened to them, what they saw happen, what they heard was right and wrong as they grew up) and their expectations *vis-à-vis* themselves, you, and your siblings; each other as mates; and themselves as parents. If you are a parent, how similar or different are you from your parents?

NOTE

1 This exercise is adapted from one that is thought to have been developed by Mike Brake while he was a professor in the School of Social Work, Carleton University.

BIBLIOGRAPHY

Abella, Irving, and Harold Troper. *None is Too Many: Canada and the Jews of Europe 1933–1948*. Toronto: Lester and Orpen Dennys, 1983.

Abraham, Carolyn. "2 Million Prescriptions for Attention Deficit Disorder Written for Kids." *Globe and Mail*, 19 October 2010: A1, 12 and 13.

Abramovitz, Mimi. *Under Attack, Fighting Back: Women and Welfare in the United States*. New York: Monthly Review Press, 2000.

Adams, Brian R., and Joan MacKenzie Davies. Editorial, "Social Work Profession Speaks Out about Press Coverage of Heikamp Inquest." Press Release, 26 March 2001: 2.

Addams, Jane. "Charity and Social Justice." *Proceedings* of the National Conference of Charities and Corrections. St. Louis, MO: The Archer Printing Co., 1910.

——. *Peace and Bread in Time of War*. New York: MacMillan, 1922.

Akamatsu, Norma. "The Talking Oppression Blues." In McGoldrick, *Revisioning Family Therapy*, 129–43.

Alderson-Gill & Associates Consulting Inc. "Evaluation Prepared for the National Homeless Initiative: Shepherds of Good Hope, Harm Reduction Program, Ottawa, Ontario." 2002. http://www.homelessness.gc.ca/projects/casestudies/docs/ottawa/shepherds_e.pdf.

Alexander, Bruce K. "The Empirical and Theoretical Bases for an Adaptive Model of Addiction." *The Journal of Drug Issues* 20.1 (1990): 37–65.

——. *Globalization of Addiction: A Study of Poverty of the Spirit*. Oxford: Oxford University Press, 2008.

Alexander, Leslie, Philip Lichtenberg, and Dennis Brunn. "Social Workers in Unions: A Survey." *Social Work* (May 1980): 216–23.

Al-Krenawi, Alean, and John R. Graham, eds. *Multicultural Social Work in Canada*. Don Mills, ON: Oxford University Press, 2003.

——. "Social Work Practice with Canadians of Arab Background: Insight into Direct Practice." In Al-Krenawi and Graham, *Multicultural Social Work in Canada*, 174–201.

Allahar, Anton L., and James E. Coté. *Richer and Poorer.* Toronto: Lorimer, 1998.

Allen-Meares, Paula. "Cultural Competence: An Ethical Requirement." *Journal of Ethnic and Cultural Diversity in Social Work* 16.3/4 (2007): 83–92.

American Association of Social Workers. *Social Case Work, Generic and Specific: An Outline, A Report of the Milford Conference.* New York: American Association of Social Workers, 1929.

American Psychiatric Association. *Diagnostic and Statistical Manual of Mental Disorders.* 4th ed., Text Revision. Washington, DC: APA, 2000.

Applewhite, Larry W., and M. Vincentia Joseph. "Confidentiality: Issues in Working with Self-harming Adolescents." *Child and Adolescent Social Work Journal* 11.4 (August 1994): 279–94.

Arches, Joan L. "Burnout and Social Action." *Journal of Progressive Human Services* 8.2 (1997): 51–62.

Arnold, Rick, Bev Burke, Carl James, D'Arcy Martin, and Barb Thomas. *Educating for a Change.* Toronto: Between the Lines Press and Doris Marshall Institute for Education and Action, 1991.

Aronson, Jane. "Lesbians in Social Work Education: Processes and Puzzles in Claiming Visibility." *Journal of Progressive Human Services* 6.1 (1995): 5–26.

Ashencaen, Sara, Fatima Husain, and Basia Spalek. *Islam and Social Work: Debating Values, Transforming Practice.* Bristol, UK: The Policy Press, 2008.

Atherton, Charles R., and Kathleen A. Bollard. "Postmodernism: A Dangerous Illusion for Social Work." *International Social Work* 45.4 (2002): 421–33.

Atkinson, Moya. "The National Association of Social Workers—Supporting Social Justice and Peace—Recent Actions Opposing US Torture." NASW, 28 June 2008.

Atwood, Nicola. "Working with Adults Who are Parenting." In Nash, Munford, and O'Donoghue, *Social Work Theories in Action*, 223–38.

Austin, Juliet, and Juergen Dankwort. "A Review of Standards for Batterer Intervention Programs." http://www.vawnet.org/Assoc_Files_VAWnet/AR_standards.pdf.

Backhouse, Constance. *Colour-Coded: A Legal History of Racism in Canada 1900–1950.* Toronto: University of Toronto Press, 1999.

Backwith, Dave, and Greg Mantle. "Inequalities in Health and Community-oriented Social Work: Lessons from Cuba." *International Social Work* 52.4 (2009): 499–511.

Bailey, Roy, and Mike Brake, eds. *Radical Social Work.* New York: Pantheon Books, 1975.

Baines, Donna. "Feminist Social Work in the Inner City: The Challenges of Race, Class, and Gender." *Affilia: Journal of Women and Social Work* 12.3 (1997): 297–317.

Baker, Raymond W. Shereen T. Ismael, and Traeq Y. Ismael, eds. *Cultural Cleansing in Iraq.* New York: Pluto Press, 2010.

Ball, Brenda, John Gaventa, John Peters, Myles Horton, and Paulo Freire. *We Make the Road by Walking: Conversation on Education and Social Change.* Philadelphia: Temple University Press, 1990.

Barlow, Maude. *Blue Covenant: The Global Water Crisis and the Coming Battle for the Right to Water.* Toronto: McClelland and Stewart, 2007.

———. "The Fourth Ministerial Meeting of the World Trade Organization—An Analysis."

16 October 2001. http://www.canadians.org/campaigns/campaigns-tradepub-4min mtg.html.

———. *The Free Trade Areas of the Americas and the Threat to Social Programs, Environmental Sustainability, and Social Justice in Canada and the Americas.* Ottawa: Council of Canadians, 18 January 2001.

———. "The World has Divided into Rich and Poor as at No Time in History." *Democracy Now!*, 2 July 2010: 1. http://www.commondreams.org.

Barter, Ken. "Reclaiming Community: Shaping the Social Work Agenda." *Canadian Social Work* 2.2 (Fall 2000): 6–18.

Beck, Aaron T., Neil A. Rector, Neal Stolar, and Paul Grant. *Schizophrenia: Cognitive Theory, Research and Therapy.* New York: The Guilford Press, 2009.

Belanger, Yale D. "The United Declaration on the Rights of Indigenous Peoples and Urban Aboriginal Self-Determination in Canada: A Preliminary Assessment." *Aboriginal Policy Studies* 1.1 (2011): 132–61.

Bellamy, Donald, and Allan Irving. "Pioneers." In Turner and Turner, *Canadian Social Welfare*, 89–117.

Bentley, Kia J., and Joseph Walsh. *The Social Worker and Psychotropic Medication.* 3rd ed. Belmont, CA: Brooks/Cole, 2006.

Bentley, Kia J., Joseph Walsh, and Rosemary Farmer. "Referring Clients for Psychiatric Medication: Best Practices for Social Workers." *Best Practices in Mental Health* 1.1 (Winter 2005): 59–71.

Berberoglu, Berch. "Conclusion: Globalization for a New Century." In Berberoglu, *Globalization in the 21st Century* 199–202.

———, ed. *Globalization in the 21st Century: Labor, Capital, and the State on a World Scale.* New York: Palgrave MacMillan, 2010.

Berg, Insoo. *Family-Based Services: A Solution-Focused Approach.* New York: Norton, 1994.

Bernard, Wanda, and Veronica Marsman. "The Association of Black Social Workers (ABSW): A Model of Empowerment Practice." In *Structural Social Work in Action*, edited by Steven F. Hick, Heather I. Peters, Tammy Corner, and Tracy London, 191–208. Toronto: Canadian Scholars' Press, 2010.

Best, Katherine. "Another Point of View on Staff Associations." *The Social Worker* 12.2 (November 1943): 16.

Bishop, Anne. *Becoming an Ally: Breaking the Cycle of Oppression.* Halifax: Fernwood, 1994.

Bisno, Herbert. "How Social Will Social Work Be?" *Social Work* 1.2 (April 1956): 12–18.

Bitensky, Reuben. "The Influence of Political Power in Determining the Theoretical Developments of Social Work." *Journal of Social Policy* 2, Pt. 2 (April 1973): 119–30.

Blackstock, Cindy. "Leaders in the Social Work Community 2008." *OASW Newsmagazine* 34.3 (June 2010): 1–3.

———. "Reconciliation Means Not Saying Sorry Twice: Lessons from Child Welfare in Canada." In *From Truth to Reconciliation: Transforming the Legacy of Residential Schools*, edited by Marlene Brant Costellano, Linda Archibald, and Mike DeGagne, 165–78. Ottawa: Aboriginal Healing Foundation, 2008.

Blakeney, Jill, Fadumo Jama Dirie, and Mary Ann MacRae. "Empowering Traumatized Somali Women: A Support Group Model for Helping Survivors to Cope." In *Community Support for Survivors of Torture*, edited by Karen Price, 50–58. Toronto: Canadian Centre for Victims of Torture, n.d.

Blatchford, Christie. "CAS Failed to Answer Mother's Cry for Help." *Globe and Mail*, 14 April 2011: A10.

———. "Children Died Where Welfare Workers Feared to Tread." *Globe and Mail*, 2 April 2011: A13.

———. "A Desperate Call, a Lost File, Brought This Woman's Story to its Deadly, Tragic Close." *Globe and Mail*, 16 April 2011: A2.

Blau, Judith R., and Albert Moncado. "Constitution and Human Rights." In *Globalization and America*, edited by Angela J. Hattery, David G. Embrick, and Earl Smith, 219–30. New York: Rowman and Littlefield, 2008.

Bock, Scott. "Conscientization: Paulo Freire and Class-based Practice." *Catalyst* 6 (1980): 5–25.

Boggs, James. *Racism and the Class Struggle: Further Pages from a Black Worker's Notebook*. New York: Monthly Review Press, 1970.

Bograd, Michelle, and Fernando Mederos. "Battering and Couples Therapy: Universal Screening and Selection of Treatment Modality." *Journal of Marital and Family Therapy* 25.3 (1999): 291–312.

Bolt, Clarence. "Our Destiny to be Decided More by TNCs Than by MPs." *The CCPA Monitor* 6.6 (1999): 18.

Bourgeon, Michele, and Nancy Guberman. "How Feminism Can Take the Crazy out of Your Head and Put it Back into Society: The Example of Social Work Practice." In *Limited Edition: Voices of Women, Voices of Feminism*, edited by Geraldine Finn, 301–21. Halifax: Fernwood, 1993.

Boyle, Edward R. *Feed People First*. Ottawa: Canadian Centre for Policy Alternatives, February 2009.

Bradimore, Ashley, and Harald Bauer. *Mystery Ships and Risky Boat People: Tamil Refugee Migration in the Newsprint Media*. Working Paper Series. Vancouver: Metropolis British Columbia Centre of Excellence for Research on Immigration and Diversity, January 2011. 1–46. Also at http://riim.metropolis.net/wp_2011.html.

Bradley, Brent, and Sue M. Johnson. "EFT: An Integrative Contemporary Approach." In *Handbook of Couples Therapy*, edited by Michele Harway, 179–93. Hoboken, NJ: John Wiley and Sons, 2005.

Brager, George, and Harry Specht. *Community Organizing*. New York: Columbia University Press, 1973.

Brenner, Johanna. *Women and the Politics of Class*. New York: Monthly Review Press, 2000.

Bricker-Jenkins, Mary. "Hidden Treasures: Unlocking Strengths in the Public Social Services." In *The Strengths Perspective in Social Work Practice*. 2nd ed., edited by Dennis Saleeby, 133–50. New York: Longman, 1997.

Bride, Brian E. "Prevalence of Secondary Traumatic Stress among Social Workers." *Social Work* 52.1 (January 2007): 63–69.

Brodsky, Gwen. "Human Rights and Poverty: A Twenty-First Century Tribute to J.S. Woodsworth and Call for Human Rights." In Pulkingham, *Human Welfare, Rights, and Social Activism* 136–60.

Brookfield, Stephen. *Developing Critical Thinkers: Challenging Adults to Explore Alternative Ways of Thinking and Acting.* London: Jossey-Bass, 1987.

Brotman, Shari, and Shoshana Pollack. "Loss of Context: The Problem of Merging Postmodernism with Feminist Social Work." *Canadian Social Work Review* 14.1 (Winter 1997): 9–21.

Brown, Allan, and Tara Mistry. "Group Work with Mixed Membership Groups: Issues of Race and Gender," *Social Work with Groups* 17.3 (1994) 14.

Brown, Pam A., and Claire E. Dickey. "Facilitating Critical Thinking in an Abused Women's Group." *Proceedings* of the Eleventh Annual Symposium of the Association for the Advancement of Social Work with Groups, Montreal, 26–29 October 1989.

Bruni, Frank. "Child Psychiatrist and Pedophile." *The New York Times*, 19 April 1998: 35, 40.

Bryan, Laura A. "Neither Mask nor Mirror: One Therapist's Journal to Ethically Integrate Feminist Family Therapy and Multiculturalism." *Journal of Feminist Family Therapy* 12.2/3 (2011): 105–21.

Buergenthal, Thomas, Dinah Shelton, and David P. Stewart. *International Human Rights in a Nut Shell.* 4th ed. St. Paul, MN: West Publishing, 2009.

Bunch, Charlotte. "Transforming Human Rights from a Feminist Perspective." In *Women's Rights: Human Rights*, edited by Julie Peters and Andrea Wolpe, 11–17. New York: Routledge, 1995.

Burnham, G., R. Lafta, S. Doocy, and L. Roberts. "Mortality after the 2003 Invasion of Iraq: A Cross-Sectional Cluster Sample Survey." *The Lancet* 368.9545 (2006): 1421–28.

Burrell, Gibson, and Gareth Morgan. *Sociological Paradigms and Organizational Analysis.* London: Heinemann Educational Books, 1979.

Burstow, Bonnie. "Freirian Codifications and Social Work Education." *Journal of Social Work Education* 272 (1991): 196–207.

Burton, Neil. "'War on Terror' a Convenient Excuse for the New Global Arms Race." *The CCPA Monitor* 13.6 (November 2006): 29–30.

Butler, Sandra, and Claire Wintram. *Feminist Groupwork.* Newbury Park, CA: Sage, 1992.

Callahan, Marilyn. "Feminist Community Organizing in Canada." In *Community Organizing,* edited by Brian Wharf and Michael Clague, 181–204. Don Mills, ON: Oxford University Press, 1997.

Campaign 2000. "Annual Report Card on Child and Family Poverty." 24 November 2009. http://www.campaign2000.ca/reportCards/national/2009EnglishC2000National ReportCard.pdf.

Canada. Canadian Human Rights Act (rev. 1996). http://www.chrc-ccdp.ca/en/timePor tals/milestones/139mile.asp.

———. Citizen and Immigration Canada. http://www.cic.gc.ca.

Canadian Association of Social Workers. *Code of Ethics.* Ottawa: CASW, 1983.

———. *Guidelines for Ethical Practice.* Ottawa: CASW, 2005.

———. *Social Work Code of Ethics.* Ottawa: CASW, 2005.

Canadian Centre for Policy Alternatives. Editorial, "Structurally Maladjusted." *The CCPA Monitor* 9.2 (June 2002): 2.

——. *Getting Canada Working Again: A Six Point Jobs Plan*. Alternative Federal Budget. Ottawa: Canadian Centre for Policy Alternatives, March 2010.

——. *Getting the Job Done Right*. Alternative Federal Budget. Ottawa: Canadian Centre for Policy Alternatives, 2010.

Canda, Edward R. "Spiritual Connection in Social Work: Boundary Violations and Creating Common Ground." Key Note Address to the First North American Conference on Spirituality and Social Work, Renison College, University of Waterloo, Waterloo, ON (25–27 May 2006) 1–50.

——. "Spiritually Sensitive Social Work: An Overview of American and International Trends." Plenary Address to the International Conference on Social Work and Counseling Practice, City University of Hong Kong, China, 2009. 1–19.

Canda, Edward R., and Leola Dyrud Furman. *Spiritual Diversity in Social Work Practice: The Heart of Helping*. 2nd ed. New York: Oxford University Press, 2010.

Carniol, Ben. "Analysis of Social Location and Change: Practice Implications." In *Social Work: A Critical Turn*, edited by Steven Hick, Jan Fook, and Richard Pozzuto, 153–63. Toronto: Thompson Educational, 2005.

——. *Case Critical: Challenging Social Work in Canada*. 2nd ed. Toronto: Between the Lines, 1990.

——. "Clash of Ideologies in Social Work Education." *Canadian Social Work Review* (1984): 184–99.

——. "Social Work and the Labour Movement." In Wharf, *Social Work and Social Change in Canada* 114–43.

Carniol, Ben, and Brigitte Kitchen. "OAPSW Proposal is a Disaster and Must be Defeated." *Canadian Review of Social Policy* 25 (May 1990): 62.

Carpenter-Song, Elizabeth, Edward Chu, Robert E. Drake, Meika Ritsems, Beverly Smith, and Hoyt Alverson. "Ethno-Cultural Variations in the Experience and Meaning of Mental Illness and Treatment: Implications for Access and Utilization." *Transcultural Psychiatry* 47.2 (2010): 224–51.

Castillo, R.J. *Culture and Mental Illness*. Pacific Grove, CA: Brooks/Cole, 1997.

Castro, Fidel. "Third World Must Unite or Die: Opening of the South Summit, Havana." In *Capitalism in Crisis: Globalization and World Politics Today*, edited by David Deutschman, 279–87. New York: Ocean Press, 2000.

Cattell-Gordon, David. "The Appalachian Inheritance: A Culturally Transmitted Traumatic Stress Syndrome?" *Journal of Progressive Human Services* 1, vol. 1 (1990): 41–57.

CBC News. "Foster Care System Needs Improvement: Prentice." 6 February 2007. http://www.cbc.ca/canada/north/story/2007/02/06/foster-care.html.

Centre for Human Rights. *Human Rights and Social Work: A Manual for Schools of Social Work and the Social Work Profession*. New York and Geneva: International Federation of Social Workers, United Nations, 2000.

Chadwick, Peter K. *Schizophrenia: The Positive Perspective: In Search of Dignity for Schizophrenic People*. London: Routledge, 1997.

Chambers, Clarke A. "Women in the Creation of the Profession of Social Work." *Social Service Review* (March 1986): 1–33.

Chambers, Natalie A., and Soma Ganesan. "Refugees in Canada." In Waxler-Morrison et al., *Cross Cultural Caring* 289–321.

Chambon, Adrienne S., and Allan Irving, eds. *Essays on Postmodernism and Social Work.* Toronto: Canadian Scholars Press, 1994.

Chandrasekera, Uppala. "Multiple Identities, Multiple Barriers," *Network* 26.1 (2010): 5–8.

Chau, Ruby C.M., Sam W.K. Yu, and Cam T.L. Tran. "The Diversity Based Approach to Culturally Sensitive Practices." *International Social Work* 54.1 (2011): 21–33.

Chossudovsky, Michel. *The Globalization of Poverty: Impacts of IMF and the World Bank Reforms.* London: Zed Books, 1997.

Choudry, Aziz. "What's Left? Canada's 'Global Justice' Movement and Colonial Amnesia." *Race and Class* 52.1 (2010): 97–102.

Chulov, Martin. "Research Links Rise in Falluja Birth Defects and Cancers to US Assault." *Guardian*, 30 December 30, 2010. http://www.guardian.co.uk/world/2010/dec/30 /faulluja-birth-defects-iraq.

Chung, Raymond C.Y., and Maria Lo. "Mental Health and Migration: Journey to Promote Mental Health." *INSCAN* 23.4 (2010): 7–9.

Citizen and Immigration Canada. "Facts and Figures 2008" (2009). http://www.cic.gc.ca /english/pdf/research-stats/facts2008.pdf.

———. "Facts and Figures 2009—Immigration Overview: Permanent and Temporary Residents." http://www.cic.gc.ca/english/resources/statistics/facts2009/temporary /01.asp.

———. "Government of Canada Will Welcome More Economic Immigrants in 2010." News Release (26 June 2010). http://www.cic.gc.ca/english/department/media/re leases/2010/2010-06-26.asp.

Clarke, Tony. "Transitional Corporation Agenda behind the Harris Regime." In *Mike Harris's Ontario: Open for Business: Closed to People,* edited by Diana Ralph, Andre Regimbald, and Nérée St-Amand, 28–36. Halifax: Fernwood, 1990.

Clement, Wallace. "Canada's Social Structure: Capital, Labour, and the State, 1930–1980." In *Modern Canada 1930–1980s,* edited by Michael S. Cross and Gregory S. Kealey, 81–102. Toronto: McClelland and Stewart, 1984.

———. *The Challenge of Class Analysis.* Ottawa: Carleton University Press, 1988.

Clement, Wallace, and John Myles. *Relations of Ruling: Class and Gender in Postindustrial Societies.* Montreal: McGill-Queen's University Press, 1994.

Cloward, Richard, and Francis Fox Piven. "The Acquiescence of Social Work." In *Strategic Perspectives on Social Policy,* edited by John E. Tropman, Milan J. Dluhy, and Roger M. Lind, 276–95. New York: Pergamon Press, 1981.

———. "Disruptive Dissensus: People and Power in the Industrial Age." In *Reflections on Community Organization: Enduring Themes and Critical Issues,* edited by Jack Rothman, 165–93. Itasca, IL: F.E. Peacock, 1999.

Coalition on Human Needs. http://www.chn.org/humanneeds/.

Coates, John. "Ideology and Education for Social Work Practice." *Journal of Progressive Human Services* 3.2 (1992): 15–30.

Cobb, Chris. "Victims Recount Horrors of Cluster Bombs." *Ottawa Citizen,* 4 December 2008: A9.

Cohen, Marcia, and Audrey Mullender. "The Personal is Political: Exploring the Group Work Continuum from Individual to Social Change Goals." *Social Work with Groups* 22.1 (1999): 13–31.

Cole, Mike. *Critical Race Theory and Education: A Marxist Response.* New York: Palgrave Macmillan/St. Martin's Press, 2009.

Collins, Robert O. *A History of Modern Sudan.* Cambridge: Cambridge University Press, 2008.

Colton, Matthew. "Editorial." *British Journal of Social Work* 32 (2002): 659.

Commission on the School of Social Work. *Report.* Ottawa: Carleton University, June 1972.

Congress, E. "Teaching Social Work Values, Ethics and Human Rights." In Hall, *Social Work*, 71–87.

———. "What Social Workers Should Know about Ethics Understanding and Resolving Practice Dilemmas," *Advances in Social Work* 1.1 (2000): 1–25.

Congress, Elaine P., and Manny J. Gonzalez, eds. *Multicultural Perspectives in Working with Families.* 2nd ed. New York: Springer, 2005.

Congress, Elaine P., and Winnie W. Kung. "Using the Culturagram to Assess and Empower Culturally Diverse Families." In Congress and Gonzalez, *Multicultural Perspectives in Working with Families* 3–21.

Coombs, Mary. "Transgenderism and Sexual Orientation: More Than a Marriage of Convenience?" In *Queer Families: Queer Politics*, edited by Mary Bernstein and Renate Reimann, 397–419. New York: Columbia University Press, 2001.

Cooper, Marlene. "Life-Threatening Disability in Adolescence: Adjusting to a Limited Future." *Clinical Social Work Journal* 22.4 (1994): 435–48.

Corey, Gerald, Marianne Scheider Corey, Patrick Callanan, and J. Michael Russell. *Group Techniques.* 2nd ed. Pacific Grove, CA: Brooks/Cole, 1992.

Corey, Marianne Schneider, and Gerald Corey. *Group Process and Practice.* 4th ed. Belmont, CA: Brooks/Cole, 1992.

Corrigan, Patrick W. "How Clinical Diagnosis Might Exacerbate the Stigma of Mental Illness." *Social Work* 52.1 (January 2007): 31–39.

Corrigan, Paul, and Peter Leonard. *Social Work Practice under Capitalism: A Marxist Approach.* London: Macmillan, 1978.

Council of Canadians. "Win! UN General Assembly Passes Historic Human Right to Water and Sanitation Resolution." council-of-canadians@topica.email-publisher.com.

Council on Social Work Education. *Educational Policy and Accreditation Standards.* Alexandria, VA: CSWE, 2008.

Craig, Gary. "Poverty, Social Work, and Social Justice." *British Journal of Social Work* 32 (2002): 669–82.

Craig, Tom, Peter Jaujua, and Nasir Warfa. "Mental Healthcare Needs of Refugees." *Psychiatry* 5.11 (2006): 405–08.

Cronin, Michael, Robin Sakina Mama, Charles Mbugua, and Ellen Mouravieff-Apostol. "Social Work and the United Nations." In Hall, *Social Work* 209–24.

CUPE. *Overloaded and under Fire.* Report of the Ontario Social Services Work Environment

Survey. Ottawa: CUPE, 1999. http://cupe.ca/updir/overloaded%20%20underfire.pdf.

Dance Network News 9.35 (Winter–Spring 2002).

Davidson, Larry, Stacey Lambert, and Thomas H. McGlashan. "Pychotherapeutic and Cognitive-behavioral Treatments for Schizophrenia: Developing a Disorder-specific Form of Psychotherapy for Persons with Psychosis." In Perris and McGorry, *Cognitive Psychotherapy of Psychotic and Personality Disorders* 1–20.

Davis, Rebecca Meghan, and Henry Davis. "PTSD Symptom Change in Refugees." *Torture* 16.1 (2006): 10–19.

Day, Shelagh. "Cutbacks Leave Poorest Women Trapped in 'Vicious Circle.'" *CCPA Monitor* 17.3 (July/August 2010): 2.

de Feyter, Koen. *Human Rights: Social Justice in the Age of the Market.* Dhaka: University Press, 2005.

de Mello, Sergio Vieira. "Five Questions for the Human Rights Field." *SUR—International Journal of Human Rights* 1 (2004): 165–71. http://www.surjournal.org/eng.

de Shazer, Steven. *Keys to Solution in Brief Therapy.* New York: Norton, 1985.

de Shazer, Steven, Insoo Kim Berg, Eve Lipchick, Elam Nunnally, Alex Molnar, Wallace Gringerich and Michele Weiner-Davis. "Brief Therapy: Focused Solution Development." *Family Process* 25.2 (1986): 207–21.

Degado, Melvin. *Community Social Work Practice in an Urban Context: The Potential of a Capacity-Enhancement Perspective.* New York: Oxford University Press, 2000.

Derman-Sparks, Louise, and Carol Brunson Phillips. *Teaching/Learning Anti-Racism: A Developmental Approach.* New York: Teachers College Press, 1997.

DiAngelo, Robin. "Heterosexism: Addressing Internalized Dominance." *Journal of Progressive Human Services* 8.1 (1997): 5–21.

Diebel, Linda. "It's Time to Renegotiate NAFTA, Critics Tell Harper." *The Star*, 14 February 2009. http://www.thestar.com/News/Canada/article/587628.

Directory of International Contacts and Social Work and Spiritual Diversity. http://www.socwel.ku.edu/canda.

Disability Statistics Canada. http://www.disabled-world.com/disability/statistics/disability-statistics-canada.php.

Dodds, Imelda, and Tom Johannesen. "Go on Using Your Voice for Peace." Sydney/Bern: IFSW, 18 March 2003.

Doidge, N. *The Brain that Changes Itself.* New York: Penguin 2007.

Dominelli, Lena. *Anti-Racist Social Work.* London: Macmillan, 1988.

Dore, Martha M. "Functional Theory: Its History and Influence on Contemporary Social Work Practice." *Social Service Review* 64.3 (1990): 358–74.

Doyal, Len, and Ian Gough. *A Theory of Human Need.* New York: Guilford Press, 1991.

Drar, Yohannes F. "Mental Health Social Work Practice with Refugees from the Horn of Africa: A Personal Experience." Eastern Branch, Ontario Association of Social Workers *Bulletin* 36.2 (Summer 2010): 11–13.

Dreikosen, Denise. "Radical Social Work: A Call to Link Arms." *Journal of Progressive Human Services* 20 (2009): 107–09.

DuBois, W.E.B. *The Soul of Black Folks.* New York: Bantam Books, 1989.

Eisenhower, Dwight D. Speech to the American Society of Newspaper Editors, 16 April 1953. http://www.quotationspage.com/quote/9556.html.

Elliott, Catherine Canfield. "A Board Member Speaks Out." *The Social Worker* 12.2 (November 1943): 15.

Ephross, Paul H., and Michael Reisch. "The Ideology of Some Social Work Texts." *Social Service Review* (June 1982): 273–91.

Eriksen, Karen, and Victoria E. Kress. *Beyond the DSM Story: Ethical Quandaries, Challenges, and Best Practices*. Thousand Oaks, CA: Sage, 2005.

Este, David, and Wanda Bernard. "Social Work Practice with African Canadians: An Examination of the African Nova Scotian Community." In Al-Krenawi and Graham, *Multicultural Social Work in Canada* 306–37.

Etherden, Laura. "Criminalization of the Poor: Government Complicity in the Death of Kim Rogers." *NAPO News* 81 (December 2001): 9.

Evans, Estalla Norwood. "Liberation Theology, Empowerment Theory and Social Work Practice with the Oppressed." *International Social Work* 35.2 (1992): 135–47.

Evans, Nikki, and Marie Connolly. "Attachment Issues and Work with Adolescents." In Nash, Munford, and O'Donoghue, *Social Work Theories in Action* 239–50.

FAFIA. "Join the December 10th Campaign for Women's Equality and Human Rights in Canada." http://www.fafia-afai.org/en/node/381.

Falicov, Celia. "Working with Transnational Immigrants: Expanding Meanings of Family, Community, and Culture." *Family Process* 46.2 (2007): 157–71.

Farwell, Nancy. "In War's Wake." *International Journal of Mental Health* 32.4 (Winter 2003–04): 20–50.

Fazel, Mina, Jeremy Wheeler, and John Danesh. "Prevalence of Serious Mental Disorder in 7000 Refugees in Western Countries: A Systematic Review." *The Lancet* 35 (9 April 2005): 1309–14.

Ferguson, Iain. "Identity Politics or Class Struggle? The Case of the Mental Health Users' Movement." In *Class Struggle and Social Welfare*, edited by Michael Lavalette and Gerry Mooney, 228–49. London: Routledge, 2000.

Ferguson, Iain, and Michael Lavalette. "Beyond Power Discourse: Alienation and Social Work." *British Journal of Social Work* 34 (2004): 298.

———. "Globalization and Global Justice: Towards a Social Work of Resistance," *International Social Work* 49 (2006): 309–18.

Fernando, Gaithri A. "Interventions for Survivors of the Tsunami Disaster: Report from Sri Lanka." *Journal of Traumatic Stress* 18.3 (June 2005): 267–68.

Finkel, Alvin. *Social Policy and Practice in Canada: A History*. Waterloo, ON: Wilfrid Laurier University Press, 2006.

Fisher, Dena. "Problems for Social Work in a Strike Situation: Professional, Ethical, and Value Considerations." *Social Work* 32.3 (1987): 252–54.

Fisher, Jacob. "The Rank and File Movement 1930–1936." *Social Work Today* 3.5/6 (February 1936); repr. *Journal of Progressive Human Service* 1.1 (1990): 95–99.

———. *The Response of Social Work to the Depression*. Cambridge, MA: Schenkman, 1980.

Flexner, Abraham. "Is Social Work a Profession." *Proceedings* of the National Conference of Charities and Corrections. 576–90. Baltimore, MD: Hildmann Printing Co., 1915.

Foley, Duncan K. *Understanding Capital: Marx Economic Theory*. Cambridge, MA: Harvard University Press, 1986.

Foley, Juliet. "Professional Associations in Canada." In *Social Work Practice: A Canadian Perspective*, edited by Francis J. Turner, 477–91. Scarborough, ON: Prentice Hall, 1999.

Food Banks Canada. *HungerCount 2010*. Toronto: Food Banks Canada, 2010. http://foodbankscanada.ca/HungerCount.htm.

Fook, Janis. *Radical Casework: A Theory of Practice*. St. Leonards, NSW: Allen and Unwin, 1993.

Fook, Jan, Martin Ryan, and Linette Hawkins. "Toward a Theory of Social Work Expertise." *British Journal of Social Work* 27 (1997): 399–417.

Foreign Affairs and International Trade Canada. "Free Trade Area of the Americas." http://www.international.gc.ca/trade-agreements-accords-commerciaux/agr-acc/ftaa-zlea/f.

Foster, John. "Afghanistan Vital to US as a Natural Gas Pipeline Route." *CCPA Monitor* 15.1 (May 2008): 1.

Foster, John Bellamy, Hannah Holleman, and Robert McChesney. "The US Imperial Triangle and Military Spending." *Monthly Review* 60.5 (October 2008): 1–19.

Foster, John Bellamy, and Fred Magdoff. *The Great Financial Crisis: Causes and Consequences*. New York: Monthly Review Press, 2009.

Frame, Marsha Wiggins. "The Spiritual Genogram in Family Therapy," *Journal of Marital and Family Therapy* 26.2 (April 2000): 211–16.

Frances, Allen. "A Warning Sign on the Road to DSM-V: Beware of the Unintended Consequences." *Psychiatric Times* 26.8 (26 June 209): 1–6. http://www.psychiatrictimes.com/print/article/10168/1425378?printable=true.

Franklin, Donna L. "Mary Richmond and Jane Addams: From Moral Certainty to Rational Inquiry in Social Work Practice." *Social Service Review* (December 1986): 504–25.

Freire, Paulo. "A Critical Understanding of Social Work." *Journal of Progressive Human Services* 1.1 (1990): 3–9.

———. *Pedagogy of the Oppressed*. New York: Continuum, 2001.

Freire, Paulo, and Donaldo Macedo. *Ideology Matters*. Boulder, CO: Rowman and Littlefield, 2011.

Freud, Sophie, and Stefan Krug. "Beyond the Code of Ethics, Part 1: Complexities of Ethical Decision-Making in Social Work Practice." *Families in Society: The Journal of Contemporary Human Services* 83.5/6 (2002): 474–82.

Gairdner, William D. *The Book of Absolutes: A Critique of Relativism, and a Defence of Universals*. Montreal: McGill-Queen's University Press, 2008.

Galper, Jeffry H. *The Politics of Social Services*. Englewood Cliffs, NJ: Prentice-Hall, 1975.

———. *Social Work Practice: A Radical Perspective*. Englewood Cliffs, NJ: Prentice-Hall, 1980.

Garfield, Robert. "Male Emotional Intimacy: How Therapeutic Men's Groups Can Enhance Couples Therapy." *Family Process* 49.1 (2010): 109–22.

George, Purnima, and Sara Marlowe. "Structural Social Work in Action: Experiences from Rural India." *Journal of Progressive Human Services* 16.1 (2005): 5–24.

Germain, Carel B., and Alex Gitterman. *The Life Model of Social Work Practice*. New York: Columbia University Press, 1996.

Gil, David G. *Confronting Injustice and Oppression: Concepts and Strategies for Social Workers*. New York: Columbia University Press, 1999.

Gilbert, Neil. "The Search for Professional Identity." *Social Work* 22.5 (1977): 401–06.

Gilligan, Carol. *In a Different Voice: Psychological Theory and Women's Development*. Cambridge, MA: Harvard University Press, 1982.

Gindin, Sam. "Social Justice and Globalization: Are They Compatible?" *Monthly Review* 54.2 (June 2002): 1–11.

Ginsburg, Norman. *Class, Capital and Social Policy*. London: Macmillan, 1979.

Gitterman, Alex. "Developing a New Group Service: Strategies and Skills." In Gitterman and Shulman, *Mutual Aid Groups and the Life Cycle* 53–71.

Gitterman, Alex, and Lawrence Shulman, eds. *Mutual Aid Groups and the Life Cycle*. Itasca, IL: F.E. Peacock, 1986.

Globe and Mail. "Bleak House," 18 August 2001.

——. "Canadian Family Income Slips over Past Decade." 27 January 2000: A6.

——. "Child Welfare Time Lost on Paperwork, Report Says." 25 February 2002: A1.

——. "Female, Seeking Public Office? Better Try Sweden." 7 March 2003: A7.

——. "Mother Nature's Wrath: The Year the Earth Struck Back." 20 December, 2010: A15.

——. "New Poverty Gauge Based on Survival." 9 January 2003: A3.

——. "Ontario to Maintain Lifetime Welfare Ban." 20 December 2002: A11.

——. "Tragedy in Chicoutimi: Kids Killed in Parents' Suicide Pact: Police." 5 January 2009: A1 and A4.

——. "US Sets Firm Date for Iraq Pullout." 28 February 2009: A1.

Globerman, Judith. "Regulating Social Work: Illuminating Motives." *Canadian Social Work Review* 9.2 (Summer 1992): 229–43.

Gold, Nora. "Putting Anti-Semitism on the Anti-Racism Agenda in North American Schools of Social Work." *Journal of Social Work Education* 32.1 (Winter 1996): 77–89.

Goldberg, Gale. "Structural Approach to Practice: A New Model." *Social Work* (March 1974): 150–55.

Goldberg Wood, Gale, and Ruth R. Middleman. *The Structural Approach to Direct Practice in Social Work*. New York: Columbia University Press, 1989.

Goldstein, Howard. *Social Work Practice: A Unitary Approach*. Columbia, SC: University of South Carolina Press, 1979), 31.

Goodman, Amy. *Democracy Now!*, 20 February 2009.

Gottlieb, M.C. "Avoiding Dual Relationships: A Decision-making Model." *Psychotherapy* 30.1 (1993): 41–48; also at http://kspope.com/gottlieb.html.

Gough, Ian. *The Political Economy of the Welfare State*. London: Macmillan, 1979.

Gould, Ellen. *First, Do No Harm: The Doha Round and Climate Change*. Ottawa: Canadian Centre for Policy Alternatives (March 2010).

Graham, John R., Cathryn Bradshaw, and Jennifer L. Trew. "Cultural Considerations for Social Service Agencies Working with Muslim Clients." *Social Work* 55.4 (October 2010): 337–46.

Graham, John. "A History of the University of Toronto School of Social Work." Ph.D. dissertation, University of Toronto, 1996.

Greenberg, Leslie, Serine Warwar, and Wanda Malcolm. "Emotion-focused Couples Therapy and the Facilitation of Forgiveness." *Journal of Marital and Family Therapy* 36.1 (January 2010): 28–42.

Greene, Gilbert. "Using the Written Contract for Evaluating and Enhancing Practice Effectiveness." *Journal of Independent Social Work* 4.2 (1990): 135–55.

Greenspan, Miriam. *A New Approach to Women and Therapy*. 2nd ed. Bradenton, FL: Human Services Institute, 1993.

———. "Out of Bounds." In Lazarus and Zur, *Dual Relationships and Psychotherapy*, 425–31.

Greenwood, E. "Attributes of a Profession." *Social Work* 2 (1957): 45–55.

Guest, Krysti Justine. "Exploitation under Erasure: Economic, Social, and Cultural Rights Engage Economic Exploitation." *Adelaide Law Review* 19 (1997): 73–93.

Guevara, Che. *To His Children: Che's Letter of Farewell*. Translated by Carmen Gonzalez, edited by José Marti. Havana: Artex, 1995.

Guru, Surinder. "Social Work and the 'War on Terror.'" *British Journal of Social Work* 40 (2010): 272–89.

Gutiérrez, Lorraine M., Ruth J. Parsons, and Enid Opal Cox. *Empowerment in Social Work Practice: A Sourcebook*. Pacific Grove, CA: Brooks/Cole, 1998.

Hall, Barbara. "Guest Editorial: Mental Health and Human Rights." *Network* 26.1 (Spring 2010): 3.

Hall, Nigel, ed. *Social Work: Making a World of Difference*. IFSW and FAFO, 2006. http://www.ifsw.org/home; http://icsw.org/index.htm; and http://www.iassw-aiets .org/.

Halverson, Glenn, and Keith Brownlee. "Managing Ethical Considerations around Dual Relationships in Small Rural and Remote Canadian Communities." *International Social Work* 53.2 (2010): 247–60.

Hanmer, Jalna, and Daphne Statham. *Women and Social Work: Towards a Woman-Centered Practice*. London: Macmillan, 1989.

Harding, A.K., L.A. Gray, and M. Neal. "Confidentiality Limits with Clients Who Have HIV: A Review of Ethical and Legal Guidelines and Professional Policies." *Journal of Counseling and Development* 71.3 (1993): 297–305.

Harding, Scott, "Man-made Disaster and Development," *International Social Work* 50.3 (2007): 295–306.

Hardy, Kenneth V., and Tracy A. Laszloffy. "The Dynamics of a Pro-Racist Ideology: Implications for Family Therapists." In McGoldrick, *Revisioning Family Therapy* 118–28.

Harney, Stefano. "Anti-racism, Ontario Style." *Race and Class* 37.3 (1996): 35–45.

Harris, Jerry. "US Imperialism after Iraq." *Race and Class* 50.1 (2008): 37–58.

Harrison, Gai, and Rose Melville. *Rethinking Social Work in a Global World*. New York: Palgrave MacMillan, 2010.

Hart, Michael Anthony. "Critical Reflections on an Aboriginal Approach to Helping." In *Indigenous Social Work around the World: Toward Culturally Relevant Education and Practice*, edited by Mel Gray, John Coates, and Michael Yellow Bird, 130–39. Burlington, VT: Ashgate, 2008.

Hartman, Ann. "Diagrammatic Assessment of Family Relations." *Social Casework* (October 1978): 465–76.

Hartman, Ann, and Joan Laird. *Family-Centered Social Work Practice*. New York: The Free Press, 1983.

Healy, Karen. "Power and Activist Social Work." In Pease and Fook, *Transforming Social Work Practice* 115–34.

Healy, Lynne M. "Exploring the History of Social Work as a Human Rights Profession." *International Social Work* 51.6 (2008): 735–48.

Henwood, Doug. "The 'New Economy' and the Speculative Bubble: An Interview with Doug Henwood." *Monthly Review* 52.11 (April 2000): 72.

———. *Wall Street: How It Works and for Whom*. New York: Verso, 1999.

Herd, Dean. Ernie Lightman, and Andrew Mitchell."Searching for Solutions: Making Welfare Policy on the Ground in Ontario." *Journal of Progressive Human Services* 20.2 (2009): 129–51.

Herman, Judith. *Trauma and Recovery*. New York: Basic Books, 1992.

Hicks, Jack, and the Working Group for a Suicide Prevention Strategy for Nunavut. "Qaujiausimajuni Tunngaviqarniq: Using Knowledge and Experience as a Foundation for Action: A Discussion Paper on Suicide Prevention in Nunavut." Nunavut: Working Group for a Suicide Prevention Strategy for Nunavut, 2009.

Hill-Collins, Patricia. *Black Feminist Thought: Knowledge, Consciousness, and the Politics of Empowerment*. London: Unwin Hyman, 1990.

Hipple, Steven F. "The Labor Market in 2009: Recession Drags On." *Monthly Labour Review* (March 2010): 1–20. http://www.bls.gov/opub/mlr/2010/03/artfull.pdf.

Hodge, David R. "Social Work and the House of Islam: Orienting Practitioners to the Beliefs and Values of Muslims in the United States." *Social Work* 50.2 (April 2005): 162–70.

———. "Spiritual Ecomaps: A New Diagrammatic Tool for Assessing Marital and Family Spirituality." *Journal of Marital and Family Therapy* 26.2 (April 2000): 217–28.

Hodge, David R., and Suzanne Bushfield. "Developing Spiritual Competence in Practice." *Journal of Ethnic and Cultural Diversity in Social Work* 15.3/4 (2006): 101–27.

Hoekman, Bernard M., and Michel M. Kostecki. *The Political Economy of the World Trading System*. New York: Oxford University Press, 2001.

Hollis, Ernest V., and Alice L. Taylor. *Social Work Education in the United States*. New York: Columbia University Press, 1951.

Hollis, Florence. *Casework: A Psycho Social Therapy*. New York: Random House, 1964.

———. "The Psycho Social Approach to Casework." In *Theories of Social Casework*, edited by Robert W. Roberts and Robert H. Nee, 33–78. Chicago: University of Chicago Press, 1970.

Hopwood, Kate. "The Sad Story of Kashechewan." *Guelph Mercury News*, 28 April 2008. http://news.guelphmercury.com/news/article/321826.

Horn, Kahn-Tineta. "Interview: Oka and Mohawk Sovereignty." *Studies in Political Economy* 35 (Summer 1991): 29–41.

Horn, Michiel. *The League for Social Reconstruction: Intellectual Origins of the Democratic Left in Canada 1930–1942*. Toronto: University of Toronto Press, 1980.

Horton, John. "Order and Conflict Theories of Social Problems as Competing Ideologies." *The American Journal of Sociology* 71.6 (May 1966): 701–13.

Howe, David. *An Introduction to Social Work Theory.* Aldershot, UK: Wildwood House, 1987.

Human Resources and Skills Development Canada. 27 May 2011. http://www4.hrsdc.gc .ca/.3ndic.1t.4r@-eng.jsp?iid=16.

Hurtado, Aida. *The Colour of Privilege: Three Blasphemies on Race and Feminism.* Ann Arbor, MI: University of Michigan Press, 1996.

Hurtig, Mel. "Danger of a Nuclear Holocaust is Becoming Even Greater," *The CCPA Monitor* 13.4 (October 2006): 36–37.

Ibbitson, John, and Tara Perkins. "Secret Origins and the New Order." *Globe and Mail*, 19 June 2010: F1 and F6–7.

Ife, J. *Human Rights and Social Work: Towards a Rights-Based Practice.* Rev. ed. Cambridge: University of Cambridge Press, 2008.

Inter Parliamentary Union. "Women in National Parliaments," 1 March 2002 and 31 July 2010. http://www.ipu.org/wmn-e/classif.htm.

International Federation of Social Workers. "Definition of Social Work." IFSW General Meeting, Montreal, July 2000. http://www.ifsw.org/p38000208.html.

———. "Human Rights." *International Policy Papers.* Geneva: IFSW, 1988.

———. *Human Rights and Social Work: A Manual for Schools of Social Work and the Social Work Profession.* Geneva: United Nations Centre for Human Rights, 1994, repr. 2000.

Irving, Allan. "From Image to Simulacra: The Modern/Postmodern Divide and Social Work." In Chambon and Irving, *Essays on Postmodernism and Social Work* 19–32.

Irving, Allan, Harriet Parsons, and Donald Bellamy. *Neighbours: Three Social Settlements in Downtown Toronto.* Toronto: Canadian Scholars Press, 1995.

Ismi, Asad, and Kristin Schwartz. "Canada is Violating the Nuclear Non-Proliferation Treaty." *CCPA Monitor* 15.4 (October 2008): 20–21.

Ives, Nicole, and Jill Witmer Sinha. "The Religious Congregation as Partner in Refugee Settlement," *Canadian Social Work* 12.1 (2010): 210–17.

James, Carl E. *Perspectives on Racism and the Human Services Sector: A Case for Change.* Toronto: University of Toronto Press, 1996, 19.

James, Gayle Gilchrist, Richard Ramsey, and Glenn Drover, eds. *International Social Work: Canadian Perspectives.* Toronto: Thompson Educational, 2009.

Jennissen, Therese, and Colleen Lundy. *One Hundred Years of Social Work: A History of the Profession in English Canada, 1900–2000.* Waterloo, ON: Wilfrid Laurier University Press, 2011.

Jessel, Ethel. "Staff Associations." *The Social Worker* 11.4 (May 1943): 20.

Johnson, Holly. *Dangerous Domains: Violence against Women in Canada.* Scarborough, ON: Nelson, 1996.

Johnson, Sue. *Hold Me Tight: Seven Conversations for a Lifetime of Love.* New York: Little, Brown and Company, 2008.

Johnson, Yvonne M., and Shari Munch. "Fundamental Contradictions in Cultural Competence." *Social Work* 54.3 (July 2009): 220–31.

Jones, A., and L. Rutman. *In the Children's Aid: J.J. Kelso and Child Welfare in Ontario.* Toronto: University of Toronto Press, 1981.

Jones, David N., and Tom Johannesen. "Statement on the Gaza Conflict." London: IFSW, 13 January 2009.

Kadushin, Alfred, and Goldie Kadushin. *The Social Work Interview: A Guide for Human Service Professionals.* 4th ed. New York: Columbia University Press, 1997.

Kagle, Jill Donner. "Record Keeping in the 1990s." *Social Work* 38.2 (March 1993): 190–96.

Kagle, Jill Donner, and Sandra Kopels. "Confidentiality after Tarasoff." *Health and Social Work* 193 (1994): 217–22.

Kahn, Si. "Leadership: Realizing Concepts through Creative Process." In *Community Practice: Models in Action,* edited by Marie Weil, 109–36. Binghamton, NY: The Haworth Press, 1997.

Kain, C.D. "To Breach or Not to Breach: Is That the Question? A Response to Gray and Harding." *Journal of Counseling and Development* 66.5 (1988): 224–25.

Kardon, Sidney. "Confidentiality: A Different Perspective." *Social Work in Education* 15.4 (October 1993): 247–50.

Karger, Howard Jacob. *Social Work and Labor Unions.* New York: Greenwood Press, 1988.

Kazemipur, A. and S.S. Halli. *The New Poverty in Canada: Ethnic Groups and Ghetto Neighbourhoods.* Toronto: Thompson Educational , 2000.

Keefe, Thomas. "Empathy: The Critical Skill." *Social Work* 21.1 (1976): 10–14.

———. "Empathy Skill and Critical Consciousness." *Social Casework* 61.7 (September 1980): 387–93.

Khayatt, Didi. "The Boundaries of Identity at the Intersection of Race, Class, and Gender." *Canadian Women's Studies* 14.2 (1994): 6–12.

King, Martin Luther. *The Strength to Love.* New York: Harper Row, 1963.

Kenny, Colin. "Afghan Mission Numbers Don't Add Up to Success." *Ottawa Citizen,* 14 July 2011: A13.

Kira, Ibrahim A., Asha Ahmed, Vanessa Mahmoud, and Fatima Wassim. "Group Therapy Model for Refugee and Torture Survivors." *Torture* 20.2 (2010): 108–13.

Kirby, Michael. "Everybody Hurts in a Social Recession." *Globe and Mail,* 26 August 2009: A13.

Kirkey, Sharon. "Psychiatric Drugs Carry Serious Physical Risks, Researchers Find." *Ottawa Citizen,* 15 June 2010: A5.

———. "The Sickening of Society." *Ottawa Citizen,* 26 April 2010: A1 and A4.

Klosterman, Eleanor M., and Dorothy C. Stratton. "Speaking Truth to Power: Jane Addams's Value Base for Peacemaking." *Affilia* 21.2 (Summer 2006): 158–68.

Knitter, Paul F. "Social Work and Religious Diversity: Problems and Possibilities." *Journal of Religion and Spirituality in Social Work* 29 (2010): 256–70.

Kopels, Sandra. "Confidentiality and the School Social Worker." *Social Work in Education* 14.4 (October 1992): 203–04.

Koring, Paul. "Almost 44 Million Americans Living below the Poverty Line." *Globe and Mail,* 17 September 2010: A14.

Kortman, Frank. "Transcultural Psychiatry: From Practice to Theory." *Transcultural Psychiatry* 47.2 (2010): 203–23.

Koven, Peter. "Despite Deal, Vale Tensions Remain." *Ottawa Citizen,* 6 July 2010: C7.

Kubler-Ross, Elizabeth, and David Kessler. *On Grief and Grieving.* New York: Scribner, 2005.

Kucinich, Dennis. Letter to members of Congress, 17 August 2010. CommonDreams. http://www.commondreams.org.

Kumsa, Martha Kuwee. "Wounds of the Gut, Wounds of the Soul": Youth Violence and Community Healing among the Oromos in Toronto." *Canadian Social Work* 12.1 (2010): 123–30.

Kutchins, Herb, and Stuart A. Kirk. *Making Us Crazy, DSM: The Psychiatric Bible and the Creation of Mental Disorders.* New York: The Free Press, 1997.

Kuyek, Joan Newman. *Fighting for Hope: Organizing to Realize Our Dreams.* Montreal: Black Rose Books, 1990.

Kwong, Miu Ha. "Applying Cultural Competency in Clinical Practice: Findings from Multicultural Experts' Experience." *Journal of Ethnic and Cultural Diversity in Social Work* 18 (2009): 146–65.

La Violette, Nicole, and Craig Forcese, eds. *The Human Rights of Anti-Terrorism.* Toronto: Irwin Law, 2008.

Lafond, Virginia. "The Grief of Mental Illness: Context for the Cognitive Therapy of Schizophrenia." In Perris and McGorry, *Cognitive Psychotherapy of Psychotic and Personality Disorders* 237–56.

———. *Grieving Mental Illness: A Guide for Patients and Their Caregivers.* 2nd ed. Toronto: University of Toronto Press, 2002.

Laird, Joan. "Changing Women's Narratives: Taking Back the Discourse." In Peterson and Lieberman, *Building on Women's Strengths* 271–301.

———, ed. *Revisioning Social Work Education: A Social Constructionist Approach.* New York: The Haworth Press, 1993.

Lamoureux, Henri, Robert Mayer, and Jean Panet-Raymond. *Community Action.* Montreal: Black Rose Books, 1989.

Larson, Magali Sarfatti. *The Rise of Professionalism: A Sociological Analysis.* Berkeley, CA: University of California Press, 1977.

Lazarus, Arnold, and Ofer Zur, eds. *Dual Relationships and Psychotherapy.* New York: Springer, 2002.

Lebow, Jay L., ed. *Handbook of Clinical Family Therapy.* Hoboken, NJ: John Wiley and Sons, 2005.

Lecomte, Roland. "Connecting Private Troubles and Public Issues in Social Work Education." In Wharf, *Social Work and Social Change in Canada* 31–51.

Lee, Mo Yee, Siu-Man Ng, Pamela Pui Yu Leung, and Cecilia Lai Wan Chan. *Integrative Body-Mind-Spirit Social Work.* New York: Oxford University Press, 2009.

Leighninger, Leslie. *Creating a New Profession: The Beginnings of Social Work Education in the United States.* Alexandria, VA: Council on Social Work Education, 2000.

———. "The Generalist-Specialist Debate in Social Work." *Social Service Review* (March 1980): 1–12.

Leighninger, Leslie, and Robert Knickmeyer. "The Rank and File Movement: The Relevance of Radical Social Work Traditions to Modern Social Work Practice." *Journal of Sociology and Social Welfare* 4.2 (1976): 166–77.

Leonard, Peter. "Knowledge/Power and Postmodernism: Implications for the Practice of a Critical Social Work Education." *Canadian Social Work Review* 11.1 (Winter 1994): 11–24.

———. *Personality and Ideology: Toward a Materialist Understanding of the Individual.* London: Macmillan, 1984.

———. *Postmodern Welfare: Reconstructing an Emancipatory Project.* London: Sage, 1997.

———. "Postmodernism, Socialism, and Social Welfare." *Journal of Progressive Human Services* 6, no. 2 (1995): 3–19.

———. "Three Discourses on Practice: A Postmodern Re-appraisal." *Journal of Sociology and Social Welfare* 23.2 (June 1996): 7–26.

Levine, Helen. "The Personal is Political: Feminism and the Helping Professions." In *Feminism in Canada*, edited by Angela Miles and Geraldine Finn, 175–210. Montreal: Black Rose Books, 1982.

Lewey, Laurel. "Anti-Communism in the Cold War and Its Impact on Six Canadian Social Workers." *Canadian Social Work* 12.2 (2010): 10–24.

Lewin, Kurt. "Problems of Research in Social Psychology (1943–1944)." In *Field Theory in Social Psychology: Selected Theoretical Papers*, edited by D. Cartwright, 155–69. Chicago: University of Chicago Press, 1976.

Li, Peter. *Race and Ethnic Relations in Canada.* Toronto: Oxford University Press, 1990.

Lightman, Ernie. "Social Workers, Strikes, and Service to Clients." *Social Work* 28.2 (March–April 1983): 142–47.

Lightman, Ernie. *Social Policy in Canada.* Don Mills, ON: Oxford University Press, 2003.

London Edinburgh Weekend Return Group. *In and against the State.* London: Pluto Press, 1979.

Longres, John F. "Marxian Theory and Social Work Practice." *Catalyst* 20 (1986): 30.

———. "Reactions to Working Statement on Purpose." *Social Work* 26.1 (1981): 85–87.

Lubove, Roy. *The Professional Altruist: The Emergence of Social Work as a Career 1880–1930.* Cambridge, MA: Harvard University Press, 1965.

Lundblad, Karen. "Jane Addams and Social Reform: A Role Model for the 1990s." *Social Work* 40.5 (1995): 661–69.

Lundy, Colleen, and Katherine van Wormer. "Social and Economic Justice, Human Rights, and Peace: The Challenge for Social Work in Canada and the USA." *International Social Work* 50.6 (2007): 727–39.

Lundy, Colleen. "The Role of Social Work in the Peace Movement." *The Social Worker/ Le Travailleur* 55.2 (1987): 61–65.

Lundy, Colleen, and Larry Gauthier. "Social Work Practice and the Master-Servant Relationship." *The Social Worker* 57.4 (1989): 190–94.

Lundy, Colleen, and Therese Jennissen. "The Shifting Terrain of Social Work." *OASW Eastern Branch Bulletin* 37 (2011): 9–10.

———. "Social Development and Human Rights during Economic Transition: Women in Russia and Cuba." In James, Ramsey, and Drover, *International Social Work* 127–49.

MacKenzie, Hugh. *A Soft Landing: Recession and Canada's 100 Highest Paid CEOs.* Ottawa: Canadian Centre for Policy Alternatives, January 2010.

Maglin, Arthur. "Alienation and Therapeutic Intervention." *Catalyst* 2 (1978): 70.

Magnus, Peter. "Preparation for Social Work Students to do Cross-cultural Clinical Practice." *International Social Work* 52.3 (2009): 375–85.

Mahrouse, Gada. "'Reasonable Accommodation' in Quebec: The Limits of Participation and Dialogue." *Race and Class* 52.1 (2010): 85–96.

Mahtani, Minelle K. "Polarity versus Plurality." *Canadian Women's Studies* 14.2 (1994): 16.

Maines, Joy. "Through the Years in CASW." NAC, FA 1713, MG 281441: 2.

Malik, Kenan. "Universalism and Difference: Race and the Postmodernists," *Race and Class* 37.3 (1996): 1–17.

Marable, Manning. "Beyond Racial Identity Politics: Towards a Liberation Theory for Multicultural Democracy." *Race and Class* 35.1 (July–September 1993): 113–30.

———. "History and Black Consciousness: The Political Culture of Black America." *Monthly Review* (July–August 1995): 71–88.

Marchant, Helen, and Betsy Wearing, eds. *Gender Reclaimed: Women in Social Work.* Sydney, NSW: Hale and Iremonger, 1986.

Marshall, Brandon D.L., M-J Milloy, Evan Wood, Julio S.G. Montaner, and Thomas Kerr. "Reduction in Overdose Mortality after the Opening of North America's First Medically Supervised Safe Injecting Facility: A Retrospective Population-based Study." *The Lancet*, Early Online Publication (18 April 2011), doi:10.1016/S0140-6736 (10) 62353-7. http://www.thelancet.com.

Marx, Karl, and Friedrich Engels. "*The Communist Manifesto* (1848)." In *The Communist Manifesto Now: Socialist Register*, edited by Leo Panitch and Colin Leys, 240–68. Halifax: Fernwood, 1998.

Maslow, A. *Toward a Psychology of Being.* New York: Van Nostrand, 1962.

Maté, Gabor. "Dr. Maté on the Stress-Disease Connection, Addiction, Attention Deficit Disorder and the Destruction of American Childhood." *Democracy Now!* (24 December 2010): 1–19. http://www.democracynow.org/2010/12/24/dr_gabor_mat_on_the_stress.

———. In *the Realm of Hungry Ghosts: Close Encounters with Addiction.* Toronto: Vintage Canada, 2009.

———. *When the Body Says No: The Cost of Hidden Stress.* Toronto: Alfred A. Knopf, 2003.

———. "When the Body Says No: Understanding the Stress-Disease Connection." An interview with Amy Goodman, *Democracy Now!* (15 February 2010). http://www.democracynow.org/2010/2/15/dr_gabor_mat_when_the_body.

McCarthy, Shawn. "Goals Modest for Environmental Summit." *Globe and Mail*, 30 November 2010: A9.

McClung, Nellie. *In Times Like These.* Social History of Canada Series. Toronto: University of Toronto Press, 1972.

McCorquodale, Shannon. "The Role of Regulators in Practice." In Turner and Turner, *Canadian Social Welfare*, 462–76.

McGoldrick, Monica, ed. *Revisioning Family Therapy: Race, Culture, and Gender in Clinical Practice.* New York: The Guilford Press, 1998.

McGoldrick, Monica, and Joe Giordano. "Overview: Ethnicity and Family Therapy." In *Ethnicity and Family Therapy.* 2nd ed., edited by Monica McGoldrick, Joe Giordano, and John K. Pearce, 1–27. New York: The Guilford Press, 1996.

McGowan, Kelly, and Nancy McKenzie. "A Community Response to the Needs of Drug Users, Stand Up Harlem." *Health/PAC Bulletin* (Winter 1993): 4–13.

McIntyre, Deborah. "Domestic Violence: A Case of the Disappearing Victim." *Australian Journal of Family Therapy* 5.4 (1984): 249–58.

McQuillan, Kevin, and Marilyn Belle. "Who Does What? Gender and the Division of Labour in Canadian Households." In *Social Inequality in Canada: Patterns, Problems and Policies*, edited by James Curtis, Edward Grabb, and Neil Guppy, 186–98. Scarborough, ON: Prentice-Hall, 1999.

Mederos, Fernando. "Batterer Intervention Programs: Past and Future Prospects." In *Coordinated Community Response to Domestic Violence: Lessons from the Duluth Model*, edited by Melanie F. Shepherd and Ellen L. Pence, 127–50. Newbury Park, CA: Sage, 1998.

Mehrotra, Gita. "Toward a Continuum of Intersectionality Theorizing for Feminist Social Work Scholarship." *Affilia* 25.4 (2010): 417–30.

Meister, Joan. "Keynote Address: The More We Get Together." In *The More We Get Together*, edited by Houston Stewart, Beth Percival, and Elizabeth R. Epperley, 11–18. Charlottetown, PEI: CRIAW and Gynergy Books, 1992.

Mickleburgh, Rob. "Vancouver Gay Bashing Ruled a Hate Crime." *Globe and Mail*, 9 November 2010: A7.

Middleman, Ruth R., and Gale Goldberg. *Social Service Delivery: A Structural Approach to Social Work Practice*. New York: Columbia University Press, 1974.

Middleman, Ruth R., and Gale Goldberg Wood. "So Much for the Bell Curve: Constructionism, Power/Conflict, and the Structural Approach to Direct Practice in Social Work." In Laird, *Revisioning Social Work Education* 129–46.

Mikkonen, Juha, and Dennis Raphael. *Social Determinants of Health: The Canadian Facts*. Toronto: York University School of Health Policy and Management, 2010. http://www.thecanadianfacts.org/.

Mikulincer, Mario, and Phillip R. Shaver. *Attachment in Adulthood: Structure, Dynamics, and Change*. New York: The Guilford Press, 2007.

Miller, Dorothy C. "What is Needed for True Equality: An Overview of Policy Issues for Women." In Peterson and Lieberman, *Building on Women's Strengths*, 45–65.

Mills, C. Wright. *Power, Politics and People*. New York: Oxford University Press, 1963.

Minahan, Anne. "Introduction to Special Issue." *Social Work* 261 (1981): 5–6.

Minahan, Anne, and Allan Pincus. "Conceptual Framework for Social Work Practice." *Social Work* 22.5 (1977): 352.

Mizrahi, Terry. "A Legacy of Peace: The Role of the Social Work Profession." *NASW News* (April 2003): 1–2. http://www.socialworkers.org/pressroom/events/peace/default.asp.

Morales, Armando T., Bradford W. Sheafor, and Malcolm E. Scott. *Social Work: A Profession of Many Faces*. 12th ed. Boston: Allyn and Bacon, 2010.

Moreau, Maurice. "Empowerment through Advocacy and Consciousness-Raising: Implications of a Structural Approach to Social Work." *Journal of Sociology and Social Welfare* 17.2 (June 1990): 53–67.

——. *Empowerment through a Structural Approach to Social Work: A Report from Practice*. Ottawa: Carleton University, 1989.

——. "A Structural Approach to Social Work Practice." *Canadian Journal of Social Work Education* 5.1 (1979): 78–94.

Moreau, Maurice, and Sandra Frosst. *Empowerment II: Snapshots of the Structural Approach in Action*. Ottawa: Carleton University Press, 1993.

Moyo, Otrude Nontobeko. "A Commitment to Social Justice in a Capitalist Democracy: Are We Being Critical Citizens or Just Moving Along Clichés?" *Journal of Progressive Human Services* 21.1 (2010): 3–7.

Mullaly, Bob. *Challenging Oppression: A Critical Social Work Approach*. Don Mills, ON: Oxford University Press, 2002.

——. *The New Structural Social Work*. Don Mills, ON: Oxford University Press, 2007.

——. *Structural Social Work: Ideology, Theory, and Practice*. Don Mills, ON: Oxford University Press, 1997.

Mulroney, Michael. *Formative Influences and Early Social Welfare Work of J.J. Kelso 1864–1891*. An Independent Enquiry Project. Ottawa: Carleton University, 1993.

Munford, Robyn, and Wheturangi Walsh-Tapiata. "Community Development: Principles in Practice." In Nash, Munford and O'Donoghue, *Social Work Theories in Action* 97–112.

Myer, Carol H. "The Search for Coherence." In *Clinical Social Work in the Eco-Systems Perspective*, edited by Carol H. Myer. 5–34. New York: Columbia University Press, 1983.

——. "Social Work Purpose: Status by Choice or Coercion?" *Social Work* 26.6 (1981): 69–75.

Nagoshi, Julie L., and Stephanie Brzuzy. "Transgender Theory: Embodying Research and Practice," *Affilia* 25.4 (2010): 431–43.

Naiman, Joanne. *How Societies Work: Class, Power, and Change in a Canadian Society*. Concord, ON: Irwin, 1997.

Nash, Mary, Robyn Munford, and Kieran O'Donoghue, eds. *Social Work Theories in Action*. London: Jessica Kingsley, 2005.

Nash, Mary. "Responding to Settlement Needs: Migrants and Refugees and Community Development." In Nash, Munford, and O'Donoghue, *Social Work Theories in Action* 140–54.

National Archives of Canada. "Through the Years." FA 1713, MG 28 I 441.

National Association of Social Workers. "Cultural Competence in Social Work Profession." In *Social Work Speaks: NASW Policy Statements 2000–2003*. 5th ed. Washington, DC: NASW, 2000.

——. *Indicators for the Achievement of the NASW Standards for Cultural Competence in Social Work Practice*. Washington, DC: NASW, 2007.

——. "International Policy on Human Rights." *Social Work Speaks: NASW Policy Statements*. Washington, DC: NASW Press, 2002.

——. "Peace and Social Justice." *Social Work Speaks: National Association of Social Workers Policy Statements 2000–2003*. Washington, DC: NASW Press, 2000.

Networker. "An Interview with Mara Selvini Palazzoli." September–October 1987: 26–33.

Neville, Robert. "Commentary." *CBC Morning* January 2000.

New York Times. "Immigration and Emigration." 18 April 2011. http://topics.nytimes
.com/top/reference/timetopics/subjects/i/immigration-and-emigration/ .

Newdom, Fred. "Progressive and Professional: A Contradiction in Terms?" *BCR Reports*
8.1 (1996): 1.

Nolan, Faith. "Nobody Knows My People." *Africville*, 1986.

North York Health Network. *Inequality is Bad for Our Hearts: Why Low Income and Social
Exclusion are Major Causes of Heart Disease in Canada*. Toronto: North York Health
Network, 2001. Also at http://www.yorku.ca/wellness/heart.

O'Brien, Anne-Marie, and Kimberly A. Calderwood. "Living in the Shadows: A Canadian
Experience of Mental Health Social Work." *Social Work in Mental Health* 8 (2010):
319–35.

OAPSW, Strategic Planning Committee. *Interim Report*. Toronto: Ontario Association of
Professional Social Workers, September 1987.

OASW, Eastern Branch Survey. "Observations of Social Workers in Eastern Ontario on
Effects on Clients/Families of Recent Funding and Policy Changes and Strategies
Clients/Families are Using to Cope." January–February 1996.

O'Connor, James. *The Fiscal Crisis of the State*. New York: St. Martin's Press, 1973.

Ohmer, Mary, Pamela Meadowcroft, Kate Freed, and Erica Lewis. "Community Gardening
and Community Development: Individual, Social and Community Benefits of
a Community Conservation Program." *Journal of Community Practice* 17 (2009):
377–99.

Oliver, Michael. *Social Work with Disabled People*. London: Macmillan, 1983.

———. *Understanding Disability: From Theory to Practice*. New York: St. Martin's Press,
1996.

Oliver, Michael, and Colin Barnes. "Disability Studies, Disabled People and the Struggle
for Inclusion." *British Journal of Sociology of Education* 31.5 (September 2010):
547–60.

Ontario. Ministry of the Solicitor General and Correctional Services, "Implementation
of the 'Interim Accountability and Accessibility Requirements for Male Batterer Programs.'" Toronto: Ministry of the Solicitor General and Correctional Services, March
1994.

Ottawa Citizen. "Canada New Base of Tamil Tigers." 18 January 2011: A1 and A2.

———. Editorial. 16 April 2001: A2.

———. "Families Stuck in Costly 'Last Resort' Motels," 22 October 2001.

———. "G20 Abuses 'Will Live in Infamy,' Watchdog Says in Scathing Report." 8 December
2010: A3.

———. "Humble Computer Station Links Global Village," 16 October 2001: 13.

———. "A Matter of Honour." 17 June 2010: A3.

———. "Mission to Add Hospice for Homeless," 15 March 2001: F6.

———. "Where Do I Go From Here? It is Heartbreaking Baby." 26 June 2010: A14.

Pagliaro, Jennifer, and Jill Mahoney. "Ontario Loses as Immigration Funds Shifted." *Globe
and Mail*, 24 December 2010: A3.

Palmer, Bryan. "Repression and Dissent: The OCAP Trials." *Canadian Dimension* (May/June 2003). http://www.canadiandimension.mb.ca.

Pancevski, Bogan. "Germany Turning against Muslims." *Ottawa Citizen*, 11 October 2010: A9.

Pantoja, Antonia, and Wilhelmina Perry. "Community Development and Restoration: A Perspective and Case Study." In Rivera and Erlich, *Community Organizing in a Diverse Society* 220–42.

Parry, Alan, and Robert E. Doan. *Story Re-visions: Narrative Therapy in a Postmodern World*. New York: The Guilford Press, 1994.

Parsons, Ruth J., Lorraine M. Gutiérrez, and Enid Opal Cox. "A Model for Empowerment Practice." In Parsons, Gutiérrez, and Cox, *Empowerment in Social Work Practice* 3–51.

Paterson, Rosemary, and Salli Trathen. "Feminist In(ter)ventions in Family Therapy." *ANZ Journal of Family Therapy* 15.2 (1994): 91–98.

Patricia, Hannah. "Preparing Members for the Expectations of Social Work with Groups: An Approach to the Preparatory Interview." *Social Work with Groups* 22.4 (2000): 51–66.

Patterson, Brent. "Challenging the Monstrosity of the G8 and G20 and Winning over Public Opinion along the Way." *Canadian Perspectives* (Autumn 2010): 21–22.

Payne, Malcolm. "The Code of Ethics, the Social Work Manager and the Organization." In Watson, *A Code of Ethics for Social Work* 104–22.

———. *Modern Social Work Theory: A Critical Introduction*. Chicago: Lyceum Books, 1991.

Pease, Bob, and Jan Fook, eds. *Transforming Social Work Practice: Postmodern Critical Perspectives*. London: Routledge, 1999.

Pence, Ellen, and Michael Paymar. *Education Groups for Men Who Batter: The Duluth Model*. New York: Springer, 1993.

Pennell, Joan. "Consensual Bargaining: Labor Negotiations in Battered Women's Programs." *Journal of Progressive Human Services* 1.1 (1990): 59–74.

———. "Feminism and Labor Unions: Transforming State Regulation of Women's Programs." *Journal of Progressive Human Services* 6.1 (1995): 45–72.

Perlman, Helen Harris. *Relationship: The Heart of Helping People*. Chicago: University of Chicago Press, 1979.

———. *Social Casework: A Problem Solving Process*. Chicago: University of Chicago Press, 1957.

Perris, Carlo, and Patrick D. McGorry, eds. *Cognitive Psychotherapy of Psychotic and Personality Disorders: Handbook of Theory and Practice*. New York: John Wiley and Sons, 1998.

Peterson, Jean K., and Alice A. Lieberman, eds. *Building on Women's Strengths: A Social Work Agenda for the Twenty-First Century*. New York: The Haworth Social Work Practice Press, 2001.

Pharr, Suzanne. *Homophobia: A Weapon of Sexism*. Little Rock, AR: Chardon Press, 1988.

Pincus, Allen, and Anne Minahan. *Social Work Practice: Model and Method*. Itasca, IL: F.E. Peacock, 1973.

Pinderhughes, Elaine B. "Empowerment for Our Clients and for Ourselves." *Social Case-work* (June 1983): 331–38.

Piva, Michael J. *The Condition of the Working Class in Toronto—1900–1921.* Ottawa: University of Ottawa Press, 1979.

Piven, Frances Fox, and Richard A. Cloward. *Regulating the Poor: The Functions of Public Welfare.* Rev. ed. New York: Vintage Books, 1993.

Podur, Justin. "The G20 Debacle." *The Bullet*, E-Bulletin No. 380, 2 July 2010: 1–6. http://www.socialistproject.ca/bullet/380.php.

Pogge, Thomas. *World Poverty and Human Rights.* 2nd ed. Cambridge: Polity Press, 2008.

Pollack, Daniel. "Social Workers and the United Nations: Effective Advocacy Strategies." *International Social Work* 50.1 (2007): 113–19.

Pon, Gordon. "Cultural Competency as a New Racism: An Ontology of Forgetting." *Journal of Progressive Human Services* 20.1 (2009): 59–71.

Popay, Jennie, and Yvonne Dhooge. "Unemployment, Cod's Head Soup, and Radical Social Work." In *Radical Social Work Today*, edited by Mary Langan and Phil Lee. 140–64. London: Unwin Hyman, 1989.

Posner, Wendy B. "Common Human Needs: A Story from the Prehistory of Government by Special Interests," *Social Service Review* (June 1995): 188–223.

Pottie, Kevin, Peter Tugwell, J. Freightner, Vivian Welch, Christine Grenaway, H. Swinkels, Meb Rashid, Lavanya Narasiah, Lawrence Kirmayer, Erin Ueffing, and N. MacDonald. "Summary of Clinical Preventative Care Recommendations for Newly Arriving Immigrants and Refugees to Canada." Canadian Collaboration for Immigrant and Refugee Health. *CMAJ* (2010): 1–12. Also at http://www.cmaj.ca.

Price, Karen, ed. "Doing the Right Thing: Suggestions for Non-Medical Caregivers: An Interview with Rosemary Meier." *Community Support for Survivors of Torture: A Manual.* Toronto: Canadian Centre for Victims of Torture, n.d.

Pridmore, Saxby, and Mohamed Iqbal Pasha. "Psychiatry and Islam." *Australasian Psychiatry* 12.4 (2004): 380–85.

Pross, Christine. "Burnout, Vicarious Traumatization and its Prevention." *Torture* 16.1 (2006): 1–9.

Pulkingham, Jane, ed. *Human Welfare, Rights, and Social Activism: Rethinking the Legacy of J.S. Woodsworth.* Toronto: University of Toronto Press, 2011.

Rak, Carl F., and Lewis E. Patterson. "Promoting Resilience in At-Risk Children." *Journal of Counseling and Development* 74 (March/April 1996): 368–72.

Raphael, Dennis. *Poverty and Policy in Canada: Implications for Health and Quality of Life.* Toronto: Canadian Scholars Press, 2007.

Reamer, Frederic G. *Ethical Standards in Social Work: A Critical Review of the NASW Code of Ethics.* Washington, DC: NASW Press, 1998.

———. *Ethics Education in Social Work.* Alexandria, VA: Council on Social Work Education, 2001.

———. *Social Work Malpractice and Liability: Strategies for Prevention.* New York: Columbia University Press, 1994.

———. *Social Work Values and Ethics.* 2nd ed. New York: Columbia University Press, 1999.

————. *Tangled Relationships: Managing Boundary Issues in the Human Services.* New York: Columbia University Press, 2001, 194.

Reamer, Frederic G., and S.R. Gelman. "Is *Tarasoff* Relevant in AIDS-Related Cases?" In *Controversial Issues in Social Work*, edited by E. Gambrill and R. Pruger, 342–55. Boston: Allyn and Bacon, 1997.

Rebick, Judy. "New, Stronger Feminism to Renew Fight for Social Justice." *CCPA Monitor* 17.3 (July/August 2010): 11.

Regehr, Cheryl. "Secondary Trauma in Social Workers." *Newsmagazine: Journal of the Ontario Association of Social Workers* 28.3 (2001): 11.

Regehr, Cheryl, and Graham Glancy. *Mental Health Social Work Practice in Canada.* Don Mills, ON: Oxford University Press, 2010.

Regehr, Cheryl, and Karima Kanani. "Chapter 8: Immigration and Refugee Law." In *Essential Law for Social Work Practice in Canada.* Don Mills, ON: Oxford University Press, 2006.

————. *Essential Law for Social Work Practice in Canada.* Don Mills, ON: Oxford University Press, 2006.

Rehm, J., and J. Weekes. "Abuse of Controlled Prescription Drugs." In *Substance Abuse in Canada: Current Challenges and Choices.* Ottawa: Canadian Centre on Substance Abuse, 2005: 1–44. http://www.ccsa.ca.

Reichert, Elisabeth. *Social Work and Human Rights.* New York: Columbia University Press, 2003.

————, ed. *Challenges in Human Rights: A Social Work Perspective.* New York: Columbia University Press, 2007.

Reisch, Michael. "Defining Social Justice in a Socially Unjust World." *Families in Society: The Journal of Contemporary Human Services* 83.4 (2002): 343–54.

Reisch, Michael, and Janice Andrews. *The Road Not Taken: A History of Radical Social Work in the United States.* New York: Bruner-Routledge, 2002.

Reitsma-Street, Marge, and Jennifer Keck. "The Abolition of a Welfare Snitch Line." *The Social Worker* 64.3 (Fall 1996): 35–66.

Reynolds, Bertha C. "Social Case Work: What is it? What is its Place in the World Today?" *Child and Family Welfare* 11.6 (March 1936): 1–12.

————. *An Uncharted Journey, Fifty Years of Growth in Social Work.* New York: The Citadel Press, 1963. 143.

Rian, Emily, and David R. Hodge. "Developing Cultural Competency with Mandaean Clients: Synchronizing Practice with the Light World." *International Social Work* 53.4 (2010): 542–55.

Riches, Graham. "Right to Food within Canada: International Obligations, Domestic Compliance." In James, Ramsey, and Drover, *International Social Work* 45–62.

Richmond, Mary. *Friendly Visiting among the Poor.* New York: Macmillan, 1899.

————. *The Good Neighbor.* Philadelphia: Russell Sage Foundation, 1908.

————. *Social Diagnosis.* Philadelphia: Russell Sage Foundation, 1917.

————. *What is Social Casework?* New York: Russell Sage Foundation, 1922.

Ritzer, George. *Contemporary Sociological Theory.* 2nd ed. New York: Alfred A. Knopf, 1988.

Rivera, Felix G., and John L. Erlich. "A Time of Fear; A Time of Hope." In Rivera and Erlich, *Community Organizing in a Diverse Society* 1–24.

———, eds. *Community Organizing in a Diverse Society*. 3rd ed. Toronto: Allyn and Bacon, 1998.

Roberts, Sam. "1 in 5 Americans Have Close Ties Elsewhere." *New York Times*, 19 October 2010. http://www.nytimes.com/2010/10/20/us/20brfs-1IN5AMERICAN_BRF.html ?scp =1&sq=&st=nyt.

Robinson, Bill. *Canadian Military Spending 2009*. Ottawa: Canadian Centre for Policy Alternatives, December 2009.

———. *Canadian Military Spending 2010–11*. Ottawa: Canadian Centre for Policy Alternatives, March 2011.

Robinson, Virginia. *A Changing Psychology in Social Case Work*. Chapel Hill, NC: University of North Carolina Press, 1930.

Roche, Douglas. *The Human Right to Peace*. Toronto: Novalis, 2003.

Rogan, Mary. "Girl, Interrupted," *Toronto Life*, December 2008. http://www.torontolife .com/features/girl-interrupted.

Rogers, Carl R. "The Interpersonal Relationship." In *Interpersonal Helping: Emerging Approaches for Social Work Practice*, edited by Joel Fisher, 381–91. Springfield, IL: Charles C. Thomas, 1973.

Roosevelt, Eleanor. "In Your Hands: A Guide for Community Action for the Tenth Anniversary of the Universal Declaration of Human Rights." 1958. http://www.udhr.org/history/inyour.htm.

Rose, Stephen M. "Advocacy/Empowerment: An Approach to Clinical Practice for Social Work." *Journal of Sociology and Social Welfare* 17.2 (1990): 41–51.

———. "Reflections on Empowerment-Based Practice" *Social Work* 45.5 (October 2000): 403–12.

Rose, Stephen M., and Stephanie Hatzenbuehler. "Embodying Social Class: The Link between Poverty, Income Inequality and Health." *International Social Work* 52.4 (2009): 459–71.

Rosenberg, Jessica, and Samuel Rosenberg. "Do Unions Matter? An Examination of the Historical and Contemporary Role of Labor Unions in the Social Work Profession." *Social Work* 51.4 (2006): 295–302.

Rosenhan, David L. "On Being Sane in Insane Places." *Science* New Series 179.4070 (19 January 1973): 250–58.

Ross, Lynda R. "Mom's the Word: Attachment Theory's Role in Defining the 'Good Mother.'" In *Feminist Counselling: Theory, Issues and Practice*, edited by Lynda R. Ross, 51–76. Toronto: Women's Press, 2010.

Rossiter, A., Richard Walsh Boweres, and Isaac Prilleltensky. "Learning from Broken Rules: Individualism, Bureaucracy and Ethics," *Ethics and Behaviour* 6.4 (1996): 307–20.

Rothman, Gerald C. *Philanthropists, Therapists and Activists*. Cambridge, MA: Schenkman, 1985.

Rothman, Jack. "Approaches to Community Intervention." In *Strategies of Community Intervention*. 5th ed., edited by J. Rothman, J.L. Erlichs, and J.E. Tropman, with F.M. Cox, 26–63. Itasca, IL: F.E. Peacock, 1995.

———. "Three Models of Community Practice." In *Strategies of Community Organization*. 2nd ed., edited by Fred Cox et al., 22–39. Itasca, IL: F.E. Peacock, 1974.

Rothman, Juliet Cassuto. *Contracting in Clinical Social Work*. Chicago: Nelson-Hall, 1998.

Royal Commission on Aboriginal Peoples. *Final Report*. http://www.parl.gc.ca/Content /LOP/researchpublications/prb9924-e.htm.

Rubin, Lillian B. *Families on the Fault Line: America's Working Class Speaks about the Family, the Economy, Race and Ethnicity*. New York: Harper Collins, 1994.

Ryan, William. *Blaming the Victim*. New York: Pantheon Books, 1971.

Sakamoto, Izumi. "A Critical Examination of Immigrant Acculturation: Toward and Anti-oppressive Social Work Model with Immigrant Adults in a Pluralistic Society." *British Journal of Social Work* 37 (2007): 515–35.

Saleebey, Dennis, ed. *The Strengths Perspective in Social Work Practice*. 3rd ed. Boston: Allyn and Bacon, 2002.

Sanders, Richard. "Fuelling Wars, Supplying the Warmongers: Canadian Government Heavily Subsidizing Our Military Companies." *The CCPA Monitor* (March 2010): 12–15.

Satir, Virginia. *Peoplemaking*. Palo Alto, CA: Science and Behaviour Books, 1972.

Satzewich, Vic. "Race, Racism, and Racialization: Contested Concepts." In *Racism and Social Inequality in Canada*, edited by Vic Satzewich, 25–45. Toronto: Thompson Educational, 1998.

Saul, John S. "Identifying Class, Classifying Difference." In *Fighting Identities: Race, Religion, and Ethno-Nationalism*, edited by Leo Panitch and Colin Leys, 347–74. London: Merlin Press, 2002.

Saulny, Susan. "Race Remixed; In a Multiracial Nation, Many Ways to Tally." *New York Times*, 10 February 2011. http://query.nytimes.com/gst/fullpage.html?res=9E01E5DA1E 3BF933A25751C0A9679D8B63&scp=1&sq=race+remixed&st=nyt.

Schacht, Rebecca L., Sona Dimidjian, William H. George, and Sara B. Berns. "Domestic Violence Assessment Procedures among Couples Therapists." *Journal of Marital and Family Therapy* 35.1 (2009): 47–59.

Schacter, Noel, Jim Beebe, and Luigi Zanasi. *Globalization and the North*. Ottawa: Canadian Centre for Policy Alternatives, 2004.

Schwartz, William. "Private Troubles and Public Issues." *The Social Welfare Forum*. New York: Columbia University Press (1969): 22–43.

Selekman, M.D. *Solution-Focused Therapy with Children: Harnessing Family Strength for Systemic Change*. New York: Guilford Press, 1997.

Selmi, Patrick. "Social Work and the Campaign to Save Sacco and Vanzetti." *Social Service Review* 75.1 (March 2001): 115–34.

Selmi, Patrick, and Richard Hunter. "Beyond the Rank and File Movement: Mary van Kleeck and Social Work Radicalism in the Great Depression, 1931–1942." *Journal of Sociology and Social Welfare* 27.2 (June 2001): 75–100.

Selvini-Palazzoli, M., L. Boscolo, G. Cecchin, and G. Prata. *Paradox and Counter Paradox*. New York: Jason Aronson, 1978.

Senate Standing Committee on Social Affairs, Science and Technology. *Out of the Shadows at Last: Transforming Mental Health, Mental Illness, and Addiction Services in Canada.* Ottawa: Statistics Canada, May 2006.

——. "In from the Margins: A Call to Action on Poverty, Housing, and Homelessness" (December 2009): 42. http://www.parl.gc.ca/Content/sen/Committee/402/citi/rep /rep02dec09-e.pdf.

Sepehri, Ardeshir, and Robert Chernomas. "Who Paid for the Canadian Welfare State between 1955–1988?" *Review of Radical Political Economics* 24.1 (Spring 1992): 71–88.

Settee, Pricilla. "The Struggle to Right Historical Wrongs: Grim Legacy of Colonialism Blights Indigenous Peoples." *The CCPA Monitor* (December 2008–January 2009): 12–14.

Sharma, Sohan, and Surinder Kumar. "The Military Backbone of Globalisation." *Race and Class* 44.3 (January–March 2003): 23.

Sheehy, Elizabeth. "Misogyny is Abetted by Women's Inequality." In *Speaking Truth to Power*, edited by Trish Hennessy and Ed Finn, 107–10. Ottawa: Centre for Social Policy Alternatives, 2010.

Shera, Wes, and Lillian M. Wells. *Empowerment Practice in Social Work.* Toronto: Canadian Scholars Press, 1999.

Shewell, Hugh. "Social Rights are Human Rights." In Pulkingham, *Human Welfare, Rights, and Social Activism* 114–35.

Shor, Ira. "Education is Politics: Paulo Freire's Critical Pedagogy." In *Paulo Freire: A Critical Encounter,* edited by Peter McLaren and Peter Leonard, 25–35. London: Routledge, 1993.

——. *Empowering Education: Critical Teaching for Social Change.* Chicago: University of Chicago Press, 1992.

Shulman, Lawrence. "Group Work Method." In Gitterman and Shulman, *Mutual Aid Groups and the Life Cycle* 23–51.

——. *The Skills of Helping Individuals, Families, and Groups.* 3rd ed. Itasca, IL: F.E. Peacock, 1992.

——. *The Skills of Helping Individuals, Families, Groups and Communities.* 4th ed. Itasca, IL: F.E. Peacock, 1999.

——. *The Skills of Helping Individuals, Families, Groups and Communities.* 6th ed. Belmont, CA: Brooks/Cole, 2009.

——. *The Skills of Helping Individuals, Families, Groups and Communities,* 7th ed. Belmont, CA: Wadsworth, 2011.

Siddiqui, Haroon. *Being Muslim.* Toronto: House of Anansi Press, 2006.

Simmons, Catherine A., and Joan R. Rycraft. "Ethical Challenges of Military Social Workers Serving in Combat Zone." *Social Work* 55.1 (January 2010): 9–18.

Simmons, Clara, Leticia Diaz, Vivian Jackson, and Rita Takahashi. "NASW Cultural Competence Indicators: A New Tool for the Social Work Profession." *Journal of Ethnic and Cultural Diversity in Social Work* 17.1 (2008): 4–20.

Simon, Barbara Levy. *The Empowerment Tradition in American Social Work: A History.* New York: Columbia University Press, 1994.

Sims, Jessica. "Increased Demand for Shelter Beds Points to 'Community Situation.'" *Ottawa Citizen,* 22 December 2010: C1 and C5.

Sinclair, Scott. *Negotiating from Weakness: Canada-EU Trade Treaty Threatens Canadian Purchasing Policies and Public Services.* Ottawa: Canadian Centre for Policy Alternatives, April 2010, 1–27.

Skegg, Anne-Marie. "Human Rights and Social Work." *International Social Work* 48.5 (2005): 667–72.

Skodra, Eleni E. "Counselling Immigrant Women: A Feminist Critique of Traditional Therapeutic Approaches and Reevaluation of the Role of Therapist." *Counselling Psychology Quarterly* 2.2 (1989): 185–204.

Solomon, Barbara Bryant. *Black Empowerment: Social Work in Oppressed Communities.* New York: Columbia University Press, 1976.

Solomon, R. *A Legal Guide for Social Workers.* 2nd ed. Toronto: Ontario Association of Social Workers and Family Service Ontario, 2009.

Sommers, Christina Hoff, and Sally Satel. *One Nation under Therapy.* New York: St. Martin's Press, 2005.

Specht, Harry, and Mark E. Courtney. *Unfaithful Angels: How Social Work Has Abandoned Its Mission.* New York: The Free Press, 1994.

Spector, Alan J. "Neoliberal Globalalization and Capitalist Crises in the Age of Imperialism." In Berberoglu, *Globalization in the 21st Century* 33–56.

Standing, Guy. *Work after Globalization: Building Occupational Citizenship.* Cheltenham, UK: Edward Elgar, 2009.

Stanford, Jim. *Out of Equilibrium: The Impact of the EU-Canada Free Trade on the Real Economy.* Ottawa: Centre for Policy Alternatives, October 2010. 1–42.

Staples, Lee H. "Powerful Ideas about Empowerment." *Administration in Social Work* 14.2 (1990): 29–42.

Staples, Steven. *Breaking Rank: A Citizen's Review of Canada's Military Spending.* Ottawa: The Polaris Institute, 2002.

———. *Pilot Error: Why the F-35 Stealth Fighter is Wrong for Canada.* Foreign Policy Series. Ottawa: Canadian Centre for Policy Alternatives, October 2010.

Stark, Evan. *Coercive Control: How Men Entrap Women in Personal Life.* New York: Oxford University Press, 2007.

Statistics Canada. "Aboriginal Peoples in Canada in 2006: Inuit, Métis and First Nations." Census 2006. http://www12.statcan.ca/english/census06/analysis/aboriginal/children.cfm.

———. Census 2006. http://www.statcan.gc.ca/daily-quotidien/080402/dq080402a-eng.htm.

———. "Educational Portrait of Canada." Census 2006 (March 2008). http://www.statcan.ca.

———. *Projections of the Diversity of the Canadian Population 2006–2031* (2010). http://www.statcan.gc.ca/pub/91-551-x/91-551-x2010001-eng.pdf.

Steiner, Claude. *Scripts People Live: Transactional Analysis of Life Scripts.* New York: Grove Press, 1974.

Steven F. Hick, ed. *Mindfulness and Social Work.* Chicago: Lyceum, 2009.

Stiglitz, Joseph E. *The Stiglitz Report: Reforming the International Monetary and Financial Systems in the Wake of the Global Crisis.* New York: New Press, 2010.

Stirling, Blair, Leola Dyrud Furman, Perry W. Benson, Edward R. Canda, and Cordelia Grimwood. "A Comparative Survey of Aotearoa New Zealand and UK Social Workers on the Role of Religion and Spirituality in Practice." *British Journal of Social Work* 40 (2010): 602–21.

Stith, Sandra M., Eric E McCollum, Karen H. Rosen, Lisa D. Locke, and Peter D. Goldberg. "Domestic Violence-Focused Couples Treatment." In Lebow, *Handbook of Clinical Family Therapy* 406–30.

Suarez, Zulema E., and Edith A Lewis. "Spirituality and Culturally Diverse Families: The Intersection of Culture, Religion, and Spirituality." In Congress and Gonzales, *Multicultural Perspectives in Working with Families* 425–41.

Sullivan, Maura. "Social Work's Legacy of Peace: Echoes from the Early 20th Century." *Social Work* 38.5 (September 1993): 513–26.

Swain, Harry. *Oka: A Political Crisis and its Legacy.* Vancouver: Douglas and McIntyre, 2010.

Swigonski, Mary E., Robin S. Mama, and Kelly Ward. "Introduction." *Journal of Gay and Lesbian Social Services* 13.1/2 (2001): 1–6.

Tafoya, Terry. "Finding Harmony: Balancing Traditional Values with Western Science in Therapy." *Canadian Journal of Native Education* 21 (1995): 7–27.

Taft, Jessie. *Family Casework and Counseling, A Functional Approach*. Philadelphia: University of Pennsylvania Press, 1935.

Taylor, Sharon, Keith Brownlee, and Kim Mauro-Hopkins. "Confidentiality versus the Duty to Protect," *The Social Worker* 64.4 (Winter, 1996): 9–17.

Teeple, Gary. *Globalization and the Decline of Social Reform: Into the Twenty-First Century*. Toronto: Garamond, 2000.

———. *The Riddle of Human Rights*. Aurora, ON: Garamond, 2004.

Terman, Rochelle L. "To Specify or Single Out: Should We Use the Term 'Honor Killing.'" *Muslim World Journal of Human Rights* 7.1 (2010): 1–39.

The Social Worker. "What Happened in Ottawa." 5.2 (November 1936): 1–8.

Thompson, Allison. "Radical Social Work in These Contemporary Times." *Journal of Progressive Human Services* 20 (2009): 110–11.

Thompson, Elizabeth. "Majority of Canadians Say Muslims Don't Share Their Values." *Ottawa Citizen*, 11 September 2010: A3.

Thompson, Neil. *Anti-discriminatory Practice*. London: Macmillan, 1993.

———. "Social Movements, Social Justice and Social Work." *British Journal of Social Work* 32 (2002): 711–22.

Thyer, Bruce A., and Marilyn A. Biggerstaff. *Professional Social Work Credentialing and Legal Regulation: A Review of Critical Issues and An Annotated Bibliography*. Springfield, IL: Charles C. Thomas, 1989.

Timms, Noel. "Taking Social Work Seriously: The Contribution of the Functional School." *British Journal of Social Work* 27 (1997): 723–37.

Tomm, Karl. "The Ethics of Dual Relationships." In Lazarus and Zur, *Dual Relationships and Psychotherapy* 32–43.

Toronto Star, 25 July 2000: A20.

Towle, Charlotte. *Common Human Needs*. London: George Allen and Unwin, 1973.

Townson, Monica. *Women's Poverty and the Recession*. Ottawa: Canadian Centre for Policy Alternatives, September 2009.

Tracy, Elizabeth M., and James K. Whittaker. "The Social Network Map: Assessing Social Support in Clinical Practice." *Families in Society: The Journal of Contemporary Human Services* (October 1990): 461–70.

Trevithick, Pam. "Unconsciousness Raising with Working-class Women." In *In Our Experience: Workshops at the Women's Therapy Centre*, edited by Sue Krzowski and Pat Land. 63–83. London: Women's Press, 1988.

Trolander, Judith Ann. "The Response of Settlements to the Great Depression." *Social Work* (September 1973): 92–102.

Tsetung, Mao. "On Practice." *Selected Readings from the Works of Mao Tsetung*. 65–84. Peking: Foreign Languages Press, 1971.

Turner, Frank. "Legislative Protection against Malpractice." *Canadian Review of Social Policy* 25 (May 1990): 63–64.

Turner, Joanne C., and Francis J. Turner, eds. *Canadian Social Welfare*. 3rd ed. Scarborough, ON: Allyn and Bacon, 1995.

UN Treaty Collection. Declarations and Reservations. http://treaties.un.org/.

UNHCR. "Number of Forcibly Displaced Rises to 43.3 Million Last Year, the Highest Level Since mid-1990s." 15 June 2010. http://www.unhcr.org/print/4c176c969.html.

United Nations. Refugee Convention (1951). http://www.unhcr.org/pages/49dao e466 .html.

US National Association of Black Social Workers. "Code of Ethics." http://www.nabsw .org/mserver/CodeofEthics.aspx.

Valtonen, Kathleen. *Social Work and Migration: Immigrant and Refugee Settlement and Integration*. Surrey, UK: Ashgate, 2008.

Van Voorhis, Rebecca, and Marion Wagner. "Coverage of Gay and Lesbian Subject Matter in Social Work Journals." *Journal of Social Work Education* 37.1 (Winter 2001): 147–59.

Vanier Institute of the Family. *Families Count: Profiling Canada's Families*. Ottawa: The Vanier Institute of the Family, 2010.

Vodde, Rich, and J. Paul Gallant. "Bridging the Gap between Micro and Macro Practice: Large Scale Change and a Unified Model of Narrative-Deconstructive Practice." *Journal of Social Work Education* 38.3 (2002): 439–58.

Wadden, Marie. *Where the Pavement Ends*. Vancouver: Douglas and McIntrye, 2008.

Wagner, David. "Radical Movements in the Social Services: A Theoretical Framework." *Social Service Review* (June 1989): 264–84.

———. "Radical Social Work as Conceit." *Journal of Progressive Human Services* 20 (2009): 104–06.

Wake, Bev. "CAS Workers Warn Child 'Disaster' Awaits." *Ottawa Citizen* 29 June 2001: A1, 2.

Wakefield Jerome C. "Does Social Work Need the Eco-Systems Perspective? Part 1: Is the Perspective Clinically Useful?" *Social Service Review* (March 1996): 1–32.

———. "Does Social Work Need the Exo-Systems Perspective? Part 2: Does the Perspective Save Social Work from Incoherence?" *Social Service Review* (June 1996): 183–213.

366 BIBLIOGRAPHY

Waldegrave, Charles. "Just Therapy," Social Justice and Family Therapy: A Discussion of the Work of The Family Centre, Lower Hutt, New Zealand." Special Issue. *Dulwich Centre Newsletter* 1 (1990): 1–46.

Walia, Harsha. "Transient Servitude: Migrant Labour in Canada and the Apartheid of Citizenship." *Race and Class* 52.1 (2010): 71–84.

Wallerstein, Nina. "Problem-Posing Education: Freire's Method for Transformation." *Freire for the Classroom*, edited by Ira Shor, 33–44. Portsmouth, MA: Boynton Cook/ Heinemann, 1987.

Walsh, Froma. "Spiritual Diversity: Multifaith Perspectives in Family Therapy." *Family Process* 49.3 (2010): 330–48.

Walters, Ewart. "Caribbean Airline Takes Over, Air Jamaica: The Love Bird Flies No More." *Spectrum* 27.5 (2010): 1.

Warner, Tom. *Never Going Back: A History of Queer Activism in Canada*. Toronto: University of Toronto Press, 2002.

Watson, David, ed. *A Code of Ethics for Social Work: The Second Step*. London: Routledge and Kegan Paul, 1985.

Watson, Sue. "Attachment Theory and Social Work." In Nash, Munford, and O'Donoghue, *Social Work Theories in Action* 208–22.

Watters, Ethan. *Crazy Like Us: The Globalization of the American Psyche*. New York: Free Press, 2010.

Waxler-Morrison, Nancy, and Joan M. Anderson. "Introduction: The Need for Culturally Sensitive Health Care." In Waxler-Morrison et al., *Cross Cultural Caring* 2–10.

Waxler-Morrison, Nancy, Joan M. Anderson, Elizabeth Richardson, and Natalie A. Chambers, eds. *Cross Cultural Caring*. 2nd ed. Vancouver: University of British Columbia Press, 2005.

Weaver, Hilary N. "Social Work through an Indigenous Lens: Reflections on the State of our Profession." In Hall, *Social Work* 37–51.

Weil, M. *The Handbook of Community Practice*. Thousand Oaks, CA: Sage, 2005.

Weil, Marie O. "Community Building: Building Community Practice," *Social Work* 41.5 (September 1996): 481–99.

Wenocur, Stanley, and Michael Reisch. *From Charity to Enterprise: The Development of American Social Work in a Market Economy*. Chicago: University of Illinois Press, 1989.

West, Cornel. *Race Matters*. New York: Vintage Books, 1994.

Wetzel, Janice Wood. "Human Rights in the 20th Century: Weren't Gays and Lesbians Human?" *Journal of Gay and Lesbian Social Services* 13.1/2 (2002): 15–45.

Wharf, Brian, ed. *Social Work and Social Change in Canada*. Toronto: McClelland and Stewart, 1990.

White, Michael. "Deconstruction and Therapy." In *Therapeutic Conversations*, edited by Stephen Gilligan and Resse Price, 22–61. New York: Norton, 1993.

———. *Re-Authoring Lives: Interviews and Essays*. Adelaide, AUS: Dulwich Centre Publications, 1995.

White, Michael, and David Epston. *Narrative Means to Therapeutic Ends*. New York: Norton, 1990.

Whitehorn, Alan. *Canadian Socialism: Essays on the CCF-NDP*. Toronto: Oxford University Press, 1992.

Whittington, Colin, and Ray Holland. "A Framework for Theory in Social Work." *Issues in Social Work Education* 5.1 (Summer 1985): 25–50.

WHO. Commission on Social Determinants of Health. "Final Report: Closing the Gap in a Generation: Health Equity through Action on Social Determinants of Health." Geneva: WHO, 2008.

———. "Health and Human Rights." http://www.who.int/hhr/readings/conference/en/.

———. "UN (DESA)—WHO Policy Analysis." 16 September 2010. http://www.who.int/mental _health/policy/mhtargeting/en/print.html.

Wigdor, Hazel. "Social Work and Trade Unions," *The Social Worker* 12.2 (November 1943): 18.

Wilding, Paul. *Professional Power and Social Welfare*. London: Routledge and Kegan Paul, 1982.

Wills, Gale. "Values of Community Practice: Legacy of the Radical Social Gospel." *Canadian Social Work Review* 9, no. 1 (1992): 28–40.

Wilson, Daniel, and David Macdonald. *The Income Gap between Aboriginal Peoples and the Rest of Canada*. Ottawa: Canadian Centre for Policy Alternatives, April 2010. 1–34.

Wilson, Richard, and Kate Pickett. *The Spirit Level: Why Equality is Better for Everyone*. New York: Bloomsbury Press, 2009.

Wise, Sue. "Becoming a Feminist Social Worker." In *Feminist Praxis*, edited by Liz Stanley, 236–49. London: Routledge, 1990.

Withorn, Ann. *Serving the People: Social Service and Social Change*. New York: Columbia University Press, 1984.

Witkin, Stanley L. "Human Rights and Social Work." *Social Work* 43.3 (May 1998): 197–201.

———. "If Empirical Practice is the Answer Then What is the Question?" *Social Work Research* 20.2 (June 1996): 69–74.

Wohl, Bernard J. "The Power of Group Work with Youth: Creating Activists of the Future." *Social Work with Groups* 22.4 (2000): 3–13.

Women's Unemployment Study Group. *Not for Nothing*. St. John's, NF: WUSG, 1983.

Woodsworth, David. "An Interview with Dr. David Woodsworth, Emeritus Professor of Social Work, McGill University." *Canadian Social Work* 2.2 (Fall 2000): 149.

Woolley, Scott R., and Susan M. Johnson. "Creating Secure Connections: Emotionally Focused Couples Therapy." In Lebow, *Handbook of Clinical Family Therapy* 384–405.

Wylie, Mary Sykes. "Diagnosing for Dollars?" *Networker* (May/June 1995): 23–33, 65–69.

Yalnizyan, Armine. *Exposed: Revealing Truths about Canada's Recession*. Ottawa: Canadian Centre for Policy Alternatives, April 2009. 3–43.

Yamatani, Hide, Rafael Engel, and Solveig Spjeldnes. "Child Welfare Worker Caseload: What's Just Right?" *Social Work* 54.4 (2009): 361–68.

Yan, M.C., and Y.R. Wong. "Rethinking Self-awareness in Cultural Competence: Toward a Dialogic Self in Cross-cultural Social Work." *Families in Society* 86 (2005): 181–88.

Yan, Miu Chung, and Serman Chan. "Are Social Workers Ready to Work with Newcomers?" *Canadian Social Work* 12.1 (2010): 16–23.

Yelaga, Shankar A. *An Introduction to Social Work Practice in Canada.* Scarborough, ON: Prentice-Hall, 1985.

Younge, Gary. "Islamophobia, European Style." *The Nation* 291.15 (11 October 2010): 10.

Yu, Soojin, Estelle Ouelette, and Angelun Warmington. "Refugee Integration in Canada: A Survey of Empirical Evidence and Existing Services." *Refuge* 24.2 (2007): 17–34.

Zeese, Kevin. "Obama: 'I want to end the mindset that got us into the war in the first place.'" Voters For Peace. http://votersforpeace.us/perspectives/zeese020508.html.

Zide, Marilyn R., and Susan W. Gray. "The Solutioning Process: Merging the Genogram and the Solution-Focused Model of Practice." *Journal of Family Social Work* 4.1 (2000): 3–19.

Zur, Ofer. "Guidelines for Non-Sexual Dual Relationships in Psychotherapy." http://drzur .com/dualrelationships.html.

INDEX